HOMEGROWN ECOPRAGMATICS

Edward T. Wimberley

HOMEGROWN ECOPRAGMATICS

Edward T. Wimberley

COMMON GROUND RESEARCH NETWORKS 2019

First published in 2019
as part of the On Sustainability Book Imprint
doi: 10.18848/978-1-86335-147-8/CGP (Full Book)

BISAC Codes: PHI020000, PHI019000, SCI026000

Common Ground Research Networks
2001 South First Street, Suite 202
University of Illinois Research Park
Champaign, IL
61820

Library of Congress Cataloging-in-Publication Data

Names: Wimberley, Edward T., author.
Title: Homegrown ecopragmatics / Edward T. Wimberley.
Description: Champaign, Illinois : Common Ground Research Networks, 2019. |
    Includes bibliographical references and index.
Identifiers: LCCN 2019015683 (print) | LCCN 2018061698 (ebook) | ISBN
    9781863351454 (hardback : alk. paper) | ISBN 9781863351461 (paperback :
    alk. paper) | ISBN 9781863351478 (pdf)
Subjects: LCSH: Deep ecology--United States. | Environmentalism--United
    States. | Environmental policy--United States--Citizen participation. |
    Human ecology--United States.
Classification: LCC GE197 .W563 2019 (ebook) | LCC GE197 (print) | DDC
    363.700973--dc23
LC record available at https://lccn.loc.gov/2019015683

Cover Photo Credit: Phillip Kalantzis-Cope

Table of Contents

Introduction

COOPERATION AMONG STRANGE BEDFELLOWS

It is not unusual to read a news article or hear a story on radio or television about conflict between environmental groups and others perceived to be indifferent to environmental issues, to include politicians, timber and agricultural interests, developers, manufacturers, retail companies and the like. Demonstrations, litigation, protests and boycotts have become commonplace in today's environmental news. More difficult to find are stories of cooperation and compromise between community groups and stakeholders where sincere and sustained effort is invested in solving environmental problems cooperatively and locally.

Homegrown Ecopragmatics conveys some of these stories, featuring a set of original case studies involving unusual and unexpected environmental partnerships. The book explores these unique collaborations to discover how these relationships evolved, how they serve the divergent interests of their participants and how they may be replicated elsewhere. Moreover, each case study is analyzed and interpreted in terms of the ecopragmatic principles exemplified by participants and stakeholders. These principles, derived from the earlier work *Ecopragmatics* (Wimberley & Pellegrino 2014), serve as the philosophical foundations for a pragmatic environmental ethic.

Situated at Florida Gulf Coast University in Southwest Florida it would have been tempting to begin this study of "strange bedfellows" and unexpected environmental partnerships with a case study close to the heart and geographical roots of this Florida author—the infamous Cross Florida Barge Canal. Having grown up in Florida, I vividly remember the controversy over a proposed "ditch" that would have utterly destroyed the scenic Ocklawaha River and potentially disrupted freshwater hydrology throughout northern and central Florida. Tempting as it would have been to have included that story in this book of case studies, this interesting environmental case has already been told in great nuance in Steven Noll and David Tegeder's *Ditch of Dreams* (2015).

In their remarkable book, Noll and Tegeder describe an effort spanning more than 70 years to build a canal across Florida for ship or barge traffic—an endeavor that would have rivaled the engineering of the Suez and Panama canals. At the heart of their story, however, is the epic struggle of a stalwart group of environmentalists principally situated in Alachua and Marion Counties and led by biologist Marjorie Harris Carr to halt the building of the canal in the interest of protecting the Ocklawaha River and its environs. Carr and her collaborators organized their opposition to the canal with the creation in 1962 of Citizens for Conservation. Their resistance was originally grounded in the harm such a canal would cause to the freshwater aquifer. Later, under Carr's leadership, they modified their opposition to the canal emphasizing its threat to natural scenic ecosystems and threatened species, and with this change in emphasis came a change in the organization's name—Florida Defenders of Environment (FDE).

As the organization shifted its emphasis and name so did it change its tactics. FDE aligned itself with the newly emerging Environmental Defense Fund (EDF) and used the considerable scientific expertise of its membership to document how the canal would harm the riparian ecosystem and the species residing therein, thereby empowering EDF lawyers to challenge the canal in federal court. Their efforts and the notoriety they garnered along the way ultimately influenced public support in favor of their cause and motivated President Richard Nixon to halt the project permanently in 1971 (Davis 2004).

From the outset Marjorie Carr assumed the leading role in canal opposition. However, in 1969 rebranded as Florida Defenders of Environment, another leader emerged within the organization—long time Florida businessman and civic leader John Couse. Couse had long been an opponent of the canal, in part because he owned land along the Ocklawaha River that was threatened by canal construction. In the late sixties and early seventies Couse proved valuable to canal opponents because of his ability to recruit fiscally conservative Republicans to oppose the canal by emphasizing the sizeable burden taxpayers would pay to have access to a canal of questionable value. This partnership of fiscal conservatives and environmentalists ultimately succeeded in defeating the Cross Florida Barge Canal. As Noll and Tegeder observed this "marriage of environmental liberalism and fiscal conservatism" ultimately succeeded where environmental opposition alone had failed. Accordingly, "The ultimate success of the movement lay in its ability to bridge the ideological gap between antigovernment Goldwater conservatism and activist environmental liberalism" (Noll & Tedeger 2015, 199).

ORGANIZATION OF THE TEXT

The Cross Florida Barge Canal illustrates how successful environmental partnerships can develop and function. The case studies presented herein are likewise illustrative of productive partnerships among unlikely interests. They involve four topics: solar energy in Georgia and Florida, timber and grazing in Oregon, the ecological health of the Brazos River in Texas and phosphate mining in Florida. Since these topics are inherently complicated and involved this book of case studies provides a "backgrounder" chapter (like the "white papers" used in briefing legislators on policy issues) prior to each case study. The rationale for such an inclusion is to provide a thorough context for understanding each case study.

Homegrown Ecopragmatics uses this case study methodology to demonstrate how ecopragmatic principles have been employed to build sustainable community relationships that in turn produce sustainable environmental outcomes. As such it presents a set of five case studies. Case studies involving solar energy advocates and phosphate mining opponents in Florida and timber and grazing controversies in Oregon are each preceded by a "backgrounder" chapter to provide deep context to each case study. The book also includes two case studies devoted to the health of the Brazos River in Texas, one looking at the work of the group Friends of the Brazos and another exploring the unique partnership of The Nature Conservancy with Dow

Chemical and their Freeport, Texas facility. These two case studies are preceded by a single background chapter on the ecology, hydrology and economics of the Brazos River basin.

The first four case studies demonstrate unlikely partnerships among erstwhile adversaries. However, the final case study involving opposition to phosphate mining in Florida illustrates conditions under which pragmatic action and compromise are inhibited and stymied. This important case study is included to remind the reader that sometime resistance and opposition is the only available course of action to deter and prevent environmental harm. In this regard the final case study involving opposition to phosphate mining in Florida is consistent with the legacy of Marjorie Carr, who although successful in working to forge relationships among "strange bedfellows" to avert the destruction of the Ocklawaha River and its environs, was equally successful in tireless grass-root resistance to economic and political interests that were not inclined to bend or compromise to her principles or ecological vision.

Before continuing to examine the case studies presented herein we will proceed to the first chapter which provides a conceptual framework through which each case is analyzed and evaluated. Chapter one will introduce the reader to the five guiding principles of ecopragmatics and discuss the importance of "homegrown" local environmental initiatives and partnerships. It is difficult to overstate the importance of local "homegrown" advocacy and activism on behalf of environmental issues. This text derives its title from the twin values of ecopragmatism—pursuing achievable environmental outcomes via cooperation and compromise—and dedication to developing "homegrown" local initiatives and organizations capable of pursuing environmental advocacy indefinitely. Hopefully the reader will not only find the case studies presented herein interesting and informative but will also appreciate the ecopragmatic values that are brought to bear locally and regionally to address serious environmental and socio-economic issues.

REFERENCES

Davis, Fredrick R. 2004. "Get the Facts: An Then Act": How Marjorie H. Carr and Florida Defenders of Environment Fought to Save the Ocklawaha River." *Florida Historical Quarterly*. 83(1): 46-69.

Noll, Steven and David Tegeder. 2015. *Ditch of Dreams: The Cross Florida Barge Canal and the Struggle for Florida's Future*. Gainesville: University of Florida Press.

Wimberley, Edward T. and Scott Pellegrino. 2014. *Ecopragmatics*. Champaign, IL: Common Ground Publishing.

CHAPTER 1

In Praise of Strange Bedfellows: Homegrown Values

A CONCEPTUAL FRAMEWORK

Five Essential Ecopragmatic Principles

Ecopragmatics is at work wherever multiple stakeholders holding divergent visions of environmental value, interact and find common cause. Suh approaches are particularly useful in seemingly intractable situations where conflict seems inevitable or in the case of policy stalemate when competing worldviews push important environmental concerns to the point impasse. Productive ecopragmatic efforts—like those illustrated in the case studies to follow - uniformly employ principles and practices foundational to effective problem solving.

Even a cursory analysis of the cases to follow illustrates a consistent pattern of interaction employing five guiding ecopragmatic principles to include:

1. *Partnerships among "Strange bedfellows:"* Collaboration among adversaries who normally don't cooperate or in some cases even communicate with one another.

2. *"Homegrown" Initiatives:* Grassroots efforts typically designed to deal with local problems that employ local resources and network to higher levels of community involvement.

3. *Satisficing Communitarianism:* An approach where the benefit of an entire community takes precedence over the needs of any one group. In the interest of meeting pressing community needs options are sought and then adopted that while not ideally solving all community concerns, address the most urgent needs in a way that is generally satisfactory to community members while leaving open the possibility and the community networks needed to search for and implement even better solutions.

4. *Deliberative Democracy:* Involves cooperation among communitiy groups and entities that maximize citizen input and influence or may assume a more informal and extemporaneous form when stakeholders and interest groups informally convene with one another to gauge community interests and needs to plan and program appropriately. Deliberative democracy and communitarianism are intertwined concepts and practices.

5. *Libertarian Free Market Practice:* Operates upon the principle that whenever possible private enterprise should be employed to solve community problems and conversely that when governmental regulation or

involvement is called for that only minimal governmental involvement be sought and tolerated.

These five principles insure broad community participation and practice in dealing with environmental problems first locally as grassroots efforts and then incrementally at the state, regional and national level.

The five-principle approach builds upon the research of the late Nobel Prize winning Eleanor Ostrom, favoring organic grassroots problem solving that promotes "bottom-up" solutions over hierarchical "top-down" approaches. These principles promote "community" and civic-mindedness at the most basic level and encourage individuals to assume local responsibility for environmental problems and creatively arrive at solutions employing available resources and expertise. Finally, these five ecopragmatic principles philosophically approach problems as opportunities rather than obstacles seeking to create empathy, relationships and ultimately partnerships between stakeholders who otherwise might become intractable adversaries.

The goal of ecopragmatics is to transform "either-or" mindsets into "both-and" mentalities allowing and promoting more "win-win" outcomes and fewer "win-lose" scenarios where there are "victors and victims." Ultimately, these ecopragmatic principles are designed to avoid balkanization between and among local stakeholders and replace isolation and inter-group alienation with partnerships, collaborations and ongoing cooperation capable of solving both current and emerging problems. Given this brief introduction to the ecopragmatic principles, let us proceed and take a more in-depth and nuanced look at each principle.

Strange Bedfellows: Local Initiatives

Imagine sitting down at the negotiating table—or any table for that matter—to establish an ongoing working relationship with someone or some group or organization with whom you have very little in common and whose values you fully disagree with. You might rightly ask yourself the question "Who in their right mind would do such a thing?" The answer to that question is the pragmatist. The pragmatist, you see is an individual or organization so fully committed to improving the lot of the people and the environment around them that they would be willing to sit down with almost anybody willing to make some reasonable degree of compromise to ameliorate or solve the pressing environmental problems of our day. These are the folks who avoid becoming bogged down in "analysis paralysis" or pointless posturing and instead address the pressing problems before them knowing that with ongoing contact and communication with their ideological opponents comes additional opportunities to pursue future agreements and cooperative efforts. In short, these pragmatists see more to be gained in being "strange bedfellows" with their ideological opponents than they do as "combatants" in the policy arena. Consequently, they "agree to agree" where such agreement is possible while vocally differing with one another on other important issues and "agree to disagree" on yet unaddressed and unsolved problems. This willingness among a wide array of disparate community and environmental interests to come together to forge partnerships where it is mutually advantageous while agreeing to agree to disagree (at least for the time being) on those things they can't find common ground on is what lies at the heart of a "homegrown" approach to Ecopragmatics.

Homegrown Ecopragmatics is a case study oriented follow-up to *Ecopragmatics* (Wimberley & Pellegrino 2014) and is designed to explore how ecopragmatic approaches to environmental issues have been fruitfully employed to address a variety of environmental issues throughout the nation. As the title of the book suggests, the rationale for the book is to explore a series of creative partnerships and cooperative efforts between parties and stakeholders that one might otherwise consider to be too divergent to find common ground and purpose. To that end the book presents a series of unique case studies involving *"strange bedfellows"* from around the United States to illustrate successful local initiatives that can be applied elsewhere.

Homegrown Ecopragmatics builds upon the forward-thinking research of the late Elinor Ostrom whose Nobel Prize winning research (Ostrom 2009; 2012) demonstrated how local communities can creatively and proactively address pressing environmental concerns. Rather than giving into the frustrations of market failures and the seeming inevitability of endless government regulations Ostrom's research underscores the importance of approaching environmental problems as an ongoing process directed simultaneously toward "social" and "ecological" systems—or what she calls "social-ecological systems" (SES). Ostrom's research reinforces the famous adage of former Speaker of the House Tip O'Neal who was famous for saying "all politics is local politics" (O'Neal 1995). In like manner, all environmental issues occur locally and incorporate numerous stakeholders embedded within a variety of social-ecological environments. Given this social-ecological context responses are required that reflect consideration of "natural resources" and some system of managing and using those resources (Ostrom 2012, 68-69).

The SES is part of a four-part framework Ostrom employs to conceptualize and address environmental issues locally, regionally, nationally and beyond. The framework (Figure 1) includes: (Ostrom 2009, 420)

1. "resource systems (e.g., a designated protected park encompassing a specified territory containing forested areas, wildlife, and water systems);"

2. "resource units (e.g., trees, shrubs, and plants contained in the park, types of wildlife, and amount and flow of water); "

3. "governance systems (e.g., the government and other organizations that manage the park, the specific rules related to the use of the park, and how these rules are made); and

4. "users (e.g., individuals who use the park in diverse ways for sustenance, recreation, or commercial purposes).

The sub-units of this framework system interact with one another and produce outcomes impacting every system component and the system.

Ostrom particularly focuses upon issues associated with governance systems and how they regulate users consuming natural resources within a network of resource systems. She chiefly addresses the conundrum facing modern societies who have historically relied upon a combination of market and governmental regulation. The problem that drove her concern in this regard is that neither market forces nor government regulations have consistently served to protect and sustain environmental resources and systems. Those frustrated with market failures in this regard have often called for more and more governmental regulation at every level to include increasing international regulation in a decidedly "top down" fashion. Meanwhile businesses and "libertarian" minded citizens have decried more governmental regulation as threatening trade and personal / national freedom and autonomy. Ostrom calls for a reconceptualization of environmental problems outside of the regulation versus market dichotomy arguing,

> "We need to get away from thinking about very broad terms that do not give us the specific detail that is needed to really know what we are talking about. We need to recognize that governance systems that *actually have worked in practice* fit the ecological diversity of ecological conditions that exist in a fishery, irrigation system or pasture, as well as the social systems. There is a huge diversity out there, and the range of governance systems that work reflect that diversity" (Ostrom 2009, 70).

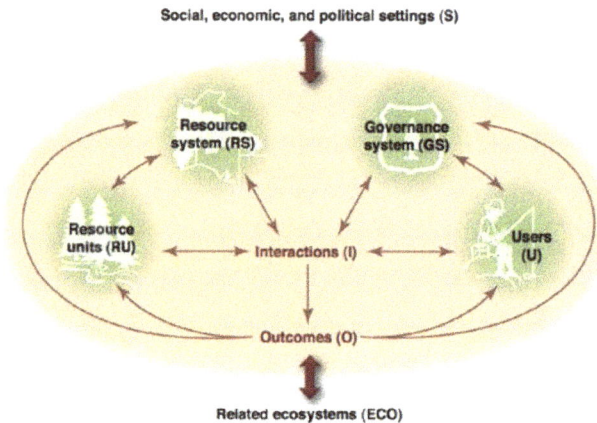

Figure 1: Framework for Analyzing Socio-Ecological Systems
Source: Ostrom 2009

Although Ostrom recognizes that local solutions to environmental problems are not always possible or effective, she favors whenever feasible fostering the local governance of natural and environmental resources within a framework of "polycentric systems" where,

> "systems exist at multiple levels with some autonomy at each level" as illustrated by "a region where there is a government agency responsible for the large regions, but there is a lot of local autonomy in the management of local resources in that region. If we create a polycentric system, then it

retains many of the benefits of local-level systems because there are people at a local level making decisions about many of the rules. But it also adds overlapping units to help monitor performance, obtain reliable information and cope with large scale resources." (Ostrom 2012, 82).

Ostrom asserts that the value in such an approach is that "it retains the benefits of local-level systems because there are people at a local level making decisions about many of the rules. But it also adds overlapping units to help monitor performance, obtain reliable information and cope with large scale resources" (Ostrom 2012, 82).

One of the central benefits of Ostrom's polycentric-system approach is that it encompasses a large pool of "actors" or stakeholders within the "social" system that consume or impact "resources." Accordingly, it is important to consider the variety of "actors" involved within a social-ecological system and to ask questions such as,

> "How many are there? What kind of socio-economic attributes do they have? What is their history of the use of a resource? Where are the actors—are they in a similar location to the location of the resource, or in places far away? What kind of leadership is there? And so on" (Ostrom 2012, 74).

This approach to partnerships and collaborative relationships fosters an abiding familiarity with and responsiveness to the jargon, language and values reflected among and between users. Meaningful and sustained local engagement necessitates garnering respect, creating partnerships and alliances and doing so to not only address immediate problems but to lay the groundwork for addressing emerging issues and problems.

Ecopragmatics presented two case studies illustrating Ostom's approach—one involving the Georgia Green Tea Coalition between the Sierra Club and the Tea Party and the other concerning community interests that coalesced to create the Carolina Thread Trail network in North Carolina and South Carolina (Wimberley & Pellegrino 2014). In each case interest groups, who could have otherwise been expected to avoid cooperation with one another given their ideological differences, found a way to agree to disagree upon some issues while closing ranks and cooperating around other issues. Decisions on the part of these disparate interests to cooperate rather than scapegoat and remain in contention with one another reflects a pragmatic desire to not let the "perfect become the enemy of the good" (Effron 2012) when engaging in problem solving. However, such pragmatic urges are purchased with compromises and a willingness to forgo scapegoating one's ideological opponent in the interest of forming a strong partnership that allows participants to incrementally engage one another time and again regarding any number of environmental concerns.

Community stakeholders eschewing collaboration fail to recognize that each entity has legitimate aims, interests, principles and values. Stakeholders can inevitably be expected to pursue courses of actions consistent with their principles, values and interests. Consequently, one might expect most environmental organizations to recoil at the prospects of partnering with an energy producer marketing petroleum products because doing so conflicts with their core organizational values. Conversely, some corporations narrowly dedicated to economic goals might uncritically label all environmentalists as "revolutionaries" and "extremists" because their environmental opposition conflicts with the company's profit orientation. Unfortunately, when such partnerships are forgone because a subset of each organizations values conflict, other opportunities for cooperation around mutual unconflicted values are also sacrificed and opportunities for collaboration are lost.

For instance, a company such as Chevron that recovers, refines and retails petroleum products must be regarded as an essential provider of goods demanded by the larger society - particularly regarding resources needed to meet transportation, heating, pharmaceutical, agricultural, and synthetic demands. An environmental group might rightly quibble about the size and nature of the society's demand for oil and criticize Chevron for the environmental harm caused through recovering, refining, transporting and disposing of its products. However, since the society clearly benefits from these products socially, economically, medically and nutritionally (despite the variety of negative environmental outcomes associated with their various uses) it is counterproductive and short sighted for any environmental advocate to refuse to cooperate with a company such as Chevron solely on the basis of its untoward environmental impacts since doing so ignores the social benefits provided by the company and only targets social and environmental costs.

Moreover, it is counterproductive to refuse to do business with a company like Chevron because it operates on a profit motive. The process of discovering and refining oil is expensive and involved—becoming increasingly more so as petroleum and gas resources must be recovered at greater depths and in more challenging geological locations. Oil companies find and produce these resources in the interest of covering their costs, rewarding investors and ultimately making a profit sufficient to maintain and marginally expand their capacity to find, produce and deliver their products to consumers. Setting aside the degree to which they achieve this through federal tax expenditures, such corporations operate via sales and investments—to include investments in renewable energy.

Any environmental organization choosing to "take on" an oil company because of its business economics or demand-driven market values would in effect commit to eliminating valuable community goods and services in the interest of pursuing narrowly environmental objectives. Doing so, would ultimately prove Pyric to the degree that environmental outcomes would have been purchased at the expense of a large array of other truly vital societal needs for energy, textiles, food, medicines, employment and more. For better or worse, environmental interest and concerns must ultimately be balanced against a wide array of other societal needs and requirements such that the resulting environmental benefits of any action cannot be allowed to exceed the social and economic costs to the society.

On the other hand, companies that depend upon maintaining a profit margin to remain in business must also recognize the legitimacy of environmental demands upon their practices. Rather than automatically construing environmental organizations and interests advocating for cleaner industry as "anti-business" or "anti-industrial" businesses would be well advised to recognize that business and market sustainability is ultimately linked to environmental sustainability. Rather than automatically regarding environmentalists as business opponents, businesses might be better advised to regard them as partners in a common cause.

Valuing cooperation over confrontation in environmental matters entails recognizing that all environmental actions are necessarily marginal rather than absolute in scope. Only revolutionaries and ideologues can afford to live and act in a theoretical world where "ideal" outcomes can be pursued without contending with "practical" consequences. Therefore, the prudent and sustainable environmental organization or actor must necessarily acknowledge the legitimate and necessary role that companies such as Chevron play in our society. Rather than seeking to run them out of business with ever more draconian rules and regulations the prudent and sustainable environmental advocate will seek to positively influence such a company or organization on the margin and work with them to operate in an ever cleaner environmental fashion rather than pursuing immediate, ideal and ultimate environmental outcomes.

Satisficing Communitarianism

An ecopragmatic approach involves the pursuit of "satisficing" rather than ideal environmental outcomes. Etzioni's "satisficing principle" (Etzioni 1997) was discussed in depth in *Ecopragmatics* (2014) and involves adopting policy options that maximize one's policy objectives at any given time rather than endlessly pursuing an unattainable ideal outcome. As such, satisficing renders all policy-making incremental—meaning that all changes in policy direction are formulated as incremental changes from existing policy orientations. Construed in the imagery of a poker game, incremental and satisficing policy outcomes seek to win the card game hand-by-hand rather than trying to win the entire game with a single hand of cards. Framed in this fashion, the prudent and sustainable environmental organization—i.e. the organization that wants to be effective and long-lived in its efforts—is one that chooses to remain in the game if necessary and to "hand-by-hand" engage their "card partners" to the end of winning the game.

However, in doing so they must be cognizant of the legitimacy of their adversary within the larger society and develop an ongoing relationship with them in the knowledge that without doubt they will need to engage adversaries again and again in future encounters and negotiations. Ultimately prudent and sustainable environmental stakeholders will establish long term mutually beneficial relationships with those with whom they are environmentally at odds. Doing so serves too underscore the environmental harm such entities produce while simultaneously acknowledging that their very existence speaks to important societal needs that must be balanced against untoward environmental harm.

Homegrown Ecopragmatics demonstrates how principles employed by social ecologists such as the communitarian Amitai Etzioni (1997; 2003) contribute to the development of sustainable social networks and relationships. These relationships embodied within and among communities serve to transform reactive community responses to emergent environmental issues into long-term cooperative relationships that address short-term environmental "emergencies" and long-term environmental concerns. Etzioni's social ecological approach compliments a deliberative democratic approach to the degree it advocates for the implementation of informal local problem solving and accommodation whenever possible in the interest of avoiding unnecessary and often inefficient laws, regulations and judicial decisions (Etzioni 1997; 2003). To that end *Homegrown Economics* encourages informal local action and cooperation whenever possible as a viable and necessary alternative to litigation, legislation and regulation.

Deliberative Democracy

The term "deliberative democracy" was coined by Joseph Bessette (1980) to describe a vision of democracy that was inherent to the founders of the American republic in the eighteenth century. Bessette conceptualizes the deliberative nature of democracy in the following fashion:

> "the framers believed that if democracy was to be successful, lawmaking must reflect what Publius called "the cool and deliberate sense of the community." Procedures and institutions must have the capacity to check or moderate unreflective popular sentiments and to promote the role of deliberative majorities. In the particular type of deliberative democracy fashioned by the American framers, the citizenry would reason, or deliberate, through their representatives; on most issues the deliberative sense of the community would emerge not so much through debate and persuasion among the citizens themselves as through the functioning of their governing institutions" (Bessette 1994,1-2).

Grounded as it is in representative government, deliberative democracy "demands that the representatives of the people share the basic values and goals of their constituents; their own deliberations about public policy must be firmly rooted in popular interests and inclinations" (Bessette 1994, 2).

While this principle may seem self-evident, in modern times the synchrony between the interests and values of local communities and their representatives cannot always be taken for granted. Per Bessette, this synchrony is central to the workings of deliberative democracy. Once communities and their representatives fall out of sync regarding policy issues then the communities and their representatives assume an adversarial rather than a collegial relationship. As Bessette goes on to observe:

> "The electoral connection is the chief mechanism for insuring such a linkage between the values and goals of the representatives and the represented. If the linkage is sufficiently strong, then the policies fashioned by the political leaders will effectively be those that the people themselves would have chosen had they possessed the same knowledge and experience as their representatives and devoted the same amount of time considering the information and arguments presented in national councils" (Bessette 1994, 2).

In the twenty-first century environmental policy issues are increasingly debated in international councils and not just at the national level. Since these international bodies do not necessarily incorporate an elected membership representative of the values of people living in local communities, there is no impetus for deliberative democracy incorporated within these geographically distant bodies. Consequently, the goals and objectives of these "higher tribunals" increasingly runs the risk of being out of sync with the desires and values of local communities world-wide. Policy initiatives that are designed among nations and implemented among communities run the risk of being ineffective unless they have the "buy-in" and support of localities.

A homegrown approach to ecopragmatics is cognizant of potential mismatches between the values of policymakers and local communities. It is for that reason that a homegrown ecopragmatic approach argues for including localities in the deliberative process as well as working to insure an increased level of community representation in the deliberations of national and international forums. Inevitably, homegrown ecopragmatic approaches associate local representative empowerment with liberty itself and consider this to be a singular value to always be pursued.

Deliberative democracy has been embraced in many quarters as an important component of effectively dealing with environmental issues at the local level. Graham Smith (2003) made significant contributions to this approach with his book *Deliberative Democracy and the Environment.* Smith defines deliberative democracy quite simply as "inclusive and reasoned political dialogue." He measures the utility of deliberative democracy in terms of a set of measurable characteristics: (Smith 2003, 80-81).

1. "Inclusiveness: are all voices heard? If not, how are they represented?

2. Unconstrained dialogue: is deliberation defended against strategic action on the part of powerful interests? Are the conditions in place for the cultivation of judgment as enlarge mentality?

3. A just decision: what type of decision rule is in operation? Does this affect the nature of the deliberations?

4. Sensitivity to environmental values and conditions: can the plurality of environmental values be articulated? Are deliberations and decisions sensitive to the scope, scale and complexity of environmental decisions?"

Given these considerations, Smith proposes three forms of deliberative democracy that can be fruitfully employed to deal with modern environmental issues: (Smith 2003, 81-105).

1. Mediation and stakeholder group engagement,

2. Citizen forums;

3. Citizen initiatives and referendums.

Mediation and stakeholder group engagement relies upon voluntary non-adversarial and cooperative interaction between citizens and stakeholders. It reflects an interactive environment where parties approach mediation as engaged citizens and stakeholders seeking to informally solve local problems—only needing the assistance of a mediator in those instances where issues have reached stalemate and require assistance in moving toward resolution. The role of the mediator in this model is entirely persuasive and facilitative - having no authority to impose a settlement.

By comparison citizen forums may consist of deliberative opinion polls, citizen juries and / or deliberative consensus conferences that serve either separately or as a series of activities to gauge the interests and values of communities. Regardless of the format employed, each approach seeks to bring together a representative cross section of the community to discuss, consider and recommend policy options. Stakeholders are usually convened by a sponsoring agency such as a community foundation that beyond convening these engagements serves to facilitate interaction and guarantee a deliberative product. While these approaches are increasingly employed to promote deliberative democracy, a perennial issue involves how representative the participants are. There is always a tendency in such opportunities for those stakeholders most invested in the issue to participate while those who perceive smaller stakes in the issue may forgo participation or be underrepresented. Likewise, regarding environmental issues there is the issue of who speaks for the environment.

Finally, citizen initiatives and referendums serve as formal policy options providing an opportunity for citizens to directly influence environmental policy. One of the more salient issues in this regard is the degree to which invested and impacted stakeholders have greater incentives to participate in the policy process than is the case for less invested stakeholders. Coupled with the voluntary nature of voting, these approaches can become inherently politically unrepresentative if only invested stakeholders participate and may produce undemocratic outcomes if a politically invested cohort of participants serves to skew outcomes.

Most of the case-study examples utilized in this text will employ a fourth model that we simply call "voluntary stakeholder collaboration" where invested stakeholders further their self-interests by establishing ongoing working relationships with competing interest groups in the pursuit of solving immediate issues and emerging issues. These policy stakeholders will remain independent of mediation or facilitation until and unless they reach a policy impasse on some issue that must be resolved in a more formal fashion or one for whom there are numerous stakeholder groups who have chosen not to participate in a voluntary collaboration.

Homegrown approaches to ecopragmatics seek to ensure that the actions of government are "justified" before the citizenry. Deliberative democracy considered from this perspective,

> "affirms the need to justify decisions made by citizens and their representatives. Both are expected to justify the laws they would impose on one another. In a democracy, leaders should therefore give reasons for their decisions, and respond to the reasons that citizens give in return. But not all issues, all the time, require deliberation. Deliberative democracy makes room for many other forms of decision-making (including bar- gaining among groups, and secret operations ordered by executives), as long as the use of these forms themselves is justified at some point in a deliberative process. Its first and most important characteristic, then, is its reason-giving requirement" (Gutmann & Thompson 2004, 3).

Deliberative democracy presupposes an inherent human agency associated with every citizen that is grounded in the moral tenant that persons "should be treated not merely as objects of legislation, as passive subjects to be ruled, but as autonomous agents who take part in the governance of their own society, directly or through their representatives" (Gutmann & Thompson, 2004, 3). This concept of "agency" is grounded in the ideas of social psychologist Albert Bandura who described human agency as interactive (Bandura, 1986) where people are "neither autonomous agents nor simply mechanical conveyers of animating environmental influences" (Bandura 1989, 1175).

Ideally, within a deliberative democracy individual, social, economic and political interaction "should be accessible to all the citizens." As Amy Gutmann and Dennis Thompson assert in their remarkable treatise on deliberative democracy—*Why Deliberative Democracy?* (2004), "[to] justify imposing their will on you, your fellow citizens must give reasons that are comprehensible to you. If you seek to impose your will on them, you owe them no less" (p. 4). Without question, fruitful cooperation and coordination between and among different social and environmental interests demands that parties be well informed and that actions and proposed actions influencing lives, interests and the environment should be wholly transparent.

Libertarian and Free-Market Oriented

Homegrown Ecopragmatics also takes a uniquely libertarian perspective to environmental policy (Sagoff 1992) by arguing that to the greatest degree possible government legislation and regulation should be relegated to a "last resort" status to be employed only when social collaboration and economic market actions fail to yield sustainable environmental outcomes. As was the case with *Ecopragmatics* (2014) *Homegrown Ecopragmatics* values individual freedom and discretion to such a high degree that it regards regulatory and legislative remedies to environmental problems as options of "last" not "first" resort. The economic corollary to this perspective is free-market environmentalism in which market solutions are employed whenever possible and when effective in lieu of the employment of legislative or regulatory solutions because free-market forces maximize the opportunity for citizens as consumers to make democratic choices by way of their purchasing power (Wimberley & Hobbs 2013; Smith & Jeffreys 1992).

A libertarian and free market outlook dovetails nicely with Ostrom's observation that meaningful environmental action can occur locally rather than imposed from above or beyond the community. Likewise, it fits with Etzioni's communitarianism that demonstrates faith in community members to both set aside individual desires and prerogatives in the interest of pursuing need common goals. Moreover, it recognizes that since citizens figuratively cast economic ballots with their purchasing decisions, they can be motivated in many cases to make consumer choices that promote environmental sustainability. This libertarian impulse, however, does not imply that it is at odds with "any" governmental regulation or oversight. Rather it implies that while governmental regulation and enforcement are necessary this should be held to a minimum.

A libertarian perspective to solving environmental problems recognizes the necessity for environmental legislation and the executive authority to enforce those laws. However, unlike those in favor of predominantly regulatory approaches to environmental issues, the libertarian approach relegates the use of regulation to those instances where informal problem-solving processes and market forces ultimately fail to produce an outcome that is both environmentally and socially sustainable. Moreover, such a perspective asserts that when it comes to moral persuasion or the inducement of people to behave in a more moral fashion regarding the environment that government is the "wrong" institution to implement such action since it rightly emanates from community institutions and values.

A libertarian perspective doesn't expect market forces to produce moral behavior—since the market by nature is "amoral." Rather a libertarian perspective posits an optimistic view of human nature and expects more times than not that when communities can create and enforce moral expectations within their boundaries that people can ultimately be expected to behave morally. By comparison, when government legislates and regulates it sets up external standards for behavior but does not instill an "inner" or "personal" standard. Instead all that is produced are expectations and the threat of sanction if these expectations are violated.

Why "Homegrown" Ecopragmatics?

Based upon this introduction, the reader might inquire as to why this book is entitled "Homegrown Ecopragmatics"? The term "homegrown" hopefully elicits images of locality, novelty, freshness and originality. For instance, tomatoes can be purchased at virtually any food store but tomatoes picked fresh from a garden and sold at a local farmer's market seem to be riper, fresher and tastier. In fact, many will pay extra to purchase such local fare. While tomatoes can be grown in many places—to include hydroponically in greenhouses—those grown close to home always seem preferable to those shipped in from afar.

Arguably the same analogy applies to environmental policy. Policy issues can be debated and "decided upon" at a distance to local communities and in many cases, can be superior to those derived locally—in part because state, federal and international governments have access to better data and research resources than is the case for localities. Even so some argue that decentralized environmental policy-making is inherently problematic since "under most practical circumstances, local environmental authority will lead to inefficient regulations" (Levinson 2003, 103). Admittedly "off-site" policymakers have the virtue of not being compromised by local issues, needs and values—they can be "objective" with a perspective born of distance from the issue. Yet distance and objectivity create their own problems including losing a sense of colloquial sentiments, values and needs as well as a diminished investment in potential outcomes.

For local citizens, home-grown environmental issues are both subjective *and* objective in nature having immediate and important local ramifications. Consequently, these local participants have a personal and community investment in issues that those more distant from the issue may lack. This investment can either lend itself to sustainable environmental policies or not. Nonetheless, the libertarian and communitarian perspective is that community involvement and decision-making is good and that if kept well informed the public will make every effort to pursue sustainable social and environmental outcomes.

Beyond providing a local perspective, objectivity and subjectivity on the issues at hand, homegrown ecopragmatics implies that local people are empowered democratically, economically and practically to solve environmental problems in a manner that promotes the environment, sustains their communities and nurtures their freedom and liberty as citizens. This does not mean that every citizen or even most engage in this democratic process of environmental problem-solving. However, it does mean that those identified in our earlier book *Ecopragmatics* as the "responsibles"—who when given an opportunity to problem-solve and innovate—can be reasonably expected to come up with good (not necessarily "perfect" or "ideal") solutions to local environmental problems.

Finally, "homegrown" approaches to environmental issues foster innovation and ultimately cooperation among communities as each community becomes a democratic laboratory for addressing issues in a way that sustains the environment and the local community. Implicit within American decentralized federalism is the idea that the various states can serve as laboratories for democratic change and experimentation (Boushey 2012). Although federalism makes policy coordination difficult, it also creates opportunities for considerable policy innovation, as municipal, county, and state governments develop new policies to address local concerns. Federalism encourages venue shopping, a process where activists and interest groups strategically exploit the multiple venues of government to secure support for their legislative programs (Baumgartner & Jones 2009; Traub & Hillary 2007). This process increases the number of new ideas entering the political system and can create conditions where innovative policy considerations migrate among a variety of stakeholder constituencies to produce positive feedback loops (Baumgartner & Jones 2009, 240). Although federalism renders policy coordination complex, it also creates opportunities for innovation and policy diffusion—contributing to an approach known as environmental federalism.

While federalism has long been associated with U.S. government as well as among a number of similar federated state systems (Belbase 2010; Millimet 2013) its success as an organizing principle and approach to environmental policy has been mixed particularly regarding "allocation distortions" in which the allocation of resources to meet national environmental issues are not always effectively allocated when political will and influence dominate more objective measures of environmental need. Accordingly,

> "The theoretical literature thus generates some diverse findings on this issue. There seem to be some basic efficiency-enhancing aspects of inter-jurisdictional competition, but there are clearly a range of "imperfections" that can be the source of allocative distortions. The real issue here is the magnitude of these distortions" (Oates 1999, 1136).

In a nation like the United States, where policies at the federal level are tempered and implemented at the level of "sub-nations" (states), environmental federalism entailing decentralized decision-making is not only inevitable, it is necessary to the successful development and implementation of any public policy (Shobe & Burtraw 2012). Essentially, American styled environmental federalism is an approach to addressing environmental issue that requires cooperation between federal and state and local governments in the interest of addressing common environmental issues. In this manner, it can also be referred to as "cooperative" environmental federalism (Percival 1995).

Of necessity, the relationship between state and federal governments in the U.S. is in great part "adversarial" rather than "cooperative" given the Constitution's system of checks and balances on governmental power. Consequently, there are constitutional and policy specific considerations that influence the effectiveness of any federal initiative implemented at the state level. In part this is because the U.S. Constitution allows a proscribed set of powers at the national level while leaving the bulk of policy discretion to the states (Beckett 1988).

Constitutional authority exists at both levels with normative constitutional tenets invested in the U.S. Constitution. Federal laws and policies may be imposed upon the states provided they are federally constitutional and can be funded (either federally or at the state level). Problems predictably arise in cases where Federal regulation extends beyond constitutional authority or when funding regulations fails at either the state or federal level. Policy considerations fail when they don't apply to conditions at the state and local level, when issues of accountability and implementation are left unresolved and when value conflicts emerge between federal regulators and the values imbued within states and localities. In such situations policy-implementation is distorted by constitutional conflicts and state and local policy resistance.

Many who look at pressing global environmental issues such as climate change argue that the stakes are just too high to rely upon decentralized approaches to environmental policy. They in turn call for more centralized approaches at the national and international level. Their perspective is understandable given the importance of so many of the issues and the degree to which issues such as climate change transcend state, regional and national borders.

Understandably these critics don't want to see the planet's fate compromised by the time spent forging consensus at state, local and national levels. Nevertheless, unless democracy is to be suspended perforce internationally to solve the world's most pressing environmental problems, there is no other option within representative republics but to respect local autonomy and constitutional authority and solve complex environmental problems locally and innovatively. Thus, while federalism of necessity implies an inherent adversarial relationship between the governing and the governed, it also offers the possibility for cooperation—what A. R. Rear (1963) refers to as "Cooperative Federalism." It is this approach to federalism that a "homegrown" approach to environmental policy embraces.

REFERENCES

Bandura, A. 1986. *Social Foundations of Thought and Action: A Social Cognitive Theory.* Englewood Cliffs: Prentice-Hall.

———. 1989. "Human Agency in Social Cognitive Theory." *American Psychologist.* 44 (9): 1175-11984.

Baumgartner, Frank R. and Bryan D. Jones. 2009. *Agendas and Instability in American Politics.* Chicago: University of Chicago Press.

Beckett, Candace H. 1988. "Separation of Powers and Federalism: Their Impact on Individual Liberty and the Functioning of Our Government." *William and Mary Law Review.* 29(3): 635-651.

Belbase, Narayan. 2010. "Environmental Federalism," *Policy Brief (April).* International for Conservation of Nature. Washington, D.C.

Bessette, Joseph. 1980. "Deliberative Democracy: The Majority Principle in Republican Government." In Robert Goldwin and William Schambra's *How Democratic is the Constitution?* Washington: AEI Press. 102–116.

———. 1994. *The Mild Voice of Reason: Deliberative Democracy & American National Government.* Chicago: University of Chicago Press.

Boushey, Graeme. 2012. "Punctuated Equilibrium Theory and the Diffusion of Innovations." *Policy Study Journal.* 40(1): 127-146.

Effron, Robin. 2012. "Letting the Perfect Become the Enemy of the Good: The Relatedness Problem in Personal Jurisdiction." *Lewis & Clark Law Review.* 16(3): 867-904.

Etzioni, Amitai. 2003. *The Monochrome Society.* Princeton: Princeton University Press.

———. 1997. *The New Golden Rule: Community and Morality in a Democratic Society.* London: Profile Books.

———. 1967. "Mixed-Scanning: A Third Approach to Decision-Making." *Public Administration Review.* 27(5): 385-392.

Gutman, Amy and Dennis Thompson. 2004. *Why Deliberative Democracy?* Princeton: Princeton University Press.

Levinson, A. 2003. "Environmental Regulatory Competition: A Status Report and Some New Evidence." *National Tax Journal.* 56(1): 91-106.

Millimet, Daniel L. 2013. "Environmental Federalism: A Survey of the Empirical Literature." Discussion Paper 7831, Bonn: Institute for the Study of Labor

Oates, Wallace E. 1999. "An Essay on Fiscal Federalism." *Journal of Economic Literature.* 37(3): 1120-1149.

O'Neal, Tip and Gary Hymel. 1995. *All Politics is Local: And Other Rules of the Game.* New York: Adams Media Corporation.

Ostrom, Elinor. 2012. *The Future of the Commons: Beyond Market Failure and Government Regulation.* London: The Institute of Economic Affairs.

———. 2009. "A General Framework for Analyzing Sustainability of Social-Ecological Systems." *Science.* 325(419): 419-422.

Percival, Robert V. 1995. "Environmental Federalism: Historical Roots and Contemporary Models." *Maryland Law Review.* 54(4): 1141-1182.

Rear, A. R. 1963. "Cooperative Federalism: A Study of the Federal Provincial Continuing Committee on Fiscal and Economic Matters." *Canadian Public Administration.* 6(1): 43-56.

Sagoff, Mark. 1992. "Free-Market versus Libertarian Environmentalism," *Critical Review.* 6 (Spring/Summer): 221-230.

Shobe, William M. and Dallas Burtraw. 2012. "Rethinking Environmental Federalism in Warming World." (January 17), Center for Economic and Policy Studies, University of Virginia, accessed July 17, 2017, http://econ.ccps.virginia.edu/RePEc_docs/ceps_docs/RethinkingEnvFederalism_wp12-01.pdf

Smith, Fred L., Jr. and Kent Jeffreys. 1992. "A Free-Market Environmental Vision." in *Market Liberalism: A Paradigm for the 21st Century.* ed. by David Boaz and Edward H. Crane. Washington: The Cato Institute.

Smith, Graham. 2003. *Deliberative Democracy and the Environment.* New York: Routledge.

Traub, Leah Goldman and Hillary Sigman. 2007. "Cooperative Federalism as a Strategic Interaction: Voluntary Decentralization in Environmental Policy." NBER Working Papers (No. 13238), National Bureau for Economic Research. Cambridge, MA.

Wimberley, Edward T. and Bradley Hobbs. 2013. "The Conservative Ecologist and Free-Market Environmentalism." *The International Journal of Sustainability Policy and Practice.* 8(4): 29-45.

Wimberley, Edward T. and Scott Pellegrino. 2014. *Ecopragmatics.* Champaign: Common Ground Publishing.

CHAPTER 2

Georgia's Green Tea Coalition

BACKGROUNDER FOR CASE STUDY ONE

Who's Sleeping with Whom?

The 2016-2017 campaign to expand homeowner-generated solar power in the State of Florida originated in a phenomenon that first emerged in Georgia several years earlier. The "Sunshine State's" quest of solar expansion was rooted in a "Peach State" initiative known as the "Green Tea Coalition" a truly unique partnership between the progressive Sierra Club and the comparatively libertarian-minded Tea Party of Georgia. The emergence of this unique partnership left many wondering what was going on between these seemingly "strange bedfellows" (Roberts 2015; Schwartz 2014; Cottle 2013). This unexpected partnership eventually influenced the solar debate in neighboring Florida contributing to yet another set of interesting and unexpected environmental collaborations.

Ironically, the unifying issue uniting the Sierra Club and the Tea Party was that of affordable solar energy in the State of Georgia. Their opponent in this quest for affordable solar energy for Georgians was the state's largest electric utility providers - Georgia Power and the Southern Company. These utilities opposed the expansion of small-scale solar roof-top projects because the cumulative impact of home-generated solar power threatened their monopoly over solar power provision statewide. From a purely market driven perspective, these two large utilities sought to thwart the expansion of solar power to prevent homeowners from generating surplus solar power to sell back to the utilities.

Historically, Georgia Power approached the state's Public Service Commission (PSC) annually to request rate increases to offset the cost of operating aging coal-powered electrical generating facilities. Conversely, environmental groups like the Sierra Club, the Southern Alliance for Clean Energy, and the Solar Energy Industries Association challenged these rate increases to force utilities to invest in renewable energy resources. In 2013 following a utility rate increase request, these environmental groups were joined by the Georgia Tea Party who favored the expansion of solar energy by homeowners as an expression of their libertarian-derived belief that consumers had the right to "go off the grid" and reduce their dependence upon utility-provided electricity. The Georgia Tea Party also supported the citizen's prerogative to generate surplus power to sell back to the utility—considering this to be an entrepreneurial right of citizens (Kidd et al. 2013). Realizing they shared similar desires though based upon differing premises, the two groups united to create Georgia's Green Tea Coalition.

Georgia gets lots of sun and the state's largest utilities wanted to cash in on the sunshine and expand their solar generation capacity as they phased out coal-fired plants (Grillo 2013). They also sought to maintain their monopoly over energy generation in Georgia. Consequently, in 2013 when approaching PSC for a rate increase they signaled their intent to dramatically expand their solar generation capacity. PSC resisted their request believing that such an expansion should come at the expense of the utility companies and should not be borne by the state's electric consumers.

Georgia Power responded to the PSC ruling in July of 2013 reporting that several solar power projects associated with the Georgia Power Advanced Solar Initiative (GPASI) and the Large-Scale Solar Initiative demonstrated the capacity for increasing power generation in a cost-effective fashion without the need to increase power rates (Chance 2013). GPASI is a solar energy purchase program adding 210 megawatts (MW) of solar capacity over a two-year period while the Large-Scale Solar Initiative involved buying up to 50 MW of additional solar power to be utilized in Georgia annually (Chance 2013). Based in part upon support from the Tea Party and state environmental groups, the PSC approved the development of large-scale solar utilities in Georgia.

A Commitment to Renewable Energy

The 2013 PSC ruling reinforced the state's commitment to expanding energy capacity as reflected in the Georgia Cogeneration and Distributed Generation Act of 2001 (GCDGA 2001). This legislation included language committing the state to provide "compensation to customers for any power produced in excess of on-site needs or for all of the power generated from the [solar] system" (USEPA 2008). Based upon the provisions of this legislation,

> "Utilities are required to purchase the excess power from an eligible customer generator until the cumulative renewable energy capacity reaches 0.2% of the utility's system peak load. Systems can be interconnected on the customer side of the meter and have a bi-directional meter to measure flows in each direction. In this scenario, net excess generation (NEG) is credited to the customer's next bill. Alternatively, customers may send all power from a system directly to the grid by connecting ahead of the customer meter and essentially selling all power (rather than meeting on-site load with part of the energy and then selling any excess generation)" (USEPA 2008).

The act also permitted private citizens generating electricity to use that energy without the restrictions of PSC regulation. In 2012 and 2013 amendments were brought before the Georgia General Assembly to amend the GCDGA 2001 to "expand consumer choice and economic competition in power production and remove artificial barriers to renewable energy development" (Smith 2012).

In 2012 SB401 was introduced to expand customer freedom to produce and consume electricity (Georgia SB401 2012). The bill met stiff opposition from both Georgia Power and Southern Power. Their resistance was based upon a desire to maintain their monopoly on solar power in Georgia by restricting the capacity of consumers to sell surplus solar power back to the utilities. Their goal was to avoid purchasing surplus solar power from citizen consumers, avoid having to expand the capacity of the grid to handle this additional power and to maintain a monopoly over solar power statewide (Cummings, 2012).

The cumulative impact of the GCDGA amendments and SB401 would have literally redefined the meaning of the term "customer generator" (those who in the original act were permitted to sell power back to the utilities), allowing for much broader citizen participation in power generation and sales. The bill also explicitly prohibited the assessment of unreasonable charges by utilities upon citizen producers of solar energy. Ultimately the Georgia General Assembly failed to enact the legislation. The bill was reintroduced in 2013 and again in 2014. In 2013, the bill was reintroduced with virtually identical language as SB51 and was reintroduced in the 2014 session of the Georgia General Assembly (Trabish 2015).

In 2015 the Georgia General Assembly finally enacted solar energy reform consistent with that advocated by the Green Tea Coalition when they passed the Solar Power Free-Market Financing Act of 2015 which allowed for third party ownership (TPO) of solar. Under the provisions of the act TPO is a finance plan permitting homes and businesses to host solar panels with no pre-installation costs or ownership responsibilities. This new law represents a compromise between solar advocates to include the Green Tea Coalition and Georgia Power Georgia's largest electricity utility—a particularly important compromise since Georgia Power had previously opposed this law. The compromise agreement that Georgia Power ultimately endorsed limits the extent of TPO financing for residential solar installations to no more than 10 kilowatts while commercial solar systems cannot generate power beyond 125% of their business electricity use (Trabish 2015).

Solar Energy Costs

The benefits to be realized by Georgia's consumers from TPO must be considered within the context of investment by Georgia's utility companies in large-scale solar plants. These infrastructure investments take into consideration the amount of solar energy produced by private homeowners if for no other reason because this energy puts additional pressure upon the state's electric grid which the public utilities maintain. From a purely economic perspective, the proliferation of small solar producers significantly impacts the nation's electric providers. A recent report by the Edison Electric Institute asserts that small-scale solar systems constitute the single greatest threat to the nation's utilities—threatening to transform the electric utility industry along the lines that cell phones transformed the telephone industry (Shulman 2013). In Georgia, the sanctioning of TPO's turns consumers into producers and as such these competitors will influence the "bottom line" for all Georgia utilities.

Beyond competitive market concerns between utility-scale and small-scale consumer energy producers, a persistent issue confronting Georgia's renewable energy policies involves operational costs for utility-scale solar energy production. Based upon recent cost-benefit analyses, based on mean energy consumption of 1200 kilowatt-hours annually it would take a full six years for a solar panel in Georgia to produce more energy than had been consumed in its construction. Moreover, the physical space required to produce large volumes of solar energy is significant and costly. Solar utility-scale systems typically require 5 acres of space to generate a single megawatt of energy, meaning that 500 megawatts of energy production require 25 acres of space. Production levels are further compromised by annual sunny day variability. Seasonal variations in sunshine coupled with predictable base-load declines after sundown also necessitates the ongoing operation of coal or natural gas driven plants or power from nuclear facilities which further drives up the cost of power generation (Rust 2013).

Solar Energy Waste Products

The toxic wastes involved in the production of solar panels are also of significant concern both for panel manufacturers and consumers who ultimately assume the costs of disposing of such byproducts. As a recent Rochester Institute of Technology report noted:

> "One drawback of policies that expand renewable technology is they do not proactively consider how the waste produced by PV panels is managed once these panels reach the end of their life span. PV cells contain economically valuable materials, such as silver, indium, and gallium, and other materials, such as silicon and tellurium, that are extremely energy intensive to produce because they can require purities as high as 99.99999 percent. An additional concern with materials contained in PV cells is the potential for toxic metals, such as arsenic and cadmium, to leach into groundwater once these materials are in landfills. For these reasons, discarded PV panel materials that become part of the waste stream must be recycled" (Goe, Tomazewski & Gaustad 2013).

Solar panel manufacturers produce millions of pounds of polluted sludge and wastewater (containing silicon tetrachloride, cadmium, selenium and sulfur hexafluoride to name but a few) annually and this waste must be transported far and wide for disposal (Dearen 2013; Gies 2013). These wastes and their disposal are typically not included in the cost of a solar panel and in Georgia little thought has been put into what will become of old discarded solar panels. Consequently, calculating the true costs of solar energy is rendered complicated since such costs include the cost of production and the cost of recycling and/or disposing of solar panels and their waste. California is illustrative of the types of issues Georgia has yet to face. Some 46 million pounds of solar waste were produced in California between 2007 and 2011. Fully 97% of that waste has been sequestered in California. The remaining 3% or 1.4 million pounds of waste was exported to Montana, Nevada and Arkansas (Dearen 2013).

California's solar waste concerns date to a 2009 report "Toward a Just and Sustainable Solar Energy Industry." This report from the Silicon Valley Toxics Coalition (SVTC) identifies several troublesome pollutants, few of which can be realistically captured for recycling or disposal. Included among these wastes is silica (SiO2) dust, hydrochloric Acid (HCL), trichlorosilane (HSiCl3), silane gas (an extremely hazardous and volatile substance), silicone tetrachloride (SiCl4), sulfur hexafluoride (SF6). The SVTC report further highlights concerns regarding fugitive air emissions involving trichloroethane, acetone, ammonia, and isopropyl alcohol while identifying an extensive number of other toxic substances requiring treatment or disposal, to include sodium hydroxide, lead, hexavalent chromium, potassium hydroxide and more. Unfortunately, as extensive as this list of waste products is there are yet other pollutants of concern, (e.g. ammonia, copper catalyst, diborane, ethyl acetate, ethyl vinyl acetate etc.) associated with the production of solar "wafers" contained on solar panels (SVTC 2009).

Recognizing that as solar power proliferates in states like California and Georgia, SVTC proposed a set of solar waste regulations to include:

- "Phase out use of chemicals already restricted by the E.U.'s Restriction of Hazardous Substances (RoHS).
- Develop chlorine-free methods for making polysilicon feedstock that eliminate the use of trichlorosilane.
- Phase out use of sulfur hexafluoride (SF6).
- Phase out use of hydrogen selenide.
- Phase out use of arsenic.
- Phase out phosphine and arsine.
- Reduce fugitive air emissions from facilities" (SCTV, 2009, 27).

SVTC also proffered suggestions on solar cell recycling to include: (SVTC, 2009, 29).

- Investing in recycling infrastructure
- Designing solar panels for recycling.
- Recycling silicon recovered from consumer electronics products.
- Developing additional recycling processes for all rare metals.

To date, these suggestions have been mostly disregarded and solar panel production facilities continue to produce a significant amount of waste that is being stored in waste sites across the nation.

The need for policies, procedures and infrastructure to manage solar product waste grows proportionately with the expansion of solar energy production. Solar energy production in the U.S. increased from approximately 14 GW of power in the first quarter of 2010 to 64 GW in third quarter of 2012 (Energy Manager Today 2012). As solar power production increases and as solar power generation infrastructure continues to expand so will the costs associated with treating and disposing of waste byproducts and discarded solar panels. Ultimately these costs are incorporated into the prices consumers pay to satisfy their energy needs.

Disposal, Treatment and Recycling Considerations

Historically the Georgia Public Service Commission has principally concerned itself with the rates public utilities charge citizens, the development and siting of new energy facilities and costs associated with these facilities that will be passed on to Georgia consumers. However, in the future PSC will also have to incorporate environmental waste costs to include solar waste treatment, disposal and recycling when setting Georgia's electric utility rates. While such benefit-loss accounting is new to the regulators and utilities, they will become increasingly common and will ultimately increase the cost of energy use.

Until recently, Georgia had only one producer of solar panels in the state— Suniva Inc. located in Norcross, Georgia (Suniva 2013). Historically, Suniva has been the leading solar panel producer in the U.S. and insists their production process "creates zero "sludge" and zero "contaminated water" (Shea 2013). Suniva also claims their monocrystaline solar modules can be produced using 88% recycled glass and 85% of solar cell material using 55% less wastewater, recycling 100% of silicon wafer scrap and utilizing 60% less raw material input than their competitors (Coker 2010).

However, in 2017, Suniva announced it was declaring bankruptcy and closing its only Georgia production facility (Duncan 2017). In so announcing Suniva claimed that they were unable to remain competitive with Asian manufacturers who are quite literally flooding the market with their products (Roselund 2017). Suiva grew rapidly since its founding in 2007 at Georgia Tech University. This growth in part was fueled by state and federal tax credits. The company was partially acquired by a Chinese solar panel producer in 2015 (Shunfeng International Clean Energy). Much of Suniva's growth was fueled by millions of dollars in local, state and federal tax credits. Trade tariffs against Chinese manufacturers made Chinese exports of solar panels prohibitive thereby motivating Shunfeng International to move part of their production capacity to the U.S. Ultimately however international pressure from other overseas markets forced investors to close their U.S. operations in Georgia. Even as Suniva filed for bankruptcy it urged the Trump administration to impose tariffs on foreign solar panel producers to protect U.S. manufacturers (Maloney 2017).

Per USEPA data, during Suniva's first two years of operation air pollution emissions increased from 45 pounds annually in 2009 to 295 pounds in 2011 while off-site transfers of pollutants increased from 35 to 171 pounds over the same period with total pollution releases and transfers increasing from 80 to 466 pounds over the period. Of these pollutants 295 pounds of hydrogen fluoride were released into the atmosphere and 171 pounds of lead was shipped off-site (USEPA, 2012). This is a remarkably small quantity of waste production, especially when considering that the total production related waste—i.e. the sum of recycled on-site, recycled off-site, energy recovery on-site, energy recovery off-site, treated on-site, treated off-site and quantities disposed of or otherwise released on- and off-site—totaled 39,371 pounds in 2011 (USEPA, 2012).

As Suniva's demise illustrates, solar panels can be purchased by Georgia homeowners from manufacturers worldwide. The quality and environmental standards involved in manufacturing these panels can vary significantly with many failing to meet the quality and environmental standards required of Suniva by the USEPA (Jai 2017; USEPA 2016; Lerner 2014; Nunez 2014; USEPA 2011). Imported solar panels are those which are most likely to be found on the homes and in the backyards of consumers across Georgia to include solar panels principally manufactured in China, such as CanadianSolar, ReneSola, Hanwha Solar One, Sharp, ET Solar, Yingli Solar, Solarland, Suntech and Talesun as well as by U.S. manufacturers like Suniva, SunEdison, SolarWorld, REC Solar and Kyocera. Solar panels manufactured in the US are regulated by the USEPA while panels manufactured in China and other Asian countries are not environmentally regulated as strictly as in the U.S. or Europe. Consequently, toxic wastes associated with solar panels produced in China are a much bigger environmental problem in Asia than in Europe or the U.S. (Nath 2010).

Admittedly, environmental pollution realized in the production of solar panels in Asia doesn't immediately impact utility consumers in Georgia since that pollution has been externalized out of state and out of the U.S. However, when it comes to disposing of spent solar panels, the costs of recycling and disposal applies to all domestic consumers. With the number of Georgians purchasing solar panels increasing and with public utilities increasing the sizes of their solar operations inevitably significant costs for managing solar waste from spent panels will increase and be passed on to the consumer.

Silicon based solar panels have a functional life of about 25-30 years before they are discarded. The glass and aluminum in the cells can be immediately recycled. In some cases the silicon wafers in the panels can be refurbished. In fact, about 90% of the content of a solar panel can be recycled. European nations have been steadily increasing the rate at which they recycle used solar panels led by the efforts of PV Recycle (PV Cycle 2013). In the United States, it is estimated that recycling solar panels should prove to be a very lucrative business generating approximately $12 billion by 2035 (Energy Matters 2012).

A new technology developed at Georgia Tech University may one day further improve the environmental safety of solar panels by constructing them with solar cells developed from trees (Cameron 2013). However, currently there are no solar panel recycling facilities available in Georgia and the organic cells being developed by Georgia Tech are not readily available on the market. Clearly if solar power is to be expanded in Georgia it will be accomplished via silicon-based panels manufactured domestically and abroad. At some point these panels will become spent and will require disposal and recycling. Clearly, thought needs to be given now to planning for facilities to collect and recycle panels currently being sold and utilized in the state by public utilities and private citizens.

Recent reports on issues associated with defective solar panels manufactured abroad and sold in the U.S. may serve to accelerate public concern regarding the recycling and disposal of spent solar panels. For instance, in the Los Angeles area accounts of defective solar panels marketed with a 25-year warranty but dysfunctional after only two years have grown in number. One New York Times story (Woody 2013) presents a series of anecdotes regarding seemingly pervasive solar generation problems throughout the central region of California. However, in the absence of any well documented study or survey of how solar panels are performing across the rest of the nation and internationally it is hard to determine the extent to which plans for solar panel recycling and disposal need to be prioritized.

A recent audit by the Massachusetts procurement and quality assurance company, SolarBuyer demonstrates the degree to which solar panel quality has come under public scrutiny. Per their recent audit of Chinese solar panel factories, SolarBuyer discovered "defect rates of 5.5 percent to 22 percent" over an 18-month period (Olen 2013). SolarBuyer's audit, directed by company founders Ian Gregory and Peter Rusch, was based upon their extensive experience with solar panel manufacturing. Their experience in working with Chinese solar panels led the to conclude that the quality of these panels was so poor that they "needed to provide buyers with solutions" (Trabish 2013). Based upon their estimates, up to 17% of solar panels procured from Chinese plants could conceivably be faulty. Clearly, if it were not for auditors such as SolarBuyer U.S. consumers might be unaware of their panel's defects until sometimes years after installation (Trabish 2013; 2012).

Given the experience of SolarBuyer and its clients, it is reasonable to expect that a significant number of solar panels—not just those manufactured in China, but also in Australia, Germany, the U.S. and elsewhere (IER 2013)—may reasonably be expected to fail within the next 20-30 years. This reality puts pressure upon states embracing the expanded utilization of solar panels such as Georgia to begin the process of anticipating the costs associated with recycling and disposing of solar panels manufactured today. These costs of necessity must be considered in expanding solar energy utilization in the state.

The Adequacy of Georgia's Electric Grid System

A final issue to be considered in expanding Georgia's solar energy capacity is the adequacy of the state and regional power grid to manage loads from intermittent energy sources such as those generated by solar panels. The current electrical grid was designed for continuous, steady-rates of electric generation fueled by coal, diesel and natural gas plants. The introduction of green energy sources from wind and solar produces variable and intermittent rates of power generation that can overwhelm the conduction capacity of the grid when both steady-stream or continuous power are being transmitted simultaneously. Accordingly, managing the flow of power can become problematic when the grid must absorb home-generated solar energy while steadily transmitting utility-based power, particularly when solar-generated power fluctuates such as when cloudy days produce a net draw on the grid, whereas very sunny days may produce a troublesome power surge (Palmer 2013). Consequently, utility companies are increasingly called upon to develop every more complex synchronization systems to insure the grid is not overloaded producing state and regional power failures (Cardwell 2013).

The development and maintenance of these systems is costly and is complicated by the reality that alternative sources of energy generated off-grid by homeowners and other energy interests serve to undercut the revenue structure of public utilities while often imposing new costs upon them—such as more sophisticated power synchronization technologies. Concern in this regard has been recently fueled by a report by Peter Kind on behalf of the Edison Electric Institute (EEI) entitled "Disruptive Challenges: Financial Implications and Strategic Responses to a Changing Retail Electric Business" (Kind 2013). What EEI is concerned about is how the growth of decentralized solar and other renewable energy resources threatens the ability of large energy utilities to maintain the electrical grid that everyone relies upon to transport power from one location to another. Per the EEI report:

> "Today, a variety of disruptive technologies are emerging that may compete with utility-provided services. Such technologies include solar photovoltaics (PV), battery storage, fuel cells, geothermal energy systems, wind, micro turbines, and electric vehicle (EV) enhanced storage. As the cost curve for

these technologies improves, they could directly threaten the centralized utility model. To promote the growth of these technologies in the near-term, policymakers have sought to encourage disruptive competing energy sources through various subsidy programs, such as tax incentives, renewable portfolio standards, and net metering where the pricing structure of utility services allows customers to engage in the use of new technologies, while shifting costs/lost revenues to remaining non-participating customers. In addition, energy efficiency and DSM programs also promote reduced utility revenues while causing the utility to incur implementation costs" (Kind 2013, 3).

It is feared that with the spread or new energy technologies such as the widespread use of solar cells that consumers will reduce their use of utility-generated power forcing utilities to raise their rates which will disproportionately impact users who aren't participating in these new energy technologies. Ultimately, the EEI report concludes that,

"The threat to the centralized utility service model is likely to come from new technologies or customer behavioral changes that reduce load. Any recovery paradigms that force cost of service to be spread over fewer units of sales (i.e., kilowatt-hours or kWh) enhance the ongoing competitive threat of disruptive alternatives" (Kind 2013, 3).

Illustrative of the technology concerns voiced by EEI are the developments occurring at the home-owned solar panel level where technological innovations are making it possible for consumers to use less electricity from the grid while selling power back to the grid as well as being able to go completely off-grid for extended periods of time. For instance, each home-based solar panel employs a grid-tied inverter that converts direct current (DC) into a grid system based upon alternating current (AC). This inverter assists in protecting the solar panel from surges from the grid, while allowing for reduced grid usage and the transmission of excess power into the grid system (Maehlum 2013). However, a problem encountered by many homeowners using a grid-tied inverter is that when the power grid is down for whatever reason, consumers are unable to use the energy being provided by their solar panel (Gahran 2014). This issue involves net-metered solar energy systems that do not include battery back-up (Aggarwal 2016).

Unfortunately, most of the approximately 300,000 solar systems employed in homes across the U.S. are net-metered and lack batteries—meaning that when the grid is down the functionality of the solar panels is completely lost (IEC 2014). However, by employing battery back-up systems and employing technology that "islands" the solar generating system such that its power is segregated from the incoming power on the electric grid, consumers are increasingly able to function comfortably both on and off the electrical grid (Wilson 2013). In this fashion "decentralized" electric producers are reducing their reliance on the electrical grid, thereby reducing demand for these energy resources while foisting upon the public utilities the complex and costly problem of synchronizing a grid system being fed by "predictable" utility-based providers and comparatively "variable" decentralized energy providers (IEC 2015).

While decentralized home solar energy production is of great concern to the viability of the electric industry, some providers are innovatively developing new ways of producing solar energy on a utility-based scale and doing so in a manner that makes that energy easier to synchronize into the electric grid (Pérez-Arriaga & Knittel 2016).

For instance, consider the case of the Ivanpah Solar Plant in Ivanpah Dry Lake, California. Per officials at the plant, solar energy is now being fed into the Pacific Gas and Electric grid (PG&E) by way of a synchronization system that is built around a large array of mirrors situated in the California desert aimed at a central tower that continuously and uniformly captures solar energy used to power a steam turbine that produces electricity in essentially the same way any conventionally fueled generator would. This steady source of energy generated throughout most of the daylight allows the Ivanpah plant to function in a manner like other non-solar facilities (Oswana 2013), with the exception that this plant heavily relies upon natural gas resources during the evening hours to maintain solar power during the daylight (Danelski 2017). This 377-megawatt facility is a joint venture between developer BrightSource Energy, project owners NRG Energy, Google and Bechtel Engineering (Hering 2014).

Ventures like the one at Ivanpah and the willingness of investors to back such projects suggest that the livelihoods of electric utilities are not going to disappear from the scene and can be expected to provide the bulk of the nation's electric energy over the foreseeable future. However, that said, there is no doubt that the advent of home energy production via solar technology will allow consumers to economize in their energy use and place a smaller demand upon utilities, compelling these large corporate entities to refashion their rate structure, refashion how they produce and transport electricity and reformulate how they manage the electric grid in a manner that insures sustainable power while doing so within a cost / reimbursement structure that the utilities and their customers can financially sustain.

These are the issues that Georgia Power and any other electrical utility operating within the State of Georgia must consider considering the Georgia Public Service Commission's decision to encourage and facilitate the ease with which Georgia consumers can employ solar panels in their homes, businesses and properties. Allowing more players in the electric industry produces more and cleaner power while increasing the autonomy of the consumer. However, it does so at a price and that price involves a degree of destabilization of the state's utilities, a marginal increase in energy costs for customers who are not using solar panels, and additional grid management costs for the state's electric utilities because of the changing nature of the electricity being transmitted across the grid (i.e. intermediately generated power versus stead electric generation).

Environmental Partnerships at Work

Given the plethora of issues to be addressed in expanding solar energy in Georgia, it is noteworthy that the Public Service Commission finally agreed to pursue a course of action that empowers consumers to both conserve energy and produce power that can be re-directed back into the electric grid. There is no doubt, however, that the Georgia Public Service Commission's decision to make solar energy more available to consumers is in great part the result of the influence of Georgia's Green Tea Coalition (Green Tea Coalition 2013). The Green-Tea Coalition is a wonderful example of a productive environmental partnership uniting two very philosophically disparate groups—the progressive Sierra Club and the libertarian-leaning Tea Party. These strange bedfellows ultimately congealed to accomplish a common goal: the expansion of solar energy in Georgia.

While their intuitive reasons for entering an agreement with one another (environmental protection versus entrepreneurism and consumer choice in the production of solar energy) emanated from very different sources their shared vision of expanded solar energy via homeowner and public utility owned solar generation made it possible for them to agree to disagree on any number of other policy issues in the interest of coming together to promote outcomes they both favored. This is classic environmental communitarianism as predictably heterogeneous intuitive group values ultimately coalesce to promote homogeneous community outcomes.

However, as valuable and functional as these partnerships can be they require ongoing compromise and the willingness to accept satisficing outcomes rather than ideal ones. Such partnerships also require that each party refrain from demonizing their ideological opponent/partner in recognition of the need to be able to negotiate future issues as they arise. Finally, partnerships such as that illustrated by the Green-Tea Coalition demonstrate the utility of an ever-expanding set of goals and objectives, proving that a willingness to incorporate a wide range of constituencies in problem solving can ultimately increase the likelihood of arriving at outcomes that are serve multiple interests.

In the case of the Green-Tea Coalition we see a group that has already successfully formed and been influential in the solar energy policy process in the State of Georgia. Yet as the case narrative illustrates, winning support from the public utility commission and the state legislature to expand solar power only sets the stage for creatively dealing with a whole host of other related policy issues such as: (1) the appropriate level of financial benefits homeowners should receive for producing solar power,(2) how public utilities will be regulated and paid in terms of their share of solar energy production, (3) what are reasonable solar energy rates for Georgia consumers, (4) how quality control and safety will be maintained for solar panels sold and manufactured in Georgia, (5) management and innovation of the state's electrical grid and (6) the manner in which solar wastes will be dealt with both in the production of solar panels and in the recycling and disposal of spent solar panels. Unavoidably, coalitions such as the one between the Tea Party and The Sierra Club necessitate the creation of ever-broader coalitions encompassing stakeholders involved in the evolving issue at hand—which in this case involves producing more solar power in Georgia and reducing the state's reliance upon fossil fuels.

Clearly there are other constituencies that will need to be brought into the policy debate (or debates) in Georgia regarding solar energy. If the quality and safety of products is to be assured then retailers, installers and suppliers must be drawn into the conversation regarding product safety, safe installation, product upgrading and recycling of spent panels, etc. The governor and the state assembly will also have to be included in the policy process as demand increases for the licensed and certified solar-panel technicians, as the accumulation of spent panels increases demand for waste disposal and product recycling and as public-safety and fire fighters cope with extinguishing fires and rescuing victims from burning or damaged homes with potentially lethal solar panels (Wong, 2014; Trabish, 2013; Riggs, 2013).

Nor are these the only issues flowing from the decision to expand the use of solar energy in Georgia. As demand for solar energy increases so will the growth of companies producing solar panels—either in terms of silicon-based panels or at some point in terms of organically engineered solar panels. With the growth of these companies comes demand not only for more workers but also for workers with the requisite education and skills to function in the solar energy. Thus, public school districts, community colleges and universities will find their niche in the solar market. Likewise, as solar panels are produced and shipped to customer's state- and nationwide as well as abroad, issues of quality assurance and safety will increasingly emerge as well as issues involving the appropriate levels of tax-levy versus tax-credit should be applied to these products.

While solar energy use is on the upswing in Georgia, it is not the only state to also be moving in this direction. Western and sun-belt states nationwide are also embracing solar power and are expanding their utility-based solar capacity as well as expanding the use of homeowner solar panels. This means that increasingly solar-produced energy will cross state lines meaning that the Congress of the United States, the federal court system and agencies within the federal executive branch will also become involved in the growth of solar power relative to the interstate commerce clause in the U.S. Constitution. Consequently, state-based coalitions such as the Green-Tea Coalition will also have to contend with federal regulators, the Congress and the courts in tailoring solar policy issues to best serve local communities.

As the efforts of the Green-Tea Coalition continues to unfold in Georgia, so will the array of solar-energy related issues that will present themselves (such as product safety, installation regulation, waste-disposal, solar related employment, training and education, economic development, etc.) as will the number of policy participants that representatives of the Sierra Club and The Tea Party will contend with. Also expanding is the number of venues within which the Green-Tea Coalition will seek influence. Of necessity the range of venues within which the Coalition will pursue policy outcomes will significantly expand beyond the Georgia Public Service Commission to the General Assembly (where all new state laws and policies will emanate), the Georgia Secretary of State's office (where corporations are formed and regulated and where professional licensure and certification occurs), the Georgia Department of Community Affairs (that oversees housing and community development and provides local government assistance including waste disposal, state and regional planning and economic development), the Georgia Department of Labor (where the solar-energy workforce will be drawn), the Georgia Office of Insurance and Safety Fire Officer (where issues of public safety and insurability are administered particularly in regard to fire safety), the Georgia Department of Education (where education and training for a solar-energy workforce will occur), and the Georgia Department of Economic Development (which concerns itself with all forms of economic development in the state to include business investing in energy resources as well as marketing Georgia-made products to the nation and world).

Conceivably, the Georgia Department of Agriculture and the Georgia Forestry Commission may also become of interest to the Green-Tea Coalition as utility-scale solar energy farms expand into agricultural and forested areas of the state as well as in regard to the emergence of organically produced plastic polymer solar cell energy along the lines of that being developed at the Georgia Institute of Technology (Hicks

2012). Similarly, the Georgia Department of Natural Resources (GADNR) may likely become involved regarding waste treatment, recycling and disposal activities involved with either the production of solar panels or their eventual disposal. These activities will be specifically a function of the Environmental Protection Division of GADNR but will also involve the U.S Environmental Protection Agency (USEPA).

In summary, the Green-Tea Coalition is a successful partnership between divergent interest groups to accomplish shared goals. To date it has proved itself to be a substantive force in Georgia energy politics and its continued successes will guarantee that it becomes more involved in policy issues relating to solar-energy that will necessitate interaction with a growing number of agencies and community groups. While current leadership is drawn from the Sierra Club and the Tea Party its continued influence and success will require it to cooperate with a growing number of public interests and organizations to realize success. It will pursue its interests in a growing array of policy venues, will seek to influence the policy and political process with the support of a growing array of other interest groups and as a result will inevitably begin to widen its scope of values and policy possibilities to reflect the pragmatic forces that make policy changes possible and sometimes thwart them.

REFERENCES

Aggarwal, Vikram. 2016. "Grid-Tied vs. Off-Grid Solar: Which is Right for You?" *Mother Earth News*. (November 16), Accessed August 17, 2017 https://www.motherearthnews.com/renewable-energy/gridtied-vs-offgrid-solar-which-is-right-for-you-zbcz1611

Cameron, Charley. 2013. "Researchers Create Efficient, Recyclable Solar Cells from Trees," *Inhabit*. (March 26), Accessed November 13, 2013 http://inhabitat.com/researchers-create-efficient-recyclable-organic-solar-cells-from-trees/

Cardwell, Diane. 2013. "Intermittent Nature of Green Power Is Challenge for Utilities," *The New York Times (Energy & Environment)*. (August 14), Accessed December 4, 2013 http://www.nytimes.com/2013/08/15/business/energy-environment/intermittent-nature-of-green-power-is-challenge-for-utilities.html?_r=0&pagewanted=print

Chance, Michael. 2013. "A Historic Day for Solar Energy in Georgia," *RenewableEnergyWorld.Com*. (July 12), Accessed October 1, 2013 http://www.renewableenergyworld.com/rea/blog/post/print/2013/07/why-today-was-a-historic-day-for-solar-energy-in-georgia.

Coker, Anthony A. 2010. "Sustainability at Suniva," Accessed November 13, 2013. http://s389705876.onlinehome.us/Joomla/images/PDFBank/Repository/2011/7AnthonyCoker.pdf

Cottle, Michelle. 2013. "The Green Tea Party: Debbie Dooley Fights Big Energy." *Daily Beast*. (September 16), Accessed August 8, 2017 http://www.thedailybeast.com/the-green-tea-party-debbie-dooley-battles-big-energy

Cummings, Katherine Helms. 2012. "SB401: A Bill Conservatives and Treehuggers Can Love," *Rural and Progressive*. (February 15), Accessed July 27, 2017 http://ruralandprogressive.org/sb-401-a-bill-conservatives-and-treehuggers-can-love/

Danelski, David. 2017. "Ivanpah Solar Plant, Built to Limit Greenhouse Gases, Is Burning More Natural Gas." *The Press-Enterprise*. (January 23), Accessed August 18, 2017 http://www.pe.com/2017/01/23/ivanpah-solar-plant-built-to-limit-greenhouse-gases-is-burning-more-natural-gas/

Dearen, Jason. 2013. "Solar Industry Grapples with Hazardous Wastes," *Associated Press*. Accessed November 11, 2013 http://news.yahoo.com/solar-industry-grapples-hazardous-wastes-184714679.html

Duncan, Todd. 2017. "Large Solar Company in Norcross Files for Bankruptcy," *Atlanta Journal Constitution*. (April 17), Accessed July 17, 2017 http://www.ajc.com/business/large-solar-company-norcross-files-for-bankruptcy/XknGicuGOSI8ourZ8rbxjJ/

Energy Manager Today. 2012. "More than 6.4 GW Solar Electric Capacity Installed in US," December 17, Accesssed November 13, 2013 at http://www.energymanagertoday.com/more-than-6-4-gw-solar-electric-capacity-installed-in-us-087753/

Energy Matters. 2012. "Solar Panel Recycling Will Be A Multi-Billion Dollar Industry," *EcoBusiness*. (January 23), Accessed November 13, 2013 http://www.eco-business.com/news/solar-panel-recycling-will-be-a-multi-billion-dollar-industry/

Gahran, Amy. 2014. "Why Residential Solar Can't Keep the Lights on (Yet)." *Inside Energy*. (August 25), Accessed August 17, 2017 http://insideenergy.org/2014/08/25/why-residential-solar-cant-keep-the-lights-on-yet/

GCDGA. 2001. "Georgia Cogeneration and Distributed Generation Act of 2001." Georgia General Assembly. Accessed August 8, 2017 http://www.legis.ga.gov/legislation/en-US/Display/20112012/SB/401

Georgia SB401. 2012. "A Bill Amending the Georgia Cogeneration and Distributed Generation Act of 2001," Georgia General Assembly. Accessed October 1, 2013 http://www.legis.ga.gov/legislation/en-US/display/20112012/SB/401.

Gies, Erica (2013) "Solar Waste Recycling: Can the Industry Stay Green?" *SF Public Press*. Retrieved from the Worldwide Web November 11, 2013 http://spot.us/pitches/352-solar-waste-recycling-can-the-industry-stay-green/story

Goe, Michele., Brian Tomaszewski, and Gabrielle Gaustad. 2013. "Infrastructure Planning for Solar Technology Recycling," *ERSI News*. (Winter), Acccessed November 13, 2013 at http://www.esri.com/esri-news/arcuser/winter-2013/~/media/Files/Pdfs/news/arcuser/0113/uncertainty.pdf

Green Tea Coalition. 2013. "Very, Very Important Issue," *Green Tea Coalition: Facebook*. Accessed October 1, 2013 https://www.facebook.com/permalink.php?id=209442799211781&story_fbid=220386671450727.

Grillo, Jerry. 2013. "Sun Dancing," *Georgia Trend*. (July), Accessed October 1, 2013 http://www.georgiatrend.com/July-2013/Sun-Dancing/.

Hering, Garrett. 2014. "4 Reasons the Ivanpah Plant is Not the Future of Solar." *GreenBiz*. (February 19), Accessed August 6, 2017 https://www.greenbiz.com/blog/2014/02/19/largest-solar-thermal-plant-completed-ivanpah

Hicks, Jennifer. 2012. "New Techniques Creates First Plastic Solar Cell," *Forbes*. (April 25), Accessed July 12, 2014 http://www.forbes.com/sites/jenniferhicks/2012/04/25/new-technique-creates-first-plastic-solar-cell/

International Electrical Commission (IEC). 2015. "Grid integration of large-capacity Renewable Energy sources and use of large-capacity Electrical Energy Storage." (White Paper), Accessed August 17, 2017 http://www.iec.ch/whitepaper/pdf/iecWP-gridintegrationlargecapacity-LR-en.pdf

———. 2014. "Grid-Tied Inverters: How They Work," *Angelfire.org*. Accessed January 15, 2014 http://www.angelfire.com/biz/themill/hydrofiles/grid-tied.html

Institute for Energy Research (IER). 2013. "America's Green Energy Problems: Defective Solar Panels," *IER News*. (June 3), Accessed November 15, 2013 http://www.instituteforenergyresearch.org/2013/06/03/americas-green-energy-problems-defective-solar-panels/

Jai, Shyrea. 2017. "Chinese Solar Panels to Face Quality Control Barrier." *Business Standard*. (May 25), Accessed August 17, 2017 http://www.business-standard.com/article/economy-policy/chinese-solar-panels-to-face-quality-control-barrier-117052500050_1.html

Kidd, Rusty, Tom Kirby, Terry Rogers, Buzz Brockway, Gloria Frazier, and Carol Fullerton. 2013. "Solar Offers Opportunity to Grow Georgia Economy," *Loganville-Grayson Patch*. (May 31),

Accessed October 1, 2013 http://loganville.patch.com/groups/going-green/p/solar-offers-opportunity-to-grow-georgia-economy.

Kind, Peter. 2013. "Disruptive Challenges: Financial Implications and Strategic Responses to a Changing Retail Electric Business," Edison Electric Institute. Accessed January 15, 2014 http://www.eei.org/ourissues/finance/Documents/disruptivechallenges.pdf

Lerner, Louise. 2014. "Solar Panel Manufacturing is Greener in Europe than China Study Says." *Argonne Now*. (May 29), Accessed August 17, 2017 http://www.anl.gov/articles/solar-panel-manufacturing-greener-europe-china-study-says

Maehlum, Mathias A. 2013. "Grid-Tied, Off-Grid and Hybrid Solar Systems." *Go Solar*. (August 14), Accessed August 20, 2017 http://energyinformative.org/grid-tied-off-grid-and-hybrid-solar-systems/

Maloney, Peter. 2017. "In the Throes of Bankruptcy, Suniva Wants Solar Power Tarrifs to Shield Manufacturing Business." *Utility Dive*. (May 11), Accessed August 6, 2017 http://www.utilitydive.com/news/in-the-throes-of-bankruptcy-suniva-wants-solar-panel-tariffs-to-shield-man/442098/

Nath, Ishan. 2010. "Cleaning Up After Clean Energy: Hazardous Waste in the Solar Industry," *Stanford Journal of International Relations*. (Spring) 11(2): 6-15.

Nunez, Christina. 2014. "How Green Are Those Solar Panels Really?" *National Geographic*. (November 11), Accessed August 17, 2017 http://news.nationalgeographic.com/news/energy/2014/11/141111-solar-panel-manufacturing-sustainability-ranking/

Olen, John. 2013. "Defective Chinese Solar Panels are Derailing Green Energy Efforts" *Economy in Crisis*. (September 26), Accessed November 15, 2013 http://economyincrisis.org/content/defective-chinese-solar-panels-are-derailing-green-energy-efforts

Oswana, Nancy. 2013. "Ivanpah Solar Plant In California Starts Energy Feed To Grid." *Phys.org*. (Sept. 27), Accessed January 15, 2014 at http://phys.org/news/2013-09-ivanpah-solar-california-energy-grid.html.

Palmer, Roseanne. 2013. "Solar Power Growing Pains: How Will Hawaii And Germany Cope with The Boom In Alternative Energy?" *International Business Times*. (December 23, 2013), Accessed January 15, 2014 http://www.ibtimes.com/solar-power-growing-pains how will hawaii germany-cope-boom-alternative-energy-1518702.

Pérez-Arriaga, Ignacio and Christopher Knittel. 2016. *Utility of the Future: An MIT Energy Initiative Response to An Industry in Transition*. Boston: Massachusetts Institute of Technology.

PV Cycle. 2013. "PV Cycle Home." Accessed November 13, 2013 at http://www.pvcycle.org.uk/

Riggs, Mike. 2013. "Why Firefighters Fear Solar Power." *Citylab*. (September 11), Accessed July 12, 2014 at http://www.citylab.com/tech/2013/09/why-firefighters-are-scared-solar-power/6854/

Roberts, John. 2015. "Green Tea Coalition: Strange Bedfellows Fight for Solar Power in the Sunshine State." *Fox News*. (January 16), Accessed August 17, 2017 http://www.foxnews.com/politics/2015/01/16/green-tea-coalition-strange-bedfellows-fight-for-solar-power-in-sunshine-state.html

Roselund, Christian 2017. "Suniva Files for Chapter 11 Bankruptcy." *PV Magazine*. (April 18), Accessed August 17, 2017 https://www.pv-magazine.com/2017/04/18/suniva-files-for-bankruptcy/

Rust, James H. 2013. "Thoughts About Utility-Scale Solar Energy." *Somewhat Reasonable: The Policy and Commentary Blog of the Heartland Institute*. (July 3), Accessed October 1, 2013 http://blog.heartland.org/2013/07/thoughts-about-utility-scale-solar-energy/.

Schwartz, John. 2014. "Fissures in G.O.P. As Some Conservatives Embrace Renewable Energy." *New York Times*. (January 25), Accessed August 3, 2017 https://www.nytimes.com/2014/01/26/us/politics/fissures-in-gop-as-some-conservatives-embrace-renewable-energy.html?emc=edit_tnt_20140125&tntemail0=y&_r=0

Shea, Stephen. 2013. "In response to an article/photo from the Associated Press that appeared in many newspapers." (February 13), Accessed August 17, 2017 http://suniva.com/documents/Response-to-AJC-article.pdf

Shulman, Seth. 2013. "Got Science? A 'Green Tea Party' May Be Brewing." *Huff Post Green.* (August 8), Accessed November 11, 2013 at http://www.huffingtonpost.com/seth-shulman/got-science-a-green-tea-p_b_3726459.html

Silicon Valley Toxics Coalition (SVTC). 2009. "Toward a Just and Sustainable Solar Energy Industry." A SVTC White Paper. (January 14), Accessed November 13, 2013 http://edward wimberley.com/courses/10580/towardjust.pdf

Smith, Stephen A. 2012. "Georgia Consumer Choice Bill Would Boost Economic Opportunities." *CleanEnergyOrg.* (February 22), Accessed October 1, 2013. http://blog.cleanenergy.org/2012/02/22/georgia-consumer-choice-bill-would-boost-economic-opportunities/.

Suniva. 2013. "Suniva, Inc. Homepage." Accessed November 13, 2013 http://www.suniva.com/

Trabish, Herman K. 2015. "Georgia Gov. Deal Signs Solar Third Party Ownership Bill into Law." *Utility Dive.* (May 13), Accessed July 27, 2017 http://www.utilitydive.com/news/georgia-gov-deal-signs-solar-third-party-ownership-bill-into-law/397173/

———. 2013. "Putting Out the Solar Panel Fire Threat." *Greentechsolar.* (September 18), Accessed July 12, 2014 https://www.greentechmedia.com/articles/read/Putting-Out-The-Solar-Panel-Fire-Threat

———. 2012 "SolarBuyer: Teaching Firms How to Spot Shoddy Solar Panels." *Greentech Media.* (March 4), Accessed November 15, 2013 http://www.greentechmedia.com/articles/read/educating-solars-long-term-risk-takers

United States Environmental Protection Agency (USEPA). 2016. "Solar Interconnection Standards and Policies." (November 18) Accessed August 17, 2017 https://www.epa.gov/repowertoolbox/solar-interconnection-standards-policies

United States Environmental Protection Agency (USEPA). 2012. "Facility Profile Report: Suniva, Inc." Accessed November 13, 2013 http://iaspub.epa.gov/triexplorer/release_fac_profile?TRI=3009WSNVNC5775P&year=2011&trilib=TRIQ1&FLD=&FLD=RELLBY&FLD=TSFD SP&OFFDISPD=&OTHDISPD=&ONDISPD=&OTHOFFD=

———. 2011. "Enforcement and Compliance History Online (ECHO): Suniva, Inc., Norcross, GA" Accessed November 13, 2013 http://www.epa-echo.gov/cgi-bin/get1cReport.cgi?tool=echo&IDNumber=110038901864

———. 2008. "State Incentives for Achieving Clean and Renewable Energy Development on Contaminated Lands: Incentives for Clean and Renewable Energy," Georgia Incentives for Clean Energy. (November), Accessed October 1, 2013 at http://www.epa.gov/oswercpa/incentives/ga_incentives.pdf.

Wilson, Alex. 2013. "Beating the Achilles Heel of Grid-Tied Solar Electrical Systems," *BuildingGreen.com.* (August 7), Accessed January 15, 2014 https://www.buildinggreen.com/blog/beating-achilles-heel-grid-tied-solar-electric-systems

Wong, Kristine. 2014. "What Risks Do Solar Panels Pose for Firefighters?" *SolarEnergy.net.* (February 25), Accessed July 12, 2013 http://solarenergy.net/News/tackling-risks-solar-panels-pose-firefighters/

Woody, Tom. 2013. "Solar Industry Anxious Over Defective Panels," *New York Times: Business Day.* (May 28), Accessed November 15, 2013 at http://www.nytimes.com/2013/05/29/business/energy-environment/solar-powers-dark-side.html?_r=1&pagewanted=all&

CHAPTER 3

Solar Friends and Foes in Florida

CASE STUDY ONE

Partnerships of Strange Bedfellows

Throughout this book case studies are presented in two parts: (1) a backgrounder chapter that provides context for the featured case study and (2) the case study proper describing the relationship between one or more environmental organizations and one or more community, governmental, non-profit or business/economic entity. The "backgrounder" for this first case study on solar energy in Florida involved a partnership that emerged in neighboring Georgia between the Georgia Tea Party and the Sierra Club to create what has come to be known as the "Green Tea Coalition." Unbeknown to participants in this Georgia coalition was the degree to which their organization and its goals would spill over the state border into Florida and become a template for solar activism in the "Sunshine State."

The "Green Tea Coalition" backgrounder case study was designed to illustrate how ecopragmatic principles could be applied to solving environmental problems at the state, local and regional level. One of the chief characteristics of this approach is the willingness of people from diverse backgrounds and value systems to agree to set aside their differences in the interest of finding common ground to solve common environmental problems. This is what we like to refer to as the "partnership of strange bedfellows."

The leader of Georgia's "Green Tea Coalition" was a feisty minister's daughter from Louisiana by the name of Debbie Dooley who led the Atlanta Tea Party and later the Green Tea Coalition. Currently Dooley serves as the Director of Conservatives for Energy Freedom (Manjarres 2014) and has set her sights on achieving in Florida what she accomplished in Georgia. To that end she collaborated with Floridians for Solar Choice to pursue an amendment to the Florida Constitution allowing consumers to contract with independent solar providers to purchase solar energy and sell back excess solar power to the utility companies.

Currently Florida citizens have the right to own and install solar panels and can sell excess power back to the utility. However, the cost of those panels, while becoming ever more affordable, can be prohibitive. Those who own panels and wish to sell excess power back to the utility company now incur a transmission fee when doing so. Consequently, Solar Choice advocates seek to make solar more affordable by delimiting the authority of the utility to regulate "private" or "independent" solar generated power and prohibiting public utilities from charging fees on solar producers (Klas 2015). In essence, Floridians for Solar Choice seeks to "allow more homes and businesses to generate electricity by harnessing the power of the sun" by revoking state legal statutes' that prohibit citizens from purchasing electricity from independent solar power companies that install solar panels on homes and businesses and charge customers for power service (Floridians for Solar Choice 2015).

The central point of contention for solar power in Florida is whether the state's public utilities will be allowed to continue their monopoly over the sale and distribution of electrical power. Since only utilities can sell power to Florida's citizens all other competitors are effectively "locked-out" thus undercutting the opportunity for competition in the energy industry that could theoretically drive down the cost of electricity to the consumer. Currently solar leasing is the fastest growing portion of the solar market led by companies such as SolarCity Corporation who provide a "no-money-down" long-term contract to purchase solar power from panels the company installs. The spread of these innovative forms of leasing arrangements coupled with the steady decline in the cost of solar panels since 1988 offers huge potential to the "Sunshine State" to get into solar in a big way saving Florida's consumers considerable energy expenses (Chediak 2015).

Historically there have been numerous state-imposed barriers to the expansion of solar power in Florida. However, rather than challenge all or even several of these issues simultaneously, Floridians for Solar Choice selected a single issue to initially focus upon in its proposed constitutional amendment—namely, opening markets for solar energy. Accordingly, they claim that,

> "Coalition groups decided to choose one regulatory barrier for the ballot initiative, so voters can understand it easily and decide whether or not to support it based on this one issue. There are other barriers to free markets in energy not addressed by this initiative, and conservatives in the coalition believe that we should eliminate those as well. But we have to start somewhere, and opening markets for solar energy in the Sunshine State is a good first step" (Floridians for Solar Choice 2015).

Controversy over Net Metering and Free-Riders

In Georgia, Dooley and her coalition grappled with the consolidated power of the state's influential utility companies seeking to outmaneuver them in the state legislature and at the state utility commission. These Georgia utilities companies—principally Georgia Power and Duke Energy - resisted the growth of rooftop solar units in part because it provided competition for their own energy resources and because of concern that when rooftop solar power was sold back to utility companies there was not an accompanying responsibility to contribute to the maintenance and expansion of the electrical grid that transmitted this additional power (Goldenberg & Pilkington 2013). Accordingly, those who sell their excess solar power back to the utility have been characterized as "free-riders" who economically benefit from the use of the grid without assuming responsibility for financially maintaining it. Georgia utility companies and their Florida cohorts (principally Florida Power and Light and Duke Energy) have criticized these solar "free-riders" and have been supported in doing so by the American Legislative Exchange Council (ALEC).

ALEC describes themselves as a "nonpartisan membership association for state lawmakers who shared a common belief in limited government, free markets, federalism, and individual liberty" (Tanton 2014) They became involved with the solar controversy regarding the issue of "net-metering." Net-metering allows customers who participate in a distributed grid system employing private solar and utility-produced power to buy and sell power to the utility. Numerous states nationwide have adopted net-metering to encourage the use of alternative energy sources and in so doing have allowed the owners of these solar panels to sell excess power back to the utility (Goldenberg & Pilkington 2013).

ALEC favors net-metering in principle but takes issue with the way it is employed in some states. Per a 2014 ALEC report entitled *Reforming Net-Metering: Providing a Bright and Equitable Future*,

> "ALEC fully supports voluntary efforts to expand and advance renewable energy so long as no technology or class of technologies is given an unfair competitive advantage. Additionally, customers who voluntarily elect to use renewables should pay for all associated expenses, including those related to being connected to the electric power grid" (Tanton 2014, i).

In a nutshell, what ALEC opposes is not net-metering *per se* but rather approaches to net-metering that allows those so engaged to derive the benefits of the practice without assuming the costs associated with maintaining the grid thus shifting those costs upon consumers who do not net-meter while giving a competitive advantage to those who do.

ALEC opposed the ballot initiative of Floridians for Solar Choice and was joined in their opposition by the Florida Chapter of Americans for Prosperity (AFP). AFP is a self-described "center-right" organization whose vision entails "an America where truly free markets allow for free and prosperous people" (AFP 2015). So, conceived, AFP's mission is to "mobilize citizens to advocate for policies that cut red tape and increase opportunity, put the brakes on government overspending, and get the economy working for hard workers– not special interests" (AFP 2015).

AFP found common cause with ALEC and the state public utilities regarding that portion of their mission involving "special interests." Accordingly, they interpreted the language of the Floridians for Solar Choice constitutional amendment as create a protected special status for independent solar providers who would constitutionally enjoy benefits of selling solar power without incurring any of the costs of maintaining the electrical power grid—thus shifting those costs upon the public utilities and their subscribers. The Florida Chapter of AFP was particularly vocal in their opposition observing that:

> "Some people think that certain proposed policies floating around Tallahassee are free market policies, when they are anything but. Requiring traditional utility companies to give their grid space to solar energy will impose a massive cost on these providers, which will be passed onto Florida consumers in the form of higher rates. Changing our constitution such that "it shall be the policy of the state to encourage and promote" equals subsidies and mandates by another name—not a free market policy. Installing solar

panels and using solar power in one's home or business is already legal. If promoters of solar really want to encourage a free market, they should focus on deregulating the utility market as a whole, not demanding that existing companies share limited grid space with an inconsistent power source" (AFP 2015).

AFP, ALEC and the Koch Brothers

Adding a whole other level of complexity to the emerging solar debate in Florida is the involvement of David and George Koch (a.k.a. "The Koch Brothers) who own Koch Industries and fund conservative causes through their foundations. The Koch brothers are contributors to Americans for Prosperity (AFP) who are in turn contributors to ALEC (Fischer 2012). What makes their support of AFP and ALEC controversial and problematic is the degree to which they have supported resistance to solar measures in other states. Koch opposition to solar energy became national news in 2014 when the New York Times editorial board published an editorial entitled "The Koch Attach on Solar Energy," in which they asserted:

> "For the last few months, the Kochs and other big polluters have been spending heavily to fight incentives for renewable energy, which have been adopted by most states. They particularly dislike state laws that allow homeowners with solar panels to sell power they don't need back to electric utilities. So they've been pushing legislatures to impose a surtax on this increasingly popular practice, hoping to make installing solar panels on houses less attractive" (Tritch 2014).

One of the approaches the Koch brothers employed to discourage the expansion of solar power involved funding "nonprofits" (i.e. ALEC and AFP) whose print, radio and television advertisements attacked solar legislative and related constitutional initiatives.

During the solar ballot initiative in Florida the Koch brothers financed opposition via the AFP as they had done in Arizona, Kansas and Ohio (Pantsios 2015). Solar stakes are highest, however, in the Sunbelt so this is the region where the Kochs concentrated their efforts. Per their critics, the Koch's can be expected to persist in their opposition to solar expansion in these states allegedly because Koch Industries generates billions of dollars in annual profits from fossil fuels. Those who challenge the Kochs can expect the brothers to "fight like a pair of angry rattlesnakes to defend their right to make still more billions" (Pantsios 2015).

Florida Style Green Tea

In Florida (as in Georgia), those advocating at Green Tea Coalition styled approach to net-metering have engendered resistance not only from the state's electric utilities but also from the AFP as well as ALEC—whose motto ironically reads "limited government, free-markets, and federalism" all values fully consistent with the

Libertarian, conservative and free market supporters of Floridians for Solar Choice. The sticking points in this controversy are two-fold.

The first point of contention involves the consumer's ability to purchase solar panels versus contracting with private energy providers (i.e. someone other than public utilties) to provide homes with solar panels. Typically, these contracts allow homeowners to lease solar panels at affordable prices while allowing the provider to sell excess power back to the utility. Advocates associated with Floridians for Solar Choice argue that homeowners should have options beyond leasing solar panels and should be able to purchase them outright and independently sell excess power back to the utility or for that matter sell it to neighboring homes and businesses—effectively making individual homeowners with solar panels independent energy providers on their own.

The second sticking point involves maintaining and expanding the electric grid upon which a distributed model depends. At issue is who pays and who benefits. In Florida, the public utility companies maintain and expand the electric grid and they legitimately assert their belief that all who use the grid should be involved in maintaining and expanding it as power needs demand. At the heart of the second sticking point is the issue of "free-riders"—those who derive benefit from cheap solar power by shifting the cost of maintaining the grid on other consumers.

While the Green Tea Coalition and Floridians for Solar Choice have advocated for statutory changes in Georgia and Florida allowing citizens to purchase solar panels from independent providers and sell excess power back to the utility, they recognize that the principal barrier to empowering local citizens is the high cost of solar panels. These steep costs prevent many citizens from utilizing solar energy. Consequently, they also favor licensing independent solar power providers to effectively lease solar power to consumers by installing panels on homes and businesses and allowing homeowners and businesses to purchase solar power directly from them. This approach serves to increase access to solar power and lower energy costs while reducing customer dependence upon public utility power.

Realizing this goal, however requires an amendment to the Florida Constitution to allow homeowners to contract with energy providers other than the utility companies - which currently is currently constitutionally prohibited). Assuming the Florida state constitution was amended in this fashion homeowners would literally overnight realize considerable energy savings and improved access to solar power. Additionally, if the Florida constitution were so amended, homeowners who purchased solar panels for their homes or businesses would also be able to enter the solar energy distribution market and sell their excess energy to neighbors, other businesses or back to the public utility provider.

At face value amending the state constitution to permit private solar energy providers to compete with public utilities should reduce the use of carbon-based fuel for power generation, reduce dependency upon the utility companies, lower energy costs and (if consumers choose to purchase solar panels) allow citizens to opt to live "off-grid" (or nearly so) while selling excess power back to the utilities. Proponents of such an amendment argue that their measure simultaneously promotes environmental, libertarian and free-market outcomes. At face value this appears to be a win-win situation for environmentalists and libertarian-conservatives alike. However, there was a "fly in the ointment"—namely the problem of "free-riders."

Strange-Bedfellows on Both Sides

Policy initiatives that promote environmental, free-market, and limited government control should have—under normal circumstances—been attractive to a group such as ALEC. However, since the Floridians for Solar Choice amendment focuses narrowly on expanding citizen access to independent solar providers without addressing the issue of free-riders to the grid system ALEC found itself opposing a cause that were it not for the free-rider issue it might have endorsed. Indeed, it is one of the paradoxes of the unfolding solar-showdown in Florida that otherwise politically conservative groups find themselves on both sides of the solar amendment controversy.

On the one hand support for the Floridians for Solar Choice emanates from disparate organizations to include some truly strange bedfellows to include more than twenty environmentalist organizations such as the Florida Alliance for Renewable Energy, The Conservancy of Southwest Florida, Earth Justice, The Environmental Defense Fund, Greenpeace, The Florida Sierra Club and more. Likewise, it draws support for its agenda from what might be considered centrist to progressive political organizations such as the Florida League of Women Voters, All WoMen Rising, and the Green Party of Florida. Conservative and Libertarian sponsors can also be found such as the Libertarian Party of Florida, and The Tea Party Network. The business sector is also represented among supporters such as the Florida Retail Association, Florida Solar Industries Association and The Florida Green Chamber of Commerce. Finally, evangelical Christian support emerged from among the Evangelical Environmental Network and The Christian Coalition of America. Probably even more so than was the case with Georgia's Green Tea Coalition, the supporters and sponsors for the initiative sponsored by Floridians for Solar Choice is truly a smorgasbord of diverse ideological interests—all pursuing a single goal for a host of different reasons. (Floridians for Solar Choice 2015).

Consumers for Smart Solar is the opposition group in this controversy. They campaigned against the proposed constitutional amendment that would have expanded the energy market in Florida to private independent solar providers empowered to sell excess energy back to the utility companies without contributing to the maintenance of the electric grid. They represent the powerful utility companies, AFP and ALEC. Their principal agenda is to protect their customers from carrying the costs of solar "free-riders" and to consolidate the monopoly power of the state utilities.

Consumers for Smart Solar have a somewhat smaller but diverse set of supporters to include the libertarian and free-market minded Koch brothers and Koch Industries and their surrogates within AFP and ALEC. They also draw support for their amendment from a major senior citizen advocacy group (60 Plus), minority business and political groups (the National Black Chamber of Commerce and the National Congress of Black Women; Florida State Hispanic Chamber of Commerce), the conservative political group Floridians for Government Accountability as well as board member Billie Tucker of the Florida Tea Party, the more progressive Democrat Party of Florida and a consumer watchdog organization (Florida Council for Safe Communities). The organization's business supporters are principally limited to the state's public utilities and particularly Florida Power and Light (FPL) and Duke Energy (Consumers for Smart Solar 2015; 2014). It is these utilities that principally financed their "smart-solar" amendment designed to undercut the efforts of Floridians for Solar Choice.

The solar issue ultimately worked its way toward the Florida ballot box as two petitions sponsored by a pair of nonprofit political organizations equally diverse in membership. One group sought to expand energy access and diversify the energy market. The other sought to protect the status quo insuring that consumers would only buy their solar power from utilities while protecting their customers from funding an electric grid system that solar providers would use for free. These are the combatants in the Florida solar controversy. At issue is how their petitions were written and how they would be practically implemented if approved in a state referendum.

Consumers for Smart Solar (the PAC principally backed by Florida utilities) had less time to circulate their amendment to the Florida Constitution than had been the case for Floridians for Solar Choice. Their "Smart Solar" amendment (Amendment One) can be summarized as follows:

> "This amendment establishes a right under Florida's constitution for consumers to own or lease solar equipment installed on their property to generate electricity for their own use. State and Local Governments shall retain their abilities to protect consumer rights and public health and safety, and to ensure that consumers who do not choose to install solar are not required to subsidize the cost of backup power and electric grid access to those who do" (Torres 2015).

Thereafter their amendment succinctly specified how it would achieve its goal—namely through the

> "(a) Establishment of Constitutional Right. Electricity consumers have the right to own or lease solar equipment installed on their property to generate electricity for their own use.
>
> (b) Retention of State and Local Governmental Abilities. State and local governments shall retain their abilities to protect consumer rights and public health and safety, and to ensure that consumers who do not choose to install solar are not required to subsidize the costs of backup power and electric grid access to those who do" (Torres 2015).

As of July 2015, the overall reception of the "Smart Solar" amendment was going well with only 66% of polled prospective voters willing to support the amendment as compared to a meager 30% support for the amendment sponsored by Floridians for Solar Choice (News Service of Florida 2015). However, when the ballot boxes closed on November 8, 2016 and votes were counted the Smart Solar amendment had been defeated—failing to meet the constitutionally defined threshold of 60% support (Pyper 2016).

By comparison Floridians for Solar Choice failed to collect enough signatures to get their constitutional amendment on the ballot. Their "Solar Choice," or "shady choice" petition as their opponents characterized it (Ammann 2015) would have allowed third-party ownership of rooftop solar units. More specifically their petition called for:

> "(1) A local solar electricity supplier, as defined in this section, shall not be subject to state or local government regulation with respect to rates, service, or territory, or be subject to any assignment, reservation, or division of service territory between or among electric utilities.
>
> (2) No electric utility shall impair any customer's purchase or consumption of solar electricity from a local solar electricity supplier through any special rate, charge, tariff, classification, term or condition of service, or utility rule or regulation, that is not also imposed on other customers of the same type or class that do not consume electricity from a local solar electricity supplier.
>
> (3) An electric utility shall not be relieved of its obligation under law to furnish service to any customer within its service territory on the basis that such customer also purchases electricity from a local solar electricity supplier.
>
> (4) Notwithstanding paragraph (1), nothing in this section shall prohibit reasonable health, safety and welfare regulations, including, but not limited to, building codes, electrical codes, safety codes and pollution control regulations, which do not prohibit or have the effect of prohibiting the supply of solar-generated electricity by a local solar electricity supplier as defined in this section" (Floridians for Solar Choice Solar Amendment 2015).

While the Smart Solar petition began with "establishing a right" for consumers the "Solar Choice" initiative opened with how it would "limit government." Observers who studied both initiatives suggested that the complexity, length and "negative" introduction to the petition—"limiting government" rather than "establishing a right"—significantly contributed to its low popularity. Based upon a survey by Mason-Dixon Polls, "The difference between the support for the two amendments can in part be attributed to the confusing wording of the first proposal and the relatively clear wording of the second" (Wilson 2015).

Despite issues regarding petition tone, length, and marketing approach it turned out that the most significant issue shaping the solar ballot petitions was money. The Floridians for Solar Choice were simply "out-gunned" by Consumers for Smart Solar when it came to funding the ballot initiative. As of September 2015, Consumers for Smart Solar had bankrolled $789,000 in two months. By comparison Floridians for Solar Choice appear to be spending more on advertisement than they had banked. For instance, per the Orlando Sun-Sentinel in August 2015,

> "Floridians for Solar Choice committee, backed in large part by the advocacy group Southern Alliance for Clean Energy, spent slightly more than $135,000 in August while raising just $591. The monthly total put the

group's overall expenses at $468,908 as of Aug. 31, which was about $31,000 more than the group had collected" (Turner & Saunders 2015).

Having failed to get their petition before the voters, Floridians for Solar Choice capitalized on the defeat of their competitor's constitutional amendment in November 2016 and shifted gears to focus upon relieving Floridians of the tax burden associated with purchasing solar panels. They put their considerable organizational effort behind Amendment Four (Solar Devices or Renewable Energy Source Devices; Exemption from Certain Taxation and Assessment). Amendment Four was placed on the ballot by a unanimous vote of both houses of the Florida legislature and was approved by voters on August 30, 2016 (Perry 2016). The language of the amendment was simple and straightforward and sought to "exempt the assessed value of solar devices or renewable energy source devices subject to tangible personal property tax from ad valorem taxation" and "prohibit the consideration of the installation of a solar device or a renewable energy source device in determining the assessed value of real property for the purpose of ad valorem taxation" (Florida Division of Elections 2016).

By April of 2017 Amendment Four passed the Florida House as HB1351 (Thomasson 2017) and in May passed the Florida Senate as SB90 (Andorka 2017). On June 16, 2017 SB90 finally made its way to the desk of Florida Governor Rick Scott and was signed into law (Hanis 2017). Floridians for Solar Choice and their partners celebrated this success. Susan Glickman of the Southern Alliance for Clean Energy declared that:

> "Broad support from conservatives, the business community, the solar industry, and environmental organizations brought together volunteers, an array of elected officials and everyone in between, in a truly non-partisan effort to bring pro solar Amendment Four into law" (Schafer 2017).

Patrick Altier, President of Florida Solar Energy Industries Association—a major Florida trade association, declared that "This is a victory for Florida, solar customers and non-solar customers alike" (Schafer 2017). Altier's sentiments were shared by the President of the League of Women Voters of Florida (Pamela Goodman) when she observed that"

> "It is clear that the people of Florida demand good solar policy—the voters have spoken, as has the Legislature, and now finally the Governor." "Reducing taxes is smart energy policy, and I'm proud to see Governor Scott sign this important legislation into law" (Schafer 2017).

Finally, Tory Perfetti, Chair of Floridians for Solar Choice and Florida Director of Conservatives for Energy Freedom celebrated this legislative success and accomplishment for his organization's efforts noting that,

> "This effort has been supported by a historic coalition and unanimous legislative support, along with a resounding public vote. The Sunshine State

has spoken, and they said: We want the freedom to choose solar" (Schafer 2017).

Distributed Energy Resources and Smart Grids

As great a success as the enactment of Amendment Four into the Florida State Statutes was, it was essentially cosmetic and didn't address the deeper policy issues. The underlying issues associated with who will produce solar power and who pays for the up-keep of the electrical grid remained unaddressed. At the heart of the problem is the unwillingness of state utilities to surrender their monopoly over the production and sale of electric power and the reluctance of private distributed energy providers to contribute to the maintenance and expansion of the electrical grid in Florida and beyond. As Florida and other states increasingly embrace solar energy, they incrementally move their electrical grid system from a centralized model managed by public utilities to a distributed and shared model managed by a plethora of peripheral solar providers *and* a few centralized public utilities. As solar power generation continues to grow the pressing issue confronting Florida and other states employing solar resources is *"Who will pay to manage and expand the electrical grid within a distributed power system?"*

Figure 2 illustrates the electrical grid in Florida (FESC 2015). Florida's electric utility industry consists of municipal utilities, cooperatives and investor-owned utilities.

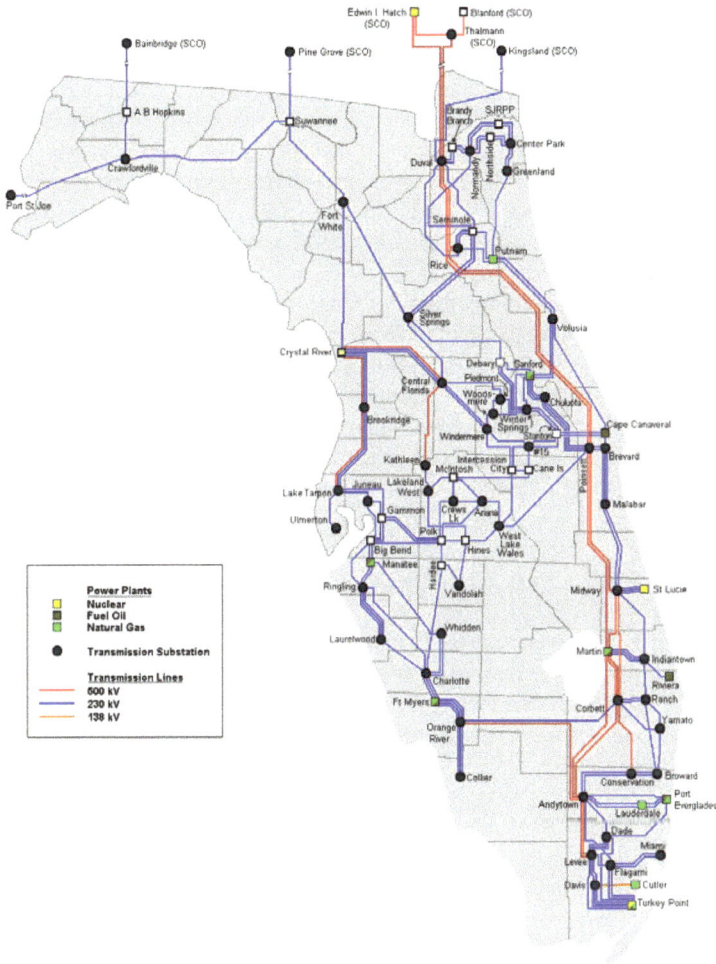

Figure 2: Florida's Electrical Grid
(Source: FESC 2015)

There are some 34 municipal utilities in the states and as their name suggests they are managed by local city councils and commissions (FMEA 2015). The state has five investor-owned public utilities to include Florida Power and Light (FPL), Progress Energy (now Duke Energy), Tampa Electric Company (TECO), Gulf Power Company, and Florida Power Utilities (FPSC 2012). Finally, Florida has 17 cooperative electrical utilities that principally provide power to rural areas and small communities statewide (FECA 2015). As a group these are the 56 Florida utilities are responsible for maintaining and expanding the state electrical grid system and authority to do so rests in state law as administered by the Florida Public Service Commission.

Although these utilities have served as the architects and custodians of Florida's electrical grid for generations a new generation of electrical generation is inevitably emerging. Nationwide demand for electricity is growing and the margin between the demand for energy and the capacity of the nation's utilities is continually shrinking (Goreham 2014; Schneider Electric 2012; Cowart 2001). More power is needed and alternative energy sources such as solar are increasingly filling the void. However, as alternative supplies materialize the principle remaining issue is how to manage demand and supply on the grid to reliably meet energy needs nationwide and day-in-day-out. What this portends is that Floridians must inevitably consider how to reconfigure the grid statewide and beyond. Inevitably solar providers such as SolarCity will become part of that distributed utility system.

What is emerging nationwide and in Florida is the "smart grid" described by the U.S. Department of Energy as a "class of technology" bringing "electricity delivery systems into the 21st century" via computer-based remote control and automation. These systems employ two-way communication technology and computer processing to manage power demand and supply. Smart grid technologies are being introduced nationwide—especially as electricity networks reflect the distributed integration of energy from power plants, wind farms and other solar sources into the electrical systems of homes and businesses. Smart grids are extremely beneficial to utilities and consumers who realize energy efficiency on the power grid and at the consumer's point of service (USDOE 2015).

Historically power generation has been a one-way affair involving production of energy by electric utilities that is transmitted to the end-user/consumer. Distributed grid systems are different and more dynamic in that power can travel from the heart of the grid to the periphery and back. One emerging development contributing to the smart grid is the ongoing development of capacity to store solar-derived power in batteries such that accumulated energy can be sold directly back to the utilities for redistribution or to the consumer for immediate consumption. Companies such as SolarCity, SunEdison, Sungevity and SunPower are teaming up with energy storage companies like Telsa, Green Charge Networks, Sonnenbatterie, Stem and Sunverge to expand solar energy storage capacity, providing continuously available energy resources (St. John 2015).

Flying Against the Winds of Inevitable Change

Inevitably the growing energy potential of solar and other alternative energy resources will drive Florida toward a distributed smart grid where everyone will pay in one way or another to maintain, modernize and expand the state's electrical grid capacity. Resisting or denying these realities is to fly aimlessly into the winds of inevitable change. There is no doubt that Florida's electrical utilities are well-aware of this reality and are employing their current resources to situate themselves as favorably as possible in anticipation of these changes. Nonetheless, the immediate and short-term issue at hand is how to entice energy stakeholders to engage one another around sharing Florida's electric market and maintaining and developing a smart grid to transmit power to consumers in a timely and predictable fashion.

Clearly everyone—including the state's public electric utilities—realizes that it is only a matter of time before the traditional utility-driven grid system is completely obsolete and replaced with a distributed network of so-called micro-grids employing solar and alternative energies to deliver the bulk of power needs for communities and businesses. The emergence of these alternative energy networks and systems are already taking place and gaining momentum. For instance, Navigant has dedicated part of its consulting and planning resources to assisting companies and municipalities better employ alternative energy sources (Navigant 2015). Their clients, to include San Francisco and Chicago, are already reducing their dependence on utility-generated power and realizing considerable savings by

- "Providing an assessment of the Smart Grid landscape and how it relates to the organization's current situation
- Creating strategies for developing, positioning and deploying Smart Grid technologies
- Developing functional requirements and business processes to align the Smart Grid with strategic objectives
- Assessing the functional benefits of Smart Grid business value for key stakeholders" (Navigant 2015).

In fact, Navigant predicts that worldwide revenue derived from the installation of solar systems will increase to $112 billion by 2018 representing a 44% increase. These revenue increases will without question siphon money away from the nation's utilities and undoubtedly will winnow away the number of public utilities. These forces will compel the remaining utilities to shift their roles away from being the principal source of electric energy and instead assume responsibility for maintaining a reliable "base load" capacity for the grid to compliment and augment power generated from and array of distributed sources (Martin, Chediak & Wells 2013).

A 2013 report produced by the Edison Electric Institute entitled *Disruptive Challenges: Financial Implications and Strategic Responses to a Changing Retail Electric Business* suggested that the U.S. electrical utility industry faces serious "disruptive challenges" due to a "convergence of factors" to include:

"falling costs of distributed generation and other distributed energy resources (DER); an enhanced focus on development of new DER technologies; increasing customer, regulatory, and political interest in demand- side management technologies (DSM); government programs to incentivize selected technologies; the declining price of natural gas; slowing economic growth trends; and rising electricity prices in certain areas of the country" (Kind 2013, 1).

These disruptive forces will inevitably transform the nation's electrical grid system and Florida will not be able to isolate itself from these emerging trends. As the 2013 EEI report concludes:

"Taken together, these factors are potential "game changers" to the U.S. electric utility industry, and are likely to dramatically impact customers, employees, investors, and the availability of capital to fund future investment. The timing of such transformative changes is unclear, but with the potential for technological innovation (e.g., solar photovoltaic or PV) becoming economically viable due to this confluence of forces, the industry and its stakeholders must proactively assess the impacts and alternatives available to address disruptive challenges in a timely manner" (Kind 2013, 1).

The consequence of these forces and trends is that solar energy produced via a decentralized grid is most definitely making its way into Florida in a big way. It is no longer a matter of "if" this will happen but "when"—if not this year or the next via the two proposed solar amendments then very soon thereafter. At issue is whether state leaders will proactively shape this new grid system or react to external market forces and "back-into" change.

The future of electric power generation in Florida will necessitate cooperation between solar providers, environmentalists, consumers and the state's electric utilities. At issue is how it happens. What typically unites policy adversaries is a "coincidence of interests" (Neu 2012, 193) where diverse parties are drawn together to realize common outcomes though they may be driven to do so based on divergent motivations. Environmental groups joined libertarian activists to pursue the expansion of solar power with full recognition that while their goal is principally environmental in nature, their libertarian partners in Floridians for Solar Choice are motivated by the exercise of citizen self-determination and free-market principles. Likewise, Florida utilities were drawn to other conservative interests to defeat the "solar choice" amendment even as the utilities sought to protect their state chartered monopoly of electrical power. Regardless of who supported which solar amendment in 2016, what will undoubtedly remain is dissension over who will maintain and develop the state's electrical power grid system.

Threats to the Grid System

There are, however, other considerations that must be incorporated into whatever form the Florida power grid system evolves into. Most pressing of all is the security of the grid system itself—an issue of utmost importance to Florida and the nation. While it may not be apparent to many, the nation's electrical grid has been under continuous attack by cyber-hackers seeking to gain control over portions of the grid, cripple it and render untold economic damage to the nation. Per an investigative study conducted by journalists at USA Today, the nation's grid comes under attack once every 4 days. Accordingly, they concluded that,

> "From 2011 to 2014, the U.S. Department of Energy received 362 reports from electric utilities of physical or cyber attacks that interrupted power services. In 2013, a Department of Homeland Security branch recorded 161 cyber attacks on the energy sector, compared to just 31 in 2011" (Toppa 2015).

Given the sheer volume of these attacks and their seriousness the U.S. Department of Homeland Security formed a task force dedicated to improving the digital defense of the nation's electrical grid (Williams 2015).

Beyond the problem cyber-attacks on the grid (Kredo 2015), physical disruption is also a very real problem with sources of these attacks coming from the deployment by an anarchistic or terrorist source of an electro-magnet pulse (EMP) weapon that could shut down electrical transmission, physical attacks by terrorist groups on key power substations and plants as well as attacks on the physical grid itself in locales where surveillance and security is lacking and disruption from natural occurrences such as earthquakes, hurricanes, and volcanoes (SecureTheGrid 2015). Federal analyses of physical these threats have confirmed them to be real and perhaps inevitable.

The most comprehensive analysis conducted to date regarding the vulnerability of the nation's power grid was published in 2012 by the prestigious National Research Council of the National Academy of Sciences (Crane et al. 2012). This report underscores the vulnerability of the nation's power grid, observing that:

> "The electric power delivery system that carries electricity from large central generators to customers could be severely damaged by a small number of well-informed attackers. The system is inherently vulnerable because transmission lines may span hundreds of miles, and many key facilities are unguarded. This vulnerability is exacerbated by the fact that the power grid, most of which was originally designed to meet the needs of individual vertically integrated utilities, is now being used to move power between regions to support the needs of new competitive markets for power generation. Primarily because of ambiguities introduced as a result of recent restructuring of the industry and cost pressures from consumers and regulators, investment to strengthen and upgrade the grid has lagged, with the result that many parts of the bulk high-voltage system are heavily stressed" (Crane et al. 2012, 1).

Likewise, a more recent report published in 2014 by the Congressional Research Service echoed the National Research Council analysis and concluded that:

> "There is widespread agreement among state and federal government officials, utilities, and manufacturers that HV transformers in the United States are vulnerable to terrorist attack, and that such an attack potentially could have catastrophic consequences. But the most serious, multitransformer attacks would require acquiring operational information and a certain level of sophistication on the part of potential attackers. Consequently, despite the technical arguments, without more specific information about potential targets and attacker capabilities, the true vulnerability of the grid to a multi-HV transformer attack remains an open question. Incomplete or ambiguous threat information may lead to inconsistency in physical security among HV transformer owners, inefficient spending of limited security resources at facilities that may not really be

under threat, or deployment of security measures against the wrong threat" (Parfomak 2014)

Undoubtedly, the U.S. power grid system has become increasingly vulnerable to cyber and physical terrorist attack. However, this potential for disruption is further exacerbated by inherent problems with the current configuration of the system. After all, the nation's power grid has been incrementally developed over almost a century, having evolved as demand increased. This gradual evolution has not contributed to system efficiency as demonstrated by power outages across many parts of the nation during periods of peak demand (Amin & Schewe 2008). In 2001 the U.S. Department of Energy (USDOE) conducted a survey to assess the state of the nation's system of electrical transmission and concluded:

> "There is growing evidence that the U.S. transmission system is in urgent need of modernization. The system has become congested because growth in electricity demand and investment in new generation facilities have not been matched by investment in new transmission facilities. Transmission problems have been compounded by the incomplete transition to fair and efficient competitive wholesale electricity markets. Because the existing transmission system was not designed to meet present demand, daily transmission constraints or "bottlenecks" increase electricity costs to consumers and increase the risk of blackouts" (Terry et. al. 2001, xi).

By 2014, these pressures were further exacerbated by federal environmental and energy policies that "are moving us toward electrical grid failure" with the "capacity reserve margin for hot or cold weather events" shrinking in many regions (Goreham 2014).

Deregulation and the emergence of interstate energy electric energy markets have also stressed the nation's power grid system. Beginning around 2001, the nation's grid was transformed into an electrical superhighway where transmission rates increased beyond original design capacity, producing a growing set of challenges to include:

1. *Declining investment.* Diminishing incentives to maintain a fragmented electrical system ultimately plunges the system into failure.
2. *Overuse of Lines between Systems.* Regularly employing emergency transmission lines to transmit increasingly heavier loads taxes system capacity.
3. *Accelerated Component Deterioration.* Pursuing profit-maximization by cycling power plants on-and-off (repeatedly heating and cooling metal parts) ultimately deteriorates system components.
4. *Unplanned Additions to Grid.* Uncritically adding alternative sources of energy to the grid without adequately determining grid capacity leads to power disruptions.
5. *Difficulty in Assigning Costs.* Fragmenting consumer power transmission costs prevents consumers from recovering costs for energy purchased in state regulated markets.

6. *Increased Line Congestion.* Increasing grid volume requires additional long distance lines that are often delayed by government regulations thereby reducing transmission rates an increasing line congestion.
7. *No Overall Plan.* Growing numbers of providers utilizing the grid makes cost assignment more complex ultimately producing system entropy.
8. *Little Incentive to Add Generating Capacity.* Expanding opportunities for purchasing electric power elsewhere and operating the grid as close as possible to full capacity accelerates infrastructure deterioration, discourages capacity expansion and inevitably produces power failures (Tverberg 2008)

One might further add the issue of the aging grid workforce and the attendant problems of recruiting and training future human resources to maintain and modernize the system (Crane et al. 2012).

Nor are these the only challenges confronting the nation's power grid. Per the U.S. Energy Information Agency (USEIA), other challenges include:

- "Siting new transmission lines (and obtaining approval of the new routes and needed land) when there is opposition to construction.
- Determining an equitable approach for recovering the construction costs of a transmission line being built within one state when the new line provides economic and system operation benefits to out-of-state customers.
- Ensuring that the network of long-distance transmission lines reaches renewable energy generation sites where high-quality wind and solar resources are located, which are often far from areas where demand for electricity is concentrated.
- Addressing the uncertainty in federal regulations regarding who is responsible for paying for new transmission lines; this uncertainty affects the private sector's ability to raise money to build them.
- Protecting the grid from physical and cybersecurity attacks" (USEIA 2014).

Clearly, the nation's electrical grid system is continually stressed by increased demand and changes in the market for electrical energy and these stresses appear to be accelerating over time as the grid transforms into an ever more distributed system.

Today the U.S. electric transmission system is Balkanized and stressed having evolved into a decentralized array of traditional and emerging energy providers. In fact, some have argued that this vulnerable system will inevitably undergo an attack that it will not withstand. Granted there are significant redundancies incorporated into the current system composed as it is of three constituent grids (Eastern, Western and Texas) fed by 7,000 generating plants and 2,000 distribution utilities (Thompson 2015; USEIA 2014). However, these redundancies do not make the grid any less vulnerable to significant local and regional blackouts.

Nationalizing the Grid

Given the issues related to system utilization and threat that have emerged some have wondered whether it is time for the entire U.S. power grid to be nationalized. In 2002 the U.S. Department of Energy took a step in that direction by forming a task force to consider "establishing a national grid and to identify transmission bottlenecks and measures to address them" (Terry et al. 2002). Ultimately the group, convened by then Secretary of Energy Spencer Abraham, championed the establishment of a national grid and further recommended "that the President direct the appropriate federal agencies to take action that will remove constraints on the interstate transmission grid so that our nation's electricity supply will meet the growing needs of our economy" (Terry et al. 2002). The recommendation to establish a "national grid" was not adopted by the President or Congress while the U.S. Department of Energy continued to work on ways to improve interstate transmission of power.

The Obama administration viewed the creation of a national power grid more favorably. In a 2008 television interview with MSNBC's Rachel Maddow, candidate Obama observed while discussion national infrastructure needs that:

> "I think, the most important infrastructure projects that we need is a whole new electricity grid. Because if we're going to be serious about renewable energy, I want to be able to get wind power from North Dakota to population centers, like Chicago. And we're going to have to have a smart grid if we want to use plug-in hybrids then we want to be able to have ordinary consumers sell back the electricity that's generated from those car batteries, back into the grid. That can create 5 million new jobs, just in new energy. But, it's huge projects that generally speaking, you're not going to have private enterprise would want to take all those risks. And we're going to have to be involved in that process" (Maddow 2008).

Upon being elected, President Obama directed the Federal Energy Regulatory Commission (FERC) to begin the process of improving upon the interconnectivity and resilience of the national power grid. The product of those efforts was FERC Order 1000 issued in 2011.

While the language of the order is complex, its intent is to clarify whether states can be compelled to coordinate their transmission planning and costs with utilities in neighboring states and regions when planning for additional electricity transmission capacity. The order was designed to achieve the goal of ensuring collaboration among energy market participants to facilitate the future and ongoing development of the nation's electrical grid while pursuing fair and economical cost allocations for newly developed regional transmission lines. The order also serves to create greater access to renewable energy resources (Kransky 2014).

FERC Oder 1000 mandates that the nation's utilities (FERC 2015)

1. Participate in a regional transmission planning process driven by public policy as expressed by state or federal laws and regulations;
2. Cooperate across neighboring transmission regions to plan and implement all changes in the grid cooperatively and on a cost-effective basis;
3. Participate in a regional transmission planning process for purposed of cost allocation employing a regional cost allocation method for new transmission facilities;

4. Employ a common interregional cost allocation method for new interregional transmission facilities;

5. Expand competition within electrical power markets by removing from state utility commission sanctioned tariffs and agreements and a federal right of first refusal (ROFR) for a transmission facility selected in a regional transmission plan;

6. Require every public utility transmission provider to amend its tariff mandating the reevaluation of regional transmission plans to determine if delays in the development of a transmission facilities required consideration of alternative solutions (FERC 2015).

FERC Order 1000 was immediately challenged in the federal courts by utility providers but in 2014 the Federal Court ultimately upheld the order paving the way for it to be widely implemented (St. John 2014).

On August 15, 2015, the U.S. Federal Court of Appeals for the District of Columbia upheld the Federal Energy Commission order. In a unanimous ruling the court found that "The Commission reasonably determined that regional planning must include consideration of transmission needs driven by public policy requirements" (SC PSA v. v. FERC 2014). More specifically, the ruling mandates that electric service providers coordinate their plans for future grid investments that impact multiple states and/or utility jurisdictions—meaning that the heretofore voluntary planning systems subject to the discretion of individual state utility commissions have now been supplanted by FERC's federal regulatory authority (St. John, 2014). Moreover, regarding the petitioner's challenges to the requirement that each region must establish and administer policies and procedures that consider the impact of grid development upon federal, state and local laws and regulatory frameworks, the court ruled that such arguments were not persuasive (Kransky, 2015).

Having been affirmed in the federal courts, FERC 1000 recasts the context in which the current solar debate is occurring. Prior to this federal order state utility commissions and electrical utilities were permitted a great deal of latitude in terms of managing and expanding their state's electric grid system. However national concerns over the security of the network of local, state and regional grid systems and emerging market concerns related to the development of interstate and regional electrical energy markets have predictably resulted in a consolidation of federal authority over what had previously been a state regulated industry. Whereas in the past constituent groups with different visions of how electric energy should be produced and distributed could reasonably expect to influence their state legislatures and utility commissions to regulate electric power along lines consistent with stakeholder interests. However now that the aegis for this planning has shifted to interstate and federal control, Floridians no longer have the kind of influence over their state's energy policy in the way they have historically enjoyed.

Floridians for Solar Choice sought changes in state law to allow for the inclusion of home-based solar providers that will further stress the existing Power grid. However, given developments at the federal level, it may be unrealistic to expect changes at the state level as locus of control over the grid increasingly falls under regional and federal regulations. Apparently regulatory authority over the power grid has shifted to the Federal Energy Regulatory Commission who will coordinate efforts between the electric utilities and state regulatory bodies. While this development does not completely negate or invalidate the emergence of grass-roots efforts to diversify the mix of energy providers in the state, it does imply that to a growing degree these decisions will be made regionally and not at the state level alone.

This suggests that the current debate in Florida over solar power, while important to the degree of expressing citizen and consumer sentiments on the issue, may be moot when it comes to influencing energy policy. The policy debate has now shifted to another level and state laws, constitutional amendments and regulatory orders emanating within the jurisdictions of any state may no longer be sufficient to produce desired changes. What may be required is a different administrative model to provide for both the requirements of FERC 1000 as well as a vehicle for providing for consumer and citizen input and influence.

Executive Order 13800 and the Sale of Public Transmission Assets

The election of Donald Trump as President in 2016 signaled that there will be a new look at the security of the nation's power system. On May 11, 2017 President Trump signed Executive Order 13800 - "Presidential Executive Order on Strengthening the Cybersecurity of Federal Networks and Critical Infrastructure" which contained a provision specifically directed toward assessing cyber-security concerns and developing a response plan. Specifically, this order mandated:

> "(e) Assessment of Electricity Disruption Incident Response Capabilities. The Secretary of Energy and the Secretary of Homeland Security, in consultation with the Director of National Intelligence, with State, local, tribal, and territorial governments, and with others as appropriate, shall jointly assess:
>
> (i) the potential scope and duration of a prolonged power outage associated with a significant cyber incident, as defined in Presidential Policy Directive 41 of July 26, 2016 (United States Cyber Incident Coordination), against the United States electric subsector;
>
> (ii) the readiness of the United States to manage the consequences of such an incident; and
>
> (iii) any gaps or shortcomings in assets or capabilities required to mitigate the consequences of such an incident" (POTUS 2017).

On June 21, 2017, the Trump administration followed through on this executive order by conducting a White House meeting with cyber-security and energy leaders where he again reiterated his commitment to security the nation's power grid (Chalfant 2017).

Prior to the issuance of Executive Order 13800 - the Trump administration signaled its attitude toward nationalizing the nation's power grid by including an item in its 2018 federal budget proposal that would have divested federal control over the

Department of Energy's four Power Marketing Administrations (PMA). These PMAs regulating power transmission in 34 states include:

- Bonneville Power Administration (Oregon, Idaho; Washington)
- Western Area Power Administration (Montana, North Dakota, South Dakota, Wyoming, Nebraska, Colorado, Nevada, Utah, California, Arizona, New Mexico, Northwestern Kansas and Central and Western Texas),
- Southwestern Power Administration (Oklahoma, Louisiana, Arkansas, Central and Western Missouri and Eastern Texas);
- Southeastern Power Administration (Kentucky, Tennessee, Mississippi, Alabama, Georgia, North Carolina, South Carolina, Virginia, West Virginia, Southern Illinois and Northwest Florida) (USEIA 2013).

These PMAs include federally financed and operated transmission assets. Among these, Bonneville Power Authority is particularly important since it manages three-quarters of the Pacific Northwest's power transmission lines extending from the 31 dams located in the Columbia River basin to energy-starved California (Postelwait 2017).

Per the Office of Management and Budget (OMB), who released the proposed executive budget, "the vast majority of the nation's electricity infrastructure is owned and operated by for-profit investor owned utilities." OMB also went on to assert that:

> "Ownership of transmission assets is best carried out by the private sector where there are appropriate market and regulatory incentives. The budget proposal to eliminate or reduce the PMA's role in electricity transmission and increase the private sector's role would encourage a more efficient allocation of economic resources and mitigate risk to taxpayers" (Linares 2017).

Given these comments contained in President Trump's very first executive budget proposal, it would seem any plans to nationalize the nation's power grid originating in the Obama administration will be rolled-back by President Trump. While the Trump administration may be interested in nationalizing a security force to protect the grid, it seems doubtful they would support the nationalization of the nation's grid system.

To date, the Trump administration has exhibited a very pro-business philosophy toward energy regulation. As of July 14, 2017, the Trump administration had nominated four pro-business individuals to head the Federal Energy Regulatory Commission (FERC). Three of these nominations have been languishing in the Senate and thwarting the work of FERC that has been without a quorum and unable to conduct its regulatory mission (Bade 2017). Trump appointed long-time Senator Mitch McConnell aide Neil Chaterjee to head the commission on August 10. This appointment will provide leadership to a commission whose membership has only recently been restored to a quorum (Wolfgang 2017; Bade 2017). However, Chaterjee's appointment as chair appears to be temporary as the Trump Administration seeks another nominee, David McIntyre, to serve as FERC chair upon Senate confirmation (Siciliano 2017).

McIntyre's final confirmation may be delayed by the efforts of some 130 environmental groups who are sworn to prevent him from assuming the chair of the commission. Todd Larsen, Executive Co-Director of Green America has signaled his group's opposition to the entire slate of Trump nominees noting that "It is imperative that all Americans voice their opposition to business as usual at FERC and oppose any Trump nominees to the agency" (Crawford & Dlouhy 2017). By comparison, Trump's nominees for FERC have pleased representatives of the nation's utilities and infrastructure contractors such as those who would build the Keystone Pipeline and expand the nation's power grid (Bade 2017).

Under the Obama administration,n FERC played a central role in opening energy markets to substitute renewable energy alternatives for coal and natural gas. The Trump administration seeks to reverse these policies and restore the place for carbon-based fuels in the nation's energy mix. McIntyre's leadership of the commission is intended to break was has heretofore been a policy stalemate on the commission between fossil fuel advocates and a coalition of states, federal agencies and business interests seeking clean fuel alternatives. Although the Trump's administration is expected to shift energy policy back toward fossil fuel advocates, tension between the competing policy camps reflected is likely to continue.

Per a joint analysis by Duke University, the University of North Carolina and Harvard University,

> "Ongoing disputes relate to the generation mix, resource adequacy, compensation for distributed energy resources, implementation of the Public Utilities Regulatory Policies Act of 1978 (PURPA), and competition policy" (Monast et al. 2016, 3).

As discussed throughout this chapter, a central point of contention between the states and the federal government regards who will oversee and develop the nation's electric power grid. Jonas Monast, senior author of the Duke/UNC/Harvard energy report and his colleagues addressed this concern directly observing that,

> "The line between federal and state jurisdiction over the electricity sector is shifting. FERC once played a limited role in sector oversight, but regionalization of the electric grid and development of interstate markets for electricity, electric capacity, and transmission development have expanded its responsibilities. At the same time, states have retained jurisdiction over generation facilities and retail markets. They have used this authority to implement policies, such as mandates for renewable energy and tariffs for rooftop solar, that may affect the federally regulated planning processes and markets. Whether and how FERC accommodates states' policy goals, and the extent to which states can regulate the industry without intruding into federal regulatory space, are questions that FERC has traditionally addressed on a case-by-case basis" (Monast et al. 2016, 3).

Interstate Compacts and the Southern States Energy Board (SSEB)

While the nation awaits the Trump administration's ultimate policies on developing and protecting the nation's power grid, there is another vehicle for regulating the grid that lies between the state and federal level. This vehicle exists in the form of interstate compacts. Interstate compacts are regional governmental bodies consisting of representatives from cooperating states who agree to affiliate together to jointly address common concerns. In this instance Florida belongs to an interstate compact organization known as the Southern States Energy Board (SSEB). SSEB was originally created by state law and consented to by Congress in 1957 as the Southern Regional Advisory Council on Nuclear Energy to promote the proliferation of seemingly cheap and safe nuclear-generated energy. By 1960, there was a perceived need among the states to revitalize this interstate compact to more effectively address emerging energy and environmental needs. To that end the organization was renamed to the Southern States Energy Board and its mission was reformulated with an emphasis upon improving "the economy of the South and to contribute to the individual and community well-being of the people of the Southern region through cooperation among member states in the creation and implementation of programs, policies and technologies in the fields of energy, science, environment and in related areas of interest" (SSEB 2010).

SSEB pursues its mission in at least a dozen ways to include continually

1. Reviewing energy and environmental issues applicable to member state and pertinent to interstate commerce and regulation,
2. Providing a collective voice on energy and environmental issues,
3. Identifying needed professional expertise and technologies,
4. Conducting pertinent research and educational dissemination activities,
5. Serving as a repository for energy and environmental research pertinent to the needs of members and to the region,
6. Presenting and advocating for energy issues at the state, regional and federal level,
7. Assisting with grant applications and supervise and administer cooperative agreements and grants,
8. Advising member state legislatures and agencies,
9. Approving and supervising supplemental agreements among member states,
10. Providing expertise to the Southern Governor's Association and the Southern Legislative Conference upon request,
11. Providing expertise and support for related interstate compacts;
12. Serving as a liaison between the states and the federal government on issues relating to energy and the environment (SSEB 2010, 1-2).

Florida's representatives to the SSEB include the governor and a representative of the Florida House of Representatives and the Florida Senate.

While subject to FERC 1000, the SSEB expressed its concerns over such regulations (SSEB 2015) with its endorsement of the Regulation Freedom Amendment that asserts:

"Whenever one quarter of the Members of the U.S. House or the U.S. Senate transmit to the President their written declaration of opposition to a proposed federal regulation, it shall require a majority vote of the House and Senate to adopt that regulation" (American Opportunity Project 2015).

Notwithstanding, issues associated with FERC 1000 fall squarely within the jurisdiction of SSEB. While this does not eliminate the important role of state executives, legislatures and the state utility commissions, it clearly suggests that effective stakeholder organization simply must consider how to influence the decisions of the SSEB.

While amending the Florida Constitution to allow entities other than the state's utilities to sell electrical power may ultimately be a necessary step for broadening the array of energy options open to Floridians, doing so in isolation from regional state compacts and federal regulation does not deal with the pressing issues at hand - to include short term concerns like paying for increased grid load as well as longer term interests like updating, expanding and securing the regional and national electric grid. New strategies and partnerships are needed and state representatives at SSEB and other interstate compacts should seriously consider engaging federal agencies under the Trump administration to update the nation's power grid while improving access to affordable solar energy.

Applied Ecopragmatic Principles

Chapter one presented a set of *ecopragmatic principles* widely illustrated throughout the Florida solar energy case study. The sponsors of both 2016 solar amendments (Floridians for Solar Choice and Consumers for Smart Solar) developed stakeholder networks built upon *collaborative relationships among "strange bedfellows."* Both groups managed to forge collaborative networks of progressive and conservative to libertarian interests that cooperated with one another for divergent motivations.

For instance, the principals behind Consumers for Smart Solar consisted of the state's utility companies seeking to maintain monopolistic control of the state's energy market. Meanwhile, their conservative-libertarian partners sought to protect consumers from the expenses of "free riders" who would utilize the grid system to transmit solar power without having to share in the cost of grid maintenance. By comparison, Floridians for Solar Choice consisted of progressive and environmentalist interests who were interests dedicated to fighting climate change by transforming energy production from fossil fuels to renewable solar energy. Their libertarian and conservative partners in this effort were principally interested in promoting energy independence among Florida's electric consumers.

The work of these solar opponents all occurred at the state and local level and involved generating voter sponsorship in local communities across Florida. Consequently, while issues associated with solar power generation clearly have national and regional ramifications that justify addressing them at a higher governmental level, the two solar coalitions competing in Florida *employed grass-root, local initiatives* to gain support for their petitions despite the reality that energy policy issues are also regional and national in scope. Rather than pursuing change at the regional and national levels that would in turn "trickle-down" to localities, both amendment groups chose to employ a "homegrown" bottom-up approach to problem-solving and policy change.

The entire debate over the future of solar energy in Florida might have never happened had each coalition narrowly pursued ideological or outcome purity and only advocated for outcomes that narrowly served their self-interests. All interests involved recognized the futility of sacrificing achievable improvements in solar policy by pursuing ideal solutions and wisely chose to compromise and partner with stakeholders who cooperated for divergent reasons. This process of forgoing partnerships to realize acceptable rather than ideal policy options is known as *communitarian satisficing*.

Florida's debate over the future of solar energy was a textbook example of *deliberative democracy* in action. Deliberative democracy seeks to engage the broadest constituency possible in resolving policy issues and ideally works at the most basic level possible. In this case study the formation of diverse stakeholder coalitions established a foundation for deliberative democracy that ultimately engaged the citizens of Florida via a state constitutional referendum. These efforts coordinated with the Florida Legislature which eventually produced SB90 that Governor Rick Scott ultimately signed. While neither amendment sponsored by Floridians for Solar Choice or Consumers for Smart Solar Choice was enacted, the debate these groups engendered ultimately produced a dialogue in the state legislature and in the media, that produced meaningful change in state policy toward solar energy.

Florida's debate over who and where solar energy would be produced and marketed was primarily about the nature of energy markets, consumer choice and consumer rights. The act that solar energy came to the fore as a policy issue in 2016 is indicative of the efforts of Floridians for Solar Choice to challenge the dominant public-utility paradigm with a model that *promoted free-market alternatives*. Despite their failure in getting enough signatures to get their initiative before Florida's voters they successfully began a conversation about free-market energy alternatives that made its way through the Florida legislature and which continues as a policy consideration and alternative that will be explored more fully in future legislative sessions.

The Pragmatics of Florida's Solar Future

A central feature of an ecopragmatic approach to environmental policy is the realization that in politics change happens in small increments and seldom "all-at-once." In most cases that means committing to a process of making incremental changes. Such is the case with the current solar policy battle in Florida. In many respects, the campaign regarding the 2016 constitutional solar amendment was ultimately not as important as the process of coalition building which the amendment process occasioned. As the debate over the future of solar energy continues one can reasonably expect the coalitions on both sides of the solar issue to fluctuate to allow the coupling and re-coupling of various interest groups in pursuit of mutually beneficial goals and objectives. It is worth remembering that in most cases interest groups and their issues don't simply go away. Instead they form new alliances and partnerships. That is what can be expected regarding the future of solar energy in Florida.

Since the debate over the future of energy development and transmission has become regional and national in scope, it is likely that the partnerships which first emerged at the state-level in Florida will likewise become regional and national. Doing so is essential to influencing decision making at the interstate compact and federal level. Interstate alliances—such as the one between the Green Tea Coalition of Georgia and Floridians for Solar Choice—are likely to become more commonplace and their level of integration and organizational action and influence can increasingly be expected to extend locally through and beyond the state level to encompass regional and eventually national collaborations.

Florida—as Georgia before it—has witnessed the alliance of traditionally politically "right" and "left" interests to pursue the expansion of solar power via the group Floridians for Solar Choice. Likewise, among those supporting Consumer for Smart Solar one can also see the alliance of some historically conservative and progressively oriented groups and individuals who are organized to stop the Floridians for Solar Choice amendment. Some conservatives, however, were drawn to the Smart Solar alliance out of concern regarding the equity with which solar costs will be distributed. This apprehension over equity and fairness has pitted some who otherwise might have been on the same (conservative) side of the solar issue rather in opposition to one another.

Ultimately the integration of local, state, regional and national initiatives should improve the functionality and responsiveness of grass-root environmental efforts. However, it will greatly expand the range of stakeholders involved with energy policy and this plethora of participants may ultimately serve to mute local concerns in the interest of serving the interests of those located elsewhere. Such is the nature of the political process—what Glenn Snyder called "Alliance Politics" (Snyder 2007). However, it is also the nature of pragmatic policy making, embodying two of the most important principles of ecopragmatics: (1) always be ready to adapt and change one's values and goals given new information and circumstances and (2) don't make enemies out of your ideological adversaries since chances are very good you will re-engage with them at some future point either as adversaries or partners.

As the Florida, solar issue evolves we can expect to see interests from a variety of philosophical, political and economic perspectives come together to achieve common causes. Once their agendas have been either fulfilled or frustrated they will undoubtedly do what political interest groups have always done—reassess, realign, regroup and reassert their efforts. In so doing, effective policy players can be expected to exhibit a reluctance to demonize their adversaries and will be consistently open to forging new—if only temporary - partnerships. This is the nature of pragmatic and ultimately effective policymaking. It is the "give-and-take" the "dance" of creating, sustaining and recreating social stakeholder "bedfellows."

REFERENCES

Americans for Prosperity—Florida (AFP). 2015. "Americans for Prosperity: Proposed Solar Policies are Not Free Market." *AFP Florida Newsroom.* (March 11), Accessed September 16, 2015 http://americansforprosperity.org/florida/article/americans-for-prosperity-proposed-solar-policies-are-not-free-market/

American Opportunity Project. 2015. "Regulation Freedom Act." (March), Accessed October 23, 2015 http://www.americanopportunityproject.org/regulation-freedom-amendment/

Amin, Massoud and Philip F. Schewe. 2008. "Preventing Blackouts: Building a Smarter Power Grid." *Scientific American.* (August 13), Accessed August 11, 2017 https://www.scientificamerican.com/article/preventing-blackouts-power-grid/

Ammann, Phil. 2015. "Consumers for Smart Solar Launches 'Consumer-Friendly' Solar Ballot Initiative For 2016." *SaintPetersBlog.com.* (July 15), Accessed September 21, 2015 http://www.saintpetersblog.com/archives/235544

Andorka, Frank. 2017. "One More Step: Florida Bill Passes Senate—Now on to Governor's Desk." *PV Magazine.* (May 5), Accessed August 1, 2017 https://pv-magazine-usa.com/2017/05/05/one-more-step-florida-bill-passes-senate-now-on-to-governors-desk/

Bade, Gavin. 2017. "Trump Nominates Republican Energy Lawyer McIntyre to Head FERC," *Utility Dive.* (July 14), Accessed August 11, 2017 http://www.utilitydive.com/news/trump-nominates-republican-energy-lawyer-mcintyre-to-head-ferc/447142/

Chalfant, Morgan. 2017. "Trump Holds Meeting to Address Power Grid Cyber Threats." *The Hill.* (June 21), Accessed August 8, 2017 http://thehill.com/policy/cybersecurity/338790-trump-holds-meeting-to-address-power-grid-cyber-threats

Chediak, Mark. 2015. "Cloudy Prospects for Rooftop Solar Growth in Florida: Energy." *Bloomberg Business.* (February 16), Accessed September 25, 2015 http://www.bloomberg.com/news/articles/2015-02-17/cloudy-prospects-for-rooftop-solar-s-growth-in-florida-energy

Consumers for Smart Solar. 2015. "About Us." Accessed September 21, 2015 https://smartsolarfl.org/about-us/

———. 2014. "A Tale of Two Amendments" Accessed September 29, 2015 https://smartsolarfl.org/a-tale-of-two-amendments/

Cowart, Richard. 2001. *Efficient Reliability: The Critical Role of Demand-Side Resources in Power Systems and Markets.* (June), Montpelier: National Association of Regulatory Utility Commissioners.

Crane, Alan; Duncan Brown, Harrison T. Pannella, and James J. Zucchetto. 2012. *Terrorism and the Electric Power Delivery System.* Washington: National Academies Press.

Crawford, Jonathan and Jennifer A. Dlouhy. 2017. "Trump Picks McIntyre, Chaterjee for Federal Energy Agency Sources Say." *Bloomberg Politics.* (March 8), Accessed August 11, 2017 https://www.bloomberg.com/news/articles/2017 03 08/lawyer-mcintyre-said-to-be-trump-s-pick-to-lead-energy-regulator

Federal Energy Regulatory Commission (FERC). 2015. "Order No. 1000 - Transmission Planning and Cost Allocation." Accessed October 1, 2015 http://www.ferc.gov/industries/electric/indus-act/trans-plan.asp

Fischer, Brendan. 2012. "ALEC Gets Support from Koch-Funded Americans for Prosperity." *PR Watch.* (April 18), Accessed September 16, 2015 http://www.prwatch.org/news/2012/04/11465/alec-gets-support-koch-funded-americans-prosperity

Florida Division of Elections. 2016. "Proposed Constitutional Amendment to be Voted on August 30, 2016." Accessed August 8, 2017 http://dos.myflorida.com/media/696213/constitutional-amendments-2016-primary-english-booklet.pdf

Florida Electrical Cooperative Association (FECA). 2015. "Member Information." Accessed September 25, 2015 http://www.feca.com/members.html

Florida Energy Systems Consortium (FESC). 2015. "Smart Grid and Energy Storage." University of Florida, Gainesville, FL, Accessed September 25, 2015 http://www.floridaenergy.ufl.edu/contact-us/

Florida Municipal Electric Association (FMEA). 2015. "Florida Public Power." Accessed September 25, 2015 http://publicpower.com/floridas-electric-utilities-2/

Florida Public Service Commission (FPSC). 2012. *Review of Florida's Investor-Owned Electric Utilities 2011 Service Reliability Reports.* (November), Tallahassee: Florida Public Service Commission Division of Engineering.

Floridians for Solar Choice. 2015. "About," Accessed September 16, 2015 http://www.flsolar choice.org/about/

———. 2015. "Constitutional Amendment Petition Form." Floridians for Solar Choice, Accessed September 21, 2015 http://www.flsolarchoice.org/sign-the-petition/

Goldenberg, Suzanne and Ed Pilkington. 2013. "ALEC Calls for Penalties on 'Free-rider' Homeowners in Assault on Clean Energy." *The Guardian.* Accessed September 16, 2015 http://www.theguardian.com/world/2013/dec/04/alec-freerider-homeowners-assault-clean-energy

Goreham, Steve. 2014. "America's Power Grid at the Limit: The Road to Electrical Blackouts." *Daily Caller.* (April 23) Accessed September 25, 2015 http://dailycaller.com/2014/04/23/americas-power-grid-at-the-limit-the-road-to-electrical-blackouts/

Hanis, Monique. 2017. "Florida Governor Rick Scott Signs Renewables Bill." *AEE News.* (June 16), Accessed August 16, 2017 https://www.aee.net/articles/florida-gov-scott-signs-renewables-bill

Kind, Peter. 2013. *Disruptive Challenges: Financial Implications and Strategic Responses to a Changing Retail Electric Business.* Washington: Edison Electric Institute (EEI).

Klas, Mary Ellen. 2015. "Group Attempts to Undercut Solar Initiative with Rival Amendment," *Miami Herald.* (July 15), Accessed September 21, 2015 http://www.miamiherald.com/news/state/florida/article27352444.html

Kransky, Ross. 2014. "U.S. Court Upholds FERC Rules on Electric Grid Planning." *Reuters.* (August 15), Accessed October 1, 2015 http://www.reuters.com/article/2014/08/15/us-usa-courts-ferc-idUSKBN0GF1R920140815

Kredo, Adam. 2015. "U.S. Power Grid Being Hit With 'Increasing' Hacking Attacks, Government Warns." *The Washington Beacon.* (June 24), Accessed October 1, 2015 http://freebeacon.com/national-security/u-s-power-grid-being-hit-with-increasing-hacking-attacks-government-warns/

Linares, Corina Rivera. 2017. "Politicians Speak Out Against Trump's Sale of Public Transmission Assets." *Electric Light & Power.* (June 19), Accessed August 8, 2017 http://www.elp.com/articles/2017/06/politicians-speak-out-against-trump-s-proposed-sale-of-public-transmission-assets.html

Maddow, Rachel. 2008. "Transcript of the Interview with Presidential Candidate Barack Obama." (October 30), *The Rachel Maddow Show - MSNBC.* Accessed October 1, 2015 http://www.nbcnews.com/id/27464980/#.Vg7DhaJuLfg.

Manjarres, Javier. 2014. "Is The Steyer-Funded Southern Alliance For Clean Energy Funding A Tea Party Civil War?" *Florida Review.* (October 30), Accessed September 16, 2015 http://shark-tank.com/2014/10/30/steyer-funded-southern-alliance-clean-energy-funding-tea-party-civil-war/

Martin, Chris, Mark Chediak, and Ken Wells. 2013. "Why the U.S. Power Grid's Days Are Numbered." *Bloomberg Business.* (August 22) Accessed September 25, 2015 http://www.bloomberg.com/bw/articles/2013-08-22/homegrown-green-energy-is-making-power-utilities-irrelevant

Monast, John, Kate Konschnik, Ari Peskoe, Sarah Adair and Christina Reichert. 2016. "Illuminating the Energy Policy Agenda: Electricity Sector Issues Facing the Next Administration." Report NR16-01 (October), Duke University, Nicholas Institute for Environmental Policy Solutions, University of North Carolina Center for Climate, Energy, Environment and Economics and Harvard University Environmental Law Program, Accessed August 11, 2017 https://nicholasinstitute.duke.edu/sites/default/files/publications/ni_r_16-01_final.pdf

Navigant. 2015. "Energy: Smart Grid" Navigant Consulting, Chicago, IL, Accessed September 25, 2015 http://www.navigant.com/industries/energy/smart-grid/.

Neu, Jerome. 2012. *On Loving Our Enemies: Essays in Moral Psychology.* New York: Oxford University Press.

News Service of Florida. 2015. "Poll: Voters Don't Take A Shine To Solar Amendment." (July 28), *Orlando Sentinel.* Accessed September 21, 2015 http://www.orlandosentinel.com/news/politics/political-pulse/os-poll-voters-solar-amendment-20150728-post.html

Pantsios, Anastasia. 2015. "4 States Where Solar is Under Attack by Koch-Funded Front Groups." *EcoWatch*. (March 27), Accessed September 16, 2015 http://ecowatch.com/2015/03/27/solar-under-attack-koch-brothers/

Parfomak, Paul W. 2014. "Physical Security of the U.S. Power Grid: High Voltage Transformer Substations." *CRS*. (June 17), Accessed October 1, 2016 https://www.documentcloud.org/documents/1303171-2014-crs-report.html.

Perry, Mitch. 2016. "Amendment Four Wins—Measure Would Expand Solar Power in Florida." *Florida Politics*. (August 30), Accessed August 8, 2017 http://floridapolitics.com/archives/220664-amendment-4-leading-big-measure-expand-solar-power-florida

Postelwait, Jeff. 2017. "Trump Budget Proposes Selling Publicly Owned Transmission Lines." *Energy Light & Power*. (May 24), Accessed August 8, 2017 http://www.elp.com/articles/2017/05/trump-budget-proposes-selling-publicly-owned-transmission-assets.html

President of the United States (POTUS). 2017. "Executive Order 13800: Strengthening the Cybersecurity of Federal Networks and Critical Infrastructure." (May 11), Accessed August 8, 2017 https://www.whitehouse.gov/the-press-office/2017/05/11/presidential-executive-order-strengthening-cybersecurity-federal

Pyper, Julia. 2016. "Florida Voters Defeat Utility-Backed Solar Amendment." *Greentech Media*. (November 9), Accessed August 3, 2017 https://www.greentechmedia.com/articles/read/florida-voters-defeat-utility-backed-solar-amendment

Schafer, Alissa Jean. 2017. "Pro Solar Amendment Four Signed into Law by Governor Scott." *Floridians For Solar Choice*. (June 16), Accessed August 3, 2017 http://www.flsolarchoice.org/pro-solar-amendment-4-signed-into-law-by-governor-scott/

Schneider Electric. 2012. "Preparing for Distributed Energy Resources." (June), Accessed June 14, 2015 https://www.slideshare.net/SchneiderElectric/der-2012-17230126

SecureTheGrid. 2015. "The Basics of Grid Security." Secure the Grid Coalition, Washington, DC. Accessed October 1, 2015 http://securethegrid.com/the-basics-of-grid-security/

Siciliano, John. 2017. "Trump Restores GOP Chairmanship at FERC." *Washington Examiner*. (August 10), Accessed August 11, 2017 http://www.washingtonexaminer.com/trump-restores-gop-chairmanship-at-ferc/article/2631168

Snyder, Glenn. 2007. *Alliance Politics*. Ithaca: Cornell University Press.

South Carolina Public Service Authority, et al, v FERC. 2014. U.S. Court of Appeals for the District of Columbia Circuit, No. 12-1232.

Southern States Energy Board (SSEB). 2015. "Resolution Encouraging Adoption of the Regulation Freedom Amendment." (Adopted September 28), 2015 *Adopted Resolutions of the Southern States Energy Board*. Norcross, GA.

———. 2010. "Southern States Energy Board By-Laws." (September 16), Norcross, GA.

St. John, Jeff. 2015."California's Distributed Energy Grid: The Next Steps." *Greentech Media (GTM)*. (July 7) Accessed September 25, 2015 http://www.greentechmedia.com/articles/read/californias-distributed-energy-grid-plans-the-next-steps

———. 2014. "FERC Grid-Planning Rule Survives Legal Challenge, Setting Stage for Transmission Upgrades." *Greentech Media*. Accessed October 1, 2015 http://www.greentechmedia.com/articles/read/court-upholds-green-friendly-regional-grid-planning-rules.

Tanton, Tom. 2013. "Reforming Net-Metering: Providing a Bright and Equitable Future." (March), Arlington, VA: American Legislative Exchange Council (ALEC), Accessed September 16, 2015 at http://alec.org/docs/Net-Metering-reform-web.pdf

Terry, Tracy, Francis Woods, Lessly Goudazi and Paul Carrier. 2001. *National Transmission Grid Study*. Washington: U.S. Department of Energy (USDOE).

Thomasson, Scott. 2017. "Sunshine State Shows Additional Gains in Solar Energy." Vote Solar. (April 19), Accessed August 3, 2017 https://votesolar.org/usa/florida/updates/sunshine-state-shows-additional-gains-solar-energy/

Thompson, Loren. 2015. "Five Reasons The U.S. Power Grid Is Overdue For A Cyber Catastrophe." *Forbes*. (August 19), Accessed October 1, 2015 http://www.forbes.com/sites/lorenthompson/2015/08/19/five-reasons-the-u-s-power-grid-is-overdue-for-a-cyber-catastrophe/print/

Toppa, Sabrina. 2015. "The National Power Grid Is Under Almost Continuous Attack, Report Says." *Time Magazine*. (March), Accessed September 29, 2015 http://time.com/3757513/electricity-power-grid-attack-energy-security/

Torres, Frank. 2015. "Consumers for Smart Solar Launch 2016 Ballot Initiative In Orlando." *The Orlando Political Observer*. (July 15) Accessed September 21, 2015 http://orlando-politics.com/2015/07/15/consumers-for-smart-solar-launch-2016-ballot-initiative-in-orlando/

Tritch, Teresa. 2014. "The Koch Attach on Solar Energy." *New York Times*. (April 26), Accessed September 16, 2015 http://readersupportednews.org/opinion2/277-75/23356-the-koch-attack-on-solar-energy

Turner, Jim and Jim Saunders. 2015. "'Smart Solar' Initiative Soaks Up Contributions." *Orlando Sun-Sentinel*. Accessed September 21, 2015 http://www.sun-sentinel.com/business/consumer/fl-nsf-solar-initiative-contributions-20150914-story.html

Tverberg, Gail. 2008. "The U.S. Grid: Will It Be Our Undoing?" *The Oil Drum*. (May 7), Accessed October 1, 2015 http://www.resilience.org/stories/2008-05-07/u-s-electric-grid-will-it-be-our-undoing.

U.S. Department of Energy (USDOE). 2015. "Smart Grids." *Energy.Gov*. Accessed September 25, 2015 http://energy.gov/oe/services/technology-development/smart-grid

U.S. Energy Information Agency (USEIA). 2014. "What Is the Electric Power Grid & What Are the Challenges It Faces?" *Energy in Brief*. Accessed October 1, 2015 https://www.eia.gov/energyexplained/index.cfm?page=electricity_delivery

———. 2013. "Federal Power Marketing Administrations Across Much of the United States." *Today in Energy*. (June 12 Independent Statistics and Analysis), Accessed August 8, 2017 https://www.eia.gov/todayinenergy/detail.php?id=11651

Wilson, Kirby. 2015. "Poll: Majority of Floridians Would Vote Against Solar Industry-Backed Amendment." *Tampa Bay Times*. (July 28), Accessed September 21, 2015 http://www.tampabay.com/blogs/the-buzz-florida-politics/poll-majority-of-floridians-would-vote-against-solar-industry-backed/2238995

Williams, Katie Bo. 2015. "Homeland Security Moves to Prevent Attack on Power Grid." *The Hill*. (August 14), Accessed September 29, 2015 at http://thehill.com/policy/cybersecurity/251177-homeland-security-moves-to-prevent-attack-on-power-grid.

Wolfgang, Ben. 2017. "Trump Taps Former McConnell Aide to Head Federal Energy Regulatory Agency." *Washington Post*. (August 10), Accessed August 11, 2017 http://www.washingtontimes.com/news/2017/aug/10/neil-chatterjee-former-mcconnell-aide-tapped-trump/

CHAPTER 4

Cooperation and Conflict in Oregon's Forests and Valleys

BACKGROUNDER FOR CASE STUDY TWO

Cooperation Born of Conflict

Most stories need to be understood within context and some stories require more context than others. The contextual background for the Blue Mountain Forest Partners case study is more complicated than most even though the work of this partnership is relatively straightforward and easy to appreciate. It is the story of people coming together in a region shaped by the surrounding physical environment to forge an economy principally consisting of ranching, timber, recreation and associated businesses and enterprises. It is the story of how a range of interests—business, local, state and federal government, non-profits, environmental groups, ranchers, farmers and citizens—cooperated to bring jobs and economic stability to a community whose lumber industry had been debilitated by a host of economic, regulatory and environmental factors. Theirs is a compelling story worth recounting and remembering. However, it is a story rendered more remarkable because of contemporary and historical factors that produced the partnership in the first place.

What is particularly noteworthy is the degree to which members of this partnership functioned within an atmosphere of distrust and conflict to ultimately improve the economic and social well-being of their community. Since 53% of the land within Oregon is either owned or managed by the federal government, promoting the economic well-being of virtually any community necessarily entails working closely with one or more federal agencies (Vincent, Hanson & Argueta 2017). This pervasive federal control of state land has produced a sense of enmity among many Oregonians and specifically among citizens of Oregon's Harney Basin. Within this region those willing to cooperate with federal agencies are often greeted with profound suspicion. Rather than perceiving opportunity and the benefits born of compromise and collaboration, many regard cooperation with the federal government as "selling out"—pure and simple. Experience has led these Oregonians to conclude that when dealing with the "feds" one should do so distrustfully and at an arms-length. This distrust is precisely what the Blue Mountain Forest Partners sought to cooperatively address.

Given the climate of skepticism and distrust existing among some within this Eastern Oregon region, it is not only necessary but frankly imperative to understand the "back-story"—the so called "story *behind* the story." In this instance the "back-story" is what makes Oregon and many other Western states "different" from their Eastern neighbors. This is the account of a people shaped by their physical environment and historical events - a tale of exploration, exploitation, settlement, violence, and above all conflict and adaptation. This is the history of Oregon and the sub-plot for the case study situated in and around the Harney Basin and the history from which the Blue Mountain Forest Partnership (BMFP) emerged.

While recent events in Eastern Oregon have significantly influenced the emergence of private/public partnerships like BMFP, these events are themselves grounded in the longer history of the region—an ongoing history of confrontation, conflict and exploitation. Simply put, recent events such as those involving the Oregon Militia and Patriot movements and the 2016 occupation of the Malheur National Wildlife Refuge don't make sense until placed within the context of the longer history of Oregon and the West. Contemporary conflicts and issues that seemingly defy the best efforts at cooperation are rooted in Western history and values dating back to the first settlers in Oregon.

A Legacy of Conquest and Conflict: Conflicting Claims

The historical relationship between Western settlers and the land has been one of conflict. Conflicts between the desire to inhabit and settle the land combined with environmental obstacles like drought, flooding, resource scarcity and competition for control of the land and its resources have produced an ongoing history of struggle and confrontation. Not surprisingly that legacy of conflict persists to this day and is primarily reflected in conflicts involving ranchers, lumber companies and farmers and the federal government. Although protagonists have changed over the years the source of controversy remains—namely who owns the land and determines how it is to be used.

The conflict between European and American settlers for control of what would be known as "Oregon Country" began when the first European explorer - Rodriguez Cabrillo of Portugal - beheld the Oregon coast in 1543 (Nauman 1999). Later the British took interest in the region when Sir Francis Drake arrived on the Oregon coast in 1579 (Gitzen 2011) followed by the Spanish explorer Juan De Fuca who mapped the Oregon coast in 1592 (DeVoto 1952). In 1778 explorer Captain James Cook revisited Oregon on behalf of the British naming several of Oregon's capes (Ledyard 1963) while American explorer Robert Gray sailed up to Columbia River in 1792 laying claim to the Oregon territory for the United States (Scofield 1992).

In 1793, Alexander Mackenzie, a French explorer, fur trader and representative of the North-West Company (a large British fur trading organization), became the first European to cross the American continent by land, reaching the Pacific Ocean by following the Bella Coola River in British Columbia. Mackenzie's exploration ultimately led to the merger of the North-West Company and the Hudson Bay Company, promoting fur trading throughout Pacific Northwest and into Oregon. His accomplishment later inspired other explorers to include the Lewis and Clark expedition that reached the Pacific coast in 1805 (Mirsky 1946).

By 1811, a wealthy New York financier by the name of John Jacob Astor in conjunction with the Pacific Fur Company sought to compete with the British North West Company and the Hudson Bay Company and funded an expedition of explorers to round Cape Horn and explore the Pacific Northwest. This expedition, aboard the ship *Tonquin,* resulted in the establishment of the Fort Astoria in 1811 which would later become Astoria, Oregon—the oldest settlement in the state (Stark 2014) and the oldest American community on the West Coast of the United States. Unfortunately, numerous setbacks involving disease, Indian skirmishes and ill-fortune led the settlers of Fort Astoria to sell their interests to the British held North West Company in 1813 during the War of 1812 with Great Britain. The British would go on to control trade and settlement throughout this region through the North-West Company (later merged by the British parliament into the Hudson Bay Company). During this period, explorer, fur trapper and cartographer David Thompson embarked by inland route on behalf of the North West Company and between 1807 and 1811 established fur trading throughout parts of Eastern Oregon before reaching Astoria in 1811 (Dobbs 2013, 42-47).

Spain ceded its territorial claims to the United States in 1819 under the terms of the Transcontinental Treaty (Adams-Onis Treaty) allowing the United States to acquire the territories of Oregon and Florida (Bevans 1974). Despite the acquisition of this territory by the U.S. The Hudson Bay Company under the leadership of John McLoughlin established a headquarters in Fort Astoria from which his assistant Peter Skene Ogden departed in 1825 to establish a fur trading operation along the Crooked River in Southeast Oregon (Wilson 1994). The Hudson's Bay Company continued to control trade throughout most of Oregon territory until 1848 when it relinquished control to the United States with the signing of the Oregon Treaty (Barnston & Swanston 1869).

During the period 1840-1880, innumerable settlers moved to Oregon from the East by way of the 2,170 mile Oregon Trail. The trail terminated in the Willamette Valley of Oregon—a route originally established by the overland expedition originally commissioned by John Jacob Astor. By 1845 the pace of settlement in the region dramatically increased (Klingle 2009) and countless settlers occupied lands that had traditionally been the home of indigenous tribes and began subsistence farming, cattle and sheep ranching and timbering for building materials (Buck 2016).

Gold and silver deposits were discovered in the 1850's throughout the streams of Southern Oregon and a gold rush ensued attracting thousands more speculators and adventurers swarming into Oregon to engage in "placer mining" in the stream beds throughout the region (Lindgren 2014; Brooks & Ramp 2013). By the 1860s gold had also been discovered in Eastern Oregon where it was recovered using bucket line dredging to move mountains of earth to expose gold nuggets. Hydraulic mining was also employed—a process where soil is washed away from hillsides by use of high pressure steam-powered hydraulic hoses (Baker City Chamber of Commerce 2014; Lindrgen 2014). Both methods produced considerable ecological damage to hillsides and streams. Lode mining for gold likewise began in the 1860's which involved digging extensive mine shafts - all requiring timber trusses as well as rails for the railroad cars transporting gold (Johnson 2016).

Indian Wars: The Cayuse, the Rogue River and Bannock-Paiute Uprising

Upon signing the Adams-Onis Treaty and prior to the convening of the Oregon Territorial Legislature (1849), Indian wars erupted in Oregon. The conflict was fueled by the infringement of British and American settlers seeking gold, fur, grazing and timber within historically native lands. Moreover, the conflict was exacerbated by the scourge of foreign-born diseases upon the natives as well as by a backlash against attempts to "Christianize" the tribes (Victor 1894).

The most notable of the Indian conflicts - the Cayuse Indian War - was precipitated by the massacre of Methodist missionaries on November 29, 1847 by a band of Cayuse men as retribution for the introduction of measles and smallpox among their tribe and the failure of Methodist missionary and physician Dr. Marcus Whitman to cure these diseases. This massacre occurred in the Blue Mountain region of what was then known as the Oregon Territory. It was this event that shocked the United States into negotiating the Oregon Treaty on August 14, 1848 (Victor 1894).

In response, the provisional governor of Oregon Territory - George Abernathy - called for the organization of a militia to respond to the massacre. The militia, under the command of Colonel Cornelius Gilliam, was formed concurrently to Abernathy's peace negotiations with the Cayuse tribe. Ultimately, Colonel Gilliam organized a force of more than 500 volunteers and departed in January of 1848 to confront the tribe and rescue hostages. In the process Gilliam's militia needlessly provoked both friendly and unfriendly tribes further escalating violence and unrest. Finally, Governor Abernathy's negotiating committee reached an agreement with tribal leaders who agreed to surrender the perpetrators of the massacre who were ultimately charged, tried and executed by hanging in 1850 (Victor 1894).

Between 1855-56, another noteworthy conflict occurred along the Rogue River in Southern Oregon when the indigenous Rogue River Athabascan Indians commenced hostilities, provoked by the infringement upon their territory of a burgeoning population of settlers seeking homesteads and gold. This conflict pitted soldiers from the U.S. Army and local militia members against a band of Indian insurgents. Under the leadership of Chief Joapserkahar (a.k.a. Chief "Jo") the Rogue River Athabascan Indians responded to what they perceived to be hostile acts on the part of settlers seeking to displace the tribe from their native lands (Lewis 2017, Victor 1894).

Settler hostilities against Indians were deemed legally justifiable via the Oregon Land Donation Act of 1850 that disposed of federal land to white settlers - quite literally confiscating traditional native lands and awarding them to settlers from the East. Settlers found additional justification for their actions in the Rogue River Treaty that effectively forced the Indians to relinquish their lands to white settlers (Kappler 1904). The provisions of the Land Donation Act and the Rogue River Treaty were unacceptable to many Indians who responded with plundering raids upon settler homestead and communities. In October 1855—two years after the signing of the Rogue River Treaty, a contingent of settlers from the nearby mining community of Jacksonville massacred some 28 Indians near Table Rock Reservation. This event escalated the violence between the settler and Indian communities fueling a war that ended in 1856 after a force of 700 soldiers literally starved the Indians into submission (Schwartz 2010, Victor 1894).

The final Indian conflict of any significance occurred on the Malheur Indian Reservation in 1878 involving the Paiute nation indigenous to Southeastern Oregon. In 1872 President Ulysses S. Grant signed an executive order establishing the nearly 1.8 million-acre Malheur Indian Reservation to sequester the Indians. The formation of the reservation was rationalized to insure the security of settlers. However, the unstated reason for creating the reservation was to acquire Paiute land and resources. The Malheur Indian Reservation encompassed 1.8 million acres and was intended to be self- supportive of its Paiute residents (Allen 2005).

Sadly, resources were never forthcoming to make this happen and conditions on the reservation deteriorated significantly. However, as living conditions deteriorated so did the morale and health of the natives. Conditions reached a boiling point in 1878 when a group of Bannock Indians from Idaho who had rebelled against authorities were relocated to the Malheur Reservation. This contingent incited the Paiute fomenting a rebellion that closed the reservation in 1878 relocating its inhabitants to Washington's Yakama Reservation. Later, President Chester Arthur restored the Malheur Reservation to the public domain in 1882 and 1883. These events reflected the end of armed conflict between indigenous tribes and Eastern settlers in Oregon (Marion 1989).

Timber

The so-called Oregon Indian Wars ended with the closing of the Malheur Indian Reservation in 1878. By the end of this period the bulk of settlers were involved in trapping, trading, ranching, subsistence farming and missionary work—principally through the auspices of the Methodist Church (Yarnes 1961). Given their vocations the members of these communities were predominantly transient and did not become firmly rooted to specific communities. However, the discovery of rich gold deposits changed all this as once primitive settlements became booming mining towns attracting more permanent residents and a variety of businesses, entrepreneurs, tradespeople and professionals (Powell 2008a).

Accompanying the growth of these communities was the expansion of cattle ranching, sheep herding and small farming operations to feed the appetites of the growing number of townspeople. The "gold rush" of Eastern Oregon also increased demand for timber necessary to construct mines and build homes and businesses in nearby communities. Timber was likewise in demand for fencing ranches and providing rail ties for a railroad fueled by the need to transport ore to market - expanded (Powell 2008a; Campbell et al. 2003).

Logging commenced in the Pacific Northwest during the early 19th century when the first sawmill was constructed at Fort Vancouver in 1826 (Klingle 2009). By 1853 the first sawmill in Oregon opened near Canyon City, Oregon (Powell, 2008b; Engeman 2005) and within the space of fifty-years an entire network of steam-powered mills covered Eastern Oregon as demand for timber increased. Accordingly, lumber production in Oregon grew dramatically over the period 1849-2004 rising from 17 million board feet (mbf) in 1849 to 735 mbf in 1899, and 3,666 mbf in 1924. Thereafter total Oregon timber harvests increased from 6,717 mbf in 1942 to 9,802 in 1952 before declining due to diminished demand and regulatory factors to 5,742 mbf in 1992 and 4,451 in 2004 (Andrews & Katura 2005, 4-6).

Ranching

Cattle ranching originated in Western Oregon but shifted to Eastern Oregon in the 1850's and 1860's when gold deposits were discovered throughout Western Oregon and placer mines began displacing ranching. Eastern Oregon is a semi-arid area that encompasses three regions:

- *The Columbia River Region* encompassing those counties with valleys that slope down toward the Columbia River to include the Dufur, John Day and Umatilla valleys.
- *The Blue Mountain Area* with peaks ranging 9,000 feet above the Powder and Rio Rondo rivers.
- *The "Plateau Region,"* ranging in elevation from 2,000 to 5,000 feet and including the Steens Mountain in Harney County whose snow melt flows down into the Harney Valley supplying Lake's Malheur and Harney with water and making the valley floor fertile for migratory birds, cattle and for farming (Strong 1940, 252).

Understanding the modern environmental dynamics of Oregon and particularly Eastern Oregon requires an appreciation of the role ranching plays in the region.

The history of ranching in Oregon dates to 1872 when a young rancher from Sacramento, California by the name of Peter French rode into the Harney basin of Oregon to establish the first major cattle operation in the state—the Peter French Ranch. Employed by California wheat farmer and rancher Hugh Glenn, French was scouting Oregon in search of rangeland upon which Glenn's cattle operation could be expanded (Langston 2003). Ultimately French purchased some 1,200 cattle from a small rancher in the Blitzen River valley and established a ranch that would ultimately include some 200,000 acres 30,000 cattle and 6,000 horses. The original rangeland consisted of a wild riparian hay species that adapted to the saline soil of the basin. This large natural riparian pasture was dependent upon runoff from the various rivers flowing from the faces of the surrounding mountains. This snow-melt ultimately flowed into the valley where much of the moisture evaporated leaving rich salt deposits (Roth 2007).

In subsequent years, French, his successor as ranch manger—Henry Miller—and other ranchers entering the Harney basin dug channels along the Blitzen and Silves Rivers to irrigate their pastures. They also cleared the rangeland of brush and trees that sapped the area's precious water resources and grazed Steen Mountain and the highlands above the Malheur valley to fatten their cattle when feed resources were seasonally scarce upon the valley floor (Langston 2003).

A central feature of this region is a pair of large shallow lakes on the valley floor, Harney and Malheur. Water for both lakes and their extensive systems of shallow marshes originate in the snow melt of the surrounding mountains. Unlike typical rivers that flow to seas or oceans, these desert rivers empty into the Harney basin where water not captured in a marsh or lake simply evaporates leaving a salty mineral residue (Langston 2003; Clark 1932). Fortunately, the bulk of these minerals are leached from the water by plant species such as willows, sago pondweed, cottonwoods, riparian hay and hardy plant species that thrive in this saline environment (Deubbert 1969).

Waterfowl

The area's large wetland areas and their vegetation resulted in Malheur Lake becoming one of the largest migratory bird sanctuaries in North America, a location where most of the waterfowl in central and Western North America rest on their bi-annual migratory flights. Sadly, these waterfowl became threatened as they were hunted for plumes hotly sought after by Eastern millinery interests producing fashionable women's hats. Ultimately, large populations of Sandhill Cranes and other wading birds, as well as numerous duck and goose species favored by hunters and birdwatchers nationwide—were pitted against the growth of ranching and farming across the Harney Basin (Langston 2003). Among the practices employed by these ranchers and farmers to cultivate and graze the land surrounding the lakes, none was more harmful to the fate of waterfowl than the practice of irrigation to recover wetlands for hay pasturage, cattle watering, homesteading and farming.

One of the unintended consequence of irrigation efforts throughout the late 19th century in the region was a significant depletion of the bird population in and around Malheur and Harney lakes. Consequently, in 1908, President Theodore Roosevelt signed Executive Order 929 designating Lake Malheur and Lake Harney as the "Lake Malheur Reservation" placing it within the Department of the Interior's jurisdiction. The reservation was largely developed through the efforts of the Civilian Conservation Corps (CCC) of Franklin D. Roosevelt during the Great Depression and was in part administered by the U.S. Audubon Society (USDA 2016; Corn 2016).

By 1929, the U.S. Congress strengthened migratory bird protection with the passage of the Migratory Bird Conservation Act that created the Migratory Bird Conservation Commission. In 1944 the Migratory Bird Conservation Commission authorized the acquisition of all privately owned lands adjacent to lakes Malheur and Harney and initiated condemnation proceedings for some 10,943 acres. Today the Malheur Wildlife Refuge encompasses 187,167 acres (Corn 2016). Throughout most of its history the Malheur Wildlife Refuge suffered because President Teddy Roosevelt failed to pursue sufficient congressional funding required to maintain the reservation and protect its species. While funding was eventually forthcoming from the Department of Interior's U.S. Fish and Wildlife Service, the task of preserving the refuge too often diverged from conservation policies of the Department of Agriculture, the U.S. Forest Service and the Bureau of Land Management that involved improving riparian systems, managing timber harvests, and reclaiming wetlands for ranching, agricultural use and homesteading (Langston 2003).

Homesteading vs. Ranching

Historically, there has been an ongoing debate in Oregon over who owns the land around Malheur and Harney lakes. This issue has been complicated by the fact that the shoreline—also known as the "meander line"—of the lakes expands and recedes depending upon snow melt as well as the degree to which water is siphoned away by ranchers or public officials upstream and downstream of the lakes (Langston 2003). Further complicating the issue is the fact that historically most of the land in the Harney basin was unfenced and ranchers allowed their stock to graze at will. Moreover, from the outset ranchers engaged in ditching activities to dry wetlands for hay production and to insure water resources for cattle. The totality of these activities altered water levels in and around Malheur and Harney lakes and influenced the acreage suitable for farming (Langston 2003).

Further complicating matters is the degree to which federal executive actions establishing the wildlife refuge in Malheur Lake failed to secure control of the shoreline itself. Consequently, while the surface of the water is owned and managed by the federal government, the status of the shoreline and adjacent lands have been in a state of constant flux with changes in the water table leaving the state and local officials and homesteaders quarreling over who owned what in the Harney basin. Historically, these "meander line" lands have been pursued by competing interests to include:

- Cattle ranchers who fence the range and grow hay for winter forage
- Homesteaders who till the soil, stretch barbwire, dig irrigation ditches and build homes,
- State governments who assert jurisdiction under the Swamp Land Act, and
- The federal government who claim jurisdiction under the jurisdiction of the Department of Interior who oversees the national refuge (Langston 2003, 44)

Ultimately, the increased pressure on the land by ranchers and homesteaders—especially ditching activities—further destabilized the surrounding land making it ever more difficult to settle legal claims of ownership.

Homesteading in Oregon was fueled by the 1820 Sale Act which enabled settlers to purchase smaller tracts as small as 80 acres for $1.25 per acre and the Homestead Act of 1862 passed by President Abraham Lincoln during the Civil War. This act served to stimulate settlement of the Western territories to include Eastern Oregon. Under the provisions of the act citizens who had not born arms against the U.S. in the Civil War were eligible to claim up to 160 acres of land to homestead. However, they could not claim their homestead if they owed a debt and if deeded a homestead had to live on the land for five years and farm it before they could officially own the land. However, they could purchase the land outright from the federal government six months after settling on it for the price of $1.25 per acre (Anderson 2011). Homesteaders were required to continuously live on their land and cultivate crops as well as make improvements to the property to include the construction of a 12-foot by 14-foot cabin. If for any reason homesteaders abandoned their land property ownership reverted to the federal government (Homestead Act 1862).

In the Malheur Lake region of Eastern Oregon, cattle ranching reigned supreme in and around the period when the Homestead Act was enacted and signed into law unavoidably pitting cattle interests against those of homesteaders. During the post-1860 period when homesteading increased throughout Oregon, so did the size of cattle herds. As these herds grew throughout the mid to late nineteenth century so did the need for more grazing land.

Throughout the Harney basin, ranchers who ditched wetlands to produce hay and water their cattle were aided in their efforts by the federal Swamp Land Act of 1850. This act allowed for the ownership of federal land to revert to the states upon the condition they would drain the land and agriculturally improve it (Langston 2003). This act rewarded ranchers in Eastern Oregon and around Lake Malheur for draining wetlands to expand cattle operations. Moreover, the act provided a rationale for the settlement of farmers around the lake within the "meander line" which is to say along the shores of Lake Malheur amid the ebb and flow of the lake's water level.

Between 1870-72, the Oregon State Legislature augmented the provisions of the Swamp Land Act by selling so-called state-owned overflow lands to settlers for $1.25 per acre. These riparian wetlands were particularly valuable to ranchers since, when drained, they could produce vast amounts of silage for livestock. These state provisions allowed ranchers to acquire monopolistic control of wetlands and they used this control to influence the region's water supply and land fertility. Ultimately the provisions of the Swamp Land Act enabled a handful of cattle ranchers to effectively control most of the entire Harney basin. Having been granted access to these considerable grazing resources and water rights, ranchers claimed significantly more grazing land for themselves and in this way acquired property through means that subsequent settlers and homesteaders would call an abuse of the provisions of The Swamp Land Act (Langston 2003).

The acquisition of these swamp and marsh lands pitted the interests of homesteaders against those of cattle ranchers. As rangeland acreage expanded so did the size of the herds until the winter of 1879-80 when a severe cold dramatically increased cattle mortality rates across the Western U.S. During that period Clarence Gordon authored a document known as the "Gordon Report" (1880) where he first documented the problem of overgrazing the region's rangelands. In the report, Gordon observed that efforts to improve the range via fencing, planting alfalfa and channeling and ditching efforts had served to degrade it to the point where in many spots the soil had been virtually denuded of grass and vegetation (Langston 2003).

Further aggravating resource depletion during this era was the expansion of sheep ranching after cattle prices plunged in 1895. Thereafter cattle ranchers found themselves in conflict with sheep ranchers in a period just prior to the influx of a new wave of eastern settlers (Langston 2003). The conflict between the ranchers and herders inevitably escalated as both pursued scarce water and grazing resources resulting in the "Sheepshooter War" between 1895 and 1906 where cattlemen shot and killed an estimated 10,000 sheep (Nixon 2015).

Between 1885 and 1895, cattle demand declined and ranchers suffered. This period marked an era when cattle ranching retreated, fueled by numerous factors including diminished beef demand, drought, the completion of the Northern Pacific Railroad, the emergence of wheat farming and the expansion of sheep ranching into the Columbia River and Blue Mountain regions (Strong 1940). Eventually, the remaining ranching migrated to Southeastern Oregon and by the end of the nineteenth century the era of big cattle barons in Oregon ended (Braly 1978). Ranching was replaced with an agrarian populism that emerged as farming expanded in Eastern Oregon's riparian lands (Langston 2003). Large rangelands for grazing were essentially eliminated in 1934 with the passage of the Taylor Grazing Act designed to.

> "stop injury to public grazing lands by preventing over-grazing and soil deterioration, to provide for orderly use, improvement and development, to stabilize the livestock industry dependent upon the public range" (Taylor Grazing Act 1934)

Despite reductions in the scale of cattle operations, cattle production increased—growing from approximately 403,000 head of cattle in Eastern Oregon in 1890 to around 522,000 in 1930 (Strong 1940, 253). Thereafter total cattle production decreased to 300,000 cattle by the mid twentieth century (Powell 2008b, 3). However, by 2016 Southeastern Oregon alone (Baker, Harney, Grant and Malheur Counties) produced 372,500 beef cattle while total cattle production (dairy and beef cattle and calves) increased to 400,000. Thus, while the "spread" of historic ranchlands shrank total cattle production yield remains on par with what it was in 1890 (NASS 2016, 5-6; Oliver, Irwin & Knapp 1994, 12).

Water Rights and Fights

Over the years, the most significant changes in Oregon ranching and farming involve the degree to which growing portions of rangeland have been fenced (to include grazing on public lands) and farmers and homesteaders have staked out claims to fertile lands in and around the riparian systems of the Harney basin. What has remained constant is the dependency of homesteader, hunter and rancher upon the most precious substance in the West—water. By 1895 Oregon's legislature had not yet gotten around to clarifying the states' water rights. In the absence of legislative action land owners acted upon a principle known as the "riparian doctrine" which simply meant that those who owned land adjacent to a body of water owned the water rights (Hutchins & Steele 1957).

Since ranching had been going on in Eastern Oregon longer and on a larger scale than farming, ranchers claimed water rights to land they owned or had historically acquired under the Swamp Land Act while the federal government claimed water rights on forest, park and refuge land acquired through Congress. Understandably farmers claimed that ranchers had unfairly utilized the Swamp Land Act to gain access to rangeland and pastures. Moreover, ranchers had aggressively purchased the land and cattle operations of smaller ranchers in the interest of incrementally growing herd capacity and acquiring more grazing land and water resources (Langston 2003).

Meanwhile, disputes over water rights persisted until 1909 when the Oregon legislature finally enacted the Oregon Water Code. Under the terms of this code riparian rights were recognized for existing users if they could demonstrate they had put the water to "beneficial use" prior to the enactment of the code. Thereafter, all water rights would be awarded on a "first in time, first in right" basis (Bateman & Patrino 2010). Unfortunately, the Oregon Water Code proved to have devastating environmental impacts as literally thousands of streams and tributaries statewide became severely depleted after the state effectively over-issued water permits (Neuman 2004).

Beyond the environmental damage occasioned by Oregon's water code, its passage did little to dampen the growing enmity between ranchers and farmers. By 1897 violence broke out between homesteaders and prominent rancher Peter French in which French was killed. Other violence followed until the U.S. Supreme Court ruled in 1901 (Marshall v. French) determining that a homestead claim on Malheur Lake that straddled the meander line, had been initially drawn to include lands residing within the public domain as opposed to privately held land. This decision established a legal framework upon which subsequent Presidents could declare unclaimed lands adjacent to Malheur and Harney lakes as federal property (U.S. Fish & Wildlife 2016 1-8).

Despite episodic conflicts between homesteaders and ranchers over water and land rights, homesteading increased in Oregon during the early twentieth century, fueled in part by several Congressional acts designed to stimulate homesteading, to include:

- The 1902 Reclamation Act allowing for the withdrawal of federal land for reclamation through irrigation,
- The 1906 "Forest Homestead Act" setting aside up to 160 acres per homestead located in forest reserves,
- The 1909 Enlarged Homestead Act allowing for additional homesteads up to 320 acres each,
- The 1912 Three-Year Homestead Act reducing time spent improving the land to 3 years to claim ownership, and
- The 1916 Stock Raising Homestead Act permitting homesteads up to 640 acres for cattle ranching (BLM 2012).

Environmental Costs of Population Growth and Economic Expansion

From the mid-nineteenth-century onward, the growth in Oregon's settlers not only resulted in the complete displacement of indigenous peoples from their native lands, the settler's "Eastern" approaches to mining, timber production, ranching and farming also dramatically changed the nature of the landscape resulting in widespread deforestation, riparian and wetland destruction, species depletion, the introduction of invasive species, water pollution and soil erosion. Cognizant of these issues, the federal government inserted itself into Oregon's state affairs by acquiring and managing the bulk of Oregon's forests and rangelands in the interest of improving timber production and protecting species. Today the federal government controls 53% of the land within the bounds of the State of Oregon (Vincent, Hanson & Bjelopera 2014).

Unfortunately, the forest, range and stream management approaches employed upon federal lands by the U.S. Forest Service (USFS) and the Bureau of Land Management (BLM) only served to further exacerbate the environmental destruction initially produced by European and American colonization (Lamm & McCarthy 1982). These practices were further complicated by conflicting policy goals between and among the various branches of government (USFS, EPA, BLM, the National Park Service (NPS) and others) regarding whether to pursue conservation, preservation and/or production goals on federal lands. The net effect of historical "governmental" management of the federal lands in Oregon was decreased forest economic productivity which threatened the timber industry and lumber mills and increased environmental destruction (Cawley 1993). It was the convergence of these factors— decreased productivity, increased environmental destruction and conflicting land-use policies along with other environmental issues such as invasive plant species (Western Juniper and cheatgrass) and aquatic invaders (carp) (Liskey 2015)—that ultimately increased federal regulatory oversight in the region.

Over at least three decades, the aegis for addressing Oregon's environmental, natural resource and economic problems shifted from landowners, localities and states to Washington, D.C. and the halls of Congress, the White House and the offices of distant federal agency bureaucrats. In considering why this has disproportionately happened in Oregon and other Western states one is drawn to a simple yet straightforward reality. Oregon, unlike most Eastern and Midwestern states is principally owned and overseen by the federal government, which means that the values that govern the use of the bulk of the land lying within the state are derived by "out-of-state" interests principally residing in Washington. This shift in the locus of land control from the state and localities to a distant Eastern capitol serves to diminish the voices of locals as well as delegitimizing their experiences, expertise and history with the land.

Federal land, agricultural, water, forest and environmental legislation since the 1970's has increasingly included language mandating cooperation and collaboration with state and local agencies (Christiansen 2003). While these provisions serve to mitigate the extent of federal control over land use, they do not change the legislative intent of laws nor influence their regulatory language. Thus, while federal collaboration with state and local governments partially relieves the degree to which citizens and officials feel their concerns are dismissed, discounted, and delegitimized many stakeholders in land use decisions nevertheless feel as if their voices and concerns don't matter in Washington. Given their experience of de-legitimization and exclusion from distantly derived environmental and economic decisions, it is hardly surprising that some from among the ranching and farming communities of Oregon have responded with populist fervor to oppose and resist ever-growing federal power and influence.

When the Federal Government Owns Most of the Land

The bulk of case studies included in this book involve cooperative relationships between environmentalists, agencies, businesses, non-profits and civic interests that collaborated to solve an environmental problem—often doing so despite significant ideological differences. The Green Teal Coalitions in Georgia and Florida are illustrative of such cases. However, case studies set in the Western United States are different principally because in the West most of the land is owned or managed by either federal or state governments (Figures 3&4). Federal lands are principally managed by five agencies—the U.S. Fish and Wildlife Service (FWS), the U.S. Forest Service (USFS), the National Park Service (NPS), the U.S. Department of Defense (DOD) and the Bureau of Land Management (BLM) (Vincent, Hanson & Argueta 2017). Per the American Lands Council Foundation (ALCF 2014) Western States on average have jurisdiction over less than 50% of their state's land area whereas in the Eastern U.S. states have jurisdiction over 95% of their land (Figures 5 & 6) (USGSA 2017; American Lands Council 2014). Moreover, much of the remaining Western state lands consist of Native-American reservations (Figure 7) (USGS 2014).

When considering these facts, one might wonder how these statistics relate to the willingness of disparate community interest groups to compromise and collaborate regarding environmental issues. The answer is deceptively straightforward. The economies of Western states are largely dependent upon access to natural resources (timber, rangeland, water, minerals, coal, oil and natural gas) that fuel the lumber, ranching, recreation, agricultural, mining and energy industries (ACLF 2014). Most local economies and communities are dependent in one way or another on one or more of these industries and the natural resources that principally drive these resources are principally found on public lands.

Historically, the extensive ownership of Western lands by the federal government produced ongoing conflict between citizen and state interests and the principal agencies overseeing these lands. In recent years, conflicts have involved the right to access public lands and their resources resulting in controversies over recreation (Downey, Fretwell & Regan 2016), ranching (Hage 1989), energy (Lamm & McCarthy 1982), timber (Hays 2009), water (Langston 2003), gold and silver (Young & Lennon 1977) and environmental and species protection (Davis 2001). Typically, these controversies involve stakeholder protests or negotiations relative federal land use and access regulations.

The forums where these controversies are aired are numerous to include state and federal courts, the U.S. Congress, state legislatures, public hearing and meetings involving federal agencies, university forums, public media of all types, as well as through civil disobedience and unrest. However, the very fact that controversy has persisted for so long and has been expressed in so many ways suggests something very basic about the relationship between citizens of the Western states and their federal government. Underneath the tension between citizen and state lies a legacy of enmity between Western settlers and Eastern bureaucratic, business and political interests who have historically approached the West as a source of resources to be plundered and sold for profit as compared to a homeland and a region with intrinsic value and worth independent of its diverse beauty and rich natural resources.

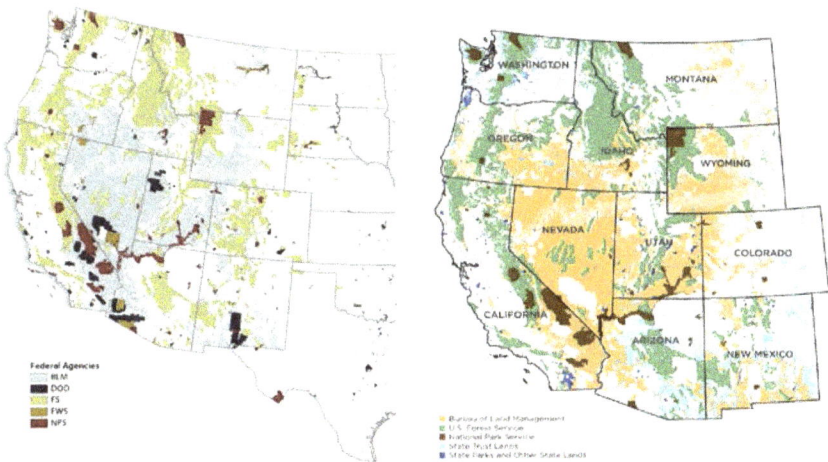

Figures 3 & 4: Federal & State Western Lands
(Source: Vincent, Hanson & Argueta 2017)

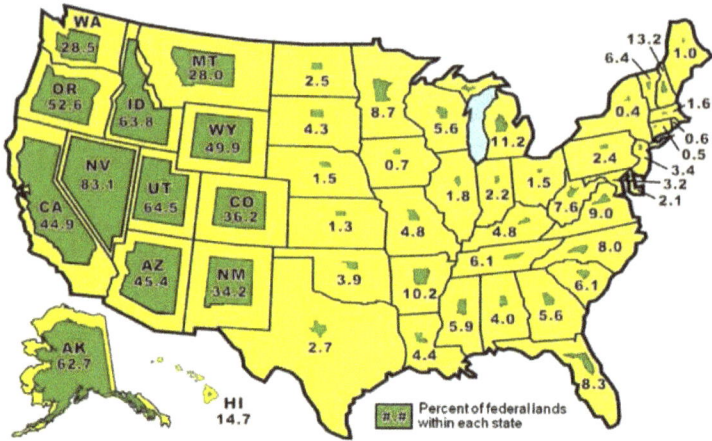

Figure 5: Federal Land as a Percentage of State Owned Land Area
(Source: O'Laughlin 2011)

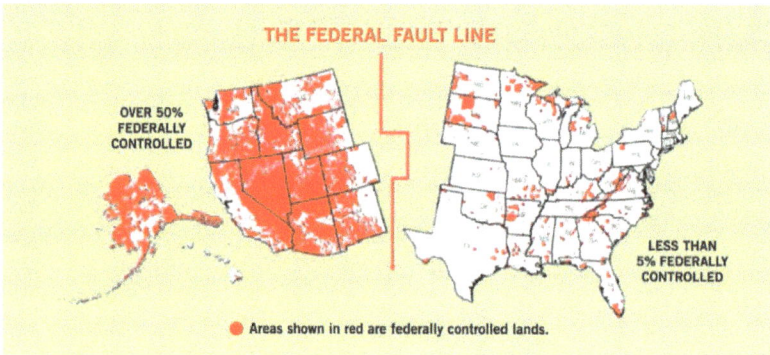

Figure 6: Federal Fault Line
(Source: American Lands Council 2014)

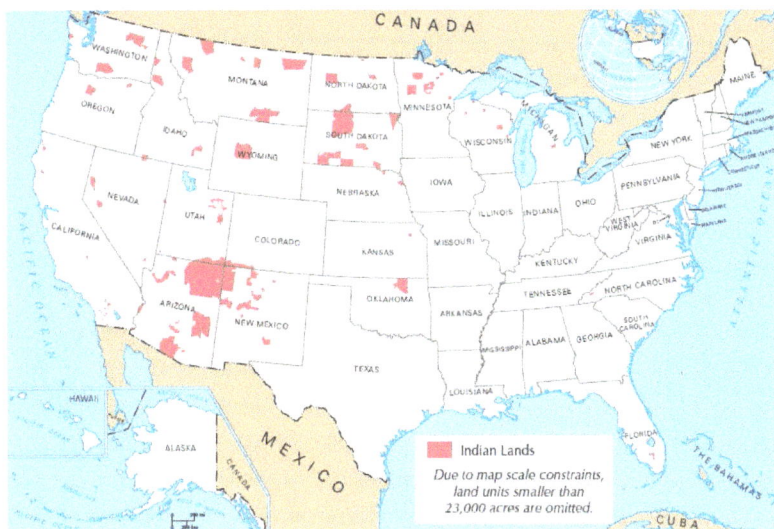

Figure 7: Indian Lands
(Source: USGS 2014)

Nobody has written more elegantly about this tension than Bernard DeVoto (1952) when in 1934 he described the West as a "plundered province" exploited by Eastern capitalists (DeVoto 1934). DeVoto observed that the West was the product of industrialism as Eastern capitalists sought to enrich themselves upon the bounteous resources of the West. Admittedly Eastern interests substantially enriched themselves but they did so at a very steep price—a price paid principally by indigenous peoples, indigenous species, a ravaged environment and ultimately by Western settlers.

Settlers from the earliest days of Westward migration from the original Eastern colonies resented their Eastern brethren because, by comparison, these Western settlers came from independent Scotch-Irish stock wholly intolerant of social or economic elitism and impatient with foreign interests meddling in their personal affairs (Fehrenbach 2000). Later, they came to associate Eastern interests of all sorts with the federal government that regulated the land upon which they had staked homesteads. For better or worse the modern legacy of this Eastern versus Western resentment is the contemporary tension between Western citizens and the federal agency officials charged with the responsibility of managing public lands.

The Sagebrush Rebellion and the Federal Five

Five federal agencies ("The Federal Five") serve as gatekeepers to all the Western federally owned or managed lands. These agencies include the Bureau of Land Management managing 38.9% of public lands, the U.S. Forest Service managing 28.7%, the Fish and Wildlife Service managing 14.2%, the National Park Service managing 11.8% (Vincent, 2004, p. CRS 3-4) and the U.S. Department of Defense who manages 2% of all public lands (14.4 million acres) (Vincent, Hanson and Bjelopera 2014). Conflict between the "Federal Five" and Western landowners and communities has long been brewing coming to a head in the late 1970's with what is now popularly referred to as the "Sagebrush Rebellion."

The "Sagebrush Rebellion" of Western landowners started as a response to federal possession of Western lands under the doctrine of "eminent domain." It began in 1891 when President Benjamin Harrison's created the two-million-acre White Timber Land Reserve in Colorado followed by acquisition of the Pikes Peak, Plum Creek, South Platte and Battlement Mesa Reserves in 1892. Thereafter, a backlash of ranchers, farmers and timber interests across the West sought to reclaim land they argued had been confiscated arbitrarily by the President. The first "Sagebrush Rebellion," ended with the introduction of the so-called McRae Act in 1893, 1896 and 1897 which sought to immobilize the federal government from managing forests to include preventing burning. Although introduced and reintroduced in various forms over the years, Congress never successfully passed the McRae Act or overturned President Harrison's land designations (McCarthy 1992).

The conflict between Western landowners and the federal government was revitalized in 1974 with the passage of the Federal Land Policy and Management Act (FLPM) which effectively ended homesteading in the West and intensified the power of federal agencies over public lands. It first emerged as a regional phenomenon in February 15, 1979 when the Nevada State Legislature acting on the grounds of long-simmering frustrations over the growing power of federal agencies enacted a bill transferring a large portion of the public domain owned by the federal government (some 48 million acres) to the State of Nevada (Rogers 2005, 1). In so doing the Nevada legislature joined other Western legislatures to oppose a law they believed to be both repressive and hostile to the interests of Westerners. John Rice, a reporter covering the legislative session, coined a term for their actions which ultimately "stuck"—"The Sagebrush Rebellion" (Rice 1979).

By July 1979, the first overt confrontation in the Sagebrush Rebellion occurred in Grand County, Utah. Grand County (80% of which consists of federal lands and 90% managed by the BLM) was hit particularly hard by the FLPM Act. The Bureau of Land Management (BLM) provided Grand County commissioners a land use inventory map in April 1979 that prohibited land use in approximately two-thirds of Southeastern Utah, to include the bulk of their county. Commissioners were incensed and in July 1979 they struck back when a county road crew destroyed a barrier to a BLM managed property to pave a strip of road on land reserved for endangered species (Wheeler 1988).

The "bulldozer war" between Grand County commissioners and the BLM continued through July 4, 1980, when 250 Fourth of July celebrants accompanied another county bulldozer into the nearby Mill Creek Canyon Wilderness Inventory Unit where county road crew staff extended a county road some 500 yards within BLM land (Wheeler 1988). The confrontation between Grand County commissioners and the BLM ended on November 20, 1980 when the local *Moab Times Independent* announced that BLM had dropped over half of the designated wilderness areas in the Moab area (county seat of Grand County) thus concluding the "squabble" between the county commissioners, the BLM (Wheeler 1988). However, the issues that fueled this confrontation was far from over and a new era of conflict between federal land, forest and environmental agencies and Western land owners was just beginning.

During this period, the so-called "rebels of '79" (McCarthy 1992) sowed their displeasure with federal regulators and managers across the West. In 1979 Utah Senator Orin Hatch introduced a bill in Congress that would begin the process of returning Federal lands to the Western states. Entitled the Western Lands Distribution and Regional Equalization Act (S.1680), the bill languished in committee and was ultimately never considered by the Senate. However, in 1980 California Governor Ronald Reagan was elected President and publicly identified with the Sagebrush Rebellion. Regan appointed conservative James Watt as Secretary of the Department of Interior as an act of solidarity with the "rebellion" and sought to rein in what westerners perceived to be the excesses of the federal agency (Bump 2016).

To the regret of many Westerners, President Regan proved unsuccessful in furthering the agenda of the rebellion and was ultimately forced into firing Interior Secretary Watt. However, in 1990 the Sagebrush Rebellions reappeared under the name of the Western States Caucus—affectionately referred to by some as "Son of Sagebrush." This group of representatives from several Western states convened a meeting in Las Vegas to develop a strategy to garner support in the Senate and White House to transfer Western Lands to the various states (Christensen 1990; 1991).

In 1992, several Western counties sought to impact federal control by shackling federal agencies in court challenges (Williams 1992). Among the strategies developed by these counties, one involved passing ordinances authorizing sheriffs to arrest federal officials who arbitrarily limited grazing on public lands. Some 45 counties spanning six states ultimately adopted similar ordinances (Swearingen & Schimel 2016). In this fashion, the seeds of what would later be called the "Patriot Movement" were sown as was the impetus for the creation of the Constitutional Sheriffs and Peace Officers Association (CSPOA) that would assert the primacy of the County Sheriff as the principal constitutionally designated law officer at the county level.

The Sagebrush Rebellion's Darker Era

While these events were unfolding, a new and darker era in the Sagebrush Rebellion began to emerge beginning in 1979. From the mid-eighties onward resistance against federal control of public lands became increasingly entwined with those of other emerging movements—particularly the Patriot and Militia Movements. Confrontations, standoffs, protracted lawsuits, and heated claims were stoked by ever increasing federal control of public lands, seemingly arbitrary bureaucratic decisions and federal actions limiting public access that seriously impacted local lifestyles, economies and livelihoods. From this point forward, the regulatory role of government was increasingly perceived by some as being both excessive and illegitimate. Those who resisted federal management ran the risk of being labeled by federal agencies and their ideological supporters as criminals and terrorists while those who chose to "play along" and cooperate with federal officials ran the risk of being labeled dupes, patsies, accomplices and or traitors to historical community values.

The Sagebrush Rebellion symbolized the idea that Westerners can exercise greater control over their land, economy, environment and political system by eschewing Eastern and federal control for enhanced local autonomy. Their critics argued that Sagebrush adherents were adopting a regressive ethic as they sought to reverse generations of history and practice in their region by quite literally jettisoning the federal government from their backyards and from local affairs. In some instances, their motivation for pursuing such political goals were born of a libertarian styled populism deeply engendered in Westerners over many generations. Yet, in other instances, this ethic appears to have been born of experience—having experienced federal officials as hostile to their values, their way of life and their property. It was these "lived experiences" that have ushered in a darker era in the Sagebrush rebellion.

A Show of Federal Force: Hage (Rancher) vs. U.S. (USFS & BLM)

Arguably, the most significant moments in the current Sagebrush Rebellion involved a series of incidents where federal officials engaged in a display of force. These actions not only escalated the level of conflict between landowners and federal agencies, they fueled the perception among some Westerners that federal force must be met with local force. Thus, the level of conflict in the region was escalated to a point where eventually lives would be lost.

The first of these incendiary incidents involved an outspoken critic of federal land authority and Nevada rancher E. Wayne Hage. Hage was the first landowner in the contemporary Sagebrush Rebellion to find his Pine Creek Ranch and livelihood threatened by the forces of the U.S. Forest Service and BLM. Hage had been cited on numerous occasions for trespassing on federal range land, destruction of federal property, failure to maintain terms of his lease and more. Hage's claim throughout all these charges was that the Forest Service and BLM were trying to force him to sell his ranch to obtain access to his water rights that were in considerable demand— particularly from the city of Las Vegas who was in negotiation with the Forest Service regarding purchasing water from them (Hage 1989).

Hage had historically been granted water rights along with his lease of federal rangeland and in 1979 was surprised to encounter Forest Service personnel surveying the rangeland to document the Forest Service's claim on those water rights. He investigated their activities and discovered that the Forest Service had filed claims on 160 sites located within his ranch and on lands he leased from the federal government. In response, Hage filed a "takings claim" petition in 1981where he asserted that the federal government had sought to acquire his ranch and property to include water rights, irrigation right of way, forage rights, rangeland improvements and his cattle (Alden 1998).

Over those ensuing years, the Forest Service effectively retaliated against Wayne Hage's taking claim, declaring his cattle were overgrazing rangeland and suspending his grazing and water permits for five years. Compounding the impact of these actions was the policy of the BLM to cancel permits in concurrence with the U.S. Forest Service. These seemingly coordinated agency actions were followed by an armed confrontation in 1991 during which Hage was informed his cattle were trespassing on the Toiyabe National Forest. At the time Hage's ranch hands were moving 2,000 cattle to highland grazing through a national forest that was completely unfenced— thus making it impossible for some number of the herd to *not* wander into the forest. Upon arriving at the Toiyabe National Forest Hage found himself confronted by 20-30 federal agents armed with assault rifles and wearing flak jackets. The agents informed Hage they were on-site to take possession of his herd that had wandered astray. Later Hage experienced two more armed incursions on to his property by federal agents who eventually confiscated and sold more than 100 cattle while sending Hage the bill for the costs of capturing and transporting the cattle (Alden 1998).

Upon losing his initial Claims Court appeal, Hage refiled his "taking claims" against the Forest Service with the U.S. Court of Appeals claiming the agency had illegally confiscated his livestock, water rights and grazing privileges on federal rangelands. In response, the Forest Service persuaded the U.S. Attorney to file felony charges against Hage and a neighbor Lloyd Seamans for taking government property while cutting and removing brush from a drainage ditch channeling water to their cattle. Ultimately these charges were dismissed and the U.S. Attorney filing them was threatened with sanctions (Alden 1998).

During this protracted legal ordeal, Hage's wife died as did Hage in 2006 leaving litigation to his son Wayne N. Hage. The Hage family was denied resolution of their claim by the initial claims court and in 2012 the Court of Appeal again ruled against the Hage family saying in part that his case lacked standing with the court. Determined to overturn this decision, the Hage family appealed to the U.S. District Court in Reno to Judge Robert C. Jones. In 2013, Jones ruled in favor of the rancher in publishing a 104-page ruling that scathingly criticized the U.S. Forest Service and the BLM for their actions against the rancher. This ruling accused the BLM of having violated federal RICO statues for harassing the Hage family over violating federal grazing rights when the agency knew full well that ranchers who hold water rights from the state can graze their cattle within a half mile of federal water resources without need of a federal permit. The judge also recommended Hage file suit against the federal government for damages (Miller 2013, Jasper 2013; Harris 2013).

The District Court's opinion, however, was reversed in 2016 when the U.S. District Court of Appeals for the Ninth Circuit rendered a judgment that:

1. *"Vacated in part and reversed* in part the district court's judgment,"

2. "Held that the *Hages violated applicable federal statutes and regulations*, as well as the Nevada state law of trespass because between 2004 and 2008,"

3. "Held that the *district court erred* in concluding that, because of their water rights, the Hages had an "easement of necessity" to access water sources,"

4. *"Remanded with instructions that the district court enter judgment for the government* on the Hages' counterclaims," and

5. *"Vacated the judgment* with respect to the government's trespass claims and remanded for reconsideration under the correct legal standard" (U.S. v. Estate of E. Wayne Hage 2016).

The Ninth Court also chastised the judge in the District Court of Nevada saying that he "was biased against the government agencies, and directed that on remand the case be assigned to a different district judge." On March 22, 2016 Wayne N. Hage appealed his family's case to the U.S. Supreme Court for reconsideration. On October

19, 2016, the Supreme Court decided that it would not hear the Hage case, thus ending this episode of the "Sagebrush Rebellion" (Lidgett 2016).

The Hage case has become emblematic among many Western populists who resented what they perceived as federal regulatory over-reach—to include a collusion between federal authorities and the federal court as embodied by the decision of the Ninth Court of Appeals (Pendley 2016). These resentments have fueled and to a degree transformed the most contemporary version of the Sagebrush Rebellion. What has been most transformative regarding this epoch of rebellion against federal land control is the degree to which it fueled the rise of the Patriot and Militia movements in the West.

The Patriot and Militia Movements

The Patriot Movement is a modern reassertion of historic Western libertarian and populist values that calls for construing the U.S. Constitution in terms of its original intent. The Patriot Movement resists what it perceives to be the illegitimate power of the federal government—power acquired and justified well beyond an "originalist" interpretation of the Constitution). They are willing to employ a variety of tools to resist what they perceive to be the illegitimate exercise of federal control to include armed resistance when deemed necessary. One of the principal tools they employ is advocacy for "county supremacy" over federal control. This doctrine embodies two key beliefs: (1) an assertion that the county sheriff is the highest law enforcement authority and (2) the contention that the United States Government has no right to public lands which constitutionally belong under local jurisdiction (Wilson 2016).

The Patriot Movement has become a central feature of the modern Sagebrush Rebellion—particularly in Oregon. One of the most controversial features of the Patriot Movement is the emergence of a parallel phenomenon known as the Militia Movement in which citizens nationwide—but particularly in Western states like Oregon—arm, train and organize themselves into a fighting force in the event of conflict with what they perceive as illegitimate federal force. This feature of the modern Sagebrush Rebellion is extremely germane to the case study to follow because of where the case is situated and the corollary events that occurred in and around the Malheur National Wildlife Refuge and in Grant and Harney County, Oregon.

Some trace the emergence of the Militia Movement to the Ruby Ridge incident that occurred in Waco, Texas in 1992 (Bigg 2010). In that incident, federal agents engaged in a shoot-out with a religious group called the Branch Davidians who barricaded themselves in a farmhouse outside of Waco, Texas. The leader of this group—Randy Weaver—was believed to have been acquiring weapons for a planned violent action. A shootout ensued in which 76 people were killed. While this incident had nothing to do with land rights, some Westerners attuned to the issue of perceived federal over-reach in to state and local affairs responded to what they believed to be excessive federal force by forming militias and arming themselves—thus birthing the Militia Movement.

The movement was further fueled by the Oklahoma City bombing in 1995 perpetrated by Militia Movement member Timothy McVeigh, as well as by a host of subsequent incidents. Per the Southern Poverty Law Center (SPLC), the timeline for the development of the Militia Movement includes:

- 1995 – the bombing of a Forest Service van in Carson City, Nevada,

- 2001 – actions by a Klamath County, Washington sheriff impeding the decision of the BLM to withhold irrigation water to downstream farmers during a severe drought in the interest of protecting the endangered sucker fish,

- 2009 – a Patriot Movement groups known as the Oath Keepers mustering in Lexington, Massachusetts,

- 2012 – the creation of the Constitutional Sheriffs and Peace Officers Association based on the premise that the county sheriff is the definitive law officer constitutionally,

- 2014 – a violent confrontation in Nevada between the BLM and rancher Clive Bundy (Lenz & Potok 2014).

SPLC's report tends to conflate those involved in or sympathetic to the Patriot Movement, the Western land transfer movement, the Tea Party movement, the Constitutional Peace Officers Association, the Council for National Policy and parts of the Republican Party into one amalgam group they consider to be extremists (Lenz & Potok 2014; Beirich & Potok 2016). In that regard its definition of extremism is likely excessively broad.

A more nuanced perspective on their chain of events might have focused upon a series of land-access confrontations occurring since 1979 involving citizens and federal agencies. Such a timeline would principally highlight the:

- 1979 Grand County, Utah confrontation with the BLM,

- 1979-2016 controversy between rancher Wayne Hage and his family with the U.S. Forest Service and BLM over grazing and water rights,

- 1995 bombing of a U.S. Forest Service office in Carson City, Nevada,

- 2001 standoff between the Klamath County Washington sheriff and the BLM over threatened irrigation water withdrawal;

- the 2014 confrontation between rancher Clive Bundy and the BLM over Bundy's refusal to pay fees for grazing rights on federal land.

Among these events, the Hage and Bundy incidents standout not simply because they involved conflicts over cattle grazing on public land, but additionally because of their direct connection to the 2016 occupation of the Malheur National Wildlife Refuge.

The refuge is partially situated in Grant County, Oregon - home of the Blue Mountain Forest Partners case study featured in this text. The Malheur occupation by members of the Patriot Movement became unavoidably linked to earlier controversies with federal agents when Clive Bundy's son, Amon, joined the occupation and thrust the Malheur Refuge and Grant County, Oregon into the public spotlight. Bundy's appearance also escalated the standoff and contributed to the death of one occupant while creating a jaded public perception of the area that placed the Blue Mountain Forest Partnership within a new and very public context. The Hage, Bundy and Malheur incidents, however, served to highlight two competing approaches to dealing with the federal government in the West—namely confrontation versus long-term negotiation, collaboration and the creation of fluid and sustainable partnerships.

The Clive Bundy / BLM Affair

To thoroughly appreciate the events surrounding the 2016 occupation of the Malheur National Wildlife Refuge, it is necessary to first understand the circumstances and events surrounding the Clive Bundy / BLM affair. Bundy's troubles with the Bureau of Land Management began in 1993, when the BLM designated thousands of acres of desert land near Las Vega, Nevada as a refuge for the endangered desert tortoise. This designation meant that ranchers who had historically grazed cattle in the desert in the vicinity suddenly found themselves ousted from rangeland they had historically come to rely upon.

Clive Bundy was one of these ranchers—a native Nevadan whose family homesteaded their ranch in 1877. The Bundy family challenged the BLM order making it clear they would neither sell nor abandon their land to make way for another national wildlife preserve. Consequently, Bundy ignored the new "protected" status of federal grazing land that historical circumstances and generations of grazing rights had bequeathed to his family. Once the land was declared a preserve in 1993 Clive Bundy stopped paying grazing fees while continuing to graze his herds as before. Given Bundy's stubbornness a confrontation with the BLM became all but inevitable (Fuller 2014).

Bundy was not alone in his resistance to BLM land management. Other ranchers also withheld payment virtually daring the agency to confiscate their cattle. As tensions rose between BLM and these dissident ranchers, so did the level of violence. In 1995 a bomb went off in a Forest Service office in Carson City, NV (mentioned earlier) and Forest Service officials all but assumed the perpetrator was one of these dissident ranchers (Fuller 2014).

By 1995, Clive Bundy had acquired $31,000 in delinquent grazing fees based upon an aerial census of his herd size. Bundy persisted in ignoring these fines knowing the agency was reluctant to either collect the fine or impound his herds for fear of starting a rancher revolt. Nevertheless, following additional bombing incidents BLM became increasingly strident in its rhetoric and actions (Fuller 2014).

In 1998, the Ninth U.S. District Court of Nevada ruled that Bundy was grazing his livestock within the bounds of the "Bunkerville Allotment" where the BLM was attempting to preserve the endangered desert tortoise. He was given until the end of November of 1998 to vacate his cattle from this allotment or face legal penalties (U.S. v Bundy 1998). The U.S. District Court decision, however, was not immediately enforced. Four years later, the first rancher from Nevada was imprisoned for failing to pay grazing fees, yet somehow, Bundy remained free. Then in 2009 the BLM began posting signage throughout federal lands warning that grazing had been banned and was punishable by fine and imprisonment. In response Bundy and other ranchers began destroying those signs (Fuller 2014).

By 2012, the BLM began formulating plans to confiscate Bundy's cattle, beginning with an injunction in federal court seeking compensation for unpaid grazing fees. In October 2013 the court issued an order directing Bundy to refrain from physically interfering with BLM agents confiscating his cattle. Ultimately, on March 15, 2014—almost 20 years after their confrontation with Bundy began, the bureau issued a letter formally informing him that his cattle were to be impounded. Soon thereafter Bundy petitioned the County Sheriff's office for protection and warned BLM that he had a virtual army of supporters ready to interfere with the cattle impoundment to include fellow rancher Cliff Gardner (Fuller 2014).

On April 1, 2014, Bundy and his relatives—some 66 individuals in all—hunkered down in the Bundy ranch house awaiting the arrival of federal agents to confiscate their cattle. The next day some 30 protesters appeared outside the ranch gates to block the cattle confiscation and seizure of his home and property. Three days later, on April 5, 2014, BLM began confiscating Bundy's cattle and arrested Bundy's son, Ammon, the next day for refusing to disperse. Ammon was quickly released but was later injured on April 9 when he and another family member got into a confrontation with BLM agents. In response, a group of militia members from across the nation made their way to the Bundy ranch and on April 10 set up an encampment threatening by their very presence to interfere with the BLM cattle confiscation. Recognizing that events were spiraling out of control and in the interest of defusing the charged atmosphere surrounding the Bundy ranch the BLM retreated and postponed enforcement of the court order to seize Bundy assets.

Later, BLM announced that although current circumstances had resulted in a standoff the agency was not abandoning their efforts to enforce the court order (Fuller 2014). Although BLM did not return the confiscated cattle (Cassini 2014) they suspended activities in the Gold Butte area near the Bundy ranch until June 2016 (Piper 2016; Suprynowicz 2016). Seemingly the Bundy's had earned a respite from BLM prosecution. However, their respite was short-lived as the family inserted themselves into a controversy in nearby Oregon, joining members of the Militia Movement to stand in solidarity with ranchers Dwight and Steve Hammond who were also being enjoined from grazing on federal land by the BLM. Ultimately the Amon Bundy joined other ranchers and representatives of the Militia Movement and occupied the Malheur National Wildlife Refuge in Eastern Oregon.

The Hammond Ranch - BLM Controversy

The dispute between the Hammond family and the BLM extends back for more than twenty years. Per local news accounts, it was alleged that Dwight Hammond had repeatedly made death threats against the managers of the Malheur National Wildlife Refuge extending back to 1986. Likewise, he was alleged to have repeatedly violated grazing permits allowing his cattle to graze on public lands at will. Prior to the family's current conflicts with the BLM to include setting fires on public lands,

Dwight Hammond was also jailed in 1994 for "disturbing and interfering" with the activities of federal officials—an incarceration that drew around 500 supporters to the Harney County seat of Burns to show solidarity (Wiles 2016).

Most recently, the Hammonds found themselves at odds with the BLM over a series of controlled burns they had initiated on their land which had inadvertently crossed over on to federal lands. On three occasions the Hammonds set fires that drifted on to adjacent BLM land. The first incident occurred in 1999 when a fire they set to control an invasive juniper species that was choking rangeland grasses crossed over into BLM land scorching some 90 acres of land. Thereafter the BLM met with the Hammonds to instruct them that heretofore they must coordinate burns with federal authorities in the interest of avoiding fires on public lands. They also warned them that failure to do so could result in criminal and/or civil penalties.

In 2001, Steve Hammond set another fire (the Hardie-Hammond fire), to also control an invasive juniper species, that again drifted off the ranch and burned a small stretch of BLM land. Steven and his father Dwight were prosecuted and found guilty of setting the fire and destroying public property. They were fined for this infraction but were not incarcerated (Cockle 2012). In 2006, following a series of nearby lightning strike fires, Steven Hammond set a backfire to protect his property. This fire—the Krumbo Butte fire—also spread to BLM land, resulting in a second conviction (Jung 2014). The Hammonds appealed both convictions and in 2016 lost those appeals and were sentenced to 5-years imprisonment each (Freda & Sepulvado 2016).

The Hammonds contended all along that the BLM charges against them had been contrived. They argued for instance that in 2001 they acquired permission from BLM via telephone to burn the juniper on their land - discovering that on that very day BLM was conducting a similar burn on public land. Moreover, after the Hammond fire drifted on federal land, BLM staffers acknowledged that the fire had "improved" federal land. Erin Maupin, a retired BLM range technician, watershed specialist and rancher in the area who worked for BLM during the Hardie-Hammond fire observed that "Juniper encroachment had become an issue on the forefront and was starting to come to a head. We were trying to figure out how to deal with it on a large scale" (Staeheim 2015).

To that end the BLM initiated the practice in 1999 of undertaking cooperative large scale burns since this practice yielded a more effective way to control invasive species over a wider area. Ideally, such planned burns were conducted in cooler weather (such as the Hammonds had chosen to do on their ranch). These autumn burns also served to improve the quality of forage as well as produce better habitat for wildfowl.

Former forester Erin Maupin recollected that, "We started to be successful on the Steens Mountain especially when we started to do it on a large watershed scale as opposed to trying to follow property lines" (Stadheim 2015). Maupin also observed that within the region it is nearly impossible to conduct a burn that narrowly follows property lines—thus the desirability of cooperative burns. As forest management experts, have noted time and again, managing such lands—particularly managing controlled burns—is extremely complex and difficult for the Forest Service, the BLM and the private landowner (Crow 2015). Also noteworthy is the fact that the Hammonds had been burning lands designated as "inholdings" or private land they owned within the bounds of BLM managed federal land—indicating that they had the legal right to be engaging in such controlled burns.

The Hammonds defended their actions contending that the 2006 fire was set defensively as a backfire against several lightning-induced blazes that threatened their entire winter feed crop (Crow 2015). They also challenged the BLM assertion that it had been their backfire that spread on to BLM land pointing out that at the time several fires had been ignited by lightning strikes and that it had been one of these blazes that had encroached upon BLM land. Their assertion was corroborated by a neighboring rancher—Ruthie Danielson - who also noted that "Lightning strikes were everywhere; fires were going off" (Stadheim 2015).

The Hammond family also pointed to the former BLM staffer Maupin's experience that in the period 1997-1999 any number of other fires originating on private land had spilled over on to BLM property—fires like the Hammond's that was set to control invasive species—but only the Hammonds were prosecuted. Maupin cited numerous instances where BLM instigated fires spilled over on to rancher land, with one incident killing some 65 cattle. He also noted that whenever these unintended crossover fires occurred the ranchers involved would as a matter of course cooperatively extinguish the blaze alongside BLM personnel. From his perspective, these were commonly understood risks associated with planned burns—risks considered preferable to allowing brush to accumulate and invite a truly catastrophic wildfire (Stadheim 2015). The appearance that BLM had singled the Hammonds out for prosecution begs the question of what would motivate such an agency to target this rancher out from among others? The answer proposed by the Hammonds and other observers is they sought to drive the ranchers off their ranch and acquire their inholdings on public lands (Zavis et al. 2016; Haun 2015; Wilson 2015).

Controversial Treatment of Inholdings by Federal Agencies

Inholdings is a term describes private land surrounded by public land, whether that be a national forest, preserve or park (Tanner 2002). Private inholdings are recognized in statutory language contained within the Wilderness Act, The Eastern Wilderness Act, The Alaska National Lands Conservation Act, and the California Desert Protection Act. Consequently, all the federal agencies involved in managing and overseeing public lands employ language pertaining to inholdings in their regulatory documents. In 2002 the extent of privately owned inholding acreage within federal lands was substantial totaling 132,603 acres of U.S. Forest Service managed land, 311,554 acres of BLM land and 2,462 acres of National Park Service land (Tanner 2002, 10).

At issue is the consistency with which the concept of inholdings is applied by various agencies in their regulations and the degree to which these regulations reflect rights of access and use of these inholdings. The various agencies overseeing public lands employ regulatory language pertinent to inholdings that seemingly confuses landowners regarding their "inholding" rights on public lands. For instance, The Bureau of Land Management approaches inholdings with the following guidelines:

> "If you own land completely surrounded by wilderness, BLM will only approve that combination of routes and modes of travel to your land that (1) BLM finds existed on the date Congress designated the area surrounding the

inholding as wilderness, and (2) BLM determines will serve the reasonable purposes for which the non-Federal lands are held or used and cause the least impact on wilderness character" (43 CFR 6305.10; Tanner 2002, 12)

The U.S. Fish and Wildlife Service (USFWS) approaches inholdings from a slightly different perspective.

"Rights of States or persons and their successors in interest, whose land is surrounded by a wilderness unit, will be recognized to assure adequate access to that land. Adequate access is defined as the combination of modes and routes of travel which will best preserve the wilderness character of the landscape. Mode of travel designated shall be reasonable and consistent with accepted, conventional, contemporary modes of travel in said vicinity. Use will be consistent with reasonable purposes for which such land is held" (50 CFR 35.13; Tanner 2002, 12).

The language of the USFWS would appear to provide quite a bit more latitude relating to landowner rights of access and use when compared to the more narrowly restrictive language of BLM. By comparison the U.S. Forest Service appears to place more discretionary authority in the hands of the Forest Service authorities overseeing a set of public lands holding that

"as appropriate, landowners shall be authorized such access as the authorized officer deems to be adequate to secure them the reasonable use and enjoyment of their land" 36 CFR 251.110 [c]; Tanner 2002, p. 12)

While this definition has the virtue of allowing flexibility in interpretation, it is flawed to the degree it appears to bestow arbitrary power to Forest Service officials—creating the potential for abuse. Finally, the National Park Service regulations on inholdings reads as follows:

"Except as specifically provided by law, there will be no permanent road, structure or installation within any study, proposed, recommended, or designated wilderness area. This includes the installation of utilities. (See the Wilderness Act 16 USC 23). The NPS will not issue any new right-of-way permits or widen or lengthen any existing rights-of-way in study, proposed, recommended, or designated wilderness areas." (At present, NPS policies target only right-of-ways to wilderness inholdings) (Director's Order #53 §10.4; Tanner 2002, p. 12).

Of these three sets of regulations, the National Park Service's language is most restrictive.

Given the disparities in these three sets of regulations it shouldn't be hard for an observer to appreciate the frustration a landowner—and in the case of this narrative ranchers—might experience when trying to use land they own which is situated in and among federal lands. Nor is it inconceivable that a landowner might come to construe a federal agency or agencies as antagonistic to their rights and interests—even to the point of defying their authority. Arguably inholding landowners are probably entitled to a set of uniform national standards regarding rights of access and use of their property. However, in the absence of such uniformity and in light of the considerable degree of discretion that BLM and Forest Service staff exercise over use and access to inholdings (discretion that can and indeed has changed over time with changes in local federal management and national political leadership) it should not be surprising to observers that periodically property owners such as the Hage Bundy, or Hammonds families would choose to defy federal authority and access, manage and alter their lands as they have historically done.

Misguided Assumptions

Having historically enjoyed grazing privileges on public lands well before the BLM came into existence, the Hammonds chose to assert what they believed was a right to land use born of historical practice and long term tolerance by BLM staff from its founding in 1946 through the early 1960's. In 2014, however that strategy ceased to serve the interests of the Hammonds when BLM suspended their grazing rights (Sepulvado & Peacher 2016). Having enjoyed reliable access to those lands for more than 40 years, the Hammonds incorrectly assumed their stable relationship with the BLM would continue into perpetuity.

The fundamental premises upon which the Hammond assumptions operated changed in 1999, when, in anticipation of acquiring virtual complete control over the Steen Mountain thanks to Congressional action, the BLM busily sought to acquire as much private land as possible within and abutting public lands. Their goal was to consolidate control over the public land and improve ecosystem management. The Hammonds represented one of the ranchers with inholdings and grazing rights on the mountain and whose ranch was adjacent to BLM land. Critics argue that the BLM was partially motivated to consolidate control over the Steens Mountain area by liquidating the Hammond's grazing rights, acquiring their inholdings and eventually driving them and their herds off the mountain and perhaps off their ranch (Brown 2016; Jasper 2016).

BLM's desire to acquire land private land was stimulated in 2000 when the agency received congressional land acquisition authority through the Federal Land Transaction Facilitation Act (FLTFA). This act allowed for the BLM in conjunction with the U.S. Forest Service, the National Park Service and the U.S. Fish and Wildlife service to purchase or acquire private properties that extend into federal wildlife refuges and national parks and forests. The presence of these private lands complicated BLM and the Forest Service's efforts to manage public lands. Conversely, acquiring these lands greatly assisted the efforts of both agencies to exercise their oversight and management responsibilities. Therefore, BLM offered $18 million to purchase 19 parcels of private land in seven Western states to include Oregon (Guinto 2007). The Hammond ranch was a prime example of the kind of property BLM wanted to acquire to make managing the Steen Mountain area easier.

Prior to the enactment of FLTFA, the BLM had acquired new authority in 1999 to impose their will upon ranchers and others who use the resources available on public lands with the Federal enactment of Public Law 106–399—The Steens

Mountain Cooperative Management and Protection Act of 2000 (Steens Act). The act was designed to "maintain the cultural, economic, ecological, and social health of the Steens Mountain area in Harney County, Oregon" (PL 106-399, Section 1(b)(1)) and "promote viable and sustainable grazing and recreation operations on private and public lands" (PL 106-399, Section 1(b)(11)). FLTFA facilitated the efforts of BLM in administering the Steens Mountain Cooperative Management Plan by providing funds to purchase the interests of adjacent ranchers.

Theoretically the key word in the Steens Mountain management plan was "cooperative" as reflected in the mandatory requirement of a citizen's advisory board. At this point the bi-word in federal management circles was the concept of cooperative or collaborative management which implied cooperation between public (BLM) and private interests (local officials, businesses, organization and constituencies) "working or acting together willingly for a common purpose or benefit" (Yarrington-Ball 1984). Unfortunately, the Steens Act failed to foster cooperation between federal agencies and the public. Specifically,

> "There is no more communication today between conservationists and ranchers than prior to the Act, and a general ambivalence, if not disdain, towards the BLM by some stakeholders continues. While there have been individual acts of cooperation between BLM and some players, a general feeling of mistrust prevails over SMAC meetings, where people continue to huddle with like-minded persons" (Brown 2006).

Distrust between BLM and advisory board members principally centered around the following issues:

- *Private Inholdings*—The Steens Mountain area contains considerable private property lying within the boundaries of federal land. BLM ultimately felt charged by Congress to incrementally eliminate these "inholdings." Since the language in the federal legislation avoided specific language on how to deal with these private lands federal agency representative on advisory committees generally tended to avoid speaking of converting private inholdings to public lands. BLM would have liked to have used the Steens Act to acquire private land such as that owned by the Hammonds within the boundaries of the Steens Mountain Wilderness area (Crow 2015). However, despite the statutory authorization of $25 million for land acquisition within the act Congress failed to appropriate funds for this purpose meaning that none of the Steen Mountain inholders and been bought out. (Brown 2006).

- *Conservation of Private Lands*—While the Steens Act authorized BLM to sign cooperative conservation management agreements with private land owners, Congress failed to appropriate funding for this purpose. The net effect was that no conservation easements had been authorized or funded

- *Grazing Permits*—While some of the Steens Mountain Wilderness was designated as a "graze free" area, only traditional guidelines were specified in the legislation (a.k.a. "Congressional Grazing Guidelines") which specified that existing livestock grazing would not be significantly impacted by the area's wilderness designation thereby requiring BLM to formulate "reasonable regulations." In effect, the traditional grazing guidelines grandfathered existing permits allowing grazing on federal lands to continue as before. However, BLM was not content with the traditional definition and imposed new and supposedly "reasonable" grazing guidelines that ranchers uniformly objected to. Ranchers, however were compensated for the loss of grazing on federal lands that were now off limits given their new wilderness designation.

- *Western Juniper Management*—The Steens Act created a Wildlands Juniper Management Area" with a dedicated advisory group to oversee the management of this invasive Western plant species. The consensus among public officials and ranchers is that this species had become a problem due to the lack of regular controlled burns. Thus, the issue of how, when and where to burn remained an unresolved controversy between federal officials and the public.

- *Wilderness Study Areas*—There was also a lack of consensus regarding the designation and implementation of wilderness study areas. Their fate remains in limbo awaiting site-specific Congressional legislation of which the Congress appears to have no current interest.

In effect, the central feature of the Steens Act is not cooperation but rather control. The act provides expansive authority for the BLM and the Forest Service to manage public lands as they see fit—which in the case of the Hage, Bundy and Hammond controversies has been portrayed as arbitrary federal action. Arguably the central feature of this act is the virtually unchecked control federal agencies are afforded over the region's public land to include water, grazing, farming and mineral rights as well as the right to acquire private lands (Kerr 2006).

Western Locus-of-Control: Competing Values

Such is the perspective "on-the-ground" as reflected in the experiences of many ranchers and Western landowners. At issue is a dynamic as old as Oregon itself—locus-of-control regarding whose values will dominate land use policies in the West? Federal and state agencies favor inclusive language and values like cooperation and coordination but these values don't appear to be uniformly translated into experience—at least for ranchers like the Hammonds, Hages and Bundys.

In truth, creating and sustaining cooperative relationships is a difficult process. As Kris Wernstedt, a Fellow in the Quality of the Environment Division at Resources for the Future (RFF) has observed, "Diverse local interests, the existence of non-local stakeholders, and the absence of strong statutory language and adequate funding all complicate efforts at local involvement" (Wernstedt 2000, 157), Accordingly,

> "Unbridled enthusiasm for greater local control over environmental management ... needs to be tempered with serious thought about how to promote statutorily grounded, effective, broad-based, and well-funded participation in the public interest" (Wernstedt 2000, 183).

Difficult as cooperation and collaboration is to achieve, the alternative is completely unacceptable—namely the top down imposition of federal authority that ignores local rights and voices. Unfortunately for some Westerners such autocratic practices are perceived throughout federal bureaucratic action despite the cooperative spin of agency values. The experiences of the Hage, Bundy and Hammond families over autocratic federal regulation—while not necessarily normative of all or most ranchers in the West—are nonetheless influential "micro" perspectives which fuel agitation and unrest across Western states.

By comparison, the "official" "macro" perspective on issues involving public lands and private landowners emanating from federal agencies and state houses is one of "cooperative processes" and "cooperative management" (Brown 2006). Emblematic of this perspective is the philosophy of the Western Governors Association (WGA) that eschews confrontation and discord between private and public interests, embracing instead a cooperative approach grounded in a variety of federal laws such as the 1960 Multiple Use and Sustained Yield Act (MUSYA), the 1984 Administrative Procedures Act (APA), portions of the National Environmental Policy Act of 1970 (NEPA), Federal Advisory Committee Act of 1972 (FACA), and the Federal Land Planning and Management Act (1976). WGA finds within these applicable laws regulatory authority for the cooperative management of public lands (Brown 2006).

Beyond the clear legal precedent for cooperative management of public lands is the pragmatic and equally clear reality that the federal government owns the overwhelming majority of Western state and county lands and that private and public interests must cooperate if they are going to reside and prosper together on those lands. While public and private partnerships may be optional in other parts of the nation where federal holdings are meager, throughout the West, this kind of cooperation is an absolute necessity. That said, the "on-the-ground" evidence suggests that cooperation is not consistently working and in the wake of the failure to realize cooperation, chaos and confrontation have emerged—particularly in the form of the Patriot and Militia movements. From their perspective, when cooperation and negotiation fail the only remaining option is demonstration, confrontation and—in the case of the Malheur National Wildlife Refuge—occupation and armed confrontation.

The Malheur National Wildlife Refuge Occupation

The Malheur National Wildlife occupation (referred to heretofore as the Malheur occupation) was ostensibly fueled by two events: (Wiles 2016)

1. The armed standoff in 2014 on the Nevada ranch of Clive Bundy regarding unpaid grazing fees and
2. The 2015 decision by the federal courts to overturn a decision by a lower court that had resulted in minimal sentences for Steve and Dwight Hammond (for arson and trespass on federal lands) and the imposition of a mandatory 5-year minimal sentence on each.

Eventually, dissenters from across the West assembled in Burns, Oregon to protest the re-imprisonment of the Hammonds as well as to object to a perceived pattern of unfair practices on the part of BLM and other federal agencies (Young 2016).

On January 2, 2016, as some 300 protesters and supporters of the Hammonds marched in solidarity through the streets of Burns another group of armed militant protesters led by Ammon Bundy—son of Clive Bundy of Nevada—took over the Malheur National Wildlife Refuge. The next day, Bundy spoke to the press saying that although the protesters were armed they had no intent of being violent unless the federal government so forced them. On January 5, Bundy dictated terms for ending the occupation, requiring the federal government to relinquish control of the refuge to local property owners. Their demand was countered with a call from the Burns Paiute Tribe, who once held claim to the refuge, to end their occupation. As the occupation continued a nighttime scuffle ensued between occupants and what was described as "another outside group" that hospitalized one person (Young 2016).

On January 11, the occupants destroyed a fence on the refuge (claiming they had the landowner's permission to do so) and on January 16 they engaged in an altercation with a group of so-called "conservationists" who met with them to end the occupation. By January 19 a community meeting in Burns was convened to negotiate ending the occupation. Amond Bundy left the refuge to attend, but the occupation continued.

The FBI began negotiating an end to the standoff on January 21. Five days later, on January 26, 2016 six of the occupiers left the refuge to travel to neighboring John Day in Grant County where they were to convene a town hall meeting with Grant County Sheriff Glenn Palmer—a controversial "constitutional sheriff" belonging to the Constitutional Sheriff and Peace Officers Association (CSPOA). Palmer was sympathetic to the views of the occupiers and was rumored to have met with them in Burns just prior to the seizure of the Refuge (Neiwert 2016; Ortiz 2016). However, before the sheriff could meet with the occupiers in Grant County they were intercepted by FBI. Five of the protesters were arrested to include Ammon Bundy. However, one of the protesters—Robert "LaVoy" Finicum—was shot and killed (Brennan 2016).

With morale among the occupiers diminishing following the arrests and Finicum's death, the remaining occupiers began leaving the refuge—eventually leaving only four occupiers by January 28. These remaining few refused to leave unless all the occupiers involved were granted full pardons. Finally, on February 11 the FBI moved into the refuge compound to dislodge the final four occupiers and on February 12 these remaining occupiers surrendered. Thus, ended a 41-day ordeal that ultimately cost the taxpayers at least $3.3 million (Wilson & Rosen 2016; Young, 2016).

Beyond the cost of the occupation, the disruption to Harney County and the community of Burns, as well as the distraction in Grant County occasioned by Sheriff Glenn Palmer's actions, the Malheur occupation underscored the degree to which tensions are running high between some in the West who not only distrust federal control over the land and resources of the area, but additionally feel the need to actively resist and / or prepare to resist the federal presence in their states. These events served to further fuel the concerns that brought the Militia and Patriot movements into existence. They likewise symbolize the degree to which federal agencies such as the BLM and the U.S. Forest Service find themselves at an impasse when interacting with local counties and communities around the cooperative and collaborative management of public lands.

From the perspective of observers among the ranks of the Patriot and Militia Movements—as well as from among those invested in eliminating federal control over Western lands and returning ownership to the states and their citizens—the themes to be found within the Hammond case and the Malheur occupation were all too familiar. These themes have repeatedly emerged within the context of the BLM and Forest Service dealings involving Nevada's Hage family, Utah's Bundy family, and the Hammond family of Oregon. In each instance, the federal government empowered the Forest Service or the BLM to consolidate their control over federal land. The regulatory rationale supporting such control was multifaceted to include protecting ecosystems and plant and animal species, managing forests, rangelands and watersheds and developing natural resources (i.e. water, oil, gas, minerals such as gold and silver). However, in each case their regulatory efforts conflicted with long-standing legally sanctioned grazing and water rights landowners had enjoyed for generations.

Arguably, a sea-change has occurred regarding who and what informs the decisions and actions of federal land agencies. As has historically been the case, Eastern voices (or at least voices outside of Oregon) have increasingly influenced federal policies and actions regarding Western lands. This is of course not a new phenomenon for Westerners since the East-West competition for control and influence is as old as the state of Oregon is itself. However, the net effect in each instance of Eastern influence is that the power of the federal government is perceived as ever growing while the power and influence of individual ranchers not only dissipates but is effectively obliterated by intimidation, litigation and imprisonment.

Control over federal lands has come to be increasingly perceived as emanating outside the region—with locals finding themselves marginalized in their control and influence (Baier 2015). As Ryan McMaken of the libertarian Mises Institute recently observed, from the perspective of U.S. Western citizens the "federal government does not respond to local needs or local demand, but to national interest groups" (McMaken 2016). These words ring true to many in Eastern Oregon and across the West since clearly relationships between ranchers and federal agencies like BLM and the Forest Service have changed significantly since the early sixties when many ranchers—like the Hammonds—first received their grazing permits.

Federal Subsidies to Support Western States

Part of what has been lost in this controversy over land-rights is an appreciation for the fact that livestock grazing on public lands involves significant congressional subsidization—a practice many question (Burns & Schick 2016; Herzog 2016; Eckoff 2015). Consider these facts from a recent study by the Center for Biodiversity:

- *"Receipts from grazing fees were $125 million less than federal appropriations in 2014.* Total federal appropriations for the USFS and BLM grazing programs in fiscal year 2014 were $143.6 million, while grazing receipts were only $18.5 million. Appropriations for the BLM and USFS grazing programs have exceeded grazing receipts by at least $120 million annually since 2002."

- *"The gap between federal grazing fees and private land fees has widened considerably.* The federal grazing fee in 2014 was set at the legal minimum of $1.35/AUM, or animal unit month, which is the amount of forage to feed a cow and calf for one month. The annual federal grazing fee has been set at the minimum required by law since 2007. The federal grazing fee is generally also considerably lower than fees charged on state-owned public lands."

- *"The federal grazing subsidy is even larger when all costs to the taxpayer are accounted for.* Indirect costs for livestock grazing include portions of different federal agencies budgets, such as the USDA Wildlife Services, which expends money to kill thousands of native carnivores each year that may threaten livestock; U.S. Fish and Wildlife Service, which expends part of its budget for listing species as threatened or endangered resulting from harm by livestock grazing; and other federal land management agencies that expend money on wildfire suppression caused by invasive cheat grass that is facilitated by livestock grazing. The full cost of the federal grazing program is long overdue for a complete analysis" (Glaser, Romaniello & Moskowitz 2015, p. 1)

Clearly federal subsidies of grazing on public lands are unjustifiable from a purely budgetary perspective.

Based upon federal statistical data (Figure 8) the BLM and the U.S. Forest service make available some 250 million acres of public land for livestock grazing. The federal government's fee of $1.35 per AUM (animal unit per month) has remained stable since about 1982. By Comparison, livestock grazing fees on private lands have doubled over the same period rising form around $10 AUM in 1982 to $20.10 AUM in 2014 (Figure 9). The implications for taxpayers regarding this federal expenditure are considerable when one considers that federal grazing subsidies cost the federal taxpayer $125,119,000 dollars in 2014 alone—an annual expense that has remained comparatively constant since 2002 (Figure 10).

Acres of federal land

Open to livestock grazing

BLM | **155 million** | **245 million acres total**

USFS | **95 million** | **193 million acres total**

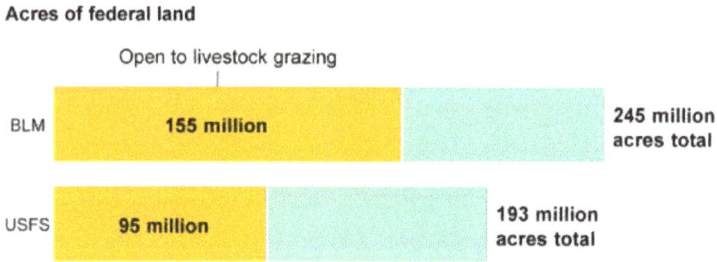

Figure 8: America's Public Grazing Lands
(Source: Zavis 2016; Glaser et al. 2015)

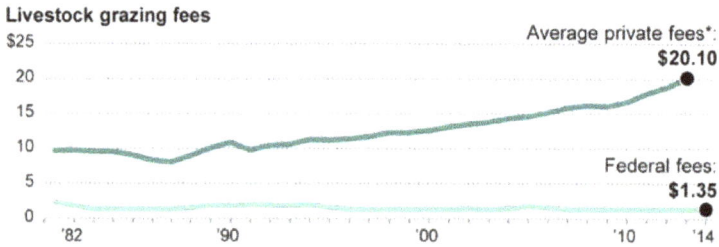

Livestock grazing fees

$25

20

15

10

5

0

'82　'90　'00　'10　'14

Average private fees*:
$20.10

Federal fees:
$1.35

Figure 9: Grazing Fees on Private and Government Land
(Source: Zavis 2016; Glaser et al. 2015)

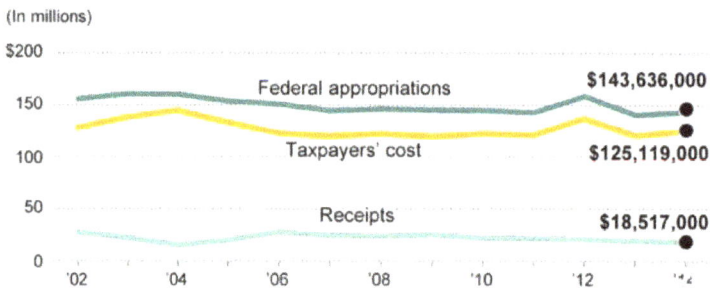

(In millions)

$200

150

100

50

0

'02　'04　'06　'08　'10　'12　'14

Federal appropriations **$143,636,000**

Taxpayers' cost **$125,119,000**

Receipts **$18,517,000**

Figure 10: Cost of the Federal Grazing Program to Taxpayers
(Source: Zavis 2016; Glaser et al. 2015)

Historically, this federal subsidy program was taken for granted as acceptable federal stewardship, but in an era of ever-competitive federal priorities such subsides have become unjustifiably excessive. These are the sorts of issues BLM and the Forest Service are increasingly confronted with as they seek to respond to local desires and needs while doing so within ever tightening federal budgetary and environmental constraints. What is lost at the local level is an appreciation of the degree to which historic private access to public has been subsidized by the nation's taxpayers.

Comparable subsides have been made available over many years on federal timber land. In fact, federal grazing subsidies pale in comparison to the amount taxpayers subsidize the timber industry on public lands (Figure 11). The total 2014 loss for timber harvested on federal lands was $349,398,231 while the total loss over a six-year period (2008-2014) was $2,810,170,273—a staggeringly high federal subsidy to the U.S. timber industry (USDA 2015). While federal timber subsidies in Oregon underwent some reduction in 2007 (Brady 2007), they were ultimately slashed dramatically in 2015 falling from $67.9 million annually to a meager $5.9 million (Barnard, 2015).

Region	Avg. Timber Program Loss (2008-2014)	Total Timber Program Loss (2008-2014)	Total Timber Program Loss - 2014 only
1 - Northern Region	-$39,258,115	-$266,251,064	-$18,207,755
2 - Rocky Mountain	-$51,561,293	-$360,929,049	-$50,912,758
3 - Southwestern	-$36,694,052	-$256,858,364	-$28,246,855
4 - Intermountain	-$37,421,812	-$261,952,683	-$26,520,912
5 - Pacific Southwest	-$63,526,377	-$444,684,642	-$62,283,699
6 - Pacific Northwest	-$79,274,269	-$554,919,884	-$57,519,792
8 - Southern	-$27,609,233	-$193,264,631	-$38,702,285
9 - Eastern	-$33,400,076	-$233,800,531	-$34,813,129
10 - Alaska	-$33,929,918	-$237,509,424	-$32,191,045
Avg. - all regions	-$44,741,683	-$312,241,141	-$38,822,026
Total - all regions		-$2,810,170,273	-$349,398,231

Figure 11: Average & Total Federal Timber Program Loss 2008-2014
(Source: USDA, 2015)

Federal Subsidies in Western States: Where Loyalties Lie

Timber subsidies, like grazing subsidies, have long been taken for granted as part of the price the nation should pay to in part compensate Western states for the tax revenue losses they suffer by having so much of their state territory owned by the Federal government. This rationale has been thoroughly explained in a CRS report of 2012 on the "fairness" of federal subsidies to states with large sections of tax-exempt public lands observing that since "the federal government owns significant amounts of land and resources" and since "these assets are exempt from state and local taxation. Congress has established a plethora of payments as compensation for this tax-exempt status" (Gorte & Corn 2012, 1). For years, this rationale has been applied as successive congressional delegations from Western states like Oregon have argued that given their narrow property tax base it is only fair and compensatory for Eastern states to subsidize Western states for timber and grazing (among other interests), while also arguing that such expenditures enable federal agencies like the Forest

Service and BLM to acquire and make "improvements" on federal land (Vincent et al. 2014).

These philosophies of fairly compensating Western States for their large federal tax exempt holdings and justifying these expenditures in the interest of improving the quality and utility of such lands have long been among the central tenets of public land management. Nancy Langston in her book *Forest Dreams, Forest Nightmares* (1995) which chronicled the successes and failures of the Forest Service in managing timber resources in Eastern Oregon and the Blue Mountains observed that "traditional management has, at its heart, assumed the human relationship with land was "improvement"—to make nature more efficient and productive" (Langston 1995, p. 275). Consequently, throughout the sixties and seventies federal agencies managing public land sought to improve the land by improving "yield" whether that be the number of trees harvested, the number of cattle grazed, the number of oil or gas wells leased, the tonnage of coal produced or the volume of sports and nature enthusiasts lured to natural environs. Regardless of the resource the task of the BLM and Forest Service throughout much of its early history was to make the land economically productive principally for those who were willing to pay for either natural resource access or products.

The constituencies that these federal agencies historically listened to—ostensibly reflecting the will of the people as articulated by elected officials—have principally consisted of their customers, namely mining, energy, ranching, timber, and agricultural interest's agencies regulated and profited from. It was these entities who put money into agency coffers with their purchase of timber, timber and grazing rights, mineral rights, water or other natural services. It was these interests who influenced decisions in Congress, the White House and in state houses across the West. Consequently, it was to their interests that Western federal agencies catered, and it is to these stakeholders that agency loyalties have been directed.

Illustrative of this is the U.S. Forest Service's relationship with the timber industry. From the post-World War II era onward the Forest Service prioritized the provision of lumber for new housing for returning veterans. This mission became so preeminent for the U.S. Forest Service that by the seventies the agency had acquired a reputation as being a virtual "timber factory" narrowly interested in the business of logs and lumber to the exclusion of all other concerns (Furnish 2015). Similar criticism can also be directed toward the Department of Interior who has long enjoyed a sweetheart relationship with the oil and gas industry (Chubb 1983).

The modern environmental movement, however, permanently altered these relationships. Following the advent of the environmentalism in the seventies, the Forest Service was forced to prioritize multiple-use policies which contributed to the sustainability and diversity of the forest land. In like fashion, the BLM's image of being "in-bed" with mineral and energy interests was challenged in the interest of protecting water, natural resources, ecosystems and habitats (Honigsberg 2011). To achieve this multi-purpose mission, BLM entered an array of relationships with environmentalists, recreational groups and businesses with the capacity to extract and produce resources from federal land, establishing a pattern of public-private partnerships (Jewell 2017).

These arrangements worked well provided the BLM's mission essentially involved sustainable resource production. However, when it became clear that historical policies based upon the exploration and production of natural resources were in fact destroying the national forests and rangelands, federal agencies had to seek another avenue for management. Such changes became particularly urgent when some of the BLM and Forest Services' most popular subsidized activities—grazing for instance—were found to be not only cost inefficient but detrimental to the environment (Hudak 1999; Wald 2002).

Shifting Agency Philosophies: From Economic to Environmental Rationales

As expected, the historical justifications for investing so many federal resources into such questionable activities have been challenged by politicians, politicians and environmentalists and significant policy changes are in the works. Such changes are frustrating for many Western ranchers principally because they originate outside the West and the timber-ranching community. Since fiscal authority for federal expenditures and subsidies originates in the nation's capital—i.e. "the East"—and "Eastern" values of cost efficiency and environmental sustainability have historically tended to conflict with local Western land management and ranching values and practices (such as maintaining historical rangeland, increasing cattle yields, maintaining a traditional presence on Western ranges and forests, etc.), more than a few Westerners have interpreted changes in federal land management and grazing policies as imposing Eastern environmental and budgetary values on Westerners who live and work on regulated federal lands (Cawley 1993; Hage 1989; Lamm & McCarthy 1989).

These critics perceive that their loyalty, experiences and values are not deemed as important in Washington as those associated with people and interests that lie along the East Coast. This disjointed perspective between locals pursuing a traditional way of life and "Easterners" who bankroll the livelihoods of Western ranchers at an exorbitant rate and in an environmentally unsustainable fashion is at the heart of why federal land policy in the West has always been and likely always will be contentious. Inevitably any significant change in federal grazing policies will be experienced by Western ranchers as Eastern interference in their way of life—an interference that has plagued Westerners and threatened federal subsidies for decades.

Whether Western ranching, timber, mineral, agricultural or energy interests like it or not historical natural resource production approaches to managing public lands based upon heavy federal subsidies for timber, grazing, energy etc. are rapidly being replaced with sustainable use policies prioritizing the intrinsic value of ecosystems and their sustainable use (as defined by environmental experts) over the utility of natural resources in the marketplace. Consequently, the mission of federal land agencies has increasingly become defined by political and policy interests that often lie far away from Western soils, sod, streams and trees while local interests such as those of ranchers, farmers, outdoor enthusiasts, timber workers and others—people to whom the BLM and Forest Service once considered to be their virtual partners in forest and land management—are seemingly relegated a diminished status.

Mutually Necessary Cooperation or Selling Out?

Given these forces, it is inevitable that many of those living and working on and among Western lands who have historically been partners if not dependents of the BLM and the U.S. Forest Service, now feel angry, abandoned and frustrated when federal agencies seemingly rely on the philosophies and values of people living a continent away to the exclusion of local values and needs. Based on such perceptions of Eastern versus Western bias upon agency practices, a sizeable number of Westerners have come to resent the authority of federal bureaucrats. As a matter of principle, they resist adopting a "cooperative ethic" that in one way or another doesn't employ them, pay their bills, feed their families or give them a local voice in land use matters of which they are huge stakeholders. Thus, in an era where community social and economic survival depends upon cooperation with the "feds" a vocal plurality within the community resist collaboration on principle and label those who so participate as "sell-outs."

Not surprisingly, creative collaborative relationships such as the one fashioned by Blue Mountain Forest Partners that seek to cooperatively engage the Forest Service in enhanced forest management are viewed skeptically by those for whom the names Forest Service and BLM have become synonyms with excessive and unchecked federal power. Their skepticism tends to undercut the best efforts of those who would seek to enter ongoing working relationships with those federal landowners who for better or worse own, control and/or manage the overwhelming majority of Western lands. Those dissident Western voices—while insufficient to significantly influence or deter cooperative efforts between local stakeholders—have become a bothersome and threatening counterforce to economic and social development in many Western communities. It is to the influence of these skeptics upon federal/state/local cooperation in the Malheur National Forest that the text now turns.

REFERENCES

Alden, Diane. 1998. "Wayne Hage's Range War: How the Monitor Valley Adjudication Came to Be." *Nevada Journal.* Accessed July 15, 2016 http://archive.nevadajournal.com/nj98/04/hage.htm

Allen, Cain. 2005. "Malheur Indian Reservation." *The Oregon History Project.* Accessed August 25, 2017 https://oregonhistoryproject.org/articles/historical-records/malheur-indian-reservation/#.WaGVqYqQzVo

American Land Council Foundation (ACLF). 2014. *Public Lands: Better Access, Better Health, Better Productivity.* South Jordan, UT: American Lands Council Foundation.

Anderson, Hannah L. 2011 "That Settles It: The Debate and Consequences of the Homestead Act of 1862." *The History Teacher.* 54(1): 117-137.

Andrews, Alicia and Kristin Katura. 2005. *Oregon's Timber Harvests: 1849-2004.* Eugene: Oregon Department of Forests.

Baier, Lowell E. 2015. *Inside the Equal Access to Justice Act: Environmental Litigation and the Crippling Battle over America's Lands, Endangered Species, and Critical Habitats.* Lanham: Rowman & Littlefield Publishers.

Baker City Chamber of Commerce. 2014. *The Gold Fields of Eastern Oregon.* Seattle: Create Space Independent Publishing Platform.

Barnard, Jeff. 2015. "Timber County Payments Shrink After Expiration of Subsidy." *Capital Press.* (January 16), Accessed June 23, 2016 http://www.capitalpress.com/Oregon/20150116/timber-county-payments-shrink-after-expiration-of-subsidy

Barnston, George and John Swanston. 1869. *The Oregon Treaty and the Hudson Bay Company*. Ottowa: Canadian Institute for Historical Microreproductions.

Bateman, Brenda and Beth Patrino. 2010. "Background Brief on Water Management," (June), Legislative Committee Services, State of Oregon, Salem, OR.

Beirich, Heidi and Mark Potok. 2016. "The Council for National Policy: Behind the Curtain." *Hatewatch*. SPLC, Accessed June 14, 2016 https://www.splcenter.org/hatewatch/2016/05/17/council-national-policy-behind-curtain

Bevans, Charles I. 1974. *Treaties and Other International Agreements of the United States of America 1776–1949, Vol. 11*. Washington: Government Printing Office.

Bigg, Matthew. 2010. "Timeline—Recent History of U.S. Militia Groups." (April 28) *Reuters*. Accessed June 15, 2016 http://www.reuters.com/article/uk-usa-militias-timeline-idUKTRE63R4M 420100428

Brady, Jeff. 2007. "Federal Subsidy Expires on Oregon Timber Towns." *National Public Radio, Morning Edition*. (February 2, 2016), Accessed June 23, 2016 at http://www.npr.org/templates/story/story.php?storyId=7122963

Braly, David. 1978. *Cattle Barons of Early Oregon*. Portland, OR: Timberline Press.

Buck, Rinker. 2016. *The Oregon Trail: A New American Journey*. New York, NY: Simon Schuster.

Bureau of Land Management (BLM). 2012. *Shaping America's History: The Homestead Act—Celebrating 150 Years—1862-2012*. Washington, DC: U.S. Department of Interior.

Burns, Jes and Tony Schick. 2016. "Controversial Federal Grazing Fees Not a Good Deal for Anyone." *Oregon Public Broadcasting*. (January 6), Retrieved from the World Wide Web June 23, 2016 at http://www.opb.org/news/series/burns-oregon-standoff-bundy-militia-news-updates/federal-grazing-fees/

Brennan, Christopher. 2016. "LaVoy Finicum Arizona Rancher and Oregon Occupation Spokesman, Killed." *New York Daily News*. (January 27), Accessed August 25, 2017 http://www.nydailynews.com/news/national/lavoy-finicum-arizona-rancher-oregon-occupation-killed-article-1.2510704

Brooks, Howard C. and Len Ramp. 2013. *Gold Mines of Oregon*. Seattle: Create Space Independent Publishing Platform.

Brown, Tim. 2016. "Just Like Bundy Ranch, The Hammonds' Ranch Is Valuable to The BLM—Here's Just How Valuable." *Freedom Outpost*. (January 5), Accessed June 22, 2016 http://freedomoutpost.com/just-like-bundy-ranch-the-hammonds-ranch-is-valuable-to-the-blm-heres-just-how-valuable/

Bump, Philip. 2016. "That Time Ronald Reagan Joined A 'Rebellion' — But Still Couldn't Change Federal Land Laws." *The Washington Post*. (January 4) Accessed June 14, 2016 at https://www.washingtonpost.com/news/the-fix/wp/2016/01/04/even-sagebrush-rebel-ronald-reagan-couldnt-change-federal-land-use-in-the-west/

Campbell, Sally, Dave Azuma and Dale Weyermann. 2003. *Forests of Eastern Oregon: An Overview*. Portland: U.S. Department of Agriculture Forest Service, Pacific Northwest Research Station.

Cassini, Gina. 2014. "MUST SEE: Citizens Rise Up—The Real Nevada Story the Media Won't Show You." *Top Right News*. (April 13), Accessed June 22, 2016 http://toprightnews.com/feds-forced-to-surrender-to-american-citizens-the-real-nevada-story-the-media-wont-report-video/

Cawley, R. McGreggor. 1993. *Federal Land, Western Anger: The Sagebrush Rebellion and Environmental Politics*. Lawrence: University Press of Kansas.

Christensen, Jon. 1991. "High Noon in Nevada: Forest Service Goes Head-to-Head with an Angry Rancher." *High Country News*. (September 9), Accessed June 14, 2016 http://s3.amazonaws.com/hcn-media/archive-pdf/1991_09_09_rfs.pdf

———. 1990. "Son of Sagebrush Rebellion Now Playing in Nevada" *High Country News*. (December 31), Accessed June 14, 2016 at http://s3.amazonaws.com/hcn-media/archive-pdf/1990_12_31_son.pdf

Christiansen, Scott. 2003. "Institutional Framework and Inter-Agency Collaboration: The U.S. Example" Plenary Session: Determinants Of Sustainable Grassland and Livestock Management, and Strategy Implementation, U.S. Department of Agriculture, Accessed July 15, 2016 http://info.worldbank.org/etools/docs/library/54262/chinalivestock2/chinalivestock2/materials/I N_ScottChritiansen_EN.pdf

Chubb, John E. 1983 *Interest Groups and the Bureaucracy: The Politics of Energy*. Stanford: Stanford University Press.

Clark, Robert. 1932. "Harney Basin Exploration, 1826-60" *Oregon Historical Quarterly* 33(2): 101-114.

Cockle, Richard. 2012. "Eastern Oregon Father-Son Ranchers Convicted of Lighting Fires on Federal Land." *The Oregonian*. (June 22) Accessed June 21, 2016 http://www.oregonlive.com/pacific-northwest-news/index.ssf/2012/06/eastern_oregon_father-son_ranc.html

Corn, M. Lynne. 2016. "Conflict and History at Malheur National Wildlife Refuge." *Congressional Research Service Insight Report*. U.S. Congressional Research Service, (January 28, IN10427).

Crow, Pete. 2015. "Hammonds Journey." *Western Livestock Journal*. (October 16), Accessed June 22, 2016 at https://wlj.net/article-permalink-12129.html

Davis, Charles. 2001. *Western Environmental Lands and Public Politics*. Boulder: Westview Press.

Deubbert, Harold F. 1969. *The Ecology of Malheur Lake and Management Implications*. Washington: United States Department of the Interior, Bureau of Sport Fisheries and Wildlife, U.S. Fish and Wildlife Service.

DeVoto, Bernard. 1952. *The Course of Empire*. New York: Houghton-Mifflin.

——. 1934. *"The West: A Plundered Province"* In *the Western Paradox: A Bernard DeVoto Conservation Reader*. (2001). Edited by Douglas Brinkley and Nelson Limerick. New Haven: Yale University Press. 2-21.

Dobbs, Gordon. 2013. *Oregon: A History*. New York: W.W. Norton & Company.

Downey, Hannah, Holly Fretwell and Shawn Regan. 2016. *Access Divided: State and Federal Recreation Management in the West*. Bozeman: The Property and Environmental Research Center (PERC).

Eckoff, Vickery. 2015. "Sustainable Cowboys or Welfare Ranchers of the West?" *Daily Pitchfork*. (February 12), Accessed June 23, 2016 http://dailypitchfork.org/?p=631

Engeman, Richard H. 2005. "Sawmills and Agricultural Structures." *The Oregon History Project*, Oregon Historical Society, Portland, OR.

Fehrenbach, T.R. 2000. *Lone Star—A History of Texas and Texans*. New York,: Open Road Media.

Freda, Kimberley and John Sepulvado. 2016. "Court Papers: Hammonds Entered Plea Deals Knowing Mandated Sentences Loomed." *Oregon Public Broadcasting*. Accessed June 21, 2016 http://www.opb.org/news/series/burns-oregon-standoff-bundy-militia-news-updates/hammonds-entered-plea-knowing-sentences-loomed/

Fuller, Jamie. 2014. "The Long Fight Between the Bundy's and the Federal Government from 1989 to Today" *The Washington Post*. (January 4), Accessed June 20, 2016 https://www.washingtonpost.com/news/the-fix/wp/2014/04/15/everything-you-need-to-know-about-the-long-fight-between-cliven-bundy-and-the-federal-government/

Furnish, Jim. 2015. "Forest Service is Still in Search of a Mission." *High Country News*. (April 14), Accessed June 21, 2016 https://www.hcn.org/articles/forest-service-is-still-in-search-of-a-mission

Gitzen, Garry. 2011. *Nehalem, Oregon and Francis Drake 1579*. Wheeler: Nehalem Publishing.

Glaser, Christine, Chuck Romaniello and Karen Moskowitz. 2015. *Costs and Consequences: The Real Cost of Livestock Grazing on Public Lands*. Tuscon: Center for Biological Diversity.

Gorte, Ross W. and Lynne M. Corn. 2012/ *Compensating State and Local Governments for the Tax-Exempt Status of Federal Lands: What Is Fair and Consistent?* Washington: U.S. Congressional Research Service.

Guinto, Lloyd D. 2013. "United States V. Bundy." Case No. 2:12-cv-0804-LDG-GWF (D. Nev. Jul. 9, 2013) *CaseText*. Accessed August 25, 2017 https://casetext.com/case/united-states-v-bundy-11

Hage, Wayne. 1989. *Storm Over Rangelands: Private Rights in Public Lands*. Bellevue: Free Enterprise Press.

Harris, Dylan Woolf. 2013. "Judge Sides with Ranch Family: Court Shocked by Actions of Forest Service, BLM." *Elko Daily Free Press*. (May 30). Accessed June 14, 2014 http://elkodaily.com/news/local/judge-sides-with-ranch-family/article_3920d17a-c8d5-11e2-b69c-001a4bcf887a.html

Haun, Marjorie. 2015. "Distrust of Federal Land Agencies Escalates with the Conviction of Oregon Ranchers." *American Thinker*. (November 27), Accessed June 22, 2016 http://www.americanthinker.com/articles/2015/11/distrust_of_federal_land_agencies_escalates_with_conviction_of_oregon_ranchers.html

Hays, Samuel P. 2009. *The American People and the National Forests: The First Century of the U.S. Forest Service*. Pittsburgh: University of Pittsburgh Press.

Herzog, Katie. 2016. "7 Kinds of Government Subsidies Those Angry Ranchers Get that You Don't." *Grist*. (January 6), Accessed June 23, 2016 http://grist.org/article/7-kinds-of-government-subsidies-those-angry-ranchers-get-that-you-dont/

Homestead Act. 1862. Public Law 37-64, (May 20), Record Group 11; General Records of the United States Government; National Archives.

Honigsberg, Peter Jan. 2011. "Conflict of Interests that Led to the Gulf Oil Disaster." *Environmental Law Reporter*. 41:10414-10418.

Hudak, Mike. 1999. "To Graze of Not to Graze: Livestock Grazing on Public Lands Policy and the Sierra Club." *Chesapeake—Newsletter of the Maryland Chapter, Sierra Club*. (September/October), 22-23.

Hutchins, Wells A. and Steele, Harry A. 1957. "Basic Water Rights Doctrines and their implications for River Basin Development," *Law & Contemporary Problems*. 22(2): 276-300.

Jasper, William. 2016. "Behind the Oregon Standoff." *The New American*. (February 11), Accessed June 22, 2016 at http://www.thenewamerican.com/usnews/constitution/item/22499-behind-the-oregon-standoff

———. 2013. "Federal Judge Rules for Property Rights, Smacks Down Abusive Feds." *The New American*. (June 3), Accessed June 14, 2016 http://www.thenewamerican.com/usnews/constitution/item/15602-federal-judge-rules-for-property-rights-smacks-down-abusive-feds

Jewell, Sally. 2017. "Toward a Bright Future: The Interior Department's Record of Progress." Exit Memo: Department of Interior. (January 5), Accessed August 25, 2017 https://obamawhitehouse.archives.gov/administration/cabinet/exit-memos/department-interior

Johnson, David. 2016. "Oregon Gold Mines." *Mining Artifacts*. Accessed June 8, 2016 http://www.miningartifacts.org/OregonMines.html

Jung, Helen. 2014. "Harney County Rancher and Son Sentenced Too Lightly For Arson Convictions, Federal Appeals Panel Says" *The Oregonian*. (February 7). Accessed June 21, 2016 http://www.oregonlive.com/pacific-northwest-news/index.ssf/2014/02/harney_county_rancher_and_son.html

Kappler, Charles J. 1904. "Treaty with Rogue River 1853." *Indian Affairs: Laws and Treaties*. 2: 603-605, Washington: U.S. Government Printing Office.

Kerr, Andy. 2006. "The Steens Mountain Cooperative Management and Protection Act of 2000 (Oregon)" In *Collaborative Conservation Strategies: Legislative Case Studies from Across the West*. Edited by Timothy Brown, Denver: Western Governors Association.

Klingle, Matthew W. 2009. *Building Nature: Topics in the Environmental History of Seattle and Spokane*. Seattle: Center for the Study of the Pacific Northwest.

Lamm, Richard D. and Michael McCarthy. 1989. *The Angry West: A Vulnerable Land and Its Future*. New York: Houghton Mifflin.

Langston, Nancy. 2003. *Where Land and Water Meet: A Western Landscape Transformed*. Seattle: University of Washington Press.

———. 1995. *Forest Dreams, Forest Nightmares: The Paradox of Old Growth in the Inland West*. Seattle: University of Washington Press.

Ledyard, John. 1963. *John Ledyard's Journal of Captain Cook's Last Voyage*. Corvallis: Oregon State University Press.

Lenz, Ryan and Mark Potok. 2014. *War in the West: The Bundy Ranch Standoff and the American Radical Right*. Montgomery: Southern Poverty Law Center, Retrieved from the Worldwide Web June 14, 2016 at https://www.splcenter.org/sites/default/files/d6_legacy_files/downloads/publication/war_in_the_west_report.pdf

Lewis, David. 2017. "Athapaskan Indians." *The Oregon Encyclopedia*. (January 26), Accessed August 18, 2017 https://oregonencyclopedia.org/articles/athapasca_indians/#.WZn-xYqQzVo

Lidgett, Adam. 2016. "Grazing Trespass Case Won't Move to Supreme Court." *Law360*. (October 19), Accessed August 17, 2017 https://www.law360.com/articles/853118/grazing-trespass-case-won-t-move-to-supreme-court

Lindgren, Waldemar. 2014. *Gold Belt of the Blue Mountains of Oregon*. Seattle: Create Space Independent Publishing Platform.

Liskey, Tracy. 2015. "Introduction: Southeast Oregon," *State of Oregon Agriculture: Industry Report to the State Department of Agriculture, January 2015*. ORS 561.378, Salem, OR: Oregon State Department of Agriculture, p. 44-46.

Marion, Louie. 1989. "History of the Malheur Paiutes." In *A Lively Little History of Harney County—A Centennial Souvenir Album*. Burns: Harney County Centennial Committee.

McCarthy, Michael. 1992. "The First Sagebrush Rebellion: Forest Reserves and States Rights in Colorado and the West, 1891-1907." In *The Origins of the National Forest: A Centennial Symposium*. Edited by Harold K. Steen. Durham: Forest History Society.

McMaken, Ryan. 2016. "How the Feds Got All that Western Land (and Why It's a Problem)." *Mises Wire*. (January 8), Accessed June 21, 2016 https://mises.org/blog/how-feds-got-all-western-land-and-why-its-problem

Miller, Steven. 2013. "Feds' War Against Rancher Takes A Body Blow." *Nevada Journal*. (June 13), Accessed June 14, 2016 http://nevadajournal.com/2013/06/13/feds-war-western-ranchers-water-rights-takes-body-blow/

Mirsky, Jeannette. 1946. *The Westward Crossings: Balboa: Mackenzie: Lewis and Clark*. New York: Knopf.

National Agricultural Statistics Service (NASS). 2016 "State-By-State Agricultural Statistics Press Release." (May 9), USDA, Accessed June 14, 2016 at https://www.nass.usda.gov/Statistics_by_State/Oregon/Publications/Livestock_Report/2016/CE_CATT.pdf

Nauman, James D. 1999. *An Account of the Voyage of Juan Rodriguez Cabrillo*. Bronx: Catholic Historical Association.

Neiwert, David. 2016. "Constitutional' Oregon Sheriff Under Investigation for Malheur Role." *Hatewatch*. (March 23), Accessed July 15, 2016 https://www.splcenter.org/hatewatch/2016/03/23/constitutional%E2%80%99-oregon-sheriff-under-investigation-malheur-role-hired-70-%E2%80%98special-deputies%E2%80%99

Neuman, Janet C. 2004 "The Good, The Bad and The Ugly: The First Ten Years of the Oregon Water Trust." *Nebraska Law Review*. 83(2): 433-484.

Nixon, Guy. 2015. *The Sheepshooter's War and Sheep Wars of the Sierra Nevada and the West*. Bloomington: Xlibris Corporation.

O'Laughlin, Jay. 2011. "Federal Land as a Percentage of Total State Land Area." Policy Analysis Group, University of Idaho College of Natural Resources, (September 26), Accessed August 25, 2017 http://www.idahoforests.org/img/pdf/CQHSNFPAG-factsheet.pdf

Oliver, Chadwick D., Irwin, Larry L. and Knapp, Walter H. 1994. *Eastside Forest Management Practices: Historical Overview, Extent of their Applications, and their Effects of Sustainability of Ecosystems*. Corvallis: U.S. Department of Agriculture, Forest Service.

Ortiz, Erik. 2016. "Embattled Sheriff Glenn Palmer, Linked to Oregon Occupiers, Under Scrutiny," *NBC News*. (March 19), Accessed July 15, 2016 http://www.nbcnews.com/news/us-news/embattled-sheriff-glenn-palmer-linked-oregon-occupiers-under-scrutiny-n541371

Pendley, William Perry. 2016. "Oregon Standoff Reveals There Is No Adult Supervision of Federal Agencies in the West." *National Review*. (January 5) Retrieved from the Worldwide Web June 15, 2016 at http://www.nationalreview.com/article/429266/oregon-rancher-protest-federal-agencies-out-control

Piper, Matthew. 2016. "BLM Returns to Work Near Bundy Ranch as Cliven And Sons Await Trial." *The Salt Lake Tribune*. (June 22), Accessed June 22, 2016 http://www.sltrib.com/news/4018764-155/blm-returns-to-work-near-bundy

Powell, David C. 2008a. "Early Timber Harvesting in the Blue Mountains." U.S. Department of Agriculture, U.S. Forest Service.

———. 2008b. "Early Livestock Grazing in the Blue Mountains." U.S. Department of Agriculture, U.S. Forest Service.

Rice, John. 1979. "They Call It the Sagebrush Rebellion." *Lewiston Evening Journal*. (June 8), 16, Accessed August 25, 2017 https://news.google.com/newspapers?nid=oQQVFBP0nzwC&dat=19790608&printsec=frontpage&hl=en

Rogers, Jedediah S. 2015. "Land Grabbers, Toadstool Worshippers, And the Sagebrush Rebellion in Utah, 1979–1981." (July 15), *All Theses and Dissertations: BYU Scholars Archive*. Provo: Brigham Young University.

Roth, Leland. 2007. "John William "Pete" French (1849-1897)." *The Oregon Encyclopedia*. Portland: Oregon Historical Society.

Sepulvado, John and Amand Peacher. 2016. "BLM Considers Reinstating Hammond Grazing Leases." *Oregon Public Broadcasting*. (January 21), Accesed June 22, 2016 http://www.opb.org/news/series/burns-oregon-standoff-bundy-militia-news-updates/hammond-blm-grazing-leases/

Suprynowicz, Vin. 2014. "Special Report: Patterns of Harassment—Onslaught at Gold Butte." *Range Magazine*. (Fall), 37-52.

Swearingen, Marshall and Kate Schimel (2016) "Timeline: A Brief History of the Sagebrush Rebellion." *High Country News*. (February 4), Accessed June 14, 2016 http://www.hcn.org/articles/a-history-of-the-sagebrush-rebellion

Schwartz, E. A. 2010. *The Rogue River Indian War and its Aftermath, 1850-1880*. Norman: University of Oklahoma Press.

Scofield, John. 1992. *Hail, Columbia! - Robert Gray, John Kendrick, and the Pacific Fur Trade (North Pacific Studies Series)*. Portland: Oregon Historical Society Press.

Stadheim, Carrie. 2015. "Where' There's Smoke." *Tri-State Livestock News*. (October 29), Accessed June 21, 2016 at http://www.tsln.com/news/18837869-113/where-theres-smoke

Stark, Peter. 2014. *Astoria: John Jacob Astor and Thomas Jefferson's Lost Pacific Empire: A Story of Wealth, Ambition, and Survival*. New York: Harper Collins.

Strong, Dexter K. 1940. "Beef Cattle Industry in Oregon, 1890-1938." *Oregon Historical Quarterly*. 41(3): 251-287.

Tanner, Randy. 2002. "Inholdings Within Wilderness: Legal Foundations, Problems and Solutions" *International Journal of Wilderness*. (December), 8(3): 9-14.

Taylor Grazing Act, 1934 48 Stat 1269, "Act of June 28, 1934" codified at 43 U.S.C. 315 et seq.

United States Department of Agriculture (USDA). 2016. "Malheur National Forest: History and Culture." U.S. Forest Service, Accessed May 23, 2016 http://www.fs.usda.gov/main/malheur/learning/history-culture

———. "Payments & Receipts." U.S. Forest Service, Accessed June 23, 2016 http://www.fs.usda.gov/main/pts/securepayments/projectedpayments

United States Fish and Wildlife Service (USFWS). 2016. "Malheur National Wildlife Refuge Conservation Plan," Accessed June 13, 2016 https://www.justice.gov/usao-or/file/851716/download.

United States General Services Administration (USGSA). 2017. "Federal Real Property Profile Summary Report Library." Accessed August 25, 2017 https://www.gsa.gov/portal/content/102880

United States Geological Survey (USGS). 2014. "Printable Maps: Federal Lands, Indian Lands." *2014 Edition of the National Atlas*. Accessed August 17, 2017 https://nationalmap.gov/small_scale/printable/fedlands.html

United States v. Clive Bundy. 1998. United States Court of Appeals for the Ninth Circuit. No. CV-S-98-531-JBR (RJJ) (D. Nev. Nov. 4, 1998) Accessed August 25, 2017 http://dohiyimir.typepad.com/bundy-1998-court.pdf

United States v. Estate of E. Wayne Hage; Wayne N. Hage. 2016. United States Court of Appeals for the Ninth Circuit. No. 2:07-cv-01154-RCJ-VCF. (D. Nev. Jan. 16, 2016) Accessed August 25, 2017 https://cdn.ca9.uscourts.gov/datastore/opinions/2016/01/15/13-16974.pdf

Victor, Frances Fuller. 1894. *The Early Indian Wars of Oregon*. Salem: Frank C. Baker State Printer.

Vincent, Carol Hardy, Laura A. Hanson and Carla N. Argueta. 2017. *Federal Land Ownership: Overview and Data*. (March 3), Washington: U.S. Congressional Research Service.

Vincent, Carol Hardy, Laura A. Hanson and Jerome P. Bjelopera. 2014. *Federal Land Ownership: Overview and Data*. (December 29), Washington: U.S. Congressional Research Service.

Vincent, Carol Hardy. 2004. *Federal Land Management Agencies: Background on Land and Resource Management*. (August 2), Washington: U.S. Congressional Research Service.

Wald, Johanna. 2002. "Livestock Grazing and the Environment," Earth Justice White Paper," Accessed June 23, 2016 http://vegetarian.procon.org/sourcefiles/livestock_grazing_and_the_environment.pdf

Wernstedt, Kris. 2000. "Terra Firma or Terra Incognita? Western Land Use, Hazardous Waste, and the Devolution of U.S. Federal Environmental Programs." *Natural Resources Journal*. 40(Winter): 157-183.

Wheeler, Raymond (1988) "Boom, Boom, Boom—War on the Colorado Plateau," *High Country News*. (September), p. 17-18; 22.

Wiles, Tay. 2016. "Malheur Occupation Explained." *High Country News*. (January 4), Accessed June 22, 2016 http://www.hcn.org/articles/oregon-occupation-at-wildlife-refuge

Williams, Florence. 1992. "Sagebrush Rebellion II: Some Rural Counties Seek to Influence Federal Land Use." *High Country News*. (February 24), Accessed June 14, 2016 http://s3.amazonaws.com/hcn-media/archive-pdf/1992_02_24_Catron.pdf

Wilson, Jason. 2016."The Rise of Militias: Patriot Candidates are Now Getting Elected in Oregon." *The Guardian*. (May 10), Accessed June 14, 2016 https://www.theguardian.com/us-news/2016/may/10/patriot-movement-oregon-militias-donald-trump-election-2016

Wilson, Julie. 2015. "OUTRAGE: Bureau Of Land Management Goes After Bundy Ranch Neighbors, Charging Them Under An Anti-Terrorism Law For Burning A Brush Fire." *Natural News*. (December 13), Accessed June 22, 2016 http://www.naturalnews.com/052301_Bundy_Ranch_Federal_government_BLM.html

Wilson, Nancy. 1994. *Dr. John McLoughlin: Master of Fort Vancouver, Father of Oregon*. Medford: Webb Research Group.

Wilson, Conrad and John Rosen. 2016. "Malheur National Wildlife Refuge Occupation Ends," *Oregon Public Broadcasting*. (February 11), Accessed June 21, 2016 http://www.opb.org/news/series/burns-oregon-standoff-bundy-militia-news-updates/malheur-occupation-ends/

Yarnes, Thomas D. 1961. *A History of Methodism*. Nashville: Parthenon Press.

Yarrington-Ball, Charlotte (1984) "Cooperative Management Agreements." *Rangelands*. Vol. 6, No. 4., (August) p. 169-171.

Young, Molly. 2016. "Oregon Standoff Timeline: How the Occupation Unfolded." The *Oregonian*. (March 8), Accessed June 23, 2016 at http://www.oregonlive.com/oregonstandoff/2016/03/oregon_standoff_timeline_how_t.html

Young, Otis E. and Robert Lennon. 1977. *Western Mining*. Norman: University of Oklahoma Press.

Zavis, Alexandra. 2016. "Oregon Standoff: Who's Really Getting Hurt by Federal Grazing Laws?" *Los Angeles Times*. (January 6), Accessed June 23, 2016 at http://www.latimes.com/nation/la-na-oregon-standoff-federal-grazing-laws-20160106-story.html

Zavis, Alexandra, Nigel Duara and Richard Winton. 2016. "How Oregon Ranchers Unwittingly Sparked an Armed Standoff." *Los Angeles Times*. (January 5) Accessed 16, 2016 at http://www.latimes.com/nation/la-na-ff-hammond-oregon-20160105-story.html

CHAPTER 5

The Blue Mountain Forest Partners

CASE STUDY TWO:

Eastern Oregon Timber Wars and Poor Timber Management

Throughout the 1980s and '90s, loggers and environmentalists across the Pacific Northwest sparred with BLM and the Forest Service over management of the nation's national forests. This conflict came to be known as the "timber wars" (Dellasala & Williams 2006). While this dispute may have superficially appeared to be about efforts to save the northern spotted owl from extinction, its roots ran much deeper involving historical conflicts between environmental, business and regulatory interests regarding who would manage and benefit from the plethora of natural resources to be realized within the nation's Western public lands (Bramen 2015).

During this period of conflict, Western national forests fell into disrepair, principally because of poor forest management practices and overharvesting. Motivated by the need to meet the nation's growing demand for timber, the U.S. Forest Service historically entered sweetheart deals with the timber industry which threatened the economic and environmental sustainability of public forest lands and local communities. More specifically, the failure of Forest Service staff to adequately oversee logging activities on federal lands enabled contractors to cut more timber than they contracted for resulting in overharvesting. The net effect of inadequate forest management and overharvesting of timber was a dramatic decline in the health of Western public forests (Knize 1991).

Illustrative of this problem is an analysis conducted in 1994 on behalf of the Center for Public Integrity (Taylor 1994). Researchers concluded "that timber interests dominate nearly all discussions and actions within the Forest Service" evidenced by the fact that,

> "The agency spends on average 70 percent of its annual total resource management budget on timber operations, and only 5 percent on fish, wildlife, soil, and water preservation. In 1992, the Forest Service budget included $1.17 billion to fund activities on national forests. Of that total, more than half—or $583.4 million—was spent on preparing trees for logging, which is a typical annual expenditure (Taylor 1994, 1-2).

During this same period, several environmental groups filed a series of lawsuits— mostly involving the Endangered Species Act—asserting that federal management of national forest "threatened and endangered and sensitive species." This litigation eventually forced the Forest Service to formulate the Northwest Forest Plan of 1994 (Davis et al. 2015; Dellasala & Williams 2006).

This plan departed with past practices that incentivized the Forest Service to enter exclusive deals with the timber industry and dramatically curtailed timber harvests on federal forests while protecting old-growth habitat for the endangered northern spotted owl and other threatened species. Since the introduction of the Northwest Forest Plan timber harvests on public lands dropped to pre-WWII levels (Davis et al. 2015; Bosworth & Brown 2007). This downturn in timber production on Western lands proved catastrophic to local economies and many blamed the Federal government and environmentalist groups for precipitating this crisis in their zeal to protect an endangered species.

In fact, structural shifts in the timber industry had been occurring for many years reducing demand for timber-related employment. These changes in timber management and harvesting practices were unrelated to the fate of endangered species and were intended to render timber harvesting and processing more efficient. The forces driving these changes stemmed from technological innovations and the emergence of competitive sources for timber—particularly from Southern pine plantations and foreign timber markets (Bosworth & Brown 2007, 272). The declining health of Western forests also depressed local timber-driven economies. By the 1990's forest resources on public lands had been degraded by overharvesting, excessive deadfall from logging, soil erosion, the intensification of wildfire hazard via the growth of undergrowth, the spread of invasive plant species such as the Western juniper as well by an increase in tree disease (Langston 2003; 1995; Hartter 2010).

One of the key markers of the health of forest is the pervasiveness of what are called "zombie trees"—dead trees standing among living trees. Normally well managed forests have fewer zombie trees than is the case in poorly managed forests. When forests are not managed effectively, trees become overcrowded and ultimately overcrowded forests exhibit a greater percentage of dead trees. Such zombie trees threaten forest health by attracting pests and fueling wildfire which in turn threaten the entire forest ecosystem. The impact of disease and fire upon forests contributes to the forest's mortality rate (Cloughesy 2015).

A dramatic difference emerged in Oregon between forest mortality rates on public versus private forest lands. Per Oregon Forest Resources Institute in Portland, Oregon:

> "Private and Native American forestlands, which have the highest timber harvest rate at 71 percent of total growth, have only 9 percent mortality. NFS forestlands have a timber harvest rate of about 8 percent of total growth, but have a mortality rate of about 55 percent" (Cloughesy 2015).

Figure 12 illustrates the disparity between federally and privately managed forest lands. This research definitively documents the negative impact that years of Forest Service mismanagement produced—practices principally driven economically and politically by catering to timber interests. These findings are provocative, clearly suggesting that any pathway to revitalizing the timber industry in Northeast Oregon entails restoring the health of public forests.

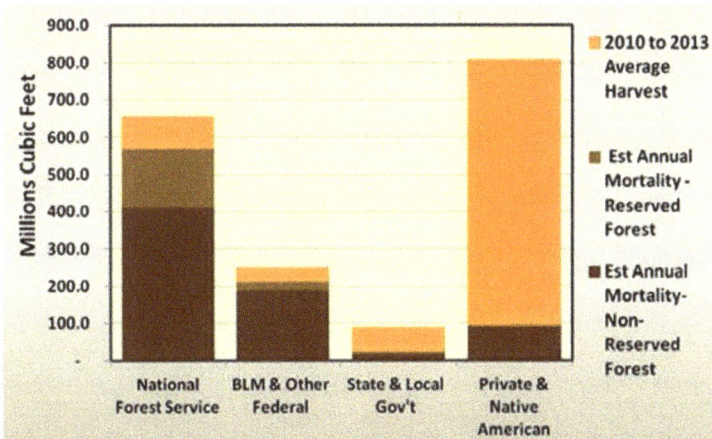

Figure 12: Annual Mortality vs. Annual Harvest on Oregon's Forests by Ownership Class
(Source: Cloughesy 2015)

Collaborative Cooperation In Lieu Of Litigation

Following the implementation of the Northwest Forest Plan timbering on public lands dramatically decreased in Northeast Oregon. In the small community of John Day, Oregon located in Grant County, the principal employer—Malheur Lumber— struggled to remain open as the volume of logs delivered to the mill from the nearby Malheur National Forest steadily dwindled. At one point the mill manager contemplated closing operations altogether, a measure that would have devastated the local economy and Grant County. Despite the desperation of their situation, however, the mill was ultimately saved thanks to community leaders like then Grant County Judge Mark Webb, timber interests and the mill's owners, and perhaps most importantly, thanks to a few visionary environmentalists—Tim Lillebo and Andy Kerr of the Oregon Natural Resources and Susan Jane Brown of the Western Environmental Law Center (Barnard 2014).

What emerged was an unlikely partnership of erstwhile adversaries. Steve Beverlin, then supervisor of the Malheur National Forest, recollects that by 2000 loggers, mill owners and the Forest Service had reached a stalemate from which no option seemed possible. Loggers wanted to cut more logs, mill owners needed more volume and the Forest Service found its hands tied by federal regulations and the influence of powerful environmental groups. Seemingly the only solutions available involved litigation against federal agencies. As bleak as prospects looked, several key stakeholders persisted in conferring together in search of solutions. Ultimately their persistence produced resilient stakeholder relationships that resulted in the discovery of common ground and a mutually acceptable path forward (Barnard 2014).

The process began when a productive relationship evolved between Malheur Lumber manager Mike Billman and Tim Lillebo of Oregon Natural Resources. Planning meetings developed into camping trips and deep friendship. Stereotypes of environmentalists and timber people rapidly evaporated as the two came to personally know one another. While their conversations began with industry and environmental concerns it ultimately shifted to family and personal beliefs, and as it did they discovered they shared a broad range of values and interests. It was from this shared common ground that they developed a path forward for Malheur Lumber that would simultaneously promote forest health and restore the region's depressed timber industry (Barnard 2014).

Parallel to the growth of this friendship, John Shelk, managing partner of Ochoco Lumber Company (Malheur Lumber's parent company) also engaged the environmental community, partnering with Andy Kerr—Tim Lillebo's colleague at Oregon Natural Resources Council. Kerr was a storied environmental activist credited with negotiating agreements with a variety of timber interests in Eastern Oregon (Mapes 2015). They too developed a strong friendship and in tandem to Mike Billman and Tim Lillebo's collaboration similarly arrived at a shared vision and plan for increasing timber production by way of restoring the national forest. In both instances, participants abandoned an "either-or" perspective that implied that either the forest could be restored *or* the timber industry could be revitalized—a win-lose proposition. Instead, they concluded that forests could sustainability be restored and maintained through a productive and ongoing partnership between environmentalists, loggers, and mill owners. In so doing, the pervasive "either-or" (win-lose) perspective was replaced with a win-win "restoration-and-harvesting" approach. As Andy Kerr recalls "We agreed that there was a lot of (timber) to be had from ecological forestry and the lumber mill weren't interested in the big trees anyway—leading us both to ultimately pose the question of "why were we fighting?" (Barnard 2014).

Beyond the evolution of these productive relationships, County Commissioner Boyd Britton likewise established a working relationship with environmental activist Susan Jane Brown, an attorney with the Western Environmental Law Center. Britton and Brown had historically engaged in an adversarial relationship as she periodically impeded timber sales to protect habitat. Having become acquainted with her first as an adversary, Britton nevertheless trusted her judgment and respected her integrity. Consequently, they too began to understand one another in greater context and in so doing concluded that forest restoration and timber harvesting need not be inherently adversarial and in fact could be mutually beneficial.

As these conversations continued, a growing consensus emerged among environmentalists that wildfires threatened the health of forests as certainly as logging. Thus, per Susan Jane Brown they came to appreciate that "the way to protect the forests was to work with the collaborative [community and business stakeholders] to approve projects that thinned overgrown stands while providing enough logs to keep the local mill running" (Barnard 2014). What ultimately emerged was a collaborative nonprofit organization—the Blue Mountain Forest Partners (BMFP)— and a plan for saving Malheur Lumber that involved forest thinning projects that reduced fire hazards while providing logs for the local mill. Soon thereafter the Forest Service via BMFP awarded a stewardship contract to a local logging company, Iron Triangle, to embark upon timber thinning to reduce excess biomass—thereby reducing wildfire risks over the period of a decade (Barnard 2014).

Pragmatic Scientific Management

The philosophical foundations of this approach involve pragmatism—doing that which is necessary to enfranchise as many stakeholders as possible in protecting the forests—and scientific decision making—managing forests based upon demonstrable reliable and valid scientific observations and practices. This perspective—the pragmatic and scientific management of forests—is the principal contribution of environmentalist Andy Kerr who asserts that,

> "Under the science-based principles and recommendations ... intact mature and old-growth forests can be conserved, degraded forests can be restored to late-successional character, and timber volume can increase from federal public forestlands" (Kerr 2012b, 3)

More specifically, Kerr's scientific management policy is based upon the following assumptions:

- ***Collaboration Is Not a Zero-Sum Game***: Collaborative efforts between timber interests, environmentalists and Forest Service personnel is no longer a "zero-sum" game where some people win and others lose.
- ***Expect a High-Probability of Success:*** Ecologically restoration thinning (ERT) produces smaller commercially available logs as a byproduct of forest management, thus eliminating controversy over old-growth timber or habitat protection for endangered species while reducing the stock of wildfire fuel.
- ***The Social License on Harvesting Older Trees Has Expired:*** The timber industry is no longer licensed by public sentiment and governmental regulation to harvest older trees or harvest in road-less areas, meaning the best available economic option involves forest restoration and a willingness to limit their cutting on public lands to ERT.
- ***Conservation Community Commitment and Collaboration:*** The more fully old growth forests are protected by federal law and effective federal forest management the greater the likelihood that conservationists and environmentalist will advocate for ERT - resulting in less resistance to timber harvests.
- ***Not All Board-Feet Are Alike:*** While under the guidelines of the NWFP a small portion of timber volume form public lands involved trees from old-growth forests, under ERT *all* timber will constitute smaller trees designated as green or salvage timber. In this way, the nation's natural forest resources are protected along with water systems and ecosystems but without engendering public resistance (Kerr 2012b).

While these tenets explain Kerr's approach to the scientific management of forests it does not include those community resources and interests that are central to success to include the need for:

- Consistent congressional funding for forest restoration,
- A willingness by federal agencies to cooperate with one another and local governments,
- Reforming federal contract approaches to streamline contracts and contain costs,

- Creating collaborative relationships between federal agencies and community stakeholders;
- Replacing timber contracts with stewardship contracts where timber resources become the byproducts of forest restoration (Kerr 2012b).

The product of these disparate yet creative conversations and collaborations was The Blue Mountain Forest Partners (BMFP). BMFP was organized as a nonprofit organization in 2006 in Grant County Oregon, a rural area in Northeast Oregon amid the Blue Mountains and the Malheur National Forest. This group emerged as a grassroots collaborative designed to convene all relevant stakeholders in the community—especially those involved with timber, ranching and the environmental community—to find a way forward in utilizing the resources of the national forest without resorting to litigation and the balkanization of interests (Barnard 2014). The BMFP operates on the north end of the Malheur National Forest in Grant County while their co-collaborators - the Harney County Restoration Collaborative - operates on the southern portion of the forest in Harney County (Sustainable Northwest 2016).

Grant County Demographics

Grant County is a rural and relatively isolated area situated 260 miles from Portland. The county encompasses 4,528 square miles of which 60.7% is federally owned. Grant County is rich in environmental resources to include the North Fork John Day Wilderness Area, Strawberry Mountain Wilderness Area, John Day Fossil Beds, the Malheur National Forest, Black Canyon Wilderness Area, and the Silvies River. Timber and lumber products and services account for the greatest portion of the local economy (Figure 13) with 24% of total employment, followed by the U.S. Forest Service (18.6%), county and municipal government (17%), public schools (13.5%), retail employment (12.6%) and healthcare (10.2%). The remaining 4% of local employees are employed in state government, public utility and transportation jobs. Major private sector employers in the County include Grayback Forestry Inc., Jackson Oil Inc., Prairie Wood Products, Grant Western Lumber, Malheur Lumber Company, Chester's Thriftway Grocery Store, and the Blue Mountain Hospital (OECD, 2006).

Grant County is situated among the Blue Mountains of Eastern Oregon and the Malheur National Forest is principally located in Grant and Harney Counties near John Day and Burns, Oregon (Figure 14). Of the 1,708,686 acres within the forest, some 1,128,920 acres lie in Grant County Oregon while 526,067 acres are sited in neighboring Harney County. Given the broad geographic expanse of the forest over five counties (to additionally include Baker County with 46,357 acres, Crook County with 9,726 acres and Malheur County with 606 acres of Malheur National Forest land) managing and restoring this vast and diverse forest requires input and cooperation from at least five counties to include environmental, business, ranch, timber, governmental and landowner stakeholders. (USDA 2009).

Employment Sector	Employees	%
Timber/Lumber	202.00	24.19
U.S. Forest Service	156.00	18.68
County/Municipal Government	140.00	16.77
Schools	113.00	13.53
Retail	105.00	12.57
Healthcare	86.00	10.30
State Government	14.00	1.68
Public Utility	12.00	1.44
Transportation	7.00	0.84
Total	835.00	100.00

Figure 13: Grant County Oregon Employment by Sector 2006
(Source: OECD 2006)

This diverse forest ecosystem ranges from 4,000 to 9,038 feet in elevation and contains vast forest reserves, alpine lakes and mountain meadows (USDA 2009). Named for the Malheur River whose headwaters lie in the Southeast region of the forest, the Malheur Forest was given "national forest" status in 1908 by President Theodore "Teddy" Roosevelt when it was carved out of previously created Blue Mountain Forest Reserve (1906). The name "Malheur" is of French origin (meaning "misfortune"), was coined in the 1820's by fur trapper Peter Ogden after a cache of supplies he had hidden along the river banks was plundered by Paiute Indians (USDA 2016).

Prior to the creation of the Malheur National Forest and its subsequent management by the U.S. Forest Service, a natural pattern of small but regular lightning-related fires kept undergrowth down thereby reducing the likelihood of larger more destructive fires. However, by the 1930's a U.S. Forest Service policy of strict fire suppression resulted in the dangerous accumulation of biomass in the understory of the forest thereby fueling larger and more catastrophic blazes. In part the practice of fire suppression was designed to protect the timber resources which began to be harvested in earnest in the 1930's and steadily continued until the mid 1990's when it began to diminish due to changes in timber demand and increasing environmental pressures. Historically the principal timber-producing species in the forest include ponderosa pine, Douglas-fir, western larch, true firs and lodgepole pine. Fully 74% of the timber harvested from the Malheur National Forest comes from "open ponderosa pine stands" (USDA/Forest Service 1987, 1-7). To this day timber sales, management and fire suppression remains the principle activities of Malheur National Forest staff (USDA 2016).

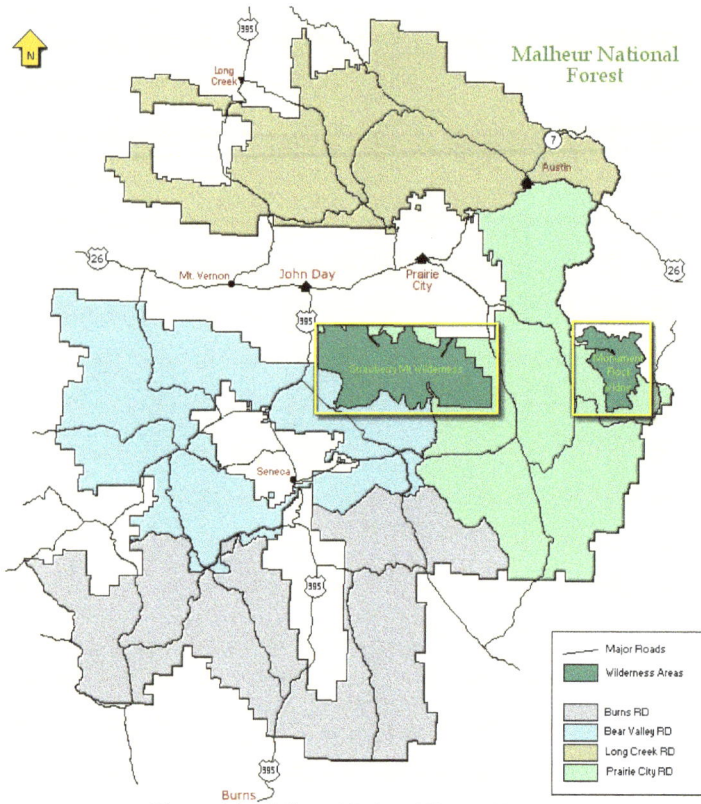

Figure 14: Malheur National Forest Zones
(Source: USDA/USFS 2016)

Conflict, Cooperation and Collaboration

Western settlers have historically found themselves in conflict with the land they inhabited, particularly regarding water and wildfires. More enduring, however, are the conflicts between and among claimants to these lands throughout the history of their settlement. What the preceding chapter makes abundantly clear is that the territorial and state history of Oregon has been inextricably shaped by successive eras of conflict, to include conflicts regarding land claims (Spain, Britain, America, Indigenous Peoples, Pioneers), natural resources (timber, grazing, agriculture, gold, energy, and water), regionalism (Eastern versus Western influence) and governmental regulation (capitalist interests, states, localities or the federal government). As was the case in neighboring states across the American West, Oregon's conflicts have been episodically violent and historically persistent. The identity of Oregon and Oregonians is one of a region and a people who have long since been compelled to learn how to creatively deal with conflict short of violence or illegality. Though independent and free-thinking in ways that only Westerners can affirm, Oregonians have of necessity learned to mediate conflict by way of cooperation and compromise.

The spirit of cooperation is probably nowhere more evident than in environmental policy and practice. Since so much of the land in Oregon falls under the aegis of one or more federal environmental laws protecting ecosystems, water and endangered species as well as EPA regulations pertaining to the production and use of carbon-based fuels that contribute to climate change, Oregonians must live with heavy federal regulation that dramatically tempers state and private land-use decisions. Federal regulators and members of Congress have learned with experience that acceptance and cooperation with federal regulatory guidelines is enhanced when collaborative arrangements with consumers and stakeholders are developed. Conversely, they have also discovered that when regulators act in ways that are seen to be unfair and arbitrary that resistance emerges—which in the case of the Patriot and Militia movements can take the form of armed resistance. Consequently, federal laws have increasingly employed the language of cooperation, collaboration and coordination with local interests to improve the effectiveness of federal authority and to minimize resistance.

Increasingly language found in federal land and environmental legislation includes specific requirements mandating collaborative, participative democracy by promoting deliberative community decision making. Chief among those federal environmental laws stipulating community involvement and deliberation is the 2009 Collaborative Forest Landscape Restoration Program (CFLRP), the National Environmental Protection Act (NEPA), the Clean Water Act (CWA), the Surface Mining Control and Restoration Act (SMCR), the Healthy Forests Restoration Act (HFRA), and the Forest Landscape Restoration Act (FLRA) (Brown 2015; Houck 2014; Sweeney, 2013; Babcock 2008). These laws each embody what has come to be known as "cooperative federalism" where "federal and state governments share some degree of regulatory authority" (Sweeney 2013; Weiser 2003).

This state/federal cooperation emerged in the 1970's when Congress passed a sizeable number of environmental laws asserting a national interest in issues associated with land, air and water resources in each state. While states were deemed to be the stewards of natural resources, responsible for their conservation as well as protecting wildlife, national interests were also at stake, particularly regarding air, water and wildlife that crossed state boundaries. Consequently, a cooperative approach to federalism emerged.

The first federal law embodying cooperative federalism was the National Environmental Protection Act (NEPA) (1970) that mandated public hearings and meetings before new environmental regulations can be implemented. Since then federal approaches to involving the public in federal decisions and actions has evolved to include small group, one-on-one interactions and surveys. In so doing the legislative intent is that a shared vision will emerge, engendering trust and fully and open communication (Emerson et al. 2007).

This shared regulatory approach differs somewhat depending upon the federal law involved. For instance, the Surface Mining Control and Reclamation Act (SMCRA) gives states the exclusive authority to regulate surface mining and the Federal government provides minimum oversight. Comparatively, the CWA presents a more restrictive form of federalism, in part because federal regulatory oversight depends upon whether surface waters are navigable (or drain into navigable waters) which in many cases means they cross state boundaries. (Sweeney & Armstrong

2013). However, the principle reason federal responsibility is defined more extensively than state authority is because historically the states have consistently failed over at least a 25-year period to clean up the nation's waters on their own. Therefore, federal latitude in cooperative federalism is much more proscribed regarding the CWA than is the case for other environmental laws (Houck 2014).

As with other environmentally oriented federal legislation, the Healthy Forests Restoration Act (2003) and the Forest Landscape Restoration Act (2009) provide "an open and inclusive process through which two or more individuals or organizations work together to address a problem/issue that concerns them all and that no one of them is likely to be able to resolve alone" (Brown 2015, 2). This approach is increasingly being applied to natural resource management and restorations programs nationwide—with groups like the Blue Mountain Forest Partners exemplifying the virtues of such a model. In fact, one of the principal architects of collaborative practice nationwide is attorney Susan Jane Brown of the Western Environmental Law Center who also serves as Vice Chair of the BMFP board.

Having worked with numerous forest restoration collaboratives (such as the Four Forests Restoration Initiative, Southwest Crown of the Continent, and Selway-Middle Fork Clearwater Collaborative), Brown asserts that as communities successfully employ collaborative approaches and reap their benefits, they engender a "spill-over" effect that is soon applied to other related areas such as landscape prioritization, project area identification, prescriptive development and more. However, Brown cautions that collaborative approaches can be controversial—as will be discussed regarding the BMFP effort. In fact, she counsels all communities considering collaborative approaches to forest management to recognize that,

> "As part of the democratic process associated with the management of public lands owned by all Americans, all citizens have the fundamental right to disagree with federal land managers and their collaborative partners about whether a particular project should be implemented. Consequently, Congress created administrative and judicial review processes to allow dissatisfied stakeholders an opportunity to be heard, and to advocate for a different course of action than that proposed by federal land managers" (Brown 2015, 2)

Excessive Federal Reach

While cooperation and compromise are the ideal products of collaborative efforts, they are often compromised politically, economically and interpersonally. This is particularly true when local authorities find their legal authority largely co-opted by state and federal agencies. Exemplary of such imbalances in power and authority are the ongoing criticisms emanating from state and local officials and other environmental stakeholders asserting that Federal agencies tend to overstep their authority (Adler 2007). The controversial cases involving the Hage, Hammond and Bundy ranches are illustrative of the degree to which such perceived over-assertion of federal authority can promote resistance and violence. The emergence of the Militia and Patriot movements also speak to the degree to which many in the West have come to question the authority federal environmental, land, air and water regulation.

In some cases, those resisting strong federal environmental control assert that federal agencies are acting beyond their constitutional authority, which they argue puts authority for environmental and conservation issues squarely in the hands of the states and their citizens and not the federal government (Tribe 2015; Johnson 2006; Kidd 2005; Adler 2005). At the heart of the issue is the question of which branch of government has authority over wildlife and natural resources residing within the boundaries of the various states. Per one environmental law scholar "Congress has not been granted the power to legislate in the name of all that is good" only having a set of "enumerated powers" specified in the constitution (Johnson 2006, 77). Consequently, when Congress grants ever-expansive authority over the environment and natural resources to federal agencies they inevitably invite constitutional challenges.

Of all the federal regulation promulgated by Congress, virtually none raises questions relative to the distributed authority of states and the federal government the way environmental regulations do. As constitutional scholar Jonathan Adler observes,

> "Environmental regulation arguably represents the most ambitious and far-reaching assertion of federal regulatory authority. The very premise of much environmental regulation is that ubiquitous ecological interconnections require broad, if not all-encompassing, federal regulation" (Adler 2005).

Without question, nature's intricacies resist constitutionally derived regulatory definitions and boundaries. As ecologist David Orr notes, there is a "mismatch between the way nature works in highly connected and interactive systems and the fragmentation of powers built into the Constitution" (Orr 2003, 1479). For Orr, and other like-minded environmentalists the Constitution is an impediment to environmental progress. Consequently, they would like to re-write the Constitution to allow for more Federal discretion in environmental matters—irrespective of state assertions of constitutional authority (Orr 2014).

Orr's sentiments, however, are not shared by many who consider the bulk of federal authority to have been unconstitutionally acquired. Rather than seeing the role of the federal government additionally strengthened, they would prefer devolving federal control back to what they perceive to be the rightful recipients of such power—the various states and "the people" as represented by state legislatures (Madsen 2016; Hawkins 2016; Fretwell & Regan 2015; Oates 2001; Hedge & Scicchitano 1992). Like sentiments are also reflected throughout the Western U.S. by advocates like the American Lands Council and the American Land Rights Association who favor transferring public lands back to the states. People who support such action associate themselves with the "TPL Movement" ("transfer public land") (Fretwell & Regan 2015; Haun 2015; Duara 2015).

Between Kowtowing and Conflict: Pragmatic Cooperation and Collaboration

Given these conditions, federal managers, local officials, citizens and stakeholders of all varieties find themselves in a turbulent environment. Either they risk excessive compliance to federal regulations and the seemingly arbitrary administration of those regulations or they exert resistance to federal rules to include civil disobedience and in the case of the Malheur occupation take up arms—if even to do so defensively. In the interest of not steering in the direction of either extreme course, most pragmatic stakeholders seek a middle course between kowtowing and conflict.

In *Ecopragmatics* (Wimberley & Pellegrino 2015), the authors specify that one of the essential requirement for collaboratively and pragmatically addressing policy issues is the need to effectively keep the "wing-nuts" (i.e. those holding inflexible and intransient opinions) away from the negotiation table and work with the "responsibles"—those people within local communities who will employ compromise and collaboration to improve conditions in their local communities. Those who fruitfully pursue truly cooperative collaboration take this principle to heart. Their motivations are typically "civic-oriented," and "outcome-oriented." Among those "responsibles" actively pursuing the promotion of cooperative community goals, idealism is a luxury that cannot be afforded and inaction a cost that cannot long be born.

Oregonians have demonstrated their pragmatism by generally concluding that cooperation and coordination is a necessity since more than half of the state's lands are federally owned and the state's economic and social needs are inextricably tied to the management and productivity derived from those lands. Such cooperation is perhaps best exemplified by an act of the Oregon legislature to create a unique center at Portland State University called The National Policy Consensus Center whose mission entails advancing "the use of innovative collaborative governance methods in Oregon and nationally by providing collaboration services, university courses, professional training, and research" (NPCC 2016). The Center promotes public deliberation specializing in policy issues that are:

- Inherently complex or controversial to include issues where not only the solutions to problems are complex but the very nature of the problem itself is complex and disputable, or regarding
- Issues where public (and arguably private) interests are involved and where stakeholder groups will need a broad public consensus to have their interests reflected in policy outcomes (NPCC 2010).

To accomplish these ends, NPCC developed several state and federal programs. Those programs most pertinent to Oregon and its environmental issues include:

- ***Oregon Solutions***: "Oregon Solutions (OS) is a state program that works with Oregon communities to implement solutions to local problems. In general, the problem and the solution are not under debate; however, finding the local support, financial resources, and best approaches to make the solution a reality demand collaboration. OS brings businesses, government, and nonprofits together to agree on what role each will play to address a community need. OS projects must meet at least two of Oregon's three sustainability objectives, which include fostering a productive economy, an equitable community, and a healthy environment.

- ***Oregon Consensus:*** Is the state's official program for public policy dispute resolution. OC provides a neutral forum to help government bodies and their stakeholders resolve or avoid conflict around contentious public policy issues in Oregon. OC facilitates group decision-making processes through consensus-seeking rather than majority rule.

- ***Oregon Kitchen Table:*** Oregon's Kitchen Table is a state program that uses online tools to allow Oregon community members to give input to elected officials, participate in civic crowdfunding, and help build prosperity through Oregonian-to-Oregonian micro-lending. These online activities are combined with other forms of community organizing" (NPCC 2016)

From the perspective of this case study the most pertinent of these programs is Oregon Solutions since it interfaces most closely with the Blue Mountain Forest Partners.

Oregon Solutions provides a system and process for problem solving known as collaborative governance, defined as "a process whereby community leaders join forces to define a problem, agree on a solution, and collaborate towards a resolution" (Oregon Solutions 2016). This concept of course flows directly from federal environmental laws and regulations that began in 1970 with NEPA. Oregon Solutions promotes collaborative governance by convening community forums to bring stakeholders (to include business interests, nonprofits, public officials and civic leaders) into deliberation with one another in the interest at arriving at a shared consensus regarding problem identification and problem solutions. They also facilitate and coordinate a process wherein participants assume solution-oriented roles and responsibilities, collaboratively commit resources, commit to shared policies and procedures and ultimately remain organized to solve future problems and address future issues (Oregon Solutions 2011). More specifically, Oregon Solutions provides:

- A neutral forum,
- A highly respected convener,
- The ability to leverage additional resources,
- Project accountability;
- Experienced, senior-level staff (Oregon Solutions 2016).

Currently, Oregon Solutions supports more than thirty initiatives statewide. Twelve sponsored initiatives are situated in Eastern Oregon alone, of which several address an array of environmental and economic issues to include the:

- Sage Grouse Conservation Partnership,
- Columbia River-Umatilla Solutions Partnership,
- Umatilla Forest Collaborative Group,
- Western Juniper Alliance,
- Wallowa County Sustainable Forestry,
- Hands on Lands,
- Harney County Restoration Collaboration;

- Milton Freewater Levee (Oregon Solutions, 2016).

Among these initiatives, the Harney County Restoration Collaborative (HCRC) is most pertinent since it is sponsored in part by the Blue Mountain Forest Partners. HCRC represents a partnership of non-profits, governmental agencies, citizens and business interests seeking to improve local forest landscape and resources to ultimately stimulate the local economy. The collaborative emerged following decades of economic decline in Harney County. Over a 40-year period, Harney County slipped from being one of the most economically prosperous counties in Oregon to being one of the poorest as the national economy slumped and with it a decline in demand for lumber by the nation's building industry. At its economic pinnacle, lumber accounted for a third of the local economy, yet by 2016 it accounted for a negligible portion. By 2009 Harney County's unemployment rate reached 17% and by 2012 two-thirds of county school children qualified for the federal school lunch program (Young 2016).

The forces behind this prolonged and seemingly permanent economic downturn are numerous and interrelated including,

1. Increased unprocessed log exports;
2. Overcutting of private timberlands matched by decreased cutting on public lands;
3. A prolonged decline in the housing market reducing demand for lumber;
4. Increased automated milling producing production efficiencies with decreased labor;
5. Efficiency driven timber-processing capacity (Kerr 2013, 2).

Events beginning in the 1980's were particularly contributory to the region's economic woes as a record volume of timber was cut across the Pacific Northwest and an unprecedented proportion of this harvest was exported as unprocessed logs overseas to Asian markets. Beginning in 1990 Japan's economy began a period of prolonged stagnation while in the U.S. a housing and financial debacle depressed the nation's building industry. Both trends decreased the volume of timber being processed in American timber mills. Nowhere was the impact of these forces felt more forcefully than in Eastern Oregon (Kerr 2012a).

The net effect of these forces and events is that Eastern Oregon was left with depleted forest reserves, a decreased volume of milled logs, persistently high unemployment, and a diminished local and state tax base coupled with an increase in demand for governmental services and public employment. These forces and their seeming permanence served in part to fuel radicalism—as portrayed in the Malheur Refuge occupation. However, they also motivated frustrated and disparate stakeholders to jump-start the local economy by regenerating timber reserves on public and private land and reinvesting in timber related industries who. They did so fully recognizing that the contemporary timber industry required a smaller workforce given increased efficiencies in timber management, harvesting and processing. Consequently, while they anticipated their efforts would stimulate employment, the recognized that it would only do so marginally in Harney County and the surrounding region.

HCRC was conceived and designed to address complex and persistent forest and community problems confronting the county. Its goals include:

- Forest restoration and the reintroduction of natural ecosystems and processes
- An improved economy based in part upon a revitalized timber industry
- Improved and targeted effectiveness and efficiency of federal initiatives administered by federal agencies on site in the county and state
- An enhanced willingness and capacity for local communities to engage in problem-solving
- Developing and sustaining improved environmental, economic and community conditions and outcomes;
- Developing plans and practices for the future to continue cooperative efforts indefinitely (HCRC 2016).

After only four years following its creation, HCRC successfully secured an important grant in 2012 to restore the forests in the Blue Mountain area. This grant from the Collaborative Forest Restoration Landscape Restoration Program (CFLRP) (a program established by Congress in 2009 as Title IV of the Omnibus Public Land Management Act of 2009) was designed to

- "Encourage ecological, economic, and social sustainability;
- Leverage local resources with national and private resources;
- Facilitate the reduction of wildfire management costs, including through re-establishing natural fire regimes and reducing the risk of uncharacteristic wildfire;
- Demonstrate the degree to which various ecological restoration techniques achieve ecological and watershed health objectives, and,
- Encourage utilization of forest restoration by-products to offset treatment costs, to benefit local rural economies, to and improve forest health" (USDA 2012).

HCRC and BMFP teamed to win this federal grant from the U.S. Department of Agriculture and the Forest Service to tackle issues of economic stimulation, employment, deforestation and wildfire prevention. Their joint effort - known as the Southern Blues Restoration Coalition (SBRC or "Southern-Blues")—created 320 new jobs within a three-year period, improved 572 miles of road, reduced wildfire hazards on 68,581 acres of forest land, restored 15,687 acres of forest and generated 264,726 CCF (CCF means "hundred cubic feet") of timber sales (Brown 2016).

The rationale for funding SBRC was based upon the reality that the local economy consists principally of timber and ranching - both of which require access to vast stretches of forest and forage. Since 60% of county land was either federally owned or managed, there was little hope of either stimulating the county's timber and ranching economy or restoring and protecting the forest and ranchland environment short of entering a cooperative and collaborative relationship with the federal government to get better access to federal timber and grazing. Since USDA had funds available to achieve some of the economic and environmental needs of the community, it was only reasonable that a group of local stakeholders decided to come together to obtain federal dollars needed to address persistent local problems. It is interesting to note, however that in pursuing this funding source for Harney County the applicants acknowledged their efforts occurred within the context of a "history of conflict and litigation" that served to virtually halt all commercially viable activity on federal lands, principally because federal lands had been so thoroughly abused and exploited over the years that they would no long support a robust economy. What emerged was a rationale for economic and environmental development that in its simplest form suggests that ongoing economic activity in the forests and on rangeland requires an ongoing program of restoration and conservation (Brown 2016).

If all proceeds as well in the future as it must the present, SBRC leadership anticipates that,

> "At the end of the ten-year period, we will have restored the aquatic and terrestrial ecosystem to a functional condition with greater ecological resilience to disturbance and created a predictable flow of work that retains current manufacturing infrastructure, supports new and emerging markets, and produces local economic benefits" (Brown 2016).

By 2016, the Southern-Blues succeeded in increasing their annual grant from USDA from $2.5 million to $4 million which continues until the project ends in 2022. To date the project has been particularly successful in the Malheur National Forest region of the Blue Mountains where Forest Service officials report that targets for timber production have tripled since the grant was first awarded—making the Malheur National Forest the only national forest to do so (Hart 2016a).

Blue Mountain Forest Partners Membership

The economic and restoration progress occurring within the Malheur National Forest would not have occurred had it not been for the existence of the Blue Mountain Forest Partners. While the Harney County Restoration Collaborative sprung from the efforts of Oregon Solutions out of Portland State University and was funded with USDA money from the Collaborative Forest Restoration Landscape Restoration Program (CFLRP), the Blue Mountain Forest Partners principally developed out of common need and deprivation in Grant County Oregon. The group was convened around 2006 under the auspices of the Portland-based nonprofit Pacific Northwest whose mission involves bringing "people, ideas, and innovations together so that nature, local economies and rural communities can thrive" (Pacific Northwest 2016). In the case of Grant County, Oregon Pacific Northwest could not have possibly found a better mission-match nor a more willing partner.

The Blue Mountain Forest Partners (BMFP) mission was to "create and implement a shared vision to improve the resilience and well-being of forests and communities in the Blue Mountains" (Webb 2016). BMFP director Mark Webb was passionate about collaborating with other stakeholders to achieve common goals, believing that,

"Collaboration is really the only way to work through the legal and legislative frameworks that are currently in place. And it is the best way for rural communities like mine to have a meaningful say and role in public lands management and decision making" (Pacific Northwest 2016).

BMFP was in part motivated to organize in response to the long period of economic decline the county had experienced over more than a decade. Compounding these economic problems was the loss of timber resources due to local wildfires as well as the imposition of a "21-Inch Rule" by the Pacific Northwest Forest Plan that restricted harvesting large trees, thereby radically reducing available timber for local mills (Antuma et al. 2014).

BMFP leaders were also concerned by the degraded state of local forests and rangelands following years of over-harvesting and poor land management. This systematic resource mismanagement robbed the county of the resources needed for economic and environmental revival. Since the county's natural resources principally involved timber and ranching, BMFP saw no reasonable way to turn their community around without simultaneously engaging in environmental restoration and economic development. Key to this process was better forest management.

Since 60% of the county's land was either federally owned or managed, forest management unavoidably involved creating collaborative partnerships with federal agencies. Consequently, one of the early obstacles challenging BMFP was achieving consensus within a community leery of cooperating with federal agencies. Doing so involved convincing the community that a better economy was unavoidably linked to forest restoration through better forest management which of necessity could only be realized by working closely with community stakeholders and federal agencies.

Given the historical community suspicion and distrust that had been simmering for generations regarding BLM and the Forest Service the partners were not surprised to encounter resistance among some quarters at the prospects of cooperation with the "feds." Likewise, it was not immediately obvious to many in the community that the county's economic doldrums were inextricably linked to poor forest management practices thus requiring forest and range restoration before economic prosperity related to timber and ranching could be realized. All of this is to say that the efforts of the BMFP was not positively received by all—nor is it today (Webb 2016).

The BMFP collaborative effort has been described by observers as notably successful due to low membership turnover and the degree to which Forest Service staff living and working in the community realized a dual identity as federal agents and as local consumers and citizens. This dual identification with role and residence lent a common purpose to their involvement in the partnership. The success of the partnership has been additionally enhanced by the strong leadership and mentorship the partners received from the outset from Pacific Northwest and other environmental organizations (Antuma et al. 2014).

Figure 15 identifies BMFP membership and Figure 16 illustrates how membership is connected to various sectors within the community. These illustrations suggest that stakeholder associations with BMFP involve a wide constituency reflecting the major political and economic interests in the community, a wide and diverse group of forest and environmental experts and key community interests. Initially as BMFP stakeholders conferred they tended to cluster based upon common interests and stakeholder group. However, as they proceeded in their work, they reorganized and integrated, finding common cause that fostered teamwork (Antuma et al, 2014).

As one participant noted, if an observer attempted to identify the different stakeholders among the membership: "You really wouldn't know. We're intermixed. We're laughing. We're talking. It's really a change. It's a great atmosphere" (Antuma 2014, p. 49). This enthusiasm and collegiality energized BMFP's efforts as they sought to restore some 700,000 acres during the lifespan of their organization. To date each organizational project success has bred enthusiasm for the next, as another member noted, "Since the collaboration, I mean our very first project, each one builds. We're being more creative, and we're getting more acres covered. So, it's been huge" (Antuma 2014, p. 49).

BMFP's initial effort involved restoring 7,200 acres of depleted forest reserves around Dad's Creek in the John Day Basin. It took the group three years just to reach agreement on pursuing this project which involved several issues to include fire suppression, riparian restoration and revitalization of the native trout population throughout the John Day River tributary system. Three years later in 2013 BLMP was involved in four additional restoration projects encompassing 117,000 additional acres of forest land (Eidger 2013).

One of the strategies employed by BMFP that has proved particularly successful is the creation of 501(c)3 nonprofit organizations to attract external funding and to finance the partnership's activities (Antuma 2014, 59). BMFP efforts in Harney County to assist in creating their collaborative as well as their cooperative work to set up the "Southern Blues" are illustrative of such efforts. Accordingly regarding the "Southern Blues" project BMFP cooperatively manages with the Harney County Restorative, each organization insists on maintaining their independent identity and autonomy despite being in neighboring counties working within the Malheur National Forest. Their resistance is based upon the fact that each county has a unique stakeholder base. Consequently, each resist merging into a single nonprofit to avoid a clash of cultures. Also, the two organizations employ different decision rules with the BMFP utilizing majority voting while the Harney group relies upon consensus. Therefore, these two groups cooperate informally on a consensus basis only when the need to do so arises, otherwise, they work independently (Antuma 2014).

Ranching

Clark Cattle Co.

Forestry & Restoration Industry

American Forest Resources Council
Backlund Logging
Boise Cascade
DR Johnson Lumber
*Greyback Forestry
Iron Triangle
*King, Inc.
*Malheur Lumber Company

Public Natural Resource Management

Grant County Public Forest Commission
N. Fork John Day Watershed Council
Oregon Department of Fish and Wildlife
Oregon Department of Forestry

US Forest Service

Blue Mountains Restoration Strategy ID Team
Malheur National Forest
*Malheur National Forest Blue Mountain RD
Malheur National Forest-Prairie City RD
National Headquarters (Washington Office)
Pacific Northwest Research Station
Wallowa-Whitman National Forest

Environmental/Conservation

Blue Mountains Biodiversity Project
Defenders of Wildlife
Oregon Wild
*Western Environmental Law Center

Research, Education, Extension

National Forest Foundation
Oregon State University
Sustainable Northwest
Univ. of Oregon-Ecosystem Workforce Project
University of Washington

Local, Regional, State Government

Grant County
Senator Ron Wyden's office

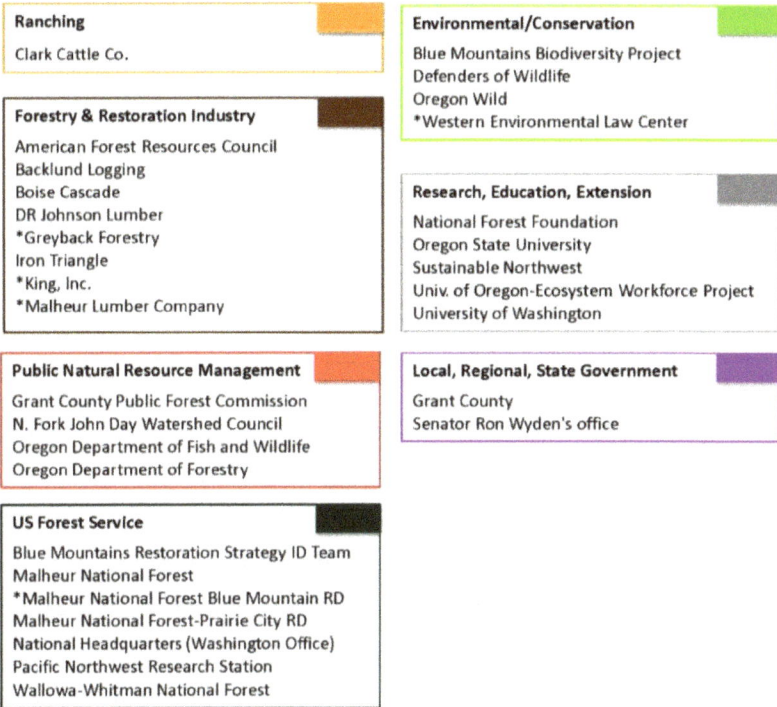

Figure 15: Blue Mountain Forest Partners Membership
(Source: McClain, et al. 2015)

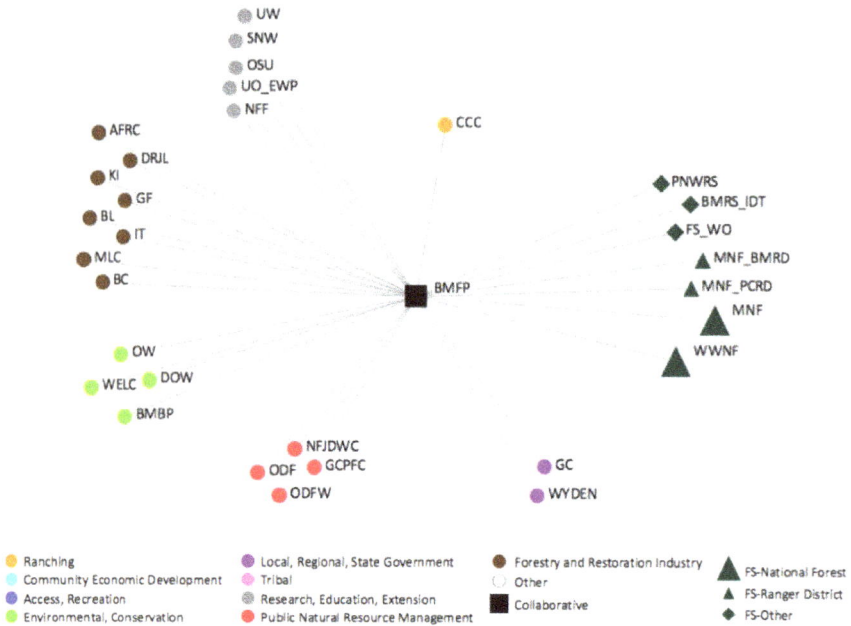

Figure 16: BMFP Membership Community Networks
(Source: McClain, et al. 2015)

While BMFP is clearly interested in the environment for its own sake and has been involved in restoring forest, ranch and riparian areas, their principle goal is socio-economic and their pursuit of restorative and environmental projects is tangential to that goal. As two of the group's former board members noted,

> "We're not doing it for ecological reasons and we're fully aware of that. We're not trying to hide that fact. We're doing it because we feel there is a need from an economic and social standpoint" and "I think our environmental groups recognize that part of the collaborative and part of the goals of the unit are social and economic, and we were put into the situation that this salvage is going to have to occur" (Antuma 2014, 99).

This emphasis upon creating economic prosperity and jobs is particularly directed toward the lumber mills in the region.

For instance, John Day, Oregon once supported three mills. Today, however, only the Malheur Lumber Company remains in business and at one point recently it too threatened to close for lack of timber throughput from local forests. Fortunately, the Blue Mountain Forest Partners via the "Southern Blues" managed to keep it in business by sending the mill salvaged logs from their restoration activities—fire damaged logs that otherwise might have gone to waste—as well as smaller timber that is cut to thin-out timber stands. In fact, the degree to which BMFP has been successful should be considered within the context of an era where federal budget cuts curtailed work throughout the entire National Forest System. BMPP's principal accomplishment in this regard is that it has tripled federal funding in Grant and Harney counties (Antuma 2014, 99).

BMFP Board Membership and Organization:

BMFP has organized for success with a flexible model illustrated in Figure 17. BMFP staff are numerically limited in their representation on the board consisting of the executive director (Mark Webb, former Grant County Judge) and a set of investigators and staff associated with the Collaborative Forest Landscape Restoration Program (CFLRP)—a total of six staff, four of whom are associated with Oregon State University along with two Forest Service staff. By employing this model, administrative overhead is kept low and the influence of the "partners" is enhanced. Of the 30 plus partners involved in BMFP, most participate in the organization via membership on one or more deliberative committees (fundraising, economic and project committees) along with an ad-hoc committee addressing issues not confined to any other standing committee. BMFP is also organized to accommodate other committees as needed. The throughput from these various committees is ultimately shared with all the partners to develop consensus and organizational direction.

Staff

Full Group

Ad hoc activity committee

Operations Committee

Fundraising Committee

Other committees as needed

Economic Committee

Project Committees

Staff: logistics, facilitation, coordination

Full group: participate in meetings and committees; elects Operations Committee, | overall collaborative decision-making, defines strategic priorities

Operations Committee: Works with staff; meeting planning, leadership on strategic priorities, liaison to full group, work with committee chairs, budget management, media liaison.

Other committees – develop and design initiatives, makes recommendations to full group.

Figure 17: Organizational Chart—Blue Mountain Forest Partners
(Source: Eidger, 2013)

Ultimate direction for the partnership however rests in a seven-member board of directors (Figure 18) chaired by Mike Billman of Malheur Lumber Company in John Day, Oregon and co-chaired by Susan Jane Brown, staff attorney with the Western Environmental Law Center in Eugene, Oregon. The remaining board includes an environmental representative (Pam Hardy of Oregon Wild), representatives from two local forest product businesses (Dave Hannibal, base manager of Grayback Forestry, Inc. in Merlin, Oregon and Glen Johnston of Backlund Logging Company from the county seat of Canyon City), a private forester and rancher (Roje Gootee, owner of 3,083 acres of forest and range land situated in the Blue Mountains on the Rush Creek Ranch) and a real estate broker (Zach Williams of King, Inc., in Canyon City).

Although representing interests in a very sparsely populated area of the West, the caliber of the board members is remarkable. For instance, Dr. Gootee (who has a Ph.D. in Environment and Natural Resources) also sits on the board of the National Forest Foundation. Susan Jane Brown is a recognized legal expert in forest management collaboration—which may explain why a collaborative approach to deliberation has been so fruitfully applied to this collaborative effort (Brown 2015). Beyond her considerable expertise in cooperative and collaborative management, she has served as legal counsel to Congressman Peter DeFazio (D-OR) and twice co-chaired the Federal Advisory Committee on the National Forest Management Act at the request of the Secretary of Agriculture. Mike Billman represents one of the principal employers in the area representing a company that may well have closed had it not been for the efforts of BMFP. Prior to joining Malheur Lumber, Billman served as coordinator of the Federal Forest Health Program of the Oregon Department of Forestry. Pam Hardy of Oregon Wild is also an attorney who sits on several collaborative forestry advisory groups (the Deschutes, Ochoco and Malheur National Forest collaborative groups) as well as serving on the Steens Mountain Advisory Council.

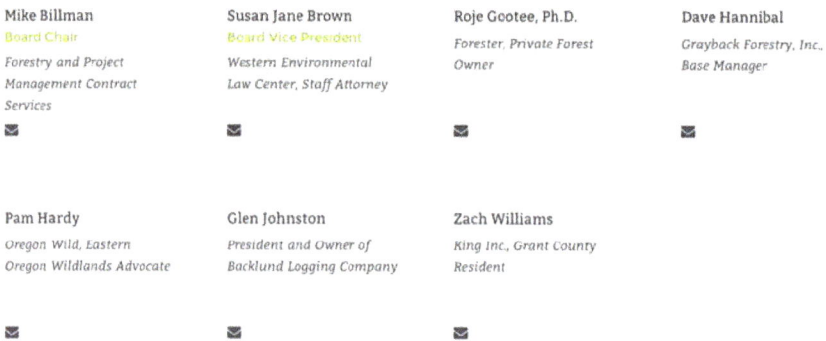

Mike Billman	Susan Jane Brown	Roje Gootee, Ph.D.	Dave Hannibal
Board Chair	Board Vice President		
Forestry and Project Management Contract Services	Western Environmental Law Center, Staff Attorney	Forester, Private Forest Owner	Grayback Forestry, Inc., Base Manager
✉	✉	✉	✉
Pam Hardy	Glen Johnston	Zach Williams	
Oregon Wild, Eastern Oregon Wildlands Advocate	President and Owner of Backlund Logging Company	King Inc., Grant County Resident	
✉	✉	✉	

Figure 18: BMFP Board of Directors
(Source: BMFP 2015)

Community Conflict

While the board of directors and partner membership of BMFP have been clearly successful in their efforts at reforestation, environmental restoration and economic development, their efforts have been frustrated in several ways. As Brown (2015) warned, collaboration is often accompanied by resistance and conflict. Chief among those resisting the efforts of BMFP is the Grant Count Public Forest Commission which is vocal in their opposition to BMFP's Elk 16 project.

The Grant County Public Forest Commission (GCPFC) was established via a county referendum in 2002 to "prescribe actions to promote the efficient beneficial and timely stewardship of public lands and resources." Commission members are elected to represent the citizenry in protecting and promoting of forest land. Per the Commission their mission is based upon the principle that "forest health is paramount to our natural environment, including watersheds, wildlife habitat, fisheries, native ecosystems, timber production, grazing and other beneficial activities" (Grant County Public Forest Commission, 2015).

The Commission became particularly concerned regarding Elk Restoration Area 16, a 43,000-acre forest parcel located along a forest road corridor near Prairie City, Oregon. Their concern emanated from a 2015 Forest Service finding regarding proposed restoration activities targeting forest ecosystems, watersheds and aquatic habitats (Blue Mountain Eagle 2015; Gubel 2011). What made the finding controversial was its impact upon several logging roads that were scheduled to be decommissioned and closed (Blue Mountain Eagle 2015). These closings generated a sharp objection from the Grant Count Public Forest Commission.

The Forest Commission, which consists of nine elected officials, objected to the Forest Service's 2015 finding by asserting that (1) public recreational access will be arbitrarily compromised by eliminating roads routinely used by ATV enthusiasts, and (2) timber interests will be harmed by closing roads utilized by loggers, thereby reducing timber harvests and further depressing an already depressed local economy. The Forest Commission noted that roads scheduled to be closed in riparian areas had been stabilized for some time and did not need to be closed to promote riparian quality. The commission likewise criticized plans to thin forests to reduce fire hazards as being excessively minimal and ineffective while asking the Forest Service to improve access to fire-damage timber so that recoverable timber could be harvested and marketed (Grant County Public Forest Commission 2015, 1).

The GCPFC objections put them at odds with BMFP who championed the Elk 16 project. In fact, the Forest Commission could be construed as a competitive voice regarding the future of forest management in the county. Some, including former County Judge Mark Webb, argued that GCPFC had no legal standing regarding oversight of timber on federal and state land. In 2016 Webb, as executive director of BMFP, joined four other BMFP board members and ran for positions on the GCPFC with the intent of shutting the commission down. These five argued that the commission's mission, which included the role of coordinating the federal management of public land on behalf of the county, had no legal standing since the bulk of the lands fell under state and federal authority. From Webb's and the BMFP perspective the actions of the commission "will never be enforced or implemented, such that it's unreasonable to treat it as a valid, legally binding county ordinance" (Hart 2016b).

The actions of controversial Grant County Sherriff Glenn Palmer further complicated the relationship between the BMFP and GCPFC. As discussed in the preceding chapter, in 2016 Palmer garnered national notoriety after inserting himself and his office into to the Malheur National Wildlife occupation in adjacent Harney County. In so doing, Palmer identified himself with the interests of the Patriot

Movement and the occupiers. Because of his actions Palmer forfeited the confidence of some of his staff, local governmental and civic leaders" (Neiwert 2016).

Prior to this incident (in 2015) Palmer managed to generate controversy in Grant county regarding the proper role of the sheriff relative to the coordination of federal agencies managing public forests with local county governments. From the perspective of the Constitutional Sherriff and Peace Officers Association (CSPOA) to which Palmer belonged, the first line of defense in preserving the citizen's constitutional rights was the county sheriff. To that end, Sheriff Palmer inserted himself into the issue of "who" manages the national forests in his county by noting that under several federal laws (previously discussed) federal agencies such as BLM and the Forest Service must collaborate and cooperate with local officials in exercising their federal management responsibilities. Since a significant portion of this federal/county interface pertained to responding to wildfires—a role that the sheriff's office was very much involved in from a public safety perspective—Palmer argued that his office played a legitimate role as a component of local government that was appropriate to be involved in assuming the local liaison role with BLM and the Forest Service. (Zaitz 2016).

Palmer deputized 11 local citizens to write what would be known as the Grant County Public Lands Natural Resources Plan (Neiwert 2016). Several of these freshly recruited "deputies" were associated with a local organization named Citizens for Public Access dedicated to "the retention of all forms of public access in Grant County and Eastern Oregon" (Plaven 2015). The Grant County Public Lands Natural Resources Plan (which was never considered by county officials) asserted that "Grant County will not support federal and state agencies on land management decisions when the social and economic impact is not carefully considered" (Plaven 2015). Palmer's abortive effort to influence forest plan management in Grant County, beyond kowtowing to members of Citizens for Public Access, served to further complicate the relationship between the BMFP and the Forest Commission (Wilson 2016).

Former County Judge Mark Webb (now director of the BMFP) disagreed with Sheriff Palmer's efforts to insert himself and his office into land and natural resource management decisions in Grant County (Selsky 2016). Webb's regulatory interpretation of mandatory federal-state-local coordination involved the interaction of legislative entities at the state and local levels with federal agencies. At the state level the pertinent legislative entity is the legislature and at the county level it is the board of county commissioners acting on behalf of voters. Moreover, in many Western counties the county judge is also a legislative officer since he/she sits on the county commission as it's chair.

At the municipal level the legislative function falls to the city or town council that is often chaired by an elected mayor. Since the Forest Commission was not a legislative entity within county government, Webb argued that it should not be called upon to coordinate or collaborate with the U.S. Forest Service (Selsky 2016). The same rationale likewise applies to the County Sheriff's Office since its mission is principally to enforce the law—not enact it. Since the Sheriff's Office is not legislative in function, Webb argues that it ineligible to play the collaborative liaison role with federal agencies (Webb 2016).

While existing federal law mandates state and local collaboration and coordination, federal regulations don't clearly delineate which local units of government are involved. In the absence of such clear language Sheriff Palmer relied upon the State of Oregon's definition which includes "all cities, counties and local service districts" as well as "all administrative subdivisions of those cities, counties and local service districts" (ORS 174.116). He argued that the county sheriff's office clearly falls within this definition (Plaven 2015). This put Palmer at odds with Judge Webb's nuanced "legislative" interpretation.

Currently, it would appear that there is no distinct entity within Grant County officially assuming the federal/state coordination role. Since wildfires greatly impact the efforts of the county sheriff, Palmer argues his agency should be the liaison. Former County Judge Mark Webb disagrees and suggests this would be a good role for the County Judge who chairs the county commission. Alternately, the Grant County Public Forest Commission sees itself as the logical body to serve as federal liaison and local coordinator.

Clearly, while the work BMFP does has been very beneficial to Grant County Oregon, there appears to be a vacuum in leadership at the county level to assume an appropriate collaborative and cooperative role relative to the U.S. Forest Service. The product of that vacuum of leadership is a competition for authority and control between the sheriff's office and the Forest Commission. While the BMFP is not officially functioning as the county's coordination liaison with the Forest Service, the fact that it is collaborating with this agency at a time when the county appears to have not clarified an official county liaison role tends to open the organization up to some criticism that otherwise might not have been forthcoming.

For instance, specific criticism has been arisen in local newspapers involving potential conflicts of interest between some BMFP partners and the Forest Commission (George 2016, Hudson 2016). In fact, one Forest Commission member, Nicky A. Sprauve, has been pointedly critical of BMFP director Mark Webb and four other BMFP partners commenting that

> "When you have five members of the Blue Mountains Forest Partners running to get on the Public Forest Commission, it looks as though you are trying to stack the Public Forest Commission (an elected body of commissioners) with people who have an agenda from an outside organization that is opposed to the interest of the voters of Grant County. I have heard that Mark Webb receives about $50,000 to $60,000 a year to be the chairman of the Blue Mountains Forest Partners, so it might not be a legal conflict of interest, but it sure looks to me like a moral conflict of interest, to you the voters of this great county. The interest of the two organizations are diametrically opposed to each other. These five individuals [from BMFP], if elected, would tip the power to the agenda of the Blue Mountains Forest Partners. Think about it! "(Sprauve 2016).

Conceivably, the work of the Forest Commission and BMFP need not be oppositional but instead collaborative and complimentary. Nonetheless, in small communities with competitive political interests it is easy to imagine how the mission and intent of BMFP and its participants could be misconstrued within the political climate of a small, stressed rural community in Eastern Oregon.

It is worth remembering that while Mark Webb has been quoted as asserting that "collaboration is really the only way to work through the legal and legislative frameworks that are currently in place" (Sprauve, 2016) Webb and other members of the BMFP have become involved in litigation, seeking to either clarify the Forest Commission's its authority and either render it effective in pursuing its mission or disband it if it serves no legally legitimate public service. At the present, a dysfunctional Forrest Commission is an impediment to the work of BMFP. However, Webb and others continued seeking to remove that impediment at the ballot box and in court in the interest of resolving the issue of who in county government will assume its complimentary collaborative role with the Forest Service and other federal agencies. On September 14, 2016, the jurisdictional issue was finally resolved when Grant County Judge William D. Cramer, Jr. ruled that2002 referendum that created the commission that "conflicts with paramount law in both the State of Oregon and federally" (Hart 2016c).

The "Responsibles" in Grant County

In *Ecopragmatics* (2014), authors Edward Wimberley and Scott Pellegrino described those who address community issues and collaborate with others to solve them as the "responsibles" of the community. In so doing they asserted that it is from among these community leaders that change happens locally. When it comes to community involvement regarding local socio-economic and environmental issues the "responsibles" may represent those who have a personal or financial stake in local issues, or may involve those whose principal interest is philosophical and primarily concerned with conserving natural resources despite their economic value. BMFP encompasses both groups in a creative and effective way. Unfortunately, Grant County government still awaits similar collaboration from among its "responsibles."

Public interest research suggests that typically, the stakeholders most willing to become involved in issues of public land management are those with an intent to use the land (i.e. "responsibles" with a financial stake) as compared to those "responsibles" whose principal desire is to conserve natural resources. Accordingly,

> "When there is a conflict over the use of public land, those who want to be able to use the land for agriculture or resource extraction have strong financial and often cultural incentives to put significant pressure on public officials. In contrast, supporters of the conservation of public lands—while larger in number—may be far less motivated to take action on the issue. The data show that farmers and ranchers—and even oil, coal, and mining companies—have great credibility with the Western voting public. If the fight comes down to pitting these interests against "environmentalists," many voters will be inclined to side with the opponents of public land conservation" (Metz, White & Weigel 2014, 13).

What this implies is that those "responsibles" within Grant County that are most likely to persevere regarding local land and natural resource management issues are those with the largest financial stake in their outcome. Since they are typically less motivated than "financial responsibles" conservationists are expected to be less influential—ultimately suggesting that financial motivations regarding the use of natural resources will typically prevail over conservation interests. Assuming this is the case, then the future of leadership in Grant County regarding forest and natural resource management will likely prioritize the county's economic needs over environmental considerations.

Assuming this is the case, then the role played locally by BMFP is vitally important since its membership appears to have found a productive way to prioritize economic *and* environmental sensibilities by assembling a diverse set of "responsibles" who don't allow their own preferences to get in the way of productive compromise. Without doubt, BMFP occupies a vital niche as a community organization with an effective track record of economic development driven by the federal desire for better forest management. Their efforts serve the needs of the Forest Service to reduce the forest biomass that fuels wildfires while the community benefits via timber jobs and regular lumber volume for the mills. A salutary outcome of BMFP's efforts is that their approach serves to meet the needs of environmentalists and businesses alike thereby completely avoiding a conflict between environmentalists and timber interests. In BMFP, "users" and "conservers" of the land have found common cause—thereby minimizing public political backlash against environmentalists. What remains is for the political forces within the county to likewise arrive at an understanding of who will represent the county's interests relative to the Forest Service.

The Role of Conflict in Collaboration:

Nevertheless, it seems all but inevitable, given the history, environment and culture of Oregon and the Pacific Northwest, that conflict and how it is managed becomes the central feature of any Western collaborative endeavor. This is, however, not a feature entirely unique to Westerners. Wherever public policy is formulated it is always created out of conflict. Conflict in public policy is not necessarily a problem. Rather it presents as an opportunity for those willing to embrace it and creatively and civilly organize to achieve cooperation, collaboration and compromise (Harper 2004).

As the State of Oregon's own Handbook for Public Policy Decision-Making and Conflict Resolution asserts:

> "Conflict is a fact of life. Actual or perceived limitations in resources, divergent or competing goals, ineffective communication, missing or erroneous information and differences in personal style are potent seeds of conflict. Although conflict is most often considered as something negative or destructive, it can have a positive side—one that promotes communication, problem solving, and positive changes for the parties involved. To be able to create positive outcomes from conflict, it is necessary to understand conflict" (Watt et al. 2000, 3).

From a pragmatic perspective understanding conflict entails not only understanding the parties to the conflict and their underlying values and motives, it also requires an appreciation that conflict is creative to the degree that it motivates people to organize and cooperate in pursuit of conflict resolution.

For instance, in a preceding case study involving a constitutional battle in Florida over the promotion of solar power, a coalition of diverse interests was created out of conflict to confront a group of concerted corporate interests—led by the state utility companies—to make solar more available and affordable statewide. The two groups did not disagree that access to solar power should be broadened and made more affordable. Their conflict involved "how" this goal would be achieved and who would benefit and/or pay.

Each stakeholder group in that case study created organizations consisting of like-minded interests and, once organized, these competing groups took their perspective on the conflict to the ballot box pursuing a Florida constitutional amendment. The "how" of their conflict led them to building grassroots stakeholder organizations, taking their case to the voters and allowing the electoral process to resolve their dispute. In this manner, each group positioned itself to pursue solar energy reform as an ongoing agenda—undoubtedly doing so based on their loyal opposition to one another's goals. However, they did so only after they organized constituencies, established principles and objectives, and pursued their goals utilizing public processes. The "how" of their disagreement serves to frame the way they relate to one another and informs "when" and by "what" means they will pursue their objectives.

In *Ecopragmatics*, similar conflicts were discussed between environmentalists and coal-powered electric utilities in Colorado, between the Georgia state utilities and the "Green Tea Coalition"—again regarding solar power—as well as between environmentalists and timber interests in the Pacific Northwest as the interests of endangered species and local economies came into conflict. Conflict—far from being foreign to ecopragmatics—is very much at the heart of its practice. Ecopragmatists are not conflict avoidant in any sense of the word. Rather, they speak to "how" conflicts are approached and resolved not "whether" they should be engaged. Ideally conflicts are resolved consensually, peacefully and democratically and in such a manner that at the end of the conflict, once-opponents can proceed anew as partners and stakeholders—even if one or more of these feel the need to identify themselves as the "loyal opposition."

One of the central tenets of ecopragmatics, beyond compromise and pursuing achievable goals incrementally, is the necessity to engage opposing stakeholders respectfully and in such a fashion that they can be fruitfully and repeatedly reengaged to address and resolve emerging issues. Equally important to ecopragmatics is the value of avoiding making enemies—especially by way of character assassinations, personal attacks and other derogatory approaches. While BMFP has done an exemplary job of modeling collaborative efforts with multiple stakeholders to improve the environmental and economic health of Grant County and surrounding areas, the conflict emerging in 2016 with local political officials regarding who will speak for the county on behalf of forest management may well result in further alienation among community leaders. It will also determine who ultimately will convene as the local governmental liaison to resolve the area's economic and environmental issues.

Extremists or what *Ecopragmatics* refers to as "wing nuts" (Wimberley & Pellegrino 2014) are unlikely to find their way to those community forums where public policy and regulations will be formulated and conflict resolved precisely because of the degree to which they alienate public discourse with their incendiary rhetoric. Unfortunately, there are many such people in Grant County who run the risk of being excluded from future public discourse, of whom County Sheriff Glenn Palmer is most illustrative. This is particularly problematic since the community has come under national scrutiny over the Malheur National Refuge occupation and the actions of the Grant County sheriff both during and after this Malheur Refuge. National media attention regarding Sheriff Palmer has served to portray the county in a controversial and uncomplimentary fashion. Moreover, the standoff at the Malheur Refuge along with the ongoing controversy surrounding Sheriff Palmer has done much to create tension within various constituencies in and around Grant and Harney Counties.

Ecopragmatic Principles Exemplified in the BMFP Case

BMFP has enjoyed success precisely because it developed a stakeholder network built upon collaborative relationships among "strange bedfellows." It successfully attracted groups that were once adversaries in the policy process (federal agencies, timber interests, environmentalists and community members) into a cooperative relationship—principally by arguing that the pursuit of environmental interests in their region was good for business and for government at all levels. To a remarkable degree BMFP organized their efforts at a grassroots level and pursued achievable rather than optimum economic and policy outcomes by not letting idealism overcome pragmatics. They have further done so by employing principles of deliberative democracy that fortunately for them had already become ingrained in state and federal policy and which was facilitated and nurtured by the presence of several effective nonprofit organizations. Finally, BMFP accomplished these goals by employing free-market economic strategies to achieve and support environmental goals and priorities—which served to increase employment while simultaneously improving the health of local forests and rangelands.

It is noteworthy that BMFP emerged as an organization from a series of conversations among an array of "*strange bedfellows*" to include environmentalists, federal officials and timber representatives. Remarkably, these conversations led to and abiding respect for one another and lasting friendships. It was this process of developing personal relationships that transformed adversaries into collaborators working in common cause with shared values. While it might be trite to say that "communication is the key" (Hodgkinson 2009), in this instance it was the basic ingredient that made everything else possible.

BMFP was born of necessity in a region principally controlled by federal landowners and manages and burdened with protracted economic decline stemming technological innovations in the timber industry, national and international economic factors, changes in timber markets, environmental pressures and federal regulatory demands. Those involved with creating and managing BMFP correctly surmised that if the local economy was going to be restored and revived it would require *grass-root initiatives and local collaboration* that reached outward and upward to state and federal agencies. BMFP effectively marshalled local resources and, with the help of several effective non-profit organizations, and linked them with state and federal programs and funding. The net effect of these collaborations was to create a local economic stimulus approach that increased timber related employment by proactively protecting the surrounding ecosystem.

Prior to the emergence of BMFP, Grant and Harney Counties were floundering in an economic morass that encouraged finger-pointing and blaming while discouraging cooperation and collaboration. This atmosphere was perpetuated by discordant stakeholder groups dedicated to narrowly realizing their personal agendas. These groups persisted in their efforts even though their idealized agendas were unresponsive to the goals of other stakeholders and in full knowledge that many of their most cherished goals such as complete environmental restoration, full employment, a robust local tax base, economic expansion etc. were unrealistic. The collaborators who organized BMFP correctly perceived the folly of interest groups pursuing unattainable "ideal" outcomes and alternately pursued workable and achievable outcomes such as marginal improvement of the environment, modest employment gains, and incremental economic growth. This process of forgoing the "ideal" in pursuit of the "achievable" is the hall mark of *satisficing communitarianism* where the welfare of the community is prioritized through the pursuit of compromise and collaboration.

Though challenged by the Grant Count Forest Commission, BMFP pursued a collaborative approach between state, federal and local entities that characterizes *deliberative democracy*. This value seems to have been deeply engrained in this community as a matter of necessity when dealing with a federal land tenet owning 60% of the county. Federal and state law had for many years recognized the inherent issues associated with local communities dominated by a federal regulatory presence. This awareness led to collaborative and cooperative requirements being introduced into a variety of state and local environmental and natural resource laws—thereby setting the stage for conversation and the negotiation of local issues and outcomes. BMFP teamed with nonprofits, state agencies and federal regulators to maximize the opportunity for local interests to voice their concerns and present the case for local environmental and economic needs. While federal guidelines ideally call for this broker role to be assumed by state and local legislative bodies (state assemblies, county commissioners, city councils etc.) BMFP successfully mediated community concerns and needs while county leadership was emerging.

BMFP emerged around a set of economic needs that began with the threat of a local lumber mill having to close its doors. It was this crisis and what it meant to Grant County that motivated County Judge Mark Webb and others to start looking for creative solutions. Throughout the process the "responsibles" in Grant County pursued market-driven solutions related to the timber industry. That they did so is hardly surprising given that this area has long been defined economically by cattle and timber. At no time was there a desire to solve local economic problems by narrowly tapping into state and federal funding. However, when it became clear to stakeholders across the ideological spectrum that *environmental needs could fuel timber-related free-market outcomes*, they did not delay in pursuing state and federal contracts that restored the regions' forest habitats while simultaneously restoring employment in the mills and in the woods.

CONCLUSION

BMFP successfully exemplified ecopragmatic problem solving by developing a broad network of responsibles, establishing cordial relationships with erstwhile adversaries and promoting and maintaining ongoing communication across the stakeholder network. Moreover, they substituted a "both-and" problem mind-set for "either-or" thinking and employed scientific research findings to inform environmental practice. These accomplishments are significant enough to be highlighted in this conclusion of the Blue Mountain Forest Partner case study.

Engaging a Network of "Responsibles"

Establishing a network of "responsibles" is inherently a two-pronged approach that involves identifying and establishing cooperative and collaborative relationships with those stakeholders in the community who value solving problems on behalf of the environment and the community (the "responsibles") *while avoiding* and *if necessary excluding* community interests who have no intent whatsoever of compromising or collaborating, instead preferring to "posture," "protest," and ultimately "prevent" collaboration and problem solving. In the Grant County case, representatives from the environmentalist community were approached by community stakeholders and conservations and negotiations began. This occurred despite agitation and criticism that emanated from a few voices in the community who by word and deed demonstrated a greater need to dominate and impose their worldview than to collaborate and arrive at a shared destination. These disruptive stakeholders were necessarily kept at "arms-length" from collaborative discussions and were not allowed to undercut fruitful partnerships and solutions.

Establishing Cordial and "Empathetic" Relationships with Erstwhile Adversaries

Even when timber and environmental interest had reached an impasse in which only litigation held any hope of resolving the conflict between timber interests and environmentalists / U.S. Forest Service stakeholders persisted in meeting with one another and straining to understand one another's values and needs. This ultimately produced relationships, friendships and common cause.

Maintaining Communication among Stakeholders

The communication patterns and networks discussed in this case study organically developed from a series of conversations, relationships, friendships and collaborations among stakeholders. What emerged, beyond a sense of common ground, was a deep appreciation for who each stakeholder was and what they valued in the community. Essentially the process of working together fostered a deep sense of empathy between and among members of the BMFP that motivated them to pursue ongoing relationships with one another and to seek one another's input whenever possible and certainly before major decisions impacting the local economy or environment were made. As hackneyed as it is to say, these individuals and groups quite literally kept the lines of communication open and still do.

Replacing "Either-Or" with "Both-And" Thinking

Participants in BMFP were painfully aware of the fact that narrowly approaching their local environmental and economic problems from an "either-or" perspective (implying that they only had options producing winners and losers) could only produce impasse and endless litigation while driving a wedge between those who benefited and those who did not. They chose instead to adopt a "both-and" mindset that sought options that would result in protecting and restoring the forest environment while also stimulating the local timber industry. Ultimately they did so by realizing that the processes needed to restore the forest and prevent wildfires created opportunities for the local timber industry and in the future, may also create a market for biomass that could be marketed to the state's electric utilities.

Employing Scientific Research Findings

Given the way this collaborative group unfolded, it is probably accurate to attribute the organization's philosophy of allowing scientific evidence to inform environmental practice to Andy Kerr of Oregon Natural Resources Council. Even so, the fact that BMFP bought into that value so significantly is a tribute to director Mark Webb and the rest of the BMFP board and partners. Employing this approach holds the best prospects for improving local forests and vouchsafing the local economy. Moreover, this approach does much to quell criticism of the organization that may claim decisions and actions are predicated upon narrowly personal gain to members or to the interests they represent. The great virtue of basing practice of research is that it tends to objectify the rationale for action beyond personal interests. BMFP was not only correct in embracing this value (a value as old as the ideas of scientific management that the Forest Service was built upon) doing so is the best defense possible against criticisms regarding conflicts of interest.

With these observations, the Blue Mountain Forest Partners case study evaluation concludes. Without question, BMFP represents one of the most successful partnerships of its kind to be found anywhere in the U.S. Arguably, the foundations of their success are rooted in their pragmatic approach to problem solving—what this book refers to as the application of ecopragmatic principles. In many respects their accomplishments could be construed in a simple and straightforward fashion and in so doing ignore or gloss over the turbulent environment within which they emerged and continue to function. Blue Mountain Forest Partners have approached conflict as opportunity and charted a thoughtful course through turbulent forces in their community. Having emerged from within a state and community long intimate with negotiating conflictual situations, BMFP exemplifies that even in the most turbulent environments reasonable and thoughtful people can yet find common ground to embrace in common causes that serve to bridge differences, overcome conflict and revitalize otherwise impoverished communities. All in all, one could hardly ask for a collaborative partnership that better exemplifies the potential for ecopragmatic problem solving.

REFERENCES:

Adler, Jonothan H. 2007. "When is Two a Crowd?" *Harvard Environmental Law Review*. 41: 67-114.

———. 2005. "What Happens When Environmental Law Meets the Constitution?" American Bar Association Section on Environment, Energy and Resources, 13th Section Meeting, (September 21-25), Nashville, TN.

Antuma, Jesse, Bryce Esch, Brendan Hall, Elizabeth Munn and Frank Sturges. 2014. *Restoring Forests and Communities Lessons from the Collaborative Forest Landscape Restoration Program*. Ann Arbor: University of Michigan School of Natural Resources and Environment.

Babcock, Hope M. 2008. "Dual Regulation, Collaborative Management, or Layered Federalism: Can Cooperative Federalism Models from Other Laws Save Our Land?" *West—Northwest*. 14(1): 449-484.

Barnard, Jeff. 2014. "Conservationists, Loggers Team Up on Forest Health" *The Register-Guardian*. (December 27), Accessed July 11, 2016 http://www.westernlaw.org/article/conservationists-loggers-team-forest-health-register-guard-122714

Blue Mountain Eagle. 2015. "Legal Notice: USDA Forest Service." *Blue Mountain Eagle*. (April 8): B6, Accessed July 5, 2016 http://oregonnews.uoregon.edu/lccn/sn96088264/2015-04-08/ed-1/seq-16.pdf

Blue Mountain Forest Partners. BMFP. 2015. "BMFP Board Members." Accessed September 2, 2017 http://www.bluemountainsforestpartners.org/about/staff-and-board/

Bosworth, Dale and Hutch Brown. 2007. "After the Timber Wars: Community Based Stewardship." *Journal of Forestry*. (July/August): 271-273.

Brown, Susan Jane. 2016. "Oregon: Southern Blues Restoration Coalition Collaborative Landscape Restoration Project—2015." *Nature Conservancy Factsheet*, Accessed July 1, 2016 http://www.nature.org/ourinitiatives/habitats/forests/cflr-factsheet-oregon-southern-blues.pdf

Brown, Susan Jane. 2015. *ERI-Issues and Forest Restoration - Administrative and Legal Review Opportunities for Collaborative Groups*. Flagstaff: Northern Arizona University Ecological Restoration Institute.

Bramen, Lisa. 2015. "Beyond the Timber Wars." *Nature Conservancy Magazine*. (August/September), Accessed July 11, 2016 http://www.nature.org/magazine/archives/beyond-the-timber-wars.xml

Cloughesy, Mike. 2015. "Study: Millions of Zombie Trees Occupy Oregon's National Forests." *Oregon Forest Resources Institute Blog*. (October 28). Accessed August 27, 2017 http://oregonforests.org/blog/study-millions-zombie-trees-occupy-oregon%E2%80%99s-national-forests-0

Davis, Raymond J., Janet L. Ohmann, Robert E. Kennedy, Warren B. Cohen, Matthew J. Gregory, Zhiquang Yang, Heather M. Roberts, Andrew N. Gray and Thomas A. Spies. 2015. *Northwest Forest Plan - The First 20 Years (1994-2013): Status and Trends of Late-Succession and Old-Growth Forests*. General Technical Report PNW-GTR-911. Portland: U.S. Department of Agriculture, Forest Service, Pacific Northwest Research Station.

Dellasala, Dominick A. and Jack E. Williams. 2006. "The Northwest Forest Plan: A Global Model of Forest Management in Contentious Times." *Conservation Biology*. 20(2): 274-276.

Duara, Nigel. 2015. "In Western States, Idea of Reclaiming Federal Land Still Has a Strong Allure." *The Los Angeles Times*. (May 10), Accessed June 29, 2016 http://www.latimes.com/nation/la-na-ff-land-battle-20150510-story.html

Eidger, Vernita. 2013. "Blue Mountain Forest Partners: Collaboration on the Malheur National Forest." *Sustainable Northwest*, (July 21), Accessed July 2, 2016 http://sustainablenorthwest.org/uploads/resources/07212013_longer_BMFP_5_Collaboratives_Meeting_Presentation_ve.ppt

Emerson, Kirk, Elena Gonzalez, Valerie Nottingham, Cliff Rader, and Horst G. Greczmiel. 2007. *Collaboration in NEPA: A Handbook for NEPA Practitioners*. Washington: CEQ.

Fretwell, Holly and Shawn Regan. 2015. *Divided Lands: State vs. Federal Management in the West*. Bozeman: The Property and Environmental Research Center (PERC).

George, John D. 2016. "Conflicts of Interest Endure." *The Voice of Grant County*. (April 25), Acessed July 5, 2016 at http://www.thevoiceofgrantcountyoregon.com/featured/conflicts-of-interest-endure/

Grant County Public Forest Commission. 2015. "Objection: Elk 16 Project, Prairie City Ranger District Malheur National Forest." Accessed July 5, 2016 http://a123.g.akamai.net/7/123/11558/abc123/forestservic.download.akamai.com/11558/www/n epa/67767_FSPLT3_2483960.pdf

Gubel, Sandra. 2011. "Blue Mountain Collaborative Embarks on Elk 16 Project." *Blue Mountain Eagle*. (August 9), Accessed July 5, 2016 http://www.bluemountaineagle.com/news/local_news/20110809/blue-mountains-collaborative-embarks-on-elk-16-project

Harney County Restoration Collaborative (HCRC). 2016 "About the Collaborative." Accessed July 1, 2016 https://sites.google.com/site/harneycountycollaborative/home/about-the-collaborative

Harper, Gary. 2004. *The Joy of Conflict*. Gabriola Island: New Societies Publisher.

Hart, Sean. 2016a. "Local Collaborative Awarded $4 Million in Federal Forest Restoration Funding." *Blue Mountain Eagle*. (April 5), Accessed July 1, 2016 http://www.bluemountaineagle.com/Local_News/20160405/local-collaborative-awarded-4-million-in-federal-forest-restoration-funding

———. 2016b. "Forest Commission Candidate Seeking to Invalidate It." *Blue Mountain Eagle*. (April 12), Accessed July 5, 2016 http://www.bluemountaineagle.com/Local_News/20160412/forest-commission-candidate-petitioning-to-invalidate-it

———. 2016c. "Judge Invalidates Public Forest Commission." *Blue Mountain Eagle*. (September 14), Accessed September 2, 2017 http://www.bluemountaineagle.com/Local_News/20160914/judge-invalidates-public-forest-commission

Hartter, J. N. 2010 "Community and Forest: Linked Human-Ecosystem Responses to Natural Disturbances in Oregon." National Institute of Food and Agriculture Competitive Grant (Project No. NHW-2009-06091), University of New Hampshire, Durham, NH.

Haun, Marjorie. 2015. "Distrust of Federal Land Agencies Escalates with the Conviction of Oregon Ranchers." *American Thinker*. (November 27), Accessed June 22, 2016 http://www.americanthinker.com/articles/2015/11/distrust_of_federal_land_agencies_escalates_with_conviction_of_oregon_ranchers.html

Hawkins, Marcus. 2015. "A Definition of Federalism: A Case for Reinvigorating State Rights." *Thought.Co*. (April 14), Accessed June 30, 2016 at http://usconservatives.about.com/od/conservativepolitics101/a/The-Conservative-Case-For-Returning-Government-Power-To-The-States.htm

Hedge, David M. and Michael J. Scicchitano. 1992. "Devolving Regulatory Authority: The Federal and State Response." *Review of Policy Research*. 11(1): 81-90.

Hodgkinson, Jeff. 2009. "Communication is the Key to Project Success." International Project Management Association (IPMA). Accessed September 2, 2017 http://www.ipma-usa.org/articles/CommunicationKey.pdf

Houck, Oliver A. 2014. "Cooperative Federalism, Nutrients and the Clean Water Act: Three Cases Revisited." *Environmental Law Reporter*. 44: 10426-10442.

Hudson, Becky. 2016. "Candidate Forum Update." *Voice of Grant County*. (April 24), Accessed July 5, 2016 http://www.thevoiceofgrantcountyoregon.com/featured/candidate-forum/

Johnson, Garrett W. 2006. "Limits to Federal Environmental Regulation: The Commerce Clause Challenge to the Safe Drinking Water Act." *Quinnipiac Health Law*. 10: 77-112.

Kerr, Andy. 2013. "Oregon Softwood Lumber Industry 1995-2012: Fewer Mills and Jobs, But Larger Timber-Processing Capacity." *Larch Occasional Paper*. 19, (February), Accessed July 5, 2016 http://static1.squarespace.com/static/573a143a746fb9ea3f1376e5/t/5787a69b03596edb2dd25bcc/1468507805230/LOP%2319ORSoftwoodLumberMillingCapacity.pdf

———. 2012a. "Oregon and Washington Raw Log Exports: Exporting Jobs and a Subsidy to Domestic Mills." *Larch Occasional Paper*. 10, (February), Accessed July 5, 2016 https://static1.squarespace.com/static/573a143a746fb9ea3f1376e5/t/5787a52259cc6802a0d085c2/1468507430738/Larch%2310LogExports.pdf

———. 2012b. "Ecologically Appropriate Restoration Thinning in the Northwest Forest Plan Area - A Policy and Technical Analysis." *Conservation Northwest.* (July), Accessed July 5, 2016 http://www.conservationnw.org/files/2012-ecologically-appropriate-restoration-thinning-in-the-nw-forest-plan-area

Kidd, Devvy. 2005. "The Environmental Protection Agency Must Be Abolished." *World News Daily.* (January 21), Accesed June 29, 2016 http://www.wnd.com/2005/01/28565/

Knize, Perri. 1991. "The Mismanagement of the National Forests." *Atlantic Monthly.* (October), Accessed August 27, 2017 https://andrewsforest.oregonstate.edu/sites/default/files/lter/pubs/pdf/pub3296.pdf

Langston, Nancy. 2003. *Where Land and Water Meet: A Western Landscape Transformed.* Seattle: University of Washington Press.

———. 1995. *Forest Dreams, Forest Nightmares: The Paradox of Old Growth in the Inland West.* Seattle: University of Washington Press.

Madsen, Sue Lani. 2016 "Its Time to Return Federal Land to the States." *The Spokesman-Review.* (April 29), Accessed June 29, 2016 at http://www.spokesman.com/stories/2016/apr/29/sue-lani-madsen-its-time-to-return-federal-land-to/

Mapes, Jeff. 2015. "Andy Kerr, The Lightning Rod of The Oregon Timber Wars, Now Plays Behind-The-Scenes Role in D.C." *The Oregonian.* (August 21), Accessed July 11, 2016 http://www.oregonlive.com/mapes/index.ssf/2015/08/andy_kerr_the_lightning_rod_of.html

McClain, Rebecca, Kristen Wright and Lee Cerveney. 2015. "Who is at the Forest Reforestation Table?" Final Report of the Blue Mountain Stewardship Network—Phase 1, (March 23), Institute for Sustainable Solutions, Portland State University, Portland, OR.

Metz, David, Emma White and Lori Weigel. 2014. *An Analysis of Western Voter Attitudes Toward Public Lands—Key Findings from Opinion Research.* Alexandria: Public Opinion Strategies.

National Policy Consensus Center (NPCC). 2016. "National Policy Consensus Center Home." NPCC, Hatfield School of Government, Portland State University, Portland, OR, Accessed June 29, 2016 at http://www.pdx.edu/npcc/home

———. 2010. *Integrating Collaborative Activities: Public Deliberation with Stakeholder Processes.* Portland: National Policy Consensus Center.

Neiwert, David. 2016. "Grant County's Glenn Palmer Faces State DOJ Criminal Investigation for His Actions During Standoff—And for Some Beforehand, Too." *Hatewatch.* (March 23), Accessed July 5, 2016 at https://www.splcenter.org/hatewatch/2016/03/23/constitutional%E2%80%99-oregon-sheriff-under-investigation-malheur-role-hired-70-%E2%80%98special-deputies%E2%80%99

Oates, Wallace E. 2001. *A Reconsideration of Environmental Federalism.* (November), Washington: Resources for the Future.

Oregon Economic and Community Development (OECD). 2006. "Grant County Community Sensitivity and Resilience," Northeast Oregon Hazard and Mitigation Plan. Portland, OR.

Oregon Solutions. 2016. "What We Do." National Policy Consensus Center, Portland State University, Portland, OR, Accessed June 29, 2016 http://orsolutions.org/about/what-we-do

———. 2011. "Solving Problems in a New Way." National Policy Consensus Center, Portland State University, Portland, OR, Accessed June 29, 2016 http://orsolutions.org/wp-content/uploads/2011/10/Brochure-updated-9.26.11.pdf

Orr, David. 2014. "Law of the Land," *Orion Magazine.* (January/February), Accessed June 29, 2016 https://orionmagazine.org/article/law-of-the-land/

———. 2003. "The Constitution of Nature," *Conservation Biology.* 17: 1478-1481.

Pacific Northwest. 2016. "What We Do." Pacific Northwest, Portland, OR, Accessed July 2, 2016 http://www.sustainablenorthwest.org/what-we-do

Plaven, George. 2015. "Grant County Sheriff Demands Coordination with Forest Service." *East Oregonian.* (October 9), Accessed July 5, 2016 http://www.eastoregonian.com/eo/local-news/20151009/grant-county-sheriff-demands-coordination-with-forest-service

Selsky, Andrew. 2016. "One Year After Malheur Takeover, Quieter Land Battle Unfolds." *Statesman Journal*. (December 21), Accessed September 1, 2017

Sustainable Northwest. 2016. "Projects and Stories: Working Together for Forest Health." Sustainable Northwest, Portland, OR, Acessed July 5, 2016 http://www.sustainablenorthwest.org/what-we-do/success-stories/collaboration-on-the-malheur-national-forest

Sprauve, Nicky A. 2016. "Letter: Voters Should Question Public Forest Commission Candidates." *Blue Mountain Eagle*. (March 22), Accessed July 5, 2016 http://www.bluemountaineagle.com/Letters/20160322/letter-voters-should-question-public-forest-commission-candidates

Sweeney, Katie M. and Armstrong, Sherrie A. 2013 "Cooperative Federalism in Environmental Law: A Growing Role for Industry." American Bar Association, Section on Environmental Energy and Resources, 21st Section Meeting (Fall, October 9-12), Baltimore, MD.

Taylor, Steven T. 1994. *Sleeping with the Enemy—The U.S. Forest Service and Timber Interests.* Washington: The Center for Public Integrity, Retrieved from the Worldwide Web July 11, 2016 at http://cloudfront-files-1.publicintegrity.org/legacy_projects/pdf_reports/SLEEPINGWITH THEINDUSTRY.pdf

Tribe, Laurence H. 2015. "EPA's Proposed 111(D) Rule for Existing Power Plants: Legal and Cost Issues." U.S. House of Representatives Committee on Energy and Commerce. Public Testimony, (March 17), Washington, DC.

United States Department of Agriculture (USDA). 2016. "Malheur National Forest: History and Culture." U.S. Forest Service, Accessed May 23, 2016 http://www.fs.usda.gov/main/malheur/learning/history-culture

———. 2012. "Collaborative Forest Landscape Restoration Program (CFLRP)." U.S. Forest Service, Accessed July 1, 2016 http://www.fs.fed.us/restoration/CFLRP/overview.shtml

———. 2009. "Forest Facts 2009: Malheur National Forest" U.S. Forest Service—Pacific Northwest Region, Malheur National Forest, John Day, Oregon, Accessed May 23, 2016 http://www.fs.usda.gov/Internet/FSE_DOCUMENTS/stelprdb5244823.pdf

Watt, Peter, Donna Silverberg, Karen Tarnow, Dale Blanton, Susan Brody, Mike Niemeyer, Margaret Weil and Karen Hartley. 2000. *Collaborative Approaches: A Handbook for Public Decision-Making and Conflict Resolutio*n. Eugene: Oregon Dispute Resolution Commission.

Webb, Mark 2016/ "Outline: The Blue Mountain Forest Partners." Personal Communication, May 6, 2016.

Weiser, Phillip J. 2003. *Cooperative Federalism and its Challenges*. Ann Arbor: Michigan State University Press.

Wilson, Jason. 2016. "A Pivotal in the West: Pro-Militia Oregon Sheriff Seeks Reelection." *The Guardian*. (November 7), Accessed September 1, 2017 https://www.theguardian.com/us-news/2016/nov/07/oregon-county-sheriff-glenn-palmer-todd-mckinley-reelection

Wimberley, Edward T. and Scott Pellegrino. 2014. *Ecopragmatics*. Champaign: Common Ground Publishing.

Young, Molly. 2016. "Behind the Harney County Standoff, Decades of Economic Decline." *The Oregonian*. (January 14), Accessed July 1, 2016 http://www.oregonlive.com/oregonstandoff/2016/01/behind_the_harney_county_standoff_decades_of_economic_decline.html

Zaitz, Les. 2016. "Sherriff Glenn Palmer Makes His Own Rules." *The Oregonian*. (August 20), Accessed September 1, 2017 http://www.oregonlive.com/oregon-standoff/2016/08/sheriff_glenn_palmer_makes_his.html

CHAPTER 6

Bleeding the Brazos Dry

BACKGROUNDER FOR CASE STUDIES THREE & FOUR

Bleeding the River Dry

Before proceeding to a pair of case studies involving environmental stakeholders along the Brazos River in Texas, it is necessary to provide context to the key environmental issues in that region. Obviously, the center of environmental concern is the Brazos River and its environs. The water resources of this major Texas tributary are the most intensely managed of any river in the state. Threatened on its Westward most region by agricultural, municipal growth and energy exploration, siphoned into dams and reservoirs along its middle length, appropriated for industrial use near its mouth and tapped for drinking water throughout, this river—which historically has been considered a "wild and unruly" stream - now finds itself freshwater resources increasingly threatened by humans and nature. This historic river along whose banks early settlers disembarked to start new lives in frontier Texas now finds it future uncertain and threatened. If it is to survive, it will be through the efforts of public and private stakeholders from Freeport and Houston to Waco and Lubbock who commit themselves to stop this great river from "bleeding to death."

Goodbye to a River?

The renowned singer-songwriter Townes Van Zandt penned and performed many memorable lyrics about his native Texas but few have touched the core of the Texas experience as deeply has his rendition of the traditional folk tune the "Texas River Song" that includes these lyrics: (Van Zandt 2006).

> "There's many a river
> That waters the land
> Now the fair Angelina
> Runs glossy and gliding
> The crooked Colorado
> Runs weaving and winding
> The slow San Antonio
> Courses and plains
> But I never will walk
> By the Brazos again!"

The original song speaks of a cowboy who would never walk the banks of the historic Brazos River with his sweetheart again. Today, however, this song takes on new meaning as the Brazos River, one of Texas's most important tributaries, finds its water threatened by excessive water demand from too many farmers, ranchers, municipalities, industries, utility companies, developers, outdoor enthusiasts, and industrial interests. In our time, we may very well be saying "goodbye to the Brazos" (Wilder 2012) as the river is quite literally bleeding to death.

To an increasing and seemingly unending degree Brazos River water is being syphoned away at an unprecedented rate by one water user after another. Freshwater resources—which, historically, have always been extremely variable—have become progressively diminished due to overuse throughout the course of the stream and intermittent drought. The consequence of these factors is that the fish, wildlife and riparian ecology of the river is threatened by a decreased freshwater flow rate that allows salt water from the Gulf of Mexico to intrude well upriver threatening riparian vegetation, fish and wildlife while jeopardizing the freshwater resources of farmers, ranchers, municipalities and industrial users.

If one were to merely track the emerging ecological crisis along the Brazos in the newspapers, or via popular media outlets on television and the internet, one might erroneously conclude that this environmental issue is relatively recent. In truth, concerns over this vital Texas tributary are long seated and most publicly emerged within the pages of John Graves' (1959) book *Goodbye to a River*. Graves wrote this book to protest plans to build numerous dams and reservoirs along the middle stretches of the river. Therein he succinctly and eloquently addresses the importance of the Brazos River, observing that,

> "The Brazos does not come from haunts of coot or hern, or even from the mountains. It comes from West Texas, and in part from an equally stark stretch of New Mexico, and it runs for something over 800 miles down to the Gulf. On the high plains it is a gypsum-salty intermittent creek; down toward the coast it is a rolling Southern river, with levees and cotton fields and ancient hardwood bottoms. It slices across Texas history as it does across the map of the state; the Republic's first capital stood by it, near the coast, and settlement flowed northwestward up its long trough as the water flowed down" (Graves 1959, 4).

With these words, Graves places the Brazos where it belongs—geographically in the heart of Texas, historically at the heart of Texas history, geologically far-flung, and ecologically diverse. His book however, is more a tribute to what the river was and has been than what its future holds for he perceives the rugged and diverse Brazos of history and his memory being transformed with the planning and building of one dam after another that—while designed for recreation, reservoirs, irrigation and municipal development—are forever changing the character of one of the Southwest's great rivers. In this regard, Graves opines:

> "If you're built like me, neither the certainty of change nor the nor the need for it, nor any wry philosophy will keep you from feeling a certain enraged awe when you hear that a river that you've known always, and that all men of that place have known always back into the red dawn of men, will shortly not exist. A piece of river, anyhow my piece.... They had not yet done more than survey the sites for the new dams, five between those two that had

already risen during my life. But the squabbling had become between their proponents and those otherwise-minded types—bottomland farmers and ranchers whose holdings would be inundated, competitive utility companies shrilling "Socialism!" and big irrigationists downstream—who would make a noise before they lost but who would lose. When someone official dreams up a dam, it generally goes in. Dams are ipso facto good all by themselves, like mothers and flags. Maybe you save a Dinosaur Monument from time to time, but in between such salvations you lose 10 Brazoses" (Graves 1959, 8).

Managing an Unruly River

The Brazos is one of Texas' major rivers and is distinctive in being the only major river in the state whose mouth empties directly into the Gulf of Mexico rather than flowing into a bay, estuary or bayou. This characteristic of the river made it most attractive for early settlers who sought to penetrate the coastal region of Texas and travel inland in search of grazing, woodlands, fertile fields and homesteading. Ironically, however, once explorers traversed the river's lower, middle and upper reaches they were forced to conclude that the upper and lower Brazos were less accommodating to human settlement given the arid nature of the upper region and the humidity and episodic flooding along the lower Brazos.

What remains is the middle Brazos where most of the region's original farming, ranching and communities developed. By comparison the remainder of the river is unruly and untamed arguably rendering it in need of human management, since after all the Brazos is a dynamic stream that,

> "becomes swollen then waterless, hostile then motionless, docile then boundless. This is a river of many faces, one that enjoys a gluttonous feast of water or no water at all. The vegetation, geology and hydrology of the river are similarly indecisive, alternately springing forth as treeless mesas, flowered hills and swampy lowlands" (Archer 2015, 2).

As a natural tributary, the Brazos is as feral and dangerous as any wild mustang that ever grazed across Texas. When tamed by human hands with dams, lagoons and pumping stations, the Brazos and its water resources can be rendered somewhat manageable. However, to imagine the Brazos River could ever be consistently and permanently tamed is to indulge in a fantasy that experience and history consistently contradict.

Texas is home to some 6,976 reservoirs (Texas Almanac 2016) of which the Brazos River basin encompasses 1,178 (Kimmel 2011) to include at least 26 major water impoundments—more dams and impoundments than any other river in Texas (Dowell 1964). Current storage capacity in the Brazos River Basin is 4,613,800 acre/feet which doesn't even include the countless smaller water tanks and impoundments along streams and drainages throughout the Brazos basin that have been developed by farmers and ranchers to water cattle (Kimmel 2011). The Brazos River basin encompasses thirty-nine reservoirs with capacities of 5,000 acre feet or more to include nine reservoirs constructed by the U.S. Corps of Engineers for flood control to include:

- Lake Whitney (the largest flood control reservoir),
- Lake Aquilla on Aquilla Creek 10 miles North of Waco,
- Lake Waco fed by the Bosque River system situated in Waco,
- Lakes Proctor, Belton, Stillhouse, Hollow, Gerogetown and Granger which contain floodwater from the Little River's tributaries that enter the Brazos above Bryan/College Station and
- Lake Somerville that controls floodwater from Yegua Creek that empties into the Brazos near Navasota (Vogl & Lopes 2009).

The final reservoir to be constructed on the Brazos River is the Allen Creek Reservoir which is to be built by the Brazos River Authority on Allen Creek near where it empties into the river in Austin County near Sealy.

Water management techniques—whether involving dams, reservoirs or water rights restrictions—typically produce benefits to some at the expense of others. However, during periods of drought these techniques arguably distribute scarcity rather than water. As Kenna Lang Archer observed in her book *Unruly Waters* (2015) settlers of every generations

> "devised projects intended to address the persistent flooding and then watched as high flows coursed over, around and sometimes through those same improvements (often in dramatic and damaging style); they wrought projects of steel and cement and wood and then lamented the destructive power of moving water over the same materials" (Archer 2015, 2).

The Brazos River is the second longest river in the state of Texas extending some 800 miles and is only exceeded in length by the Rio Grande river which is 1,250 miles in length or 48,259 square miles. Although 400 miles shorter than the Rio Grande, the Brazos encompasses an area almost as larger as that of the Rio Grande totaling 42,800 square miles (Wermund 1996). Figure 19 delimits the various river basins throughout Texas "River Basin" (Hayes, 2002). The Brazos originates in New Mexico near Clovis and travels east into the Trans Pecos region of Texas. Thereafter the river proceeds in a southeast direction through the high plains and the rolling plains of West Central Texas before crossing the Edwards Plateau (a limestone ridge in central Texas that encompasses a bioregion of some 36,680 square miles). The upper stretch of the river beginning in and around Clovis, New Mexico and extending into the Llano Estacio (Staked Plain) of West Texas has been described by some as the "lost river" of the Brazos basin since so much of the water is lost to evaporation or captured in impoundments and cattle tanks that dot the Texas plains (Kimmel 2011). At this point, the river is not so much represented by continually flowing streams as it is by a series of "draws" or "arroyos" that carry runoff water from periodic rainstorms—the most notable of which is Blackwater Draw, Running Water Draw and Yellow House Draw (Kimmel 2011).

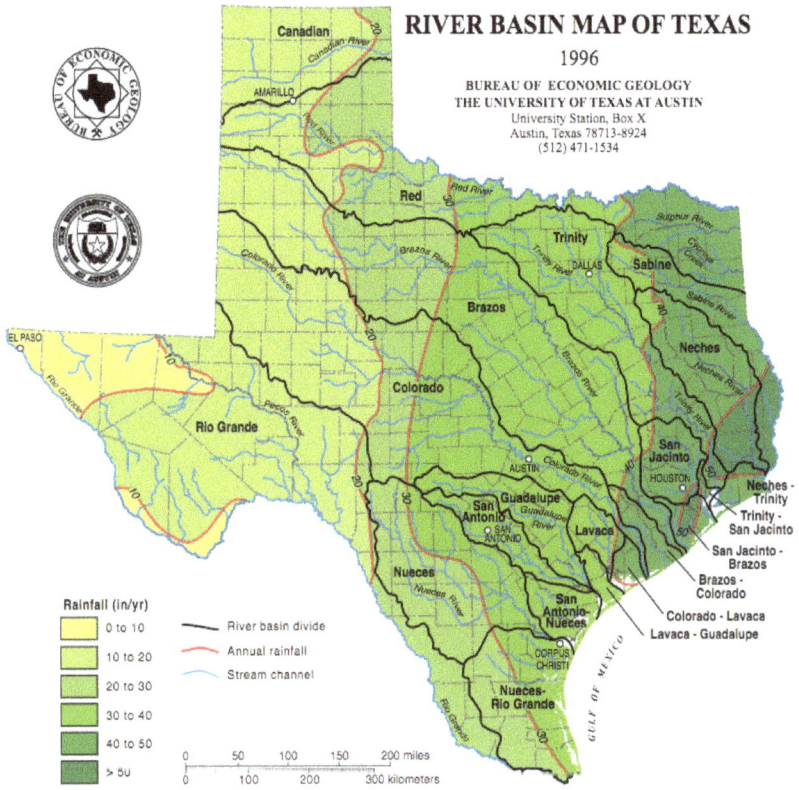

RIVER BASIN MAP OF TEXAS
1996

BUREAU OF ECONOMIC GEOLOGY
THE UNIVERSITY OF TEXAS AT AUSTIN
University Station, Box X
Austin, Texas 78713-8924
(512) 471-1534

Rainfall (in/yr)
- 0 to 10
- 10 to 20
- 20 to 30
- 30 to 40
- 40 to 50
- > 50

— River basin divide
— Annual rainfall
— Stream channel

River basins	Texas length (miles)	Texas area (sq mi)	Number of major reservoirs*	Conservation storage (acre ft)*	Storage (acre ft/sq mi)
Brazos	840	42,800	19	3,322,880	75
Canadian	200	12,700	2	560,900	44
Colorado	600	39,893	11	3,803,900	95
Guadalupe	250	6,070	2	420,000	70
Lavaca	74	2,309	1	157,900	68
Neches	416	10,011	4	3,455,500	345
Nueces	315	16,950	2	931,640	60
Red	680	30,823	7	4,593,460	149
Rio Grande	1,250	48,259	3	3,772,000	78
Sabine	360	7,426	2	6,041,300	814
San Jacinto	70	5,600	2	570,400	102
Trinity	550	17,696	14	6,969,710	388

* Data from Texas Water Development Board.

Figure 19: Historic River Basin Map of Texas
(Source: Bureau of Economic Geology 1996)

Upon entering the South Texas plains, the Brazos proceeds through the cross-timbers region (two elongated strips of forest extending from Central Texas to Oklahoma consisting of blackjack oak and post oak) through the black-land prairies, and post oak savannahs before flowing into the cypress hammocks, prairies and marshes of the Gulf Coast (Figure 20). The upper portion of the middle region of the river is recognized for its rolling hills and fertile valleys. Known by the original name given to the river by Spanish explorer—Los Brazos de Dios (The Arms of God), this area is characterized by four distinct streams emptying into the Brazos—The Salt Fork of the Brazos, the North Fork of the Double Mountain Fork of Brazos, the Double Mountain Fork of the Brazos and the Clear Fork of the Brazos (Kimmel 2011).

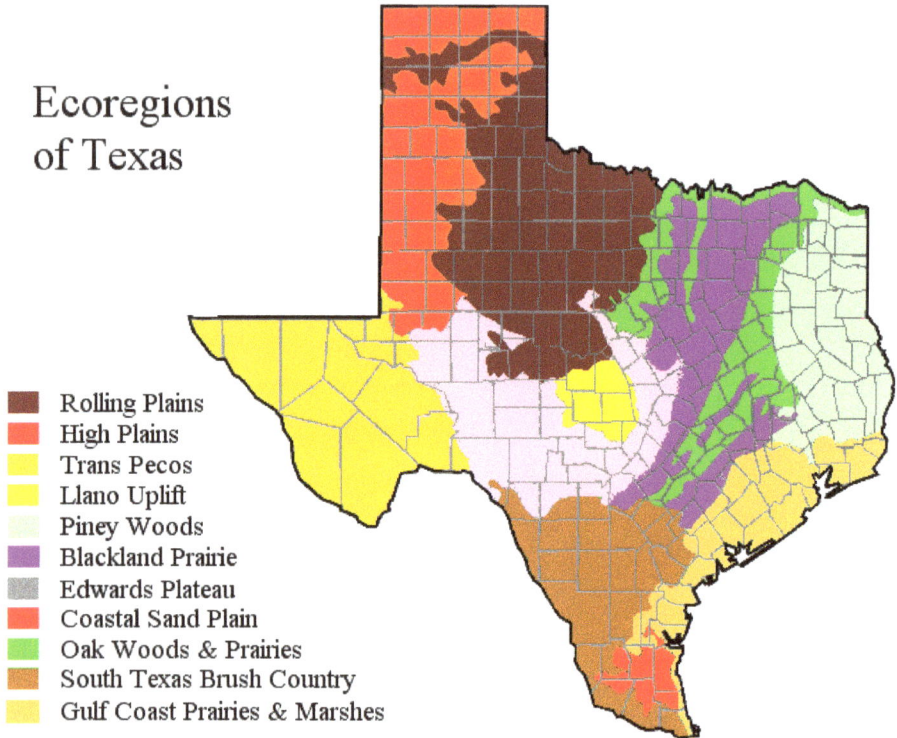

Ecoregions
of Texas

- Rolling Plains
- High Plains
- Trans Pecos
- Llano Uplift
- Piney Woods
- Blackland Prairie
- Edwards Plateau
- Coastal Sand Plain
- Oak Woods & Prairies
- South Texas Brush Country
- Gulf Coast Prairies & Marshes

Figure 20: Ecoregions of Texas
(Source: Guhlin 2016)

There are 18 man-made lakes and reservoirs within this region the to include the Hubbard Creek Reservoir (322,080 acre/feet) that serves the Abilene area and the Alan Henry Reservoir (94,808 acre/feet) along the Double Mountain Fork of the Brazos that serves as the municipal water supply for Lubbock, Texas (Texas Almanac 2016; Kimmel 2011). This rolling hills portion of the Brazos River basin includes nine other major reservoirs and lakes greater than 10,000 acre/feet in capacity to include Fort Phantom Hill Lake (70,030 acre/feet), Stamford Lake (51, 570 acre/feet), Graham Lake (45,260 acre/feet), White River Lake (29,880 acre/feet), Millers Creek Reservoir (27,888 acre/feet), Palo Pinto Lake (27, 150 acre feet), Leon Lake (26,421 acre/feet), Cisco Lake (26,000 acre/feet) and Sweetwater Lake (10,066 acre/feet) (Kimmel 2011 66). The lower portion of the middle region of the river (from the rolling plains through the post-oak savannah regions) has been referred to as the "dammed river" (Kimmel 2011) because it is in this are that the greatest volume of water is impounded behind dams.

This "dammed river" portion of the Brazos (Figure 21) begins at Possum Kingdom Reservoir and extends southward to the mouth of the Navasota River. It is in this region that the bulk of the region's farming occurs and the site of the most dramatic population growth in the Texas. The Brazos River Authority operates ten wastewater treatment plants in this region and three dams (Morris Shepherd Dam, DeCordova Bend Dam, Stirling C. Robertson Dam) (Figure 22). These dams create eleven reservoirs dominating the river to include Possum Kingdom Reservoir (750,000 acre/feet), Lake Whitney (553,344 acre/feet), Lake Belton (435,225 acre/feet), Lake Aquilla (44,566 acre/feet), Stillhouse Hollow Reservoir (227,771 acre/feet), Limestone Reservoir (208,017 acre/feet), Lake Somerville (147,104 acre/feet), Lake Granbury (128,046 acre/feet) Proctor Lake (55,456 acre/feet), and Granger Lake (50,779 acre/feet) (Texas Almanac 2016; Kimmel 2011).

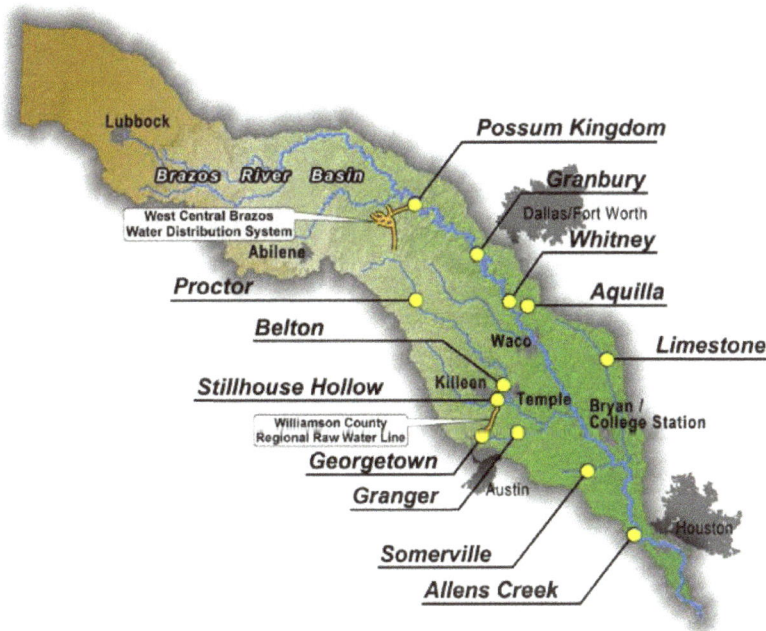

Figure 21: Brazos Reservoirs
(Source: Brazos River Authority 2017)

Figure 22: Brazos River Authority Facilities
(Source: Brazos River Authority 2017)

Rainfall and Flooding

Dependent as it is upon rainfall, water levels and flows in the Brazos can fluctuate wildly throughout its course with the upper Brazos experiencing an average of 20 inches of rain annually while at the mouth of the Brazos rainfall can exceed 50 inches annually (Figure 23). Ironically, while this river is dependent upon rainfall high, temperatures across the expanse of the river produce evaporation rates that exceed rainfall levels, meaning that parts of the river only periodically retain water whereas other parts located well downstream maintain water levels year around punctuated by periodic flooding (Kimmel 2011). The river's moisture tends to evaporate in the upper regions during summer and is recharged in the winter and spring by moisture moving south and east from the Rocky Mountains, eastward from the Pacific Ocean through Mexico and northward from the Gulf of Mexico.

Significant precipitation occurs along the mid to lower ranges of the Brazos and often rains in vast quantities sometimes dumping the bulk of average annual rainfall in a matter of weeks. River flow rates are driven by rainfall frequency which tends to peak between April and June (peaking in May) and again around October. Consequently, river flows vary widely at the mouth of the river (from 990 cubic feet per second (cps) to 29,050 cps) with the highest recorded flow at the mouth of the Brazos occurring in 1929 at 123,000 cps. By comparison peak flows on the upper reaches of the river in West Texas are comparably modest ranging from 12,000 cps at Running River Draw well up-river to 35, 600 cps at Salt Fork, 91,400 cps at Double

Mountain Fork, 149,000 cps at Clear Fork and a whopping 246,000 cps at Waco (Kimmel 2011).

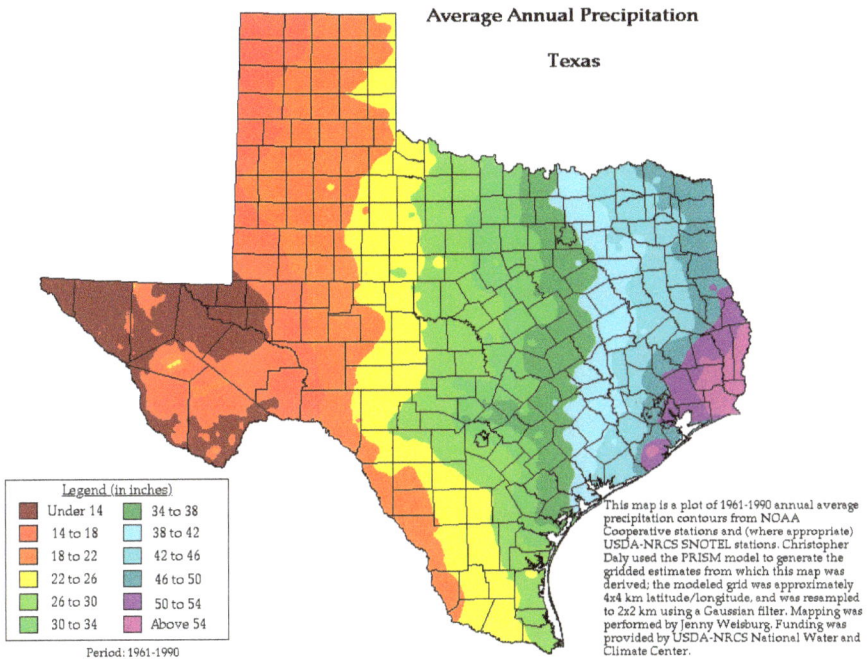

Average Annual Precipitation

Texas

This map is a plot of 1961-1990 annual average precipitation contours from NOAA Cooperative stations and (where appropriate) USDA-NRCS SNOTEL stations. Christopher Daly used the PRISM model to generate the gridded estimates from which this map was derived; the modeled grid was approximately 4x4 km latitude/longitude, and was resampled to 2x2 km using a Gaussian filter. Mapping was performed by Jenny Weisburg. Funding was provided by USDA-NRCS National Water and Climate Center.

Legend (in inches)

Under 14		34 to 38	
14 to 18		38 to 42	
18 to 22		42 to 46	
22 to 26		46 to 50	
26 to 30		50 to 54	
30 to 34		Above 54	

Period: 1961-1990

Figure 23: Annual Precipitation in Texas
(Source: OSU 2000)

Unlike other Western rivers generated from mountain snow-melt, the Brazos begins in semi-arid New Mexico and West Texas. Consequently, dams constructed along the upper portion of the river were designed for "water retention" to cope with the arid environment and provide a water supply for municipal water systems and agriculture. By comparison dams built upon the middle region of the river were constructed to both retain water for municipal and agricultural use as well as for water "detention" in the interest of alleviating flooding along the mid and lower regions of the river. Likewise, many of these dams built by the U.S. Corps of Engineers along the middle Brazos were also designed to produce hydroelectric power (Archer 2015).

The overwhelming majority of major dams and reservoirs in the Brazos River basin are situated in the middle expanse in part because of the geological characteristics of this region (limestone cliff and valleys that retain water quite well) and in part because this region of central Texas is projected to experience significant population increases requiring additional potable water and greater demand for recreational water resources. Consequently, the bulk of the water in the Brazos that is used for agriculture, municipal and industrial use is drawn from the middle and lower reaches of the river.

Historical flow data along the Brazos strongly suggests that the principal characteristic of the river is its penchant for regular and sometimes severe flooding.

Significant floods have been recorded in the 19th century (1833, 1842, 1899) as well as during the early 20th century (1908, 1913 and 1921) (Archer 2015). In response to these floods Congress provided funds for dam construction. The first of these water detention dams to be built along the Brazos River was "Lock and Dam No. 1 completed in 1915 near Navasota followed by Lock and Dam No. 8 near Waco. Lock and Dam No. 2-5 were never completed (Archer 2015). These dams were constructed principally to aid in navigation along the river south of Waco. It wasn't until 1938 that the Possum Kingdom Reservoir was constructed near Breckenridge for water retention, detention and hydroelectric generation purposes (Brazos River Authority 2016). This and subsequent dams and reservoirs were designed to reduce the frequency and severity of floods. Nevertheless, significant flooding was reported along the middle and lower stretches of the river in 1991, 1995, 1998, 2007 and in 2017 following the landfall of Hurricane Harvey (Bryan 2017; Kimmel 2011).

Saline and Freshwater Aquifers

While damming water in reservoirs and lakes throughout the Brazos basin serves to reduce flooding and provide water and hydroelectric power for farms, ranches and communities throughout the region this benefit is purchased at a cost. Water impounded behind dams is not available to maintain river flow throughout the course of the river. The implications of this are significant. Predictable freshwater flows are necessary to maintain the ecosystem within the river as well as that of the surrounding riparian environment.

Since silt and sediment picked up the flowing stream settles into the bottoms of these reservoirs water released beyond the dams does not serve to disperse sediments downstream, meaning that this relatively clear water only erodes the river downstream and does not efficiently replenish riparian environments with new soil. However, the most significant issue associated with impounding Brazos River water is that of salinization. When the rate of freshwater river flow is reduced by extensive upstream impoundment downstream river salinization becomes more extensive since persistent and vigorous freshwater flows serves to keep saltwater from the Gulf of Mexico from intruding upriver from the mouth of the river.

Water salinity threatens freshwater users throughout the course of the river, often rendering freshwater useless for agricultural, ranching, human and industrial consumption and use. Freshwater resources along the middle and lower regions of the river therefore is dependent upon regular rainfall and/ or regular freshwater releases from dams upstream to maintain a steady flow that keeps saltwater near the mouth of the river in abeyance.

Further complicating the problem of river salinity is the fact that that Brazos River water naturally contains high salt content given that some of its headwaters pass through extremely saline soil and rock sediments. The bulk of the river's upstream salt content comes from the Salt Fork of the Brazos where salinity levels associated with the Croton and Salt Fork Creek basins can reach 150 parts per thousand as compared to 35 parts per thousand found in the Gulf of Mexico (Kimmel 2011). Per a 1969 report from the U.S. Department of Interior,

"The average daily load of the Brazos River at Possum Kingdom Reservoir is about 2,800 tons of dissolved solids, of which 1,000 tons is chloride. More than 85 percent of the chloride load [in the Brazos River emptying into Possum Kingdom Reservoir] is contributed by the Salt Fork Brazos River, and more than 50 percent of the chloride load of the Brazos River originates from salt springs and seeps in Croton and Salt Croton Creeks, which are tributaries of Salt Fork Brazos River. The rest of the chloride is contributed from many small sources" (Baker, Hughes & Yost 1969).

What this means is that even before problems of saltwater intrusion from the Gulf of Mexico are considered, Brazos River water quality is already compromised by natural salt sedimentation issues. Numerous impoundments throughout the river basin and drought only serve to exacerbate this problem of natural water salinity.

A portion of the water in the Brazos River comes from groundwater resources, which consists of freshwater and saline flows. There are nine major aquifers in Texas (Figure 24) six of which lie beneath the Brazos River Basin, namely the Ogallala, Seymour, Trinity, Edwards, Carizzo-Wilcox and Gulf Coast aquifers (Texas Almanac 2015). The Brazos River basin also includes several smaller (minor) aquifers to include the Brazos River Alluvium, Woodbine, Blaine, Dockum, and High Plains aquifers (Figure 25). Aquifers provide water for agriculture and municipal use throughout the entire stretch of the river basin and produce numerous freshwater and salt springs and seeps with 17 of these discharging 330 liters/second (Texas Water Development Board 2008; George et al. 2011).

Texas is renowned for having some of the largest and most productive springs in the world, the largest of which is Comal Springs in Comal County which produces 9,000 liters/second (lps). Other "significant" springs are to be found in Hays Count (San Marcos Springs—4,300 lps), Val Verde County (Goodenough Springs—3,900 lps and San Felipe Springs - 2,600 lps), Travis Count (Barton Springs—1,400 lps) and Bexar County (San Antonio Springs (1,400 lps). Among the largest Texas springs only Salado Springs lies within the Brazos River basin (Figure 26). Texas also has many lesser magnitude springs diminished by land-use practices (Brune1981).

Major Aquifers of Texas

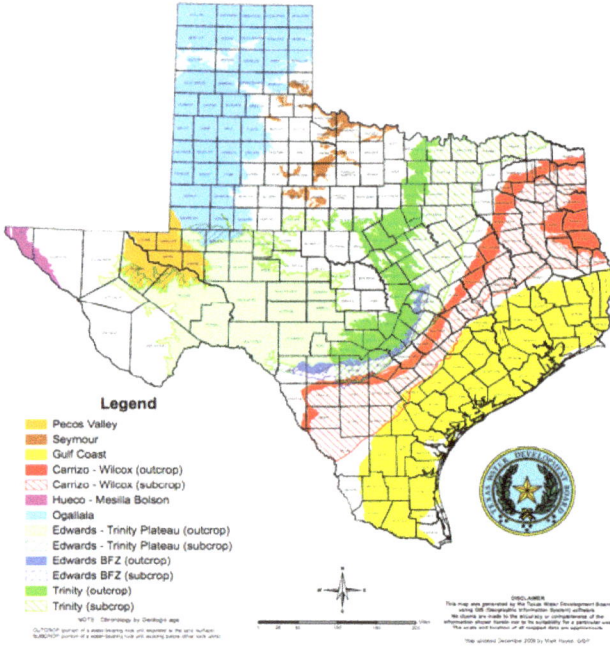

Figure 24: Major Texas Aquifers
(Source: Texas Water Development Board 2008)

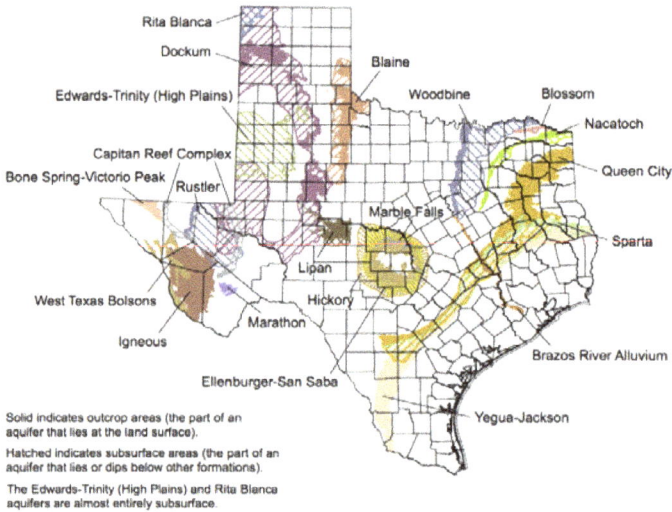

Figure 25: Minor Texas Aquifers
(Source: George et al. 2011)

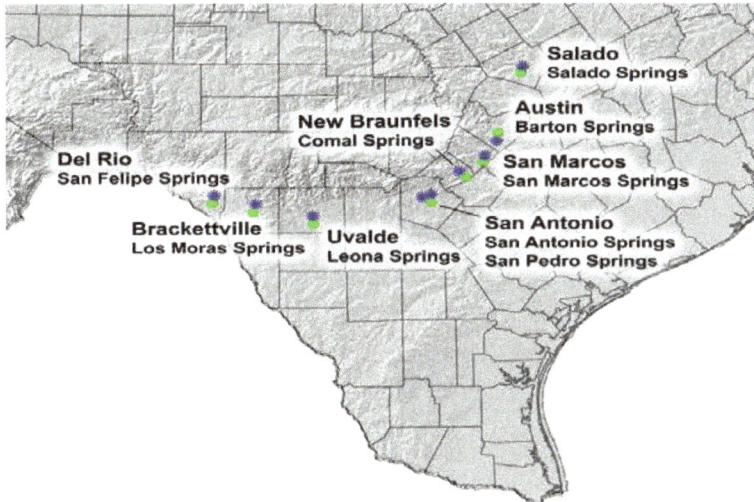

Figure 26: Largest Springs in Texas
(Source: Rosen 2017)

The Brazos River Basin encompasses some 325 springs, most of which produce an average discharge rate of well less than 400 lps. (Figures 27a and 27b). Springs provide a minor amount of water for the Brazos River basin when compared to the contribution of rainfall. The bulk of Brazos springs are freshwater except for those in King, Kent and Stonewall Counties where saline (brackish) springs and seepages are found. Saline deposits are found along the length of the Salt Fork of the Brazos extending through Crosby, Garza, Kent, and Stonewall counties (Brune 1981; 1975).

One of the most brackish of all Texas springs is Salt Creek Brine Springs in Kent County on the North Fork of Salt Creek. This spring has a saline content seven times as salty as sea water. King County also includes some extremely brackish springs, particularly Haystack Brine Springs which produces 30 tons of chloride and 3 tons of sulfate daily, and Dove Brine Springs which produces 153,000 milligrams of chlorine per liter of water. By comparison, water from Put-Off Springs in Kent County is only mildly saline and can be safely consumed while Hot Brine Springs and Short Croton Springs—also located in Kent County—contain very high chlorine levels. Many other springs throughout the Brazos basin are also highly alkaline (Brune 1981).

Brackish aquifers are found throughout the state of Texas, particularly along the Gulf Coast, the Red River and Rio Grande valleys, in West Texas into New Mexico. As Figure 28 illustrates saline groundwater deposits are widely distributed across the geography of Texas and distributed in significant concentrations within the state's major and minor aquifers (Figure 29 and 30). The most brackish aquifers are the Gulf Coast Aquifer (522,497,700 acre-feet) and the Yegua-Jackson Aquifer inland of the Gulf Coast Aquifer (517,857,300 acre-feet) (Figures 31 & 32) (Kalaswad et al. 2004).

The third largest source of brackish groundwater is in the Carrizo-Wilcox Aquifer (430,181,400 acre-feet) of central Texas that transects the state from southwest to northeast just south of the Edwards Plateau and north of the Yegua-Jackson Aquifer. The fourth largest concentration of brackish groundwater lies within the Sparta and

Queen City aquifer which is another minor aquifer located near the major Yegua-Jackson Aquifer (245,712,100 acre-feet). These four aquifers all lie beneath the Brazos River basin, as does the Trinity Aquifer containing 178,165,400 acre-feet of brackish groundwater (Kalasawad et al. 2004).

Location & No. Springs Total 325 Springs	Springs Names
Austin County (10)	Deadman, Swearingen, Wildcat, Post Oak, Shelby, Mayeye, Glenn, Coushatta, Cummings & Arroyo Dulce,
Bailey County (5)	Alkalai (saline), Barnett, Blackwater Lake &, Turnbo, Butler & White
Baylor County (9)	Buffalo, Red, Cottonwood Hole, Soap, Deadman, Shawver, Cache, Shady & Round Timber
Bell County (28)	Willow, Ransomer, McDaniel, Leon, Salado Creek, Mountain, Childress, Miller, Leon, Nolan, Taylor, Bluff, Little River, Buchanan, Elliott, Sulphur, Robertson, Dining Room, Big Boiling, Elm, Benedict, Headquarters, Warwick, Willingham, Three Chimney, Abbot & Fort Little River
Bosque County (2)	El Flechazo & Prison
Burleson County (1)	Sour
Brazoria County (3)	Brazoria, Bell, & San Bernard
Crosby County (12)	Couch, Davidson, Rock House, Carizzo, Silver Falls, Ericson, Collett, L7, Wilson, Cottonwood, C-Bar & Gholson
Dickens County (20)	Browning, Pecan Grove, White House, Cottonwood, Patton, Jackson, Sanders, Shinnery, Dripping, Law, Crow, Mitchell, Askins, Davidson, Molly Bailey, Flag, Gyp, Dockum, Spur Headquarters & Rock House
Eastland County (4)	Shinoak, Ellison, Winsett & McGough,
Erath County (5)	Dripping, Indian, Cottonwood, Rock Hole & McGinnis,
Fort Bend County (3)	Spanish, Big & Powell
Garza County (20)	Golf Course, Tipton, Barnum, Double U, Whiskey, Llano, Lane, Indian, Chimney, K, Slick Nasty, OS, Reed, Rocky, Garza, Spring Creek, Cooper, Boy Scout & Box Canyon
Grimes County (3)	Kellum, Piedmont & Gibbons
Hale County (7)	Norfleet, Morrison, Ojo de Augua, Jones, Running Water, Crawfish & Eagle
Haskell County (10)	Rice, Haskell, Willow Pond, Rice, Cook, McGregor, Willow, Buffalo, Blue Hole & Gyp .
Hockley County (3)	Silver, Devil's In Well, Yellow House,
Hood County (6)	Thorp, Parkinson, Walnut, Fort Spunky, Dripping, & Sulphur,

Figure 27a: Springs in the Brazos River Basin
(Source: Brune 1975; 1981)

Johnson County (3)	Cleburne, Big Ham & Little Ham,
Kent County (9)	Two D, Salt Creek Brine (saline), Spring Creek, Carlisle, Hot Brine (saline), Short Croton Brine (saline), Putoff (saline), Elkins & MacKenzie .
King County (15)	Hot (saline), Haystack Brine (saline), Dove Brine (saline), Camp Hollar, Water Canyon,, Finney, Hamm, Farres Spring, Pouring, Lowrance, Gunter, Cave, Lee, Blaine & Rock,
Knox County (24)	Grapevine Croton, Cedar Mountain, Weatherly, Naptha, One Minute, Sheek, Craig, Browder, Speers, China, Big Four, Turner, Hash Knife, Riley, Franklin, Cross, Redder, Watkins, W Cross, Mansfield, Wild Horse, Chalk, Cypress, Mockingbird, Bluff & Trough
Lamb County (14)	King, Alamosa, Soda Lake, Tarabe, Sod House, Rocky Ford, Fieldton, Hart, Bull, Roland, Glumpler, Green, Illusion & Yellow,
Lampasas County (13)	Hancock, Swensen (saline), Indian, Senterfitt, Beef Pen, Townsen, Hughes, Gooch, Swimming Pool, Gold Rock, Cooper & Sulphur
Lee County (14)	Darden, Knobbs, Endor, King, Lawhon, Mare, Smith, Indian Camp, Roberts, Doak, Copperas, Gum & Lincoln
Limestone County (2)	Tehuacana & Springfield
Lubbock County (4)	Lubbock, Buffalo, Johnson & Tinsley,
Lynn County (9)	Double Lakes, Tahoka, Moore, Guthrie, Blanco, Saleh Lake, Gooch, Frost & New Moore
McClennan County (1)	Waco
Milam County (16)	Ross, Hefley, Indian, Tappan, Allen, Caddo, Vineville, Nashville, Lee Garden, Smyrna, Taylor, Buer, Sipe, Sal Ildefenso, Clement & Sharp
Parker County (20)	Bear Creek, Old Soldier's, Gant, Ballou, Trapp, Stimson, Cold, Sweet, Veal, Smith, Malone, Kinnard, Reno, Bluff, Mary, Willow, Cason, Springfalls, Jones & Soda
Palo Pinto County (1)	Clayton
Scurry County (8)	Moar, Deep Creek, Dripping, Camp, Sand Rock, Dunn, Knapp, & Greene
Stonewall County (17)	Beaver, Moore, Stinking, Ward, Dripping, Beidleman, Pike, Hooker, Beaver, Rock, Whiskey, McBroom, Cottonwood, Rayner, Moore, Martin & Salt Flat Bine (saline)
Williamson County (4)	Berry, Mansche Branch, Wilson & Knight

Figure 27b: Springs in the Brazos River Basin
(Source: Brune 1975; 1981)

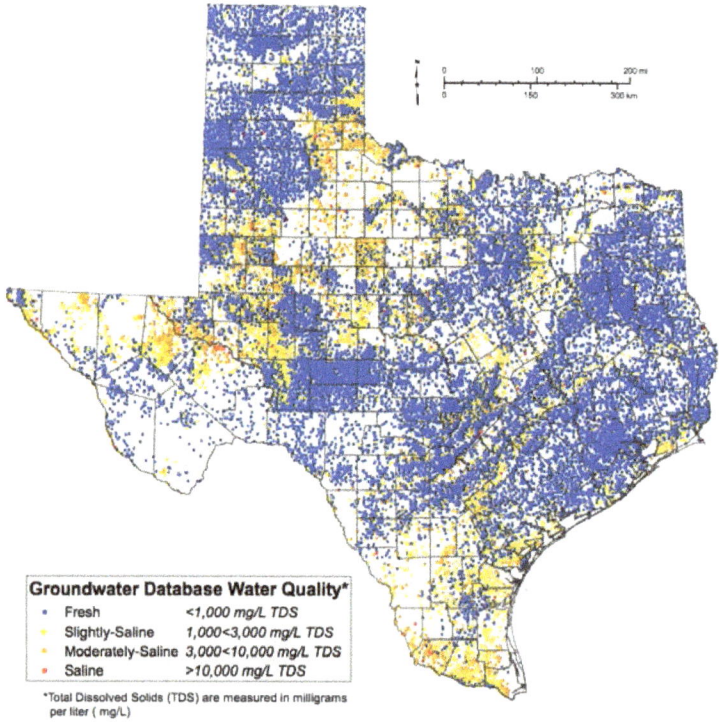

Groundwater Database Water Quality*
- Fresh   <1,000 mg/L TDS
- Slightly-Saline   1,000<3,000 mg/L TDS
- Moderately-Saline 3,000<10,000 mg/L TDS
- Saline   >10,000 mg/L TDS

*Total Dissolved Solids (TDS) are measured in milligrams
per liter (mg/L)

Figure 28: Aquifer Water Quality in Texas:
(Source: Texas Water Development Board 2017)

Brackish Aquifers of Texas

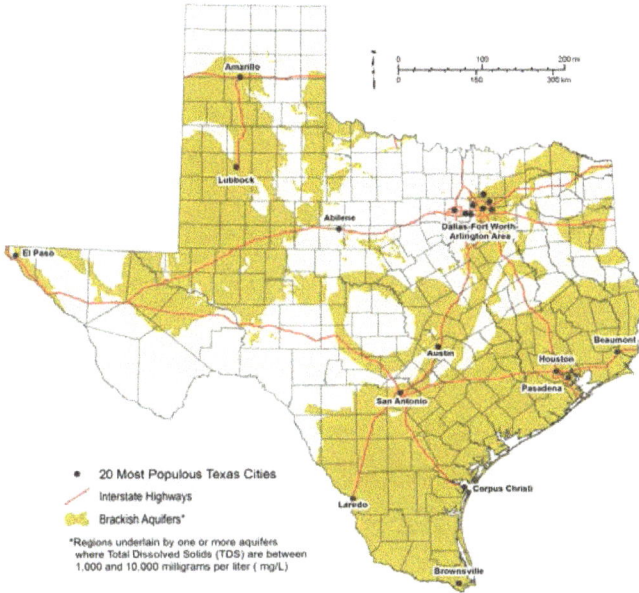

Figure 29: Brackish Aquifers, Texas
(Source: Texas Water Development Board 2017)

Brackish Wells and Brackish Aquifers

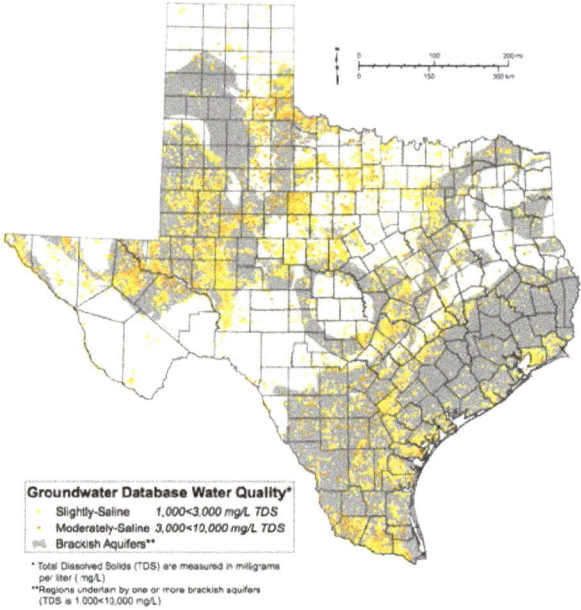

Figure 30: Texas Brackish Wells & Aquifers
(Source: Texas Water Development Board 2017)

Major Aquifer	Volume (acre-feet)		
	1,000 to 3,000 mg/l TDS	3,000 to 10,000 mg/l TDS	1,000 to 10,000 mg/l TDS
Carrizo-Wilcox	270,024,000	160,157,400	430,181,400
Cenozoic-Pecos Alluvium	114,048,000	2,534,400	116,582,400
Edwards-Balcones Fault Zone	14,302,400	24,642,700	38,945,100
Edwards-Trinity (Plateau)	22,299,900	1,960,800	24,260,700
Gulf Coast	354,429,100	168,063,600	522,492,700
Hueco-Bolson[1]	24,490,900	0	24,490,900
Mesilla-Bolson[1]	480,100	0	480,100
Ogallala	32,731,200	3,494,400	36,225,600
Seymour	2,280,000	0	2,280,000
Trinity	97,451,400	80,714,000	178,165,400
	932,537,000	**441,567,300**	**1,374,104,300**
Minor Aquifer	Volume (acre-feet)		
Blaine	8,672,000	10,944,000	19,616,000
Blossom	1,088,500	320,200	1,408,700
Bone Spring-Victorio Peak	6,400,000	2,560,000	8,960,000
Capitan Reef	54,333,500	20,375,000	74,708,500
Dockum	59,473,100	65,466,300	124,939,400
Edwards-Trinity (High Plains)	5,749,700	130,900	5,880,600
Ellenburger-San Saba	18,123,500	28,362,300	46,485,800
Hickory	68,903,000	49,221,300	118,124,300
Lipan	1,202,400	48,100	1,250,500
Nacatoch	10,858,800	3,395,400	14,254,200
Queen City and Sparta[2]	167,281,200	78,430,900	245,712,100
Rustler	18,428,800	18,428,800	36,857,700
West Texas Bolson	62,867,700	0	62,867,700
Whitehorse-Artesia[3]	898,200	16,142,600	17,040,800
Woodbine	17,273,900	26,471,600	43,745,500
Yegua-Jackson	324,864,000	192,993,300	517,857,300
	826,418,300	**513,290,800**	**1,339,709,100**

Source: Modified from data in LBG-Guyton Associates (2003)

NOTES:
TDS = total dissolved solids
Volumes have been rounded off to the nearest hundred
[1] Designated as one aquifer by TWDB
[2] Designated as two separate aquifers by TWDB

Figure 31: Major/Minor Brackish Groundwater Aquifers
(Source: Kalaswad et al. 2004, 9)

Aquifer	Type	Acre Feet Volume 1,000-10,000 mg/l TDS Chlorine
Gulf Coast	Major	522,492,700
Yegua Jackson	Minor	517,857,300
Carrizo-Wilcox	Major	430,181,400
Queen City & Sparta	Minor	245,712,100
Trinity	Major	178,165,400
Dockum	Minor	124,989,400
Hickory	Minor	118,124,300
Cenozoic-Pecos Alluvium	Major	116,582,400
Captian Reef	Minor	74,708

Figure 32: Largest Brackish Texas Aquifer Reserves
(Source: Kalaswad et al. 2004, 9)

While the Brazos River runs through some of the most brackish aquifers in Texas, the bulk of its salt load comes from the Salt Fork in Crosby, Kent, Stonewall, Garza, and King counties. Saline content in the river basin in Crosby, Kent, Stonewall, and Garza counties comes from the Ogallala Aquifer which contains 36,225,600 acre-feet of brackish water. King County additionally taps into the Blaine Aquifer—a minor aquifer containing 19,616,000 acre feet of brackish water (Kalaswad et al. 2004). The Brazos River is thus characterized as being a freshwater river with a naturally high alkaline and saline level. When rainfall is plentiful, the salinity of the river is diminished throughout its course. In periods of drought, natural saline levels increase, exacerbated by inflows of saltwater from the Gulf of Mexico. These are the principal contributors to river salinity. Additional pressures are emerging from West Texas water users (Kaiser 2002) whose demand for freshwater may outstrip the capacity of the region's largest freshwater source the Ogallala Aquifer.

Intensive agriculture and ranching practices combined with population growth around Lubbock, Midland-Odessa and San Angelo are expected to increasingly deplete the aquifer of its water and create demand for new water sources. These freshwater shortages will create incentives for the construction of additional dams and reservoirs throughout the Brazos River basin and will intensify pressure for freshwater to be pumped from other regions of the state to include the lower reaches of the Brazos. These activities will serve to even further deplete the river basin of freshwater flows and allow for increased saltwater intrusion from the Gulf of Mexico. Demand for freshwater pumped in from across Texas is particularly high in the Texas panhandle (Figure 33).

The Ogallala Aquifer (a.k.a. "High Plains Aquifer") is one of the nation's largest and oldest underground water reserves –dating back some 6,000 years. It is classified as a "closed aquifer" signifying its limited capacity for recharge. It is, therefore, entirely depletable given West Texas' arid climate. The recharge of this vast reservoir is entirely dependent upon precipitation, which in this region annually averages from 14 to 18 inches in the farthest regions of West Texas to 18 to 22 inches in West-Central Texas (OSU 2000). These precipitation rates when coupled with high rates of evaporation and the permeability of the region's sandy soils (Ashworth & Hopkins 1995) produce some of the poorest annual recharge rates in Texas (Figure 34) of less than a half-inch (Estaville & Earl 2008).

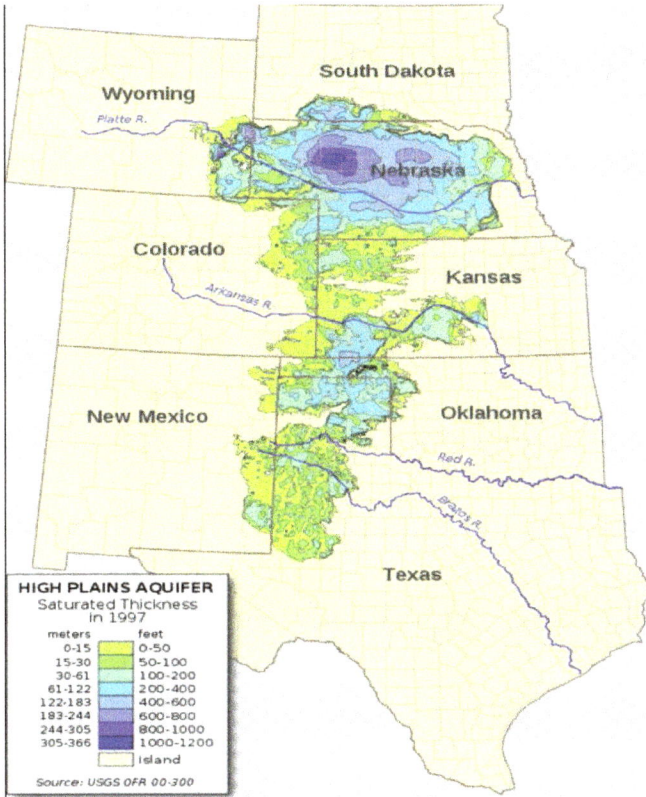

Figure 33: The High Plains (Ogallala) Aquifer
(Source: USGS 1998)

Groundwater Recharge
Estimated Mean Annual

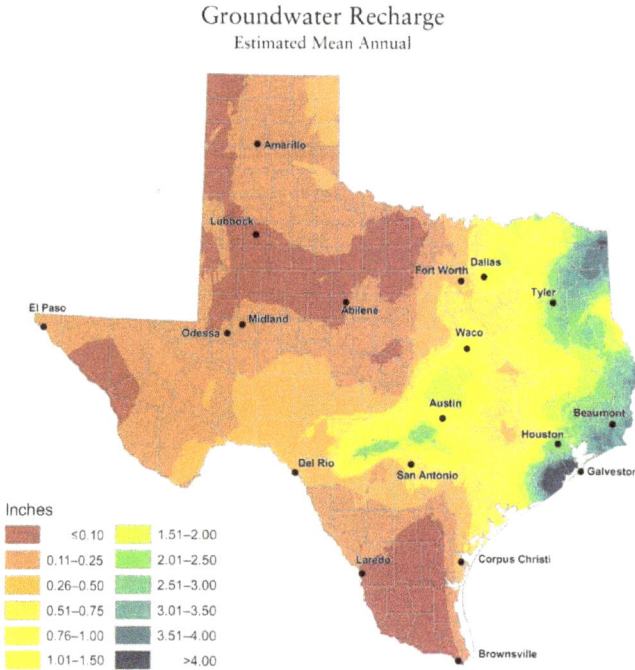

Figure 34: Estimated Mean Groundwater Recharge
(Source: Estaville & Earl 2008)

The Ogallala Aquifer extends 174,000 square miles beneath eight states; ranging in altitude from 6,000 to 1,200 feet (Hornbeck & Keskin 2012). Water contained within this aquifer generally flows at the rate of a foot a day from due west to east and generally flows in the direction of streams (Gutentag et al. 1984). At its deepest point the aquifer extends some 1,200 feet deep. However, throughout the bulk of its range the aquifer extends some 50 to 200 feet in depth (Hornbeck & Keskin 2012).

This aquifer serves as the principal water resource for countless farms, ranches and communities across its expanse. Its water has transformed farming in the region by permitting the cultivation of water-intensive crops rather than hardier, drought resistant species. Historically, more than 90% of the water pumped from the aquifer goes to agriculture producing more than $20 billion annually in food and fiber related commodities (Little 2009). Findings from a recent report, however, suggest utilizing Ogallala groundwater for crop irrigation produces both short-run and long-run effects, increasing the intensity with which the land is cultivated but rendering the crops more drought-sensitive (Hornbeck & Pinar 2012).

Past and current agricultural practices and irrigation patterns do not bode well for the future of agriculture in West Texas and threaten to tap the limited resources of this High Plains aquifer. Consequently, water-managers across West Texas are beginning to restrict water withdrawals from the aquifer forcing some farmers to adopt what is called "dry land" farming to produce crops requiring little or no irrigation. While these crops preserve the increasingly scarce water resources of the region, they result in much smaller crop production and smaller profits than in the era of extensive groundwater irrigation (Walton 2013).

Per a 2014 USGS report (McClure 2014), water levels in the Ogallala Aquifer began declining soon after significant irrigation began in 1950. Since then (through 2013) the average water table in the aquifer has declined by 15.4 feet from the pre-irrigation era for a decline in aquifer storage of 266.77 acre-feet, of which a 36 million acre-feet decline occurred between 2011 and 2013 (McClure 2014, 1). Unfortunately, the greatest aquifer decline occurred in West Texas directly beneath the Brazos River basin (Figure 35) where the water table has fallen between 100 to 150 feet.

This fact is further reflected in Figure 36 which illustrates that the most significant impact of irrigation throughout the range of the aquifer occurred in Texas—and by a significant extent (McClure 2014, 7). This 2014 report confirmed similar findings published in 2013 regarding aquifer declines between 1900 and 2008, reporting total aquifer depletion of 340.9 cubic kilometers and depletion in Texas of 181.9 cubic kilometers (Konikow 2013, 4). Projections suggest that if water use continues at its historic rate the Ogallala Aquifer will be completely depleted by 2060 (Hegeman 2013).

Population growth in cities like Lubbock and Midland-Odessa, Texas also contributes to the depletion of the Ogallala Aquifer. Currently, Lubbock—the second largest city in the region with 230,000 residents and home to Texas Tech University—is expected to experience continued growth and increase to 254,000 residents by 2020 (Rafique 2016). West Texas's largest metropolitan area—Midland-Odessa, the nation's fastest growing municipal area—grew to 326,115 residents between 2010-2015 (Durbin 2015). Known as Texas's "Petroplex," it extends to nearby San Angelo and comprises a metropolitan statistical area estimated to swell by 2018 by another 96,000 people (The Perryman Group 2015).

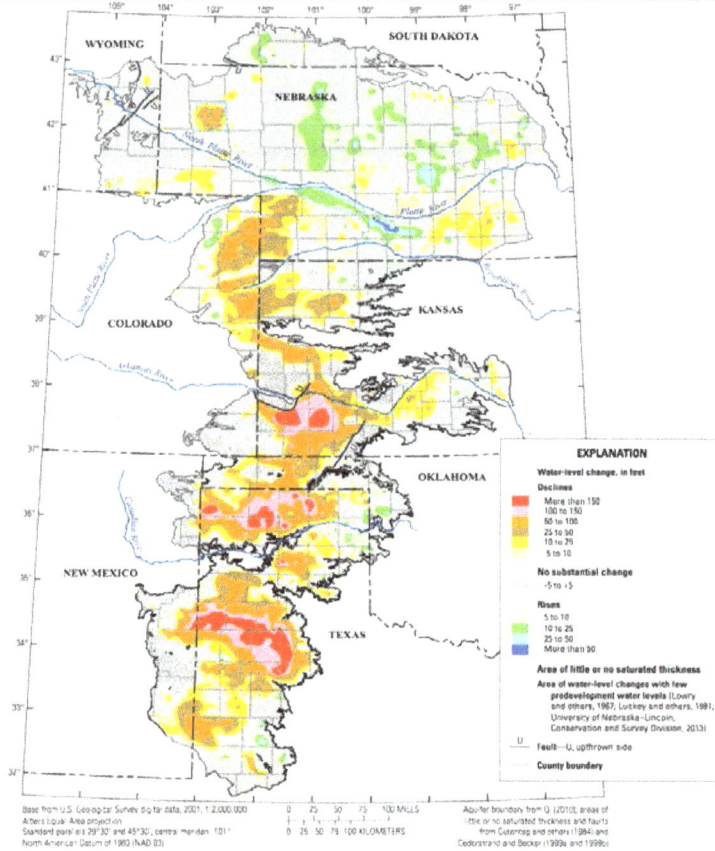

Figure 35: Water-Level Changes - Ogallala Aquifer (1949-2013)
(Source: McClure 2014, 7)

State	Area-weighted, average water-level change, in feet	
	Predevelopment to 2013	2011–13
Colorado	-14.3	-2.2
Kansas	-25.5	-3.0
Nebraska	-0.3	-1.5
New Mexico	-16.5	-0.6
Oklahoma	-12.3	-2.0
South Dakota	1.8	0
Texas	-41.2	-3.5
Wyoming	-0.8	0
High Plains aquifer	**-15.4**	**-2.1**

Figure 36: Regional Aquifer Water Changes in Feet
(Source: McClure 2014, 8)

Oil, Natural Gas and Water Reserves

At the heart of this anticipated metropolitan growth is "fracking" and the development of West Texas oil and natural gas reserves. Over the long term the nation's hunger for energy is expected to contribute to the growth of this region—even though that growth may be at times mercurial and sensitive to current oil and gas prices (Collier 2016; Klare 2016; Knoema 2016). The net effect of the growth in fracking for oil and natural gas in West Texas is a population boom that—beyond the impact of agriculture and ranching—will further exacerbate the demand for water.

Compounding this effect is the fact that fracking requires prodigious water resources to force water into underground fissures and drive oil and gas upward into the well-casing. These water resources come from the Ogallala and Edwards-Trinity Plateau aquifer that are already overdrawn for agricultural and municipal water use across the region. While water for oil and gas exploration and recovery requires less than 1% of the state's entire water demand (Clark 2014), this water is drawn from an arid region. In Texas fracking is taking place in the Barnet and Permian shale formations, both underlying the Brazos River basin (Figure 37). Moreover, much of the fracking is occurring within the bounds of the Ogallala Aquifer in areas where groundwater depletion rates range from 100 to 400 cubic kilometers (Freyman 2014).

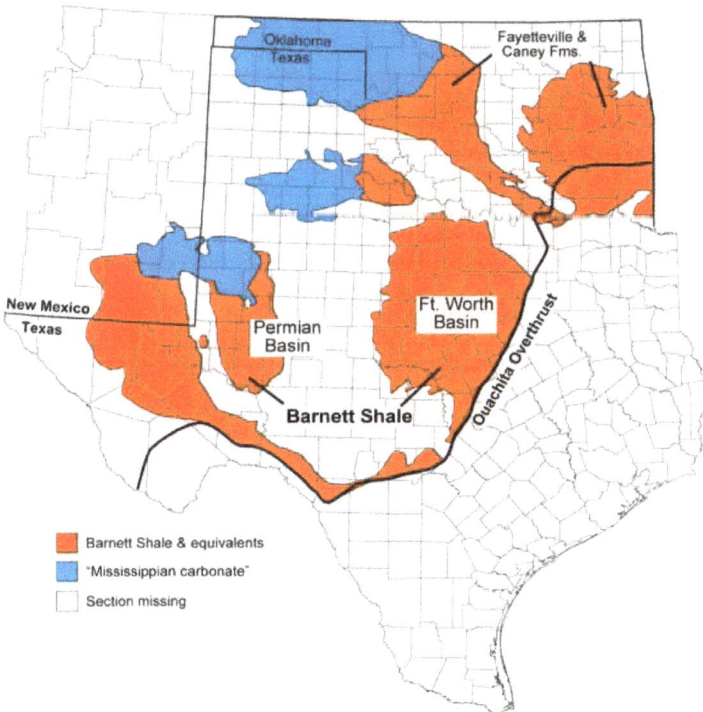

Figure 37: Texas Shale Energy Development
(Source: TCEQ 2016; 2009)

Texas is without doubt "ground-zero" for the conflict between the demand and availability of energy-related water resources. With its immense shale energy production resources, it is anticipated that Texas will be struggling over the next decade to balance energy exploration with groundwater resource management, especially since the state has experienced numerous periods of drought over the last decade and can reasonably expect to experience additional droughts in the future. In 2014 alone two-thirds of Texas experienced drought conditions that placed severe stress upon its most vital aquifers—all while the state's population grew in part driven by energy exploration and development. In fact, so severe is this stress that in counties like Karnes, Gonzales, Glasscock, Irion, Reagan and DeWitt shale producers are frantically searching to develop alternative freshwater resources (Freyman 2014).

This water crisis is particularly critical in the Permian Basin of West Texas where more than 70% of the Permian's wells are in water-stressed areas—much of which includes the already depleted Ogallala Aquifer. Some 9,300 wells have been developed in this region since 2011 and it is anticipated that by 2018 oil production is expected to grow to 1.9 million barrels of oil per day. However, energy exploration in West Texas is a risky business and companies pursuing oil production in the Permian Basin—such as Apache, Pioneer, Devon, Occidental Petroleum, Cimarex, Concho Resources, Energen and Laredo Petroleum—incur significant financial and water-stress exposure in their pursuit of oil and natural gas (Freyman 2014).

The Ongoing Issue of Salinity

Given these conditions of drought, aquifer depletion, expanded energy exploration, municipal population growth, agricultural and ranching expansion and population growth in West Texas, oil tycoon T. Boone Pickens recognized an economic opportunity to provide water for an increasingly thirsty West Texas market. In 2009 Pickens created the Mesa Water Company to meet current and future water demand by impounding freshwater resources in other parts of Texas and piping this freshwater westward to the High Plains of Texas (Berfield 2008; Patoski 2001). While this project benefits West Texas consumers and reduces pressure on the aquifer, it does so at price, depleting other streams and rivers of water, which will in turn reduce stream flow and ultimately result in additional salinity penetrating from the Gulf of Mexico or from encroaching upstream from salt and mineral deposits.

Penetration of Gulf of Mexico water upriver into the Brazos is heightened by the fact that the Gulf Coast Aquifer stretching along the coast contains a large volume of saline water that will increasingly be drawn up into the Brazos River and into freshwater wells along the river basin as freshwater flows down river decline—whether that decline be driven by river impoundment, transport of freshwater from the river to West Texas or by periodic drought. Compromising water quality in the portion of the Brazos transecting the Gulf Coast Aquifer only exacerbates the degree to which upstream salinity is increased along the Brazos River Alluvium. The Brazos River Alluvium is a shallow freshwater aquifer consisting of "water-bearing sediments, primarily gravel and sand" located along both banks of the river in parts of present day Austin, Bosque, Brazos, Burleson, Falls, Fort Bend, Grimes, Hill, McLennan, Milam, Robertson, Waller, and Washington counties. Beyond Brazos River water seepage, this aquifer is supplied with water flows from the larger Gulf

Coast Aquifer to the south as well as other smaller aquifers and is on the average some 8 miles wide and 100 feet deep (Davidson et al. 2006). Water quality in the aquifer varies regionally ranging from less than 1,000 milligrams per liter of total dissolved solids to 3,000 milligrams and is mainly used for irrigation purposes. (Davidson et al. 2006).

Population and Industrial Growth along the Middle and Lower Brazos

Given the extent to which the Brazos River has been impounded, pumped and diverted to meet municipal, agricultural, recreational and energy-related needs this stream bears little resemblance to the wild river early explorers and indigenous peoples encountered centuries earlier. The once unruly and untamed Brazos River has been domesticated over the years with the development of numerous dams and reservoirs up and down its length and across the tributary systems that flow into it. Domestication of the river has also contributed to the growth of cities and communities as well as to the growth of agriculture, recreation and industry throughout the Brazos River basin—all of which are dependent upon access to plentiful freshwater. The net effect of the region's agricultural, municipal, industrial, economic, population and energy-related growth is a seemingly endless demand for freshwater that outstrips the freshwater resources.

As of 2010, the upper, middle and lower stretches of the river encompassed approximately 3.75 million acre-feet of freshwater capacity while experiencing a demand of approximately 3.2 million acre feet. By 2020 it is anticipated that freshwater demand will almost equal water supply (which barring extreme drought conditions is expected to remain relatively constant at 3.75 million acre-feet). By 2030, demand for freshwater resources is expected to exceed supply by approximately 2.5 million acre-feet and continue to increase through 2060 when demand is expected to exceed supply by almost 1 million acre-feet annually (Figure 38) (LBB 2015, 12).

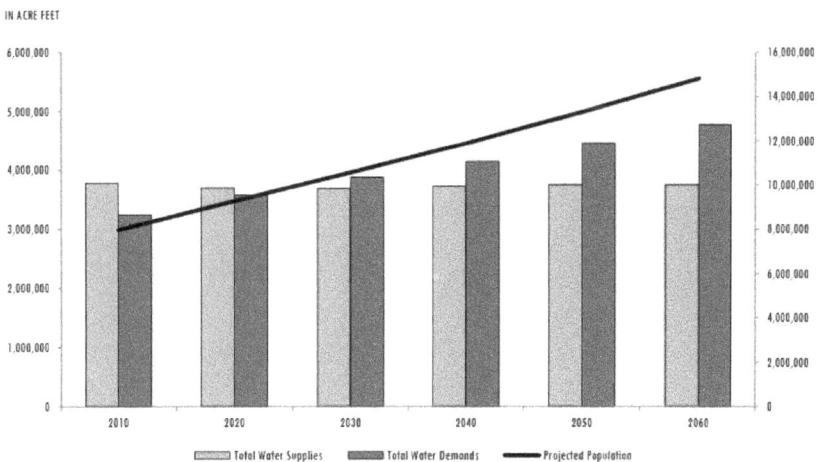

Figure 38: Demand and Supply for Brazos River Water
(Source: LBB 2015)

A significant portion of this demand is driven by population and industrial growth to include the lower Brazos basin within the greater Houston-Galveston metropolitan area - a rate that dwarfs the population growth of all the basin's West Texas communities (Houston-Galveston Area Council, 2016). In Brazoria County, southwest of Houston, increased water demand has been stimulated by industrial expansion and by Dow Chemical who operates the largest petro-chemical plant in the Western Hemisphere at the mouth of the river. This growing industrial capacity depends upon access to large quantities of freshwater—demand that is compounded by the influence of a burgeoning labor force employed by Dow Chemical and other companies.

As of 2015, the largest cities residing within the lower to middle Brazos River Basin include Waco (pop. 124,805), Temple (pop. 66,102), Galveston (pop. 47,723), Belton (pop. 18,216), Freeport (pop. 12,049) and Graham (pop. 8,771). While technically speaking Houston principally relies upon water from the San Jacinto and Trinity rivers the dramatic geographic expansion of the greater Houston metropolitan areas westward and southward into Galveston, Fort Bend and Brazoria Counties means that population growth in the region will significantly impact the Brazos River watershed. As of 2016 Houston's population included 2,296,224 people (U.S. Census Bureau 2016). By 2040 it is anticipated that the population of the Houston-Galveston area will increase to 9.6 million people (HGAC 2016), while Brazoria County increases to between 500,000 and one million people, and Galveston County swells to 427,059 residents (Office of the Texas State Demographer 2011).

Beyond the population growth anticipated along Gulf Coast and in the high plains of West Texas, significant population growth is expected along the middle Brazos River basin in central Texas. For instance, McClennan County (where Waco is situated) Bell County (Temple and Belton) and Young County (Graham) are expected to grow by between 100,000—500,000 by 2040. Figure 39 illustrates anticipated county population growth across the state of Texas and throughout the Brazos River basin. Population growth in Brazoria County has been significantly influenced by the growth in the county's petrochemical industry. While this growth in population has progressively served to increase water consumption, the principal impact upon freshwater resources has been the petrochemical industry itself. In Freeport - home to the largest petro-chemical plant in the world - industrial water usage by Dow alone in 2012 amounted to 155 million gallons of water daily, far outstripping the daily water use of the 1.3 million residents of Dallas who consumed 143 million gallons a day. In fact, between 2009 and 2012 Dow Chemical's Brazoria County facilities used more than 1 trillion gallons of water (McPhate & Sigman 2014).

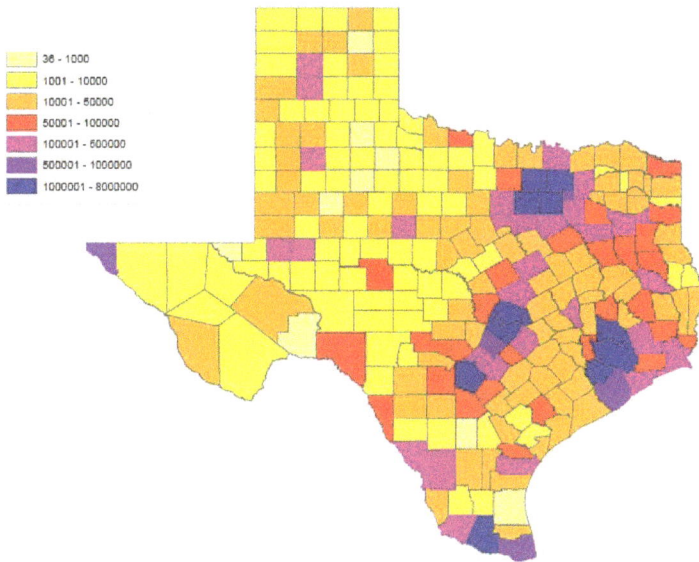

Figure 39: Projected County Population, 2040
(Source: Texas State Demographer 2011)

Water Shortfalls Statewide and in the Brazos River Basin

Texas is the third fastest growing state in the nation with a 2016 population of 26,059,203 people (Forbes 2016). The state's economy is scalding hot growing 3.8% in 2015—a rate faster than any other state except Oregon and California. Moreover, Texas has almost a third of the nation's oil reserves and although oil prices fell marginally in between 2012 and 2015, it remains a central feature of the state's long-term economic growth. Although recent declines in oil prices have depressed the local economies in any number of petroleum and gas dependent counties the overall unemployment rate in the state fell from 5.1% in 2014 to 4.5% in 2015 even though the jobless rate in many of the state's top oil-producing counties increased. By comparison the state's economic growth - led by mining - grew 12.4% (Sauter et al. 2016). The long-term outlook for the Texas economy is however optimistic. Per the Perryman Group—a leading economic forecaster:

> "The Texas economy is likely to continue to see moderate growth. Output (real gross product) is projected to more than double, expanding from about $1.5 trillion in 2015 to $3.5 trillion in 2040 (a 3.35% annual pace). Annual output in the services sector is expected to increase by about $564.9 billion between 2015 and 2040, with manufacturing up by some $338.0 billion" (Perryman Group 2015).

Approximately 6.2 million net new jobs are expected to be added over the period, a 1.64% yearly pace which will put total wage and salary employment in 2040 at more than 18.5 million. Job gains will be concentrated in the services and trade sectors, and the numbers of jobs in all major industry groups are forecast to rise" (Perryman Group 2015). Unavoidably, population expansion and economic growth requires generous water resources. Given the state's rapacious thirst for water to be used industrially, agriculturally, recreationally, municipally and to feed the burgeoning energy industry demand for Texas water is expected to exceed available supply (Callahan 2012, 175). Population growth alone will create this imbalance of resources and demand as the state's population is projected to increase from 29,650,388 in the year 2020 to 46,323,725 in 2060. During that period demand for water will increase from about 18 million acre-feet of water capacity in 2020 to more than 22 million acre-feet in 2060. However, by the year 2020 the state's water demand will have already exceeded supply by approximately 5 million acre-feet in 2020 and increase to some 8 million acre-feet in 2060 (Callahan 2012, 2-3).

This is similarly a problem within the Brazos River basin where water resources—in great part fueled by industrial water demands - are also projected to exceed supply by 2020 (LLB 2015). Consequently, a strategy for water use needs to be implemented as soon as possible and that this strategy must involve conservation efforts along with the development of new freshwater resources. Yet these considerations are narrowly drawn principally from the need to maintain water for human crops, communities and industries. Even more encompassing is the need to consider what is good for the environmental health of the river, its riparian environs and the coastal environment created by the river as it empties into the Gulf of Mexico. Put more succinctly, whatever water resources needed to support human needs in Texas must be compounded by some degree to accommodate environmental needs.

Brazos Region G

Fortunately, the Texas Water Development board has considered the issue of water resource shortfalls throughout the various regions of the Brazos River Basin. Texas monitors the water resources in Brazos River Basin within three regional planning areas: The Llano Estacado Region in West Texas (Region O), the Middle Brazos (Brazos Region G), and along the Lower Brazos to the Gulf of Mexico (Region H). While interrelated each of these region's is unique.

Brazos Region G water planning area (Figure 40) relies upon the Brazos River and its tributaries for 90% of its freshwater which ultimately serves the economic interests of manufacturing, retail trade, agriculture and the service industries. The municipalities served within this region include Abilene, Bryan, College Station, Killeen, Round Rock, Temple, and Waco. Given regional demographic trends Texas Water Development Board made the following projections and recommendations:

- "Additional supply needed in 2060—390,732 acre-feet per year
- Recommended water volume in 2060—587,084 acre-feet per year
- Total capital cost—$3.2 billion
- Conservation accounts for 7 percent of 2060 strategy volumes
- Five new major reservoirs (Brushy Creek, Cedar Ridge, Millers Creek Augmentation, Turkey Peak, Coryell County Reservoir)

- Conjunctive use strategies account for 12 percent of 2060 strategy volumes
- BRA Operation strategy accounts for 14 percent of strategy volumes
- Unmet irrigation and mining needs in all decades; limited unmet steam-electric power and municipal needs in 2010 decade" (Callahan 2012, 68).

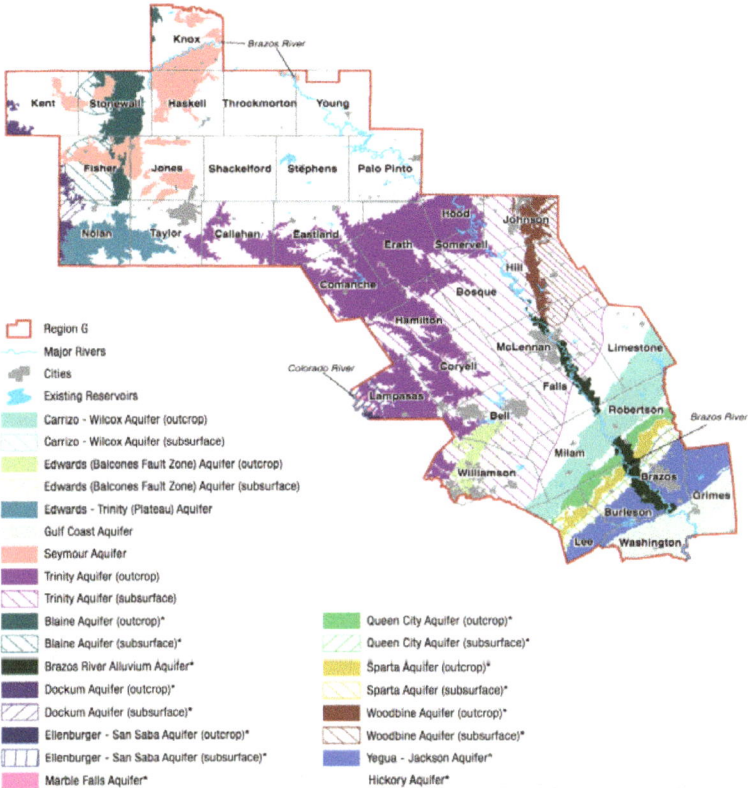

Figure 40: Water Planning Area G
(Source: Callahan 2012, 69)

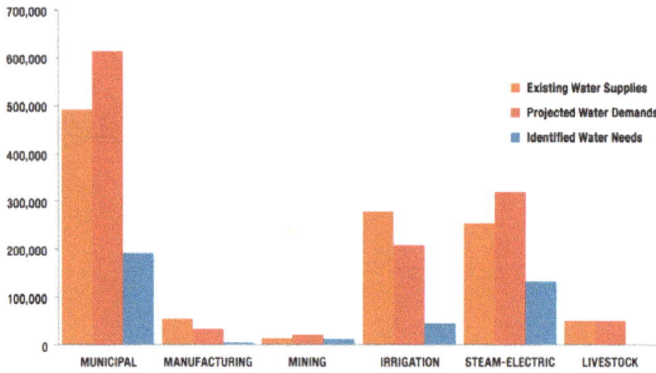

Figure 41: Existing, Projected and Identified Water Needs Region G
(Source: Callahan 2012, 71)

Figure 41 summarizes existing, projected and identified water needs in Brazos Region G. Municipal growth primarily drives future water needs as does accompanying demand for electric utilities. The remaining demand centers around agricultural and municipal irrigation, manufacturing, mining and livestock needs. It is worth noting, however, that in 2012 the Texas Water Development Board assumed that part of the solution to addressing these problems involved enhancing the systems operations capacity of the Brazos River Authority (BRA).

Region H

Region H water planning area (Figure 42) consists of a 15-county region including parts of Trinity, San Jacinto, Brazos, Neches, and Colorado river basins and the Houston metropolitan area. The most significant economic sector in this region is the petrochemical industry followed by medical services, tourism, government, agriculture, fisheries, and transportation. This region also includes the Port of Houston which is the nation's second largest port.

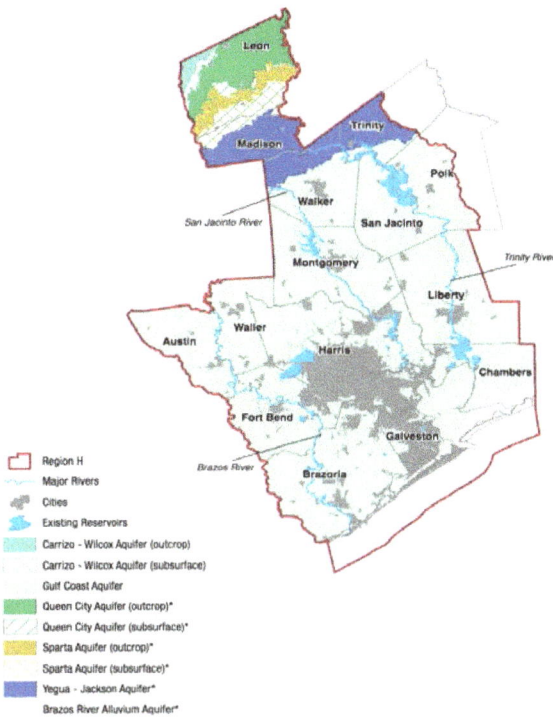

Figure 42: Water Planning Region H
(Source: Callahan 2012, 75)

Given economic and demographic trends within this planning area the Texas Water Development Board arrived at the following projections and recommendations:

- "Additional supply needed in 2060—1,236,335 acre-feet per year
- Recommended water management strategy volume in 2060—1,501,180 acre-feet per year
- Total capital cost—$12 billion
- Conservation accounts for 12 percent of 2060 strategy volumes
- Five new major reservoirs (Allens Creek, Dow Off-Channel, Gulf Coast Water Authority Off-Channel, Brazoria Off-Channel, Fort Bend Off-Channel)
- Reuse accounts for 19 percent of 2060 strategy volumes" (Callahan 2012, 74).

Approximately a quarter of the state's population resided in Region H in 2010 and by 2060 this population is expected to increase by 89% to 11.3 million people and escalate the total demand by 48% (Figure 43). The largest consumption increase involves municipalities where demand will grow by 61%. Similarly, manufacturing will also grow significantly to account for 31% of demand by 2060. By 2060 the available water supply is expected to decline .6% below its 2010 level of 2,621,660 acre feet and the region's reliance on groundwater resources from the Gulf Coast Aquifer will of necessity be further reduced to avoid additional subsidence. By 2060 surface water will supply 2,021,690 acre-feet of capacity and groundwater some 569,361 acre-feet. Reuse will provide another 148,676 acre-feet of water capacity (Callahan 2012, 76).

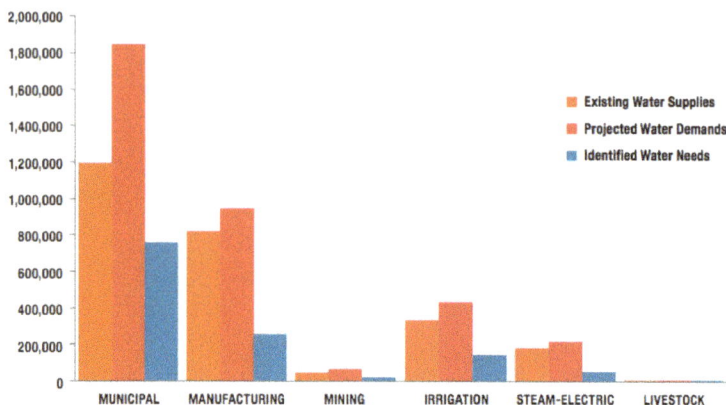

Figure 43: Supply, Demand and Water Needs Region H
(Source: Callahan 2012, 77)

Region O—Llano Estacado Region

Region O (Figure 44) encompasses 21 counties in the southern high plains situated within the Canadian, Red, Colorado and Brazos river basins. It is straddles the Ogallala Aquifer and includes the cities of Lubbock, Plainview, Levelland, Lamesa, Hereford and Brownfield. The economy of this region involves livestock and cotton, producing 60% of the state's annual cotton crop. Given economic and demographic trends within this planning area the Texas Water Development Board published a set of projections and recommendations to include:

- "Additional supply needed in 2060—2,366,036 acre-feet per year
- Recommended water management strategy volume in 2060—395,957 acre-feet per year
- Total capital cost—$1.1 billion
- Conservation accounts for 74 percent of 2060 strategy volumes
- Two new major reservoirs (Jim Bertram Lake 07, Post)
- Significant unmet irrigation and livestock needs" (Callahan 2012, 74).

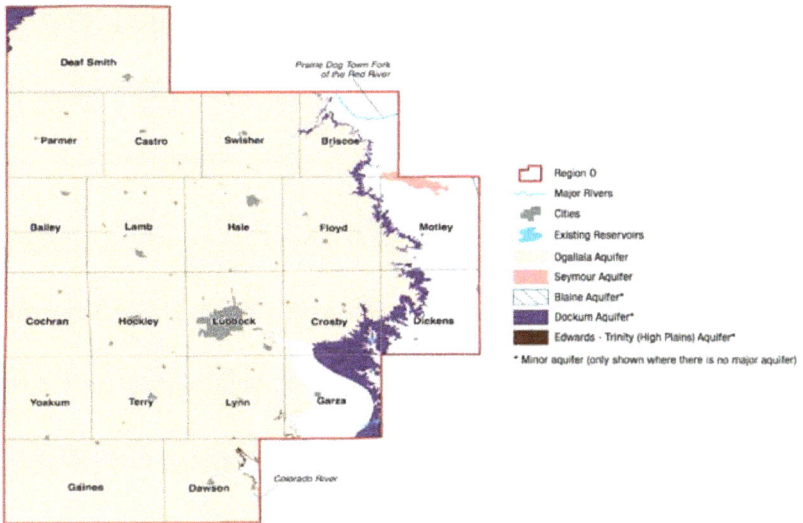

Figure 44: Water Planning Area O—Llano Estacado
(Source: Callahan 2012, 117)

Region O relies upon groundwater from the Ogallala Aquifer. Some 97% of the region's water supply was drawn from this aquifer in 2010. By 2060 total surface and groundwater resources will decline 56% with most of this reduction occurring in depleted Ogallala Aquifer resources. The principal water use is irrigation (Figure 45) with 94% of available resources dedicated to crop irrigation. Regional water needs are projected to increase 86% in 2060 with more than 90% of additional needs accountable to irrigation, followed by municipal needs (Callahan 2012, 116-120).

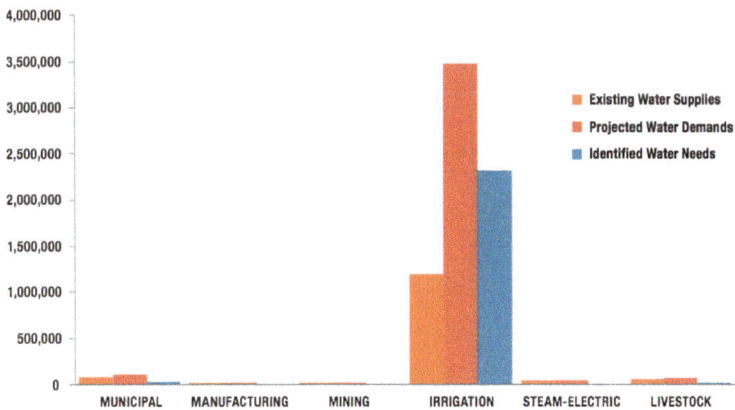

Figure 45: Region O Water Supply, Demand and Needs
(Source: Callahan 2012, 119)

As of the writing of this report only 2% of the state's population resided in the Llano Estacado Region and that population is expected to increase by 12% by 2060. Due to decreased irrigation associated with declining well yields from the Ogallala Aquifer it is anticipated that water demand will decrease by 15%. However, water supply is expected to decrease at a much faster rate as the region engages in the controlled draw-down of the Ogallala Aquifer. By 2060 total surface and groundwater resources are expected to decline 56%. Ultimately water needs in this region are expected to increase 56% by 2060 requiring an additional 2,318,004 acre-feet of water capacity (Callahan 2012, 119-120).

However, at the time this report was written, hydro fracking shale deposits for oil and natural gas had not begun in earnest therefore this report fails to account for projected needs for water for hydro fracking and to support the anticipated municipal growth that will accompany energy related economic growth in this region. Consequently, energy-related water demand and additional shortfalls are not reflected in this 2012 analysis (Callhan 2012). Energy exploration will undoubtedly contribute to municipal growth in the Lubbock area which is expected to swell to some 254,000 residents by 2020 (Rafique 2016). Moreover, hydro fracking requires water resources which are exceedingly scarce in the arid region of West Texas. Although water for oil and gas exploration and recovery requires little volume (less than 1% of the state's entire water demand (Clark 2014), this water is drawn from the already stressed Ogallala Aquifer and will additionally contribute to water woes in Region O.

Conclusion

This concludes the backgrounder on water resources within the Brazos River Basin. It describes the geological and hydrological characteristics of the river as well as the demographic, social and economic characteristics of the people and communities up and down its banks and tributaries. The backgrounder also discusses matters of public policy, regulatory oversight and water rights and has particularly focused upon the problem of salinization throughout the course of the river. What remains is a case study discussion of stakeholders residing in and around the Brazos River basin who are seeking to maintain and improve the quality of water throughout the basin.

The following two case studies address environmental and human needs across the Brazos River basin. The first case will discuss the perspective of a Brazos River stakeholder group (Friends of the Brazos) who, out of concern over the increased salinization of the river and its impact upon the surrounding riparian environment, have forged an unlikely public, private and industrial coalition to protect the Brazos. The second case study situated along the Brazos involves the Dow Chemical facility in Freeport Texas that is wholly dependent upon freshwater draws from the Brazos to maintain its chemical production processes. In both cases issues of water rights as proscribed by Texas state statute are balanced against the rights of the public and environmental rights.

REFERENCES

Amelinckx, Andrew. 2015. "Even Without a Drought, We're Depleting Groundwater at an Alarming Pace." *Modern Farmer.* (July 30), Accessed September 8, 2016 http://modernfarmer.com/2015/07/ogallala-aquifer-depletion/

Archer, Kenna Lang. 2015. *Unruly Waters: A Social and Environmental History of the Brazos River.* Albuquerque: University of New Mexico Press.

Ashworth, John B. and Janie Hopkins. 1995. *Aquifers of Texas.* Austin: Texas Water Development Board.

Baker, R.C., L. S. Hughes, and I.D. Yost. 1969. *Natural Sources of Salinity in the Brazos River, Texas—With Particular Reference to the Croton and Salt Croton Creek basins.* Washington: U.S. Department of Interior and the U.S. Government Printing Office.

Berfield, Susan. 2008. "There Will Be Water." *Bloomberg Businessweek.* (June 12), Accessed September 8, 2016 http://www.bloomberg.com/news/articles/2008-06-11/there-will-be-water

Brazos River Authority. 2017. "The Brazos River." Accessed July 17, 2017 https://www.brazos.org/About-Us/About-the-BRA/About-the-Brazos-River

———. 2016. "Brazos River," Accessed August 29, 2016 https://www.brazos.org/About-Us/About-the-BRA/About-the-Brazos-River

Brune, Gunnar. 1981. *Springs of Texas.* (Volumes 1-4), Fort Worth: Branch-Smith Inc.

———. 1975. *Major and Historical Springs of Texas.* Austin: Texas Water Board.

Bryan, Kirk. 2017. "Hurricane Harvey: Brazos River Rising After 5 Days of Unrelenting Rain." *Sugar Land Patch.* (September 1), Accessed September 2, 2017 https://patch.com/texas/houston/hurricane-harvey-brazos-river-rising-after-five-days-unrelenting-rain

Bureau of Economic Geology. 1996. "River Basin Map of Texas," University of Texas at Austin, Accessed July 17, 2017 http://www.beg.utexas.edu/UTopia/images/pagesizemaps/river_basin.pdf

Callahan, Melanie. 2012. *Water for Texas 2012 State Water Plan.* Austin: Texas State Water Development Board.

Clark, Megan. 2014. "Hydraulic Fracking in Regions Experiencing Low Water Supply Poses Risks for Investors, According to Ceres." *International Business Times.* (February 7), Accessed September 26, 2016 at http://www.ibtimes.com/hydraulic-fracking-regions-experiencing-low-water-supply-poses-risks-investors-1553978

Collier, Klah. 2016. "Despite Oil Bust, Midland is Still Booming." *The Texas Tribune.* (June 1), Accessed September 8, 2016 https://www.texastribune.org/2016/06/01/midland-leaders-confident-bust-has-bottomed-out/

Davidson, Sarah C. and Robert E. Mace, Robert E. 2006. "Aquifers of the Gulf Coast of Texas—An Overview" In *Aquifers of the Gulf Coast.* Edited by Robert E. Mace, Sarah C. Davidson, Edward S. Angle and William F. Mulllican Sarah C., Angle, Edward S. and Mullican III, William F. Austin: Texas Water Development Board, 1-22.

Dowell, C. L. 1964. "Dams and Reservoirs in Texas." *Water Bulletin.* 6408, Texas Water Commission, Austin, TX, Accessed September 8, 2016 http://www.twdb.texas.gov/publications/reports/bulletins/doc/B6408.pdf

Durbin, James. 2015. "Midland-Odessa CSA Leads the Nation in Population Growth." *Midland Reporter-Telegram.* (March 29), Accessed September 8, 2016 http://www.mrt.com/business/development/article_f8e7e142-f5fa-11e5-a58f-37c6891827a3.html

Estaville, L. E. and R.A. Earl. 2008. *Texas Water Atlas.* College Station: Texas A&M University Press.

Forbes. 2016. "The Ten Fastest Growing States in the U.S.—No. 3 Texas." *Forbes.* Accessed September 29, 2016 http://www.forbes.com/pictures/mhj45mejl/2-district-of-columbia/#76f8f614665e

Freyman, Monika. 2014. *Hydraulic Fracking and Water Stress: Water Demand by the Numbers.* Boston: CERES.

George, Peter G., Robert E. Mace and Rima Petrossian. 2011. *Aquifers of Texas.* Austin: Texas Water Development Board.

Graves, John. 1959. *Goodbye to a River.* Philadelphia: Curtis Publishing.

Guhlin, Aida. 2016. "Ecogregions of Texas." Accessed July 17, 2017 https://arguhlin.files.wordpress.com/2014/07/lab6.png

Gutentag, E.D., F. J. Heimes, N. C. Krothe, R.R. Ludkey and J. B. Weeks. 1984. "Geohydrology of the High Plains Aquifer in parts of Colorado, Kansas, Nebraska, New Mexico, Oklahoma, South Dakota, Texas, and Wyoming." (High Plains RASA Project), *U.S. Geological Survey Professional Paper 1400-B. U.S. Geological Survey*. Alexandria: U.S. Geological Survey, 1-59.

Hayes, Mark. 2002. "River Basins of Texas." Texas Water Development Board, Austin, TX. (July), Accessed September 26, 2016 https://ceprofs.tamu.edu/kbrumbelow/CVEN664/CVEN664_Handouts.htm

Hegeman, Roxana. 2013. "High Plains Aquifer Will Be 69 Percent Depleted In 50 Years, K-State Study Say.," *Wichita Eagle*. (August 26), Accessed September 8, 2016 http://www.kansas.com/news/article1121517.html

Hornbeck, Richard and Pinar Keskin. 2012. "The Historically Evolving Impact of the Ogallala Aquifer: Agricultural Adaptation to Groundwater and Drought." Harvard Environmental Economics Program, Discussion Paper 12-39, (September), Accessed September 8, 2016 https://www.hks.harvard.edu/m-rcbg/heep/papers/hornbeck_dp39.pdf

Houston-Galveston Area Council (HGAC). 2016. "2040 RTP Demographics." Accessed August 29, 2016 http://www.h-gac.com/taq/plan/2040/demographics.aspx

Kaiser, Ronald A. 2002. *Handbook of Texas Water Law: Problems and Needs*. College Station: Texas A&M University, Texas Water Resource Institute.

Kalaswad, S., B. Christian and R. Petrossian. 2004. *Brackish Groundwater in Texas*. Austin: Texas Water Development Board.

Kimmel, Jim. 2011. *Exploring the Brazos River—From Beginning to End*. San Marcos: River Books.

Klare, Michael T. 2016. "The Future of Oil is Here—And it Doesn't Look Pretty." *The Nation*. (March 8), Accessed September 29, 2016 https://www.thenation.com/article/the-future-of-oil-is-here-and-it-doesnt-look-pretty/

Knoema. 2016. "Crude Oil Price Forecast: Long Term 2016 to 2025 | Data and Charts." *Knoema Data Analysis*. (September 13), Accessed September 29, 2016 https://knoema.com/yxptpab/crude-oil-price-forecast-long-term-2016-to-2025-data-and-charts

Konikow, Leonard F. 2013. "Groundwater Depletion in the United States (1900–2008)." U.S. Geological Survey Scientific Investigations Report 2013−5079, Accessed September 8, 2016 at http://pubs.usgs.gov/sir/2013/5079/SIR2013-5079.pdf

Legislative Budget Board (LBB). 2015. "Texas Management and Performance Review: Brazos River Authority." (February), Accessed August 29, 2016 http://www.lbb.state.tx.us/Documents/Publications/Other/1860_BrazozRiverAuthority.pdf

Little, Jane Braxton. 2009. "The Ogallala Aquifer: Saving a Vital U.S. Water Source." *Scientific American*. (March 1), Accessed September 8, 2016 http://www.scientificamerican.com/article/the-ogallala-aquifer/

McClure, Virginia L. 2014. "Water-Level Changes and Change in Water in Storage in the High Plains Aquifer, Predevelopment to 2013 and 2011–13." United States Geological Survey (USGS), Groundwater Resources Program, Scientific Investigations Report 2014-52118, Accessed September 8, 2016 http://pubs.usgs.gov/sir/2014/5218/pdf/sir2014_5218.pdf

McPhate, Christian and Ashlea Sigman. 2014. "Battling Over the Brazos: Dwindling River and Reservoirs Spark Disputes Over Dam Construction." *Dallas Morning News*. (June 29), Accessed August 17, 2016 at http://res.dallasnews.com/interactives/drought/brazos/

Office of the Texas State Demographer. 2011. "Rural Health and Texas Demographic Characteristics and Trends." (September 14), Accessed August 29, 2016 http://txsdc.utsa.edu/Resources/Presentations/OSD/2011/2011_09_14_Texas_Rural_Health_Forum.pdf

Oregon State University (OSU). 2000. "Texas Annual Precipitation Map." Spatial Climate Analysis Service, Eugene, OR, Accessed July 17, 2017 at http://www.landwithminerals.com/resource_center/article/texas-average-anuual-precipitation-map/

Patoski, Joe Nick. 2001. "Boone Pickens Wants to Sell You His Water." *Texas Monthly*. (August), Accessed September 8, 2016 at http://www.texasmonthly.com/the-culture/boone-pickens-wants-to-sell-you-his-water/

Perryman Group. 2015. "West Texas." *The Perryman Group Newsletter*. 3(3), Accessed September 8, 2016 https://www.perrymangroup.com/newsletter/VOL31NO03TPR&TLpage04.pdf

Rafique, Sarah. 2016. "Lubbock Demographics Suggest Continued Growth." *Lubbock Avalanche-Journal*. (March 27), Accessed September 8, 2016 at http://lubbockonline.com/discover-lubbock/2016-03-25/lubbock-demographics-suggest-continued-growth#

Rosen, Rudolph. 2017. "Aquifers and Springs." *Texas Aquatic Science*. Produced by the Texas Parks and Wildlife, The Harte Research Institute for Gulf of Mexico Studies at Texas A&M University-Corpus Christi, and The Meadows Center for Water and the Environment at Texas State University, Accessed July 17, 2017 http://texasaquaticscience.org/aquifers-springs-aquatic-science-texas/

Sauter, Michael B., Samuel Stebbins and Evan Comen. 2016. "States with the Fastest (and Slowest) Growing Economies." *24/7 Wall Street*. (June 16), Accessed September 29, 2016 http://247wallst.com/special-report/2016/06/16/states-with-the-fastest-and-slowest-growing-economies-2/3/

Texas Almanac. 2016. "Secondary Streams of Texas." Accessed September 16, 2016 http://texasalmanac.com/topics/environment/secondary-streams-texas

———. 2015. "Texas Aquifers." Accessed February 3, 2015 http://texasalmanac.com/topics/environment/aquifers-texas

Texas Commission on Environmental Quality (TCEQ). 2016. "Rights to Surface Water in Texas." (March), Accessed August 17, 2016 http://lakesweetwater.com/sw-lake-files/RightsToSurfaceWaterInTexas.pdf

———. 2009 "Brazos River Basin Assessment." Accessed August 29, 2016 http://www.tceq.state.tx.us/waterquality/assessment/02twqi/basins/brazos.html

Texas Water Development Board. 2017. "Upper and Middle Brazos River." Accessed July 17, 2017 http://www.twdb.texas.gov/surfacewater/flows/instream/middle_lower_brazos/index.asp

———. 2008. "Major Aquifers of Texas," Accessed July 17, 2017 http://texasnuclearsafety.org/downloads/major_tx_aquifers.pdf

U.S. Census Bureau. 2016. "Five of the Nation's Eleven Fastest Growing Cities are in Texas Census Bureau Reports." (May 19), Accessed August 29, 2016 http://www.census.gov/newsroom/press-releases/2016/cb16-81.html

U.S. Geological Survey (USGS). 1998. "Digital map of the saturated thickness of the High Plains aquifer in parts of Kansas, Nebraska, New Mexico, Oklahoma, South Dakota, Texas and Wyoming, 1996-97." Accessed September 8, 2016 http://water.usgs.gov/GIS/metadata/usgswrd/XML/ofr00-300_sattk9697.xml

Van Zandt, Townes. 2006. "Texas River Song." On *K.R. Wood: Fathers of Texas* (CD). Lago, Vista: Texana Records.

Vogl, A.L. and V. Lopes. 2009. "Impacts of Water Resource Development on Flow Regimes on the Brazos River." *Environmental Monitoring and Assessment*. 157(2-4): 331-345.

Wermund, E. G. 1996. "River Basins of Texas." The Bureau of Economic Geology, University of Texas, Austin, Accessed August 29, 2016 http://www.beg.utexas.edu/UTopia/images/pagesizemaps/river_basin.pdf

Wilder, Forrest. 2012. "Goodbye to the Brazos River?" *Texas Observer*. (January 4), Accessed August 17, 2016 https://www.texasobserver.org/goodbye-to-the-brazos-river/

Walton, Brett. 2013. "Texas High Plains Prepare for Agriculture Without Irrigation." *Circle of Blue—Water News*. (April 5), Accessed September 8, 2016 http://www.circleofblue.org/2013/world/texas-ogallala-photos/

CHAPTER 7

Friends of the Brazos

CASE STUDY THREE

Origins of Friends of the Brazos

Issues of salinity and salt water intrusion from the Gulf of Mexico threaten the freshwater resources of the Brazos from its upper-reaches to the mouth of the river at Freeport. These issues—aggravated as they are by water impoundments, farming and a growing population of consumers—threaten the water supplies of homes, municipalities, farms, ranches, and energy and industrial interests throughout the course of the river. In response, a broad array of stakeholders representing these groups as well as utility providers, industrialists, outdoor enthusiasts and environmentalists from across Texas have come together to preserve the Brazos—creating some of the strangest environmental bedfellows to be found anywhere in the U.S. These diverse interests have come together for a common purpose born of many divergent motivations—namely to preserve one of the treasures of Texas and "Save the Brazos!" (Houston Chronicle 2012). Doing so involves regulating water rights throughout the Brazos River basin and managing the river's resources during droughts and floods (Wilder 2012).

Environmental Flows and Water Rights in Texas

Burgeoning industrial capacity near the mouth of the Brazos River and population growth spurred by the lure of industrial jobs, along with the urban growth in the Houston-Galveston area and the growth of population in the ever-popular Central and West Texas regions increases demand for freshwater throughout the river basin. As this demand steadily increases, so does the need to promote the health of the river by maintaining its "environmental flows." Per the Texas Water Code, an environmental flow "is an amount of water that should remain in a stream or river for the benefit of the environment of the river, bay, and estuary, while balancing human needs" (Title 2, Texas Water Code, Section 11.002.16) (TCEQ 2016). Implicit in the legal designation of "environmental flows" is the need for the state of Texas to balance withdrawal of water at any point along the river against the environmental needs of the river and its ecosystems, as well as considering the "rights" of other users up and down the river to also use the river's water resources.

Of course, this begs the question of what are the "rights" of water users, namely who gets to use how much water from what point and when and who speaks for the rights of the river as an ecosystem. Texas water law adheres to two different legal doctrines:

- The Riparian Doctrine: Water rights are tied to the ownership of the land bordering a river or stream;
- Prior Appropriation Doctrine: Water rights are acquired by compliance with state statutes (Kaiser 2002, 7-8)

Texas law also distinguishes between groundwater and surface water. Groundwater is water that emerges from underground. Groundwater belongs to the landowner from which the water is captured. Moreover, landowners have the right to pump and capture the available water even when doing so may have a deleterious impact upon other landowners. By comparison, surface water is a public good and belongs to the State of Texas (Kaiser 2002).

In 1967, the Texas State Legislature merged the riparian and prior appropriation doctrines into a single system passing the Water Rights Adjudication Act that required persons claiming a riparian right to file their claim with the Texas Water Commission by no later than 1969. The legislation also provided for a unified water permit system which required users to receive permission from the state in a so-called "water right" issued by the Texas Commission on Environmental Quality (TCEQ) (Kaiser 2002). Per the Texas Water Code, water rights can be characterized as "first-in-time, first-in-right" which means that those who first make use of the water right in time have a senior status (senior water rights) to those who acted on their water rights later. TCEQ, the agency administering these water rights, in turn creates a priority list among all water rights claimants establishing the order in which users can use water resources as well as determining the amount permitted per user and when, where and how they may acquire and store water (Kaiser 2002).

Water Rights

As the preceding background paper demonstrated, the freshwater resources of the Brazos River basin have long been threatened and given demographic trends alone—with Texas now the third fastest growing state in the nation (Forbes 2016)—the extent of that threat can only be expected to increase over time. In 2015 alone the GDP in Texas grew by 3.8% to reach $1.48 trillion making it the second largest state GDP in the U.S. Unquestionably much of this growth was driven by the energy industry to include energy exploration.

Texas's legacy of consistent economic growth has produced low unemployment (4.5%) and an annual growth rate of 1.8%, making Texas the third fastest growing state by population in the U.S. (Forbes 2016; Sauter et al. 2016). Even considering periodic downturns in the demand for oil—such as that experienced in 2016 where 50,000 oil industry jobs were lost in Texas alone (Klare 2016)—the long-term projections for the energy resources beneath Texas soils remains bullish (Knomea 2016). Consequently, it is reasonable to anticipate that the Texas economy will continue to grow and with it even greater demand for freshwater.

Unquestionably, a great deal of that future growth will occur throughout the Brazos River basin which translates into increasing competition for water rights along the course of the river and its tributaries. Given the distinct ecology of the Brazos River, increased water usage—particularly usage that results in the creation of additional reservoirs—ultimately threatens the river's flow and allows for saltwater intrusion from the Gulf of Mexico. Salinity is perennially the principal threat to the health of the Brazos River and it is a threat directly linked to water usage whenever that use outstrips the freshwater resources of the Brazos and her tributaries.

While arguably every person living within the Brazos River basin is a stakeholder in terms of access to water resources, legally speaking the principle stakeholders in the future of the river are those who hold water permits for Brazos River water use. Currently there around 1,000 permit holders allowed to draw water along the river basin representing a plethora of users to include municipalities, agricultural and industrial interests, public utilities, water districts and landowners (Carter 2016). The largest and most influential of these stakeholders is the Brazos River Authority (BRA 2016) headquartered in Waco, Texas.

The Brazos River Authority is a quasi-public agency with commissioners appointed by the Governor that manages water use over the course of the river. Accordingly, BRA staff are charged to "go forth and get water permitted so that we can put it to beneficial use"—with beneficial use legally defined as authorizing BRA to "sell it [water] to municipalities for people to drink and for industries to use in power plants" (Schutze 2012). Given their legislatively mandated mission the BRA is often criticized for seeking monopolistic control over the river's waters

In 2004 the BRA petitioned TCEQ to divert 421,449 acre-feet of water annually beyond the 670,000 acre-feet it was already authorized to divert. Fearing this move would threaten municipal water supplies along the course of the river, as well as threaten agricultural and industrial capacity, numerous water rights holders and stakeholders united in opposition to the BRA request (McPhate & Sigman 2014). These opponents or "protestants" argued that if allowed to exercise this kind of control over Brazos River water through the "banking" of freshwater resources, the BRA would acquire a monopolistic power to arbitrarily enforce compliance with environmental, agricultural, and development regulations while accruing the power to capriciously determine who will suffer or benefit from water rights. Water interests all along the Brazos feared that if the TCEQ granted the BRA's request for more water, property values would plummet and lifestyles would be irreparably altered. Figure 46 identifies the locations of the numerous permit holders authorized to withdraw water from the Brazos river (McPhate & Sigman).

Friends of the Brazos River

The Friends of the Brazos River (FBR) have been particularly persistent in contesting the BRA's water-grab (Tresauge 2012). To date, this nonprofit organization expended some $220,000 to prevent BRA from gaining virtual monopolistic authority over the river. Of this amount, some 70% went to legal fees involving litigation that effectively blocked the BRA from acquiring unlimited authority over Brazos River water. When the contributions of other opponents of the BRA (Dow Chemical, City of Granbury and others) are considered, upwards of $500,000 have been expended opposing the river authority while BRA has spent more than a million dollars (Jones 2016).

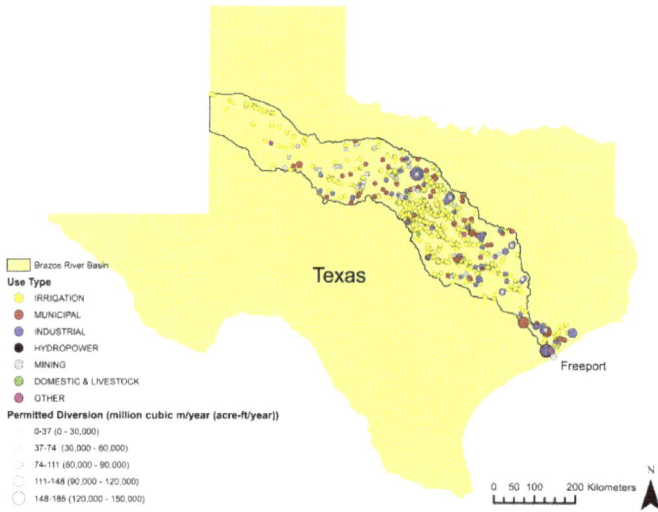

Brazos River basin water right withdrawal points and permitted annual water withdrawals. Dow's Texas Operations at Freeport is located at the mouth of the Brazos River. The most common categories of water rights are irrigation for agricultural, municipal, and industrial uses. By volume, industrial and municipal water rights comprise the majority of withdrawals. [1.5 columns].

Figure 46: Water Withdrawal Brazos River
(Source: Reddy et al, 2014)

Friends of the Brazos River emerged from the success of yet another Texas environmental advocacy group—the Brazos River Conservation Coalition (BRCC). BRCC legislative activism proved influential in shaping water use practices along the Brazos. In 2007 they successfully lobbied the Texas Legislature for the passage of SB-1354 amending Chapter 26 of the Texas Water Code to protect the Brazos River as well as regulate quarries within the newly designated John Graves Scenic Riverway. Accordingly, this influential legislation:

- "Establishes a pilot program for the protection of water quality through regulation of wastewater and storm water discharges from quarries; including requirements for financial assurance,
- Requires interagency coordination of inspections and sampling within the John Graves Scenic Riverway,
- Establishes enhanced enforcement authority and penalties;
- Provides for cost recovery if the state is required to take action to correct problems resulting from improper operation of quarries" (TCEQ 2008).

The achievements of the BRCC in part inspired other Brazos River stakeholders to create the Friends of the Brazos River who organized in 2005 in response to the BRA's unprecedented 2004 application to control the bulk of Brazos River water.

FBR was organized by Dallas restaurateur and Brazos River landowner Ed Lowe after the BRA petitioned the Texas Commission on Environmental Quality in 2004 to grant them a permit allowing for the diversion of approximately 1 million acre-feet of water from the river into eight reservoirs for selling water to municipal, industrial and other water users (Tresauge 2012). The Friends of the Brazos River principally consists of landowners along the course of the river and concerned citizens—most of whom live in the Granbury and Glen Rose areas as well as in and around the Dallas-Fort Worth area. These stakeholders are uniformly concerned about river water quality as it pertains to the river's natural ecosystems and regarding fishing, swimming and water recreation. FBR also includes a handful of small businesses and works closely with the Somervell County Commission and the city councils of the communities of Glen Rose and Granbury (Lowe 2016).

The Friends of the Brazos River is actively involved in shaping water use policies up and down the Brazos River Basin and is organized around three goals to include:

- Understanding and protecting the river's "ecological, historical, cultural, recreational and economic values,"
- Scientifically determining the adequacy of instream flows necessary to maintain the river's riparian health,
- Measuring and communicating to BRA the value of restoring a sustainable river flow (FBR 2016).

In pursuit of these goals, FBR employs an ambitious action-agenda to include:

- "Participating in the decision of the Texas Commission on Environmental Quality (TCEQ) on an application filed by the Brazos River Authority to expand its water rights."
- "Expanding its membership and capabilities through the recruitment of like-minded citizens, riverfront landowners and businesses, anglers, boaters and recreational users who are committed to a balanced allocation of water in the Brazos River for recreational uses, fish and wildlife and aesthetic values."
- "Working with the Brazos River Conservation Coalition, local officials and state representatives to extend the John Graves Scenic Riverway from Palo Pinto and Parker Counties to Hood and Somervell Counties."
- "Working with Texas Parks and Wildlife Department and the Glen Rose Convention and Visitors Bureau to establish a Texas Paddling Trail in the Glen Rose area" (FBR 2016).

Among FBR's pursuits none has been as important or noteworthy as the formal legal dispute they initiated in 2010 with BRA to curtail its water management authority. A timeline of how FBR stakeholders acted to influence the final form of the BRA authorization appears in Figure 47. By any measure, Friends of the Brazos River has been particularly persistent in contesting the BRA's water-grab (Tresauge 2012), having expended some $220,000 to prevent BRA from gaining virtual monopolistic authority over the river. Of this amount, some 70% went to legal fees involving litigation that effectively blocked the BRA from acquiring unlimited authority over Brazos River water. Combined with other opponents of the BRA (Dow Chemical, City of Granbury and others) upwards of $500,000 has been expended opposing the river authority while BRA has spent more than a million dollars (Jones 2016). Ed Lowe, President of the Friends of the Brazos River justifies these large expenditures explaining that,

> "The reason we have taken this on, and stayed in the fight, is so that we can keep enough water flowing in the Brazos to preserve the complex ecosystems from the headwaters to Freeport. We are doing this for both wildlife and people. For wildlife, it's a matter of survival. For us, it's to preserve a beautiful piece of river that we all love" (Jones 2016).

Understanding the nature of FBR's opposition to the BRA 2004 application necessitates appreciating the magnitude of the application to TCEQ. In TCEQ Permit Application Number 5851 BRA asked for control of virtually all the Brazos River water capacity between Possum Kingdom Reservoir and the Gulf of Mexico - adding one million acre-feet of capacity beyond its original 700,000 acre-feet annual water right. The volume of water requested in their application to TCEQ dwarfed the capacity that they had historically been either used or sold—some 400,000 acre-feet (Lowe 2016). BRA made its application with the ostensible purpose of more effectively fulfilling its legislatively sanctioned role as keeper of the Brazos River Basin. To that end it is empowered to engage in a variety of activities to include operating the basin's water supply, constructing and operating flood control reservoirs, operating and regulating the operation of wastewater treatment facilities and studying, monitoring and managing the basin's water supply and water quality.

While the intent of the BRA application seems benevolent, there were less benevolent incentives inherent in the sanctions that—in the minds of some observers - motivated several Texas river authority districts to exploit their legislative mandate in pursuit of power and profit (Patoski 2001). Accordingly, one critic observed that:

> "Some river authorities have embraced the lucrative and powerful business of selling water, ripening into hard-charging near-monopolies bound and determined to amass, control, and sell vast quantities of our public water. In the name of progress, the Lower Colorado, Guadalupe-Blanco, Trinity, Sabine, San Jacinto, and Brazos River authorities are involved to varying degrees in staking huge new claims on our rivers totaling well over 2.8 million acre-feet of water (an acre-foot of water is one acre, one foot deep). Their primary interest: to control and sell this water" (Parker 2005).

June 25, 2004: BRA files its application for SYSOP Permit (No. 5851) for additional 1,000,000

acre feet capacity beyond its 700,000 acre feet water rights.

2005-2010: TCEQ Director negotiates draft permit with BRA to include 1,000,000 additional

acre feet.

May 2010: TCEQ grants hearing requests from concerned stakeholders.

May 2011: First hearing on BRA challenges before Administrative Law Judge.

October 2011: Law Judges issue their decision recommending the permit be denied pending BRA

amendment of their petition application.

June 2012: BRA files an amended petition.

August 2013: Second hearing begins before Administrative Law Judge but hearing is suspended

while judges investigate appropriate law for determining instream flows.

December 2013: TCEQ commissioners decide on the appropriate law governing instream flows.

May 2014: BRA files a revised petition.

February 2015: Second hearing resumes.

July 2015: Administrative law judge issue a permit to BRA for an additional 600,000 acre feet

capacity.

August 24, 2016: TCEQ finally approves Permit 5851 awarded to BRA.

Figure 47: Summary of Key Events in BRA Permit Application No. 5851
(Source. Lowe 2016)

Given an implicit power and profit motive among designated state water authorities, many environmental, advocacy and stakeholder organizations and interests statewide, including members of the Friends of the Brazos River, have expressed an abiding concern that the unabated transfer of regulatory authority over the state's rivers to river authorities constitutes an "ominous trend" in which "river authorities—some more aggressively than others—are heading toward "locking up the very last public waters flowing in our streams" (Parker 2005). As it pertains to the Brazos River basin, a palpable concern was expressed that if the BRA application were approved "the BRA will lord over every bit of remaining water available in the basin; water never to return to the public domain" (Parker 2005).

In truth, there is much within the application that justifies these concerns regarding the BRA acquiring newly derived power over the Brazos River water. More specifically, Petition Application Number 5851 involved two parts. The first part of the petition was well known seeking control over one million acre-feet of water from within the basin for selling it. However, part two of the application was less publicized and may have been of even more importance—namely a request for permission to engage in unrestricted movement of water resources not only within the Brazos basin but also in and out of the basin to other parts of Texas. In other words, this second part of the petition allows the BRA to use the Brazos River and its tributaries as a virtual pipeline for transferring water in and out of other river basins and aquifers (Parker 2005). As discussed in the previous backgrounder chapter, this provision is consistent with the need in arid West Texas to import water from the East to meet distant municipal, agricultural, mining and energy related needs.

It was based on these concerns that FBR and several other "protestants" filed their objections to the petition in 2010 with the State Office of Administrative Hearings. FBR's "Exceptions" were offered on behalf of themselves and the Brazos River Alliance—a sister nonprofit organization organized to protect, preserve and restore the Brazos River watershed (Brazos River Alliance 2017). The remaining stakeholders filing "exceptions" with TCEQ did so individually and negotiated changes in the application to meet the needs of their constituencies (Figure 48). This allowed this diverse set of interests to cooperate in opposing the BRA application while leaving room for them to do so in a way that served their individual stakeholders.

Brazos River Authority (BRA): Supports the proposal for decision (PFD) – Permit Application No. 5851.

TCEQ Executive Director (ED): Supports the PFD.

Texas Parks and Wildlife Dept. (TPWD): Settled with BRA on all issue except the issue of adequate instream flows in the streams and rivers of the Basin. Supports the PFD in part and opposes it in part.

Friends of the Brazos River (FBR): Opposes PFD as not adequate to protect the flows needed in the streams and rivers of the Basin.

National Wildlife Foundation (NWF): Similar position to FBR.

Dow Chemical: Opposes the PFD because of its impact on Dow's water right and ability to take water from the River near the Gulf of Mexico.

Granbury Coalition: Opposes PFD as not adequate to protect water levels in Lake Granbury.

Possum Kingdom Landowners Association (PKLA): Settled with BRA for some protections for lake levels and a vague BRA promise to work with the Association in the future.

Figure 48: Principal Protestants to BRA Permit Application No. 5851
(Source: Lowe 2016)

A two-week hearing before a pair of State Office of Administrative Hearings administrative law judges occurred in 2011, producing a recommendation to deny the BRA petition, instructing them to amend their application to include an ecosystem impact of their proposal on the river basin. This outcome was heavily influenced by a 2007 report commissioned by FBR with Joe Trungale of Trungale Engineering and Science (Austin, TX). Trungale's analysis of instream flow needs in the Brazos in and around Glen Rose concluded that:

> "The Brazos River has been significantly altered from its natural condition and the BRA's proposed application for a systems operation permit has the

potential to cause further environmental degradation. The sponsors of this project propose addressing the environmental needs of the river in a future water management plan, but after they have the permit to control the remaining water in the basin, there will be little incentive for them to address these environmental needs. The BRA is currently involved in developing an instream flow study; however this study is configured on a now outdated set of assumptions and needs to be redesigned to address the ecological needs of the area that will be impacted by the proposed permit. Since the systems operation produces supplies in excess of human demands, the BRA has an opportunity to demonstrate a proactive commitment to managing the resources in an environmentally responsible manner using the surplus of water that will be available in the foreseeable future. This will also allow for experiments with adaptive management to determine which flow prescriptions are most effective in maintaining and restoring the riverine ecosystem" (Trungale Engineering & Science 2007, 34).

The upshot of Trungale's report was that BRA was attempting to co-opt all available water within the river basin without a clear understanding of who or where the water would be used in the future and do so without any real sense of how their plan would impact environmental flows and surrounding ecosystems. TCEQ commissioners responded to the administrative law judge's decision by giving BRA another opportunity to submit and "improved" application in 2013. However, once again FBR succeeded in convincing the administrative law judges that the BRA application sill lacked a proper environmental assessment of their plan's impact as mandated by Texas Senate Bill 3 which proscribes a set of environmental flow standards.

By Texas statute, an environmental flow refers to "an amount of water that should remain in a stream or river for the benefit of the environment of the river, bay and estuary while balancing human needs" (Title 2, Texas Water Code, Section 11.002.16). This code derived from The Texas Instream Flow Program that was enacted by the Texas Legislature in 2001 and later expanded in 2007 by Senate Bill 3 (SB-3). SB-3 created a joint agency cooperative involving TCEQ, the Texas Parks and Wildlife Department (TPWD) and the Texas Water Development Board (TWDB 2004) who were directed to coordinate their efforts to perform scientific studies regarding the flow conditions conducive to supporting sustainable riparian ecosystems in Texas streams and rivers. In so doing SB-3 imposed a new regulatory standard for protecting environmental flows by creating a local stakeholder mechanism that produced effective rules to be administered by TCEQ. Beyond the inclusion of water-rights holders, these stakeholder groups were also required to include representatives from the scientific and water management/use communities, as well as technical consultants (Wurbs 2013).

BRA was challenged relative to the degree to which it had conducted adequate scientific studies of instream flow consistent with the Texas Instream Flow Program. Consequently, a second hearing before the administrative law judges was scheduled in 2015 to allow BRA to produce these required studies. Once again FBR rejected this revision along with Dow Chemical, the City of Granbury and others. In so doing, they continued to rely upon the expertise of Joe Trungale to challenge the adequacy of the agency's environmental analysis. Their resistance proved fruitful and again BRA was required revise its application for final review in 2016 (Trungale Engineering & Science 2007).

Ultimately, TCEQ granted BRA a system permit in 2016 that expanded its capacity by 100,000 acre-feet - up and above its previous allocation of 661,901 acre-feet (Smith 2016). This additional water capacity is expected to enable BRA to generate $7 million annually in water sales. TCEQ also authorized BRA to operate all 11 of the middle and lower river reservoirs and to manage water rights of all permit-holders throughout the middle to lower stretches of the Brazos River on behalf of TCEQ and the State of Texas. In this manner, TCEQ effectively delegated some of its legislatively derived authority to BRA who will pursue creating a cohesive system of water management while avoiding construction of additional reservoirs (Buffam 2016; Davis 2016).

Central to the new permit is the requirement that BRA use its water resources to maximum efficiency. These resources are to be employed to create first-class (firm, dependable supply) and second-class (interruptible) water resources with first-class water used as a bulwark against drought for drinking water and second-class water used for less critical intermittent uses such as farming or to augment another water source. BRA reported that it plans to make better use of existing water resources by:

- Recalculating the "firm yield" BRA preserves its existing reservoirs by using methods the TCEQ adopted after this stored water was allocated.
- Capturing and utilizing surplus water in the Brazos River during high-flow times to serve customers instead of relying upon reservoir water.
- Including "return flows" of treated effluent from municipal sewer plants emptying into the river to contribute to water supply (Smith 2016).

The new systems operation permit also allowed BRA to import and export water resources into the basin from other regions of the state.

The water management authority ultimately granted to BRA reflects one of the most complex water regulation plans ever developed in Texas. Historically applicants seeking a water permit applied directly to the TCEQ regarding a specific permit, for a proscribed amount of water from a specific location for a specific purpose and over a delimited period. However, under the new BRA authority this one-step process became a two-step process where TCEQ would issue the water rights permit and the BRA would later allow for the actual diversion and sale of water consistent with that permit and consistent with the water capacity in the river (Tresauge 2012).

Given their new authority, BRA hoped to successfully manage water resources by considering the amount of water permitted for diversion as well as the current availability of water within the river basin from all sources and then prioritize water releases to those with the most senior water rights. Given the monolithic control over water resources now granted to BRA, the agency's activities came under the scrutiny of FBR and at least 20 other stakeholders who involved themselves in TCEQ's consideration of BRA application 5851. Involved stakeholders included Possum Kingdom Lake Association, The City of Bryan, The City of Round Rock, The City of College Station, The City of Houston, The City of Lubbock, The National Wildlife Federation, Gulf Coast Water Authority, Comanche County Growers, Freeman &

Corbett Law Firm, Turner, Guthrie, Haynes & Boone, LLC, Texas Parks and Wildlife Department, NRG Texas Power, Lake Granbury Coalition, Chisolm Trail Ventures and State Senator Mike Bingham (Lowe 2016).

Dow Chemical and the Brazos Watermaster Program

One of the most significant BRA "protestants" was Dow Chemical Company operating the world's largest petrochemical plant along the banks of the Brazos. Dow Chemical is a senior water rights holder that is entirely reliant on Brazos River water for industrial use. This water supply became critical during the period of 2009-2012 when a severe drought resulted in salinization of the river far upstream that disrupted a portion of Dow's water supply. As of 2012 permitted demand for Brazos River water exceeded supply ten to twenty percent of the year (Nature Conservancy 2012). In fact, in the eyes of many who claimed water rights along the Brazos there was simply not enough water in the river to satisfy the demands of all users. Per Brad Brunett of the Brazos River Authority, "even in normal to moderate dry times a lot of junior rights permits [those with legally diminished rights to water use] will not have enough water to divert" (McPhate & Sigman 2014).

Under Texas's "first-in-time, first-in-right" water rights doctrine, Dow is considered a "senior" water permit holder—having held water rights since 1942. This status gives Dow the right to divert millions of gallons of river water above and beyond the water rights of "junior" permit holders who must wait their turn to use water that remains after senior users have withdrawn their legislatively apportioned share. This senior rights designation is critical to Dow's operation since its Freeport plant uses a prodigious amount of water. For instance, in November 2012 alone the plant consumed 155 million gallons of water daily, far outstripping the daily water use of the 1.3 million residents of Dallas who consumed 143 million gallons. In fact, between 2009 and 2012 Dow Chemical's Brazoria County facilities used more than 1 trillion gallons of water (McPhate & Sigman 2014).

When the BRA petitioned TCEQ in 2004 for system operational water rights, Dow was compelled to enter the review proceedings along with FBR and other permit holders to protect and clarify its own water rights. This controversy over BRA authority was further exacerbated by several years of drought that resulted in a virtual water war along the Brazos over the future of the river (Wilder 2012). The prolonged drought created a second area of contention among Brazos River water users— namely whether TCEQ should appoint a watermaster to manage water withdrawal long the Brazos.

Historically, water users up and down the Brazos operated on an honor system without much direct enforcement activity from TCEQ. However, this system became dysfunctional around 2009 with the advent of prolonged drought. The protracted drought compelled Dow Chemical to petition TCEQ to recognize and honor their "priority call" to water rights as a senior rights-holder, which in turn motivated TCEQ commissioners to conclude that a more organized system was necessary to stem the tide of conflict among water users over prioritization of their rights. As Texas water rights attorney Martin Rochelle observed, in the absence of a firm water management system "there will be a land rush for water" that "can't be good for anyone, and it certainly isn't good for the Texas economy" (McPhate & Sigman 2014).

Dow Chemical found itself involved in conflicting water rights claims at a time when many perceived BRA as trying to gain a preeminent position. Since Dow's operation is dependent upon access to prodigious amounts of water they chose to avoid taking an adversarial position (like that taken by Friends of the Brazos River) regarding BRA and its Petition Application Number 5851 to TCEQ. Instead they approached the TCEQ in 2012 with a "priority call" to enforce the corporation's senior water rights and suspend the junior rights of farmers and municipalities. This allowed Dow Chemical to siphon off some 150,000 acre-feet annually so that it could lay claim to 48 billion gallons of water. By the time Dow made their call the state of Texas had already experienced three years of drought (Schalla 2015).

Dow's priority call for water rights triggered protests from other water rights holders. Their response was to remain resolute regarding their senior water rights asserting that

> "As a senior water rights holder, we need to have our consumption rights fully met and we have to be able to take the water from above the salt wedge at our diversion points" (McPhate & Sigman 2014).

Dow further claimed farmers and municipalities upstream of their plant were in effect stealing water that belongs to them—cheating Dow out of just compensation for forgone water. Sympathetic to Dow's request and cognitive of its senior-water rights, TECQ cooperated and municipalities and power plants with junior rights to Dow could divert river water while the rights of farmers were suspended (McPhate & Sigman, 2014).

This disproportionate impact upon farmers fueled the ire of the Texas Farm Bureau who argued Dow's claim was unjust and that farmers were being sacrificed to fuel the profits of Dow. The Texas Farm Bureau (representing the state's farmers and ranchers) asserted that Dow, if it so chooses, could purchase water from upstream farmers and if circumstances permit can also sell water back to these farmers. Having spurned both options, Texas Farm Bureau leadership asserted that "They're [Dow] taking without compensation." Ultimately litigation ensued that, upon resolution in the Texas 13th District Court of Appeals, upheld the so-called priority doctrine of "first in time, first in right" that has historically governed water rights within the state (Texas Farm Bureau 2015; Malewitz 2015).

In 2014 TCEQ began the process of appointing a "watermaster" to monitor and enforce surface water rights on the Brazos in the interest of mitigating against any further conflicts over water rights. Dow Chemical with its multiple "priority calls" to force recognition of its senior-water rights during the extended drought proved to be the driving force behind BRA's decision to appoint a watermaster. Dow favored the creation of this function believing it would insure reliable access to water resources in the future and avoid conflict among water users. However, upstream users to include municipalities and many agricultural users vehemently opposed the move fearing that BRA was catering to Dow and that too much power would be placed in the regulatory control of BRA who in turn would be more responsive to industrial users like Dow than to the rank-in-fil water rights holder (Schalla 2015).

While arguably a watermaster program should reduce conflicts between users through the collection of daily water use data to hold all users accountable, opponents to the program argued that it would impose regressive fees upon users and compel them to fund a program which they did not support. These users characterized the program as "state-overreach" and in contradiction to "majoritarian rule" among water rights holders. Ultimately it was the resistance of these stakeholders (led by the cities of Lubbock and Abilene) that constrained the new program to the middle and lower Brazos River basin (Figure 49) (Schalla 2015).

The newly appointed watermaster was authorized to initiate the process of metering and monitoring water removed from the Brazos and its tributaries and enforce water rights allowing senior water rights holders like Dow to have first access to water resources. This authority includes the capacity to allocate flows to water rights holders during periods of drought. The watermaster was authorized to manage the Brazos basin from Possum Kingdom Lake to the Gulf of Mexico, including population centers such as Waco, Temple-Killeen, Bryan-College Station, Williamson County, Sugar Land and Brazosport. The costs of this new program are born by the water rights users with the annual fee charge for the service varying depending upon the size of the water rights. The annual cost of the watermaster program for TCEQ is estimated to involve $500,000 and 800,000 annually (Smith 2014).

Figure 49: Brazos River Basin Watermaster Area
(Source: Zaveri 2015)

The scope of the new watermaster program exactly comports to the management area authorized by TCEQ in 2016 for the activities of the BRA. Prior to the adoption of the watermaster program by TCEQ BRA representatives testified as a neutral party arguing that if the program were created it should ideally encompass the entire Brazos River Basin. As noted, ultimately their recommendation was not accepted due to resistance from stakeholders upriver in Abilene and Lubbock and the approved program was limited to the region between Possum Kingdom and the Gulf of Mexico. BRA representatives also commented upon the inherent complexity of the proposed watermaster program—an approach that had historically only been applied in Texas along the Concho and Rio Grande river basins and never along a tributary system with as many water-users as along the Brazos (Smith 2014).

Prior to being awarded an expanded regulatory authority by TCEQ, the BRA had been authorized by the legislature to manage 60% of the water storage rights in the basin—water that it was authorized to sell to municipalities, industries and agricultural interests (Smith 2014). This authority significantly expanded under subsequent TCEQ decisions. However, what remained was for BRA and the new watermaster program to clarify to water users precisely how their regulatory roles complimented one another to produce predictable and sustainable access to Brazos water resources

Environmental vs. Economic Perspective on the Watermaster Program

While affiliated with Friends of the Brazos River in their struggle to maintain water rights on the Brazos River and concerned about the environmental health of the river and its environs, Dow Chemical (unlike Friends of the Brazos River) was not principally concerned with environmental issues since it required significant water resources to maintain its industrial production along the lower portion of the river. Consequently, Dow acted on behalf of its corporate self-interests and supported the efforts of TECQ to appoint a "watermaster" on the Brazos to manage water disputes based on water rights status.

Historically Dow made repeated "priority calls" for water rights (usually during droughts) compelling farmers to curtail irrigation and livestock watering and forcing municipalities like Waco, Texas to restrict water usage. Under Texas state statutes a "priority" or "senior" call occurs when a water rights holder demands that holders of more junior water rights cease and desist their water use so that the senior holder may exercise their right. In Dow's case this entails communicating with TCEQ to exercise enforcement action against junior rights holders (TECQ v Texas Farm Bureau 2015).

From Dow's perspective, the appointment of a watermaster was expected to routinely affirm the rights of senior permit holders thus reducing the need for Dow to issue "priority calls" that antagonized junior permit holders. Moreover, relying upon a system that automatically recognized their senior water rights also served to minimize the need for litigation. In embracing the 2014 appointment of a watermaster Dow spokesperson Trish Thompson reiterated the company's position saying

> "Once the watermaster is in place, we expect that there will be fewer priority calls in regard to the lower basin because he or she will be able to proactively manage the water resources and water rights on the Brazos River and be able to take action to address a shortage before a crisis occurs" (Thompson 2016).

Nevertheless, some took issue with the degree of unaccountable authority granted to the watermaster (Satija 2014) as well as the degree of influence Dow might exert over the program (influenced in part by being one of the largest funders of the watermaster program via proportional use fees). In researching this case study, the author contacted the Brazos River watermaster for comment and instead of responding to the request directly, the watermaster forwarded it to the public relations officer at Dow Chemical. This singularly puzzling response from a state regulatory agency left the impression that Dow and the watermaster might very well have a privileged relationship—thus lending credence to concerns among some other water rights holders that Dow might be in a very close relationship with the program. Even so, there is absolutely no collaborative evidence that such a privileged relationship exists beyond speculation from critics who did not want to be identified.

Other commentators such as Jay Bragg of Texas Farm Bureau pointed out that Dow's support for the appointment of a watermaster made a lot of sense from a corporate (economic) perspective since it lent a lot more predictability in water management decisions and hopefully reduced or eliminated the cost, inconvenience and controversy associated with filing priority claims with TECQ over water rights (Bragg 2016). In advocating for the appointment of a watermaster Dow Chemical's spokesmen argued that "a watermaster will be able to proactively manage the water resources and water rights on the Brazos River and be able to take action to address a shortage before a crisis occurs" (Satija 2014). Nonetheless, critics voiced their concern that the watermasters may act arbitrarily or in the interest of one user over others thereby eroding the opportunity for democratic input into state water policy. State Senator Troy Fraser (R-Horseshoe Bay) stated this concern succinctly when he commented the "I'm concerned that we're giving too much power to one person." Fraser's concerns were echoed by Bell County Water Control and Improvement District No. 1 manager Jerry Atkinson who called the appointment "an overreach of the government" that begged the question of "where is the justice? Where is majority rule?" (Satija 2014).

Regardless, of whether the critics of the new watermaster program are correct or not in their perceptions, one fact stands clear. From Dow Chemical's perspective, the new program should aid in providing the company with reliable freshwater resources vital to its growing industrial capacity and the growing municipal demand that accompanies company expansion and growth. Moreover, it does so without forcing the company to take an adversarial stance relative to other water rights holders, thereby contributing favorably to the company's public image. Assuming the watermaster program provides reliable access to water, it would seem Dow will minimally need to legally assert its priority rights in the future, thereby guaranteeing the water it needs while avoiding negative publicity and attorney expenses. Although Dow partnered with Friends of the Brazos River and other municipal, agricultural and private water rights holders to vouchsafe their senior water rights and improve environmental regulation of the river's resources, theirs was an essentially economic motivation rather than one based upon a principal desire to improve the environmental quality of the river and its water resources.

FBR, on the other hand, is principally concerned with the environmental health of the river. Periods of drought during which freshwater levels fall and salinity increases threatens the environmental health of the Brazos River. During such periods competition for water rights can divert attention from the environmental health of the river. These periods of low flow and higher water salinity threatens wildlife throughout the course of the river basin and can seriously impact riparian vegetation and ecosystems that are essential to the long-term health of the river. As previously discussed the environmental health of the river is dependent upon the maintenance of environmental stream flows. During periods of drought this basic requirement for environmental health can be compromised by water diversion to human use functions. What results is a pattern of season-specific water use patterns that change "when and how strongly rivers flood, damaging the surrounding environment and wildlife" (Koh 2013).

The principal mechanism by which the riparian health of the Brazos is compromised is during periods of low flows where water salinity increases while oxygen content decreases. These conditions produce a hostile environment for native and invasive freshwater species and promotes the growth of harmful vegetation such as golden algae that produce damaging toxins. For instance, two species particularly vulnerable to these environmental conditions are the "sharpnose" and "smalleye" shiners—small minnow fish that thrive in parts of the upper regions of the Brazos. These threatened species spawn eggs that must float if they are to hatch thereby requiring sufficient river flow to prevent them from settling to the bottom of the river and dying (Koh 2013). These small fish are foundational for the survival of larger fish species. These shiner species feed upon flies, caddisflies, bugs and beetles and consume plant life on the floor of the river. These shiner species in turn support larger fish species to include white bass, perch crappie and largemouth, smallmouth and spotted bass. Consequently, the depletion of this foundational species serves to threaten the viability of species further up the aquatic food chain (Wilde & Durham 2007).

Ecopragmatic Principles Exemplified

The Friends of the Brazos River case study illustrates several ecopragmatic principles that informed their activities and contributed to their accomplishments. Chief among these is the degree to which they established collaborative relationships with entities like Dow Chemical that at least from and "environmentalist" perspectives could have been characterized as the partnering of *"strange bedfellows."* The core of FBR's membership consisted of landowners up and down the Brazos River watershed. Their interests were principally related to protecting property and ecological networks. They broadened their organizational constituency by including community organizations and governmental entities throughout the course of the river to seek common cause in their efforts to protect the river's ecosystems and species. Some of these partners formally joined FBR. In other instances, FBR teamed with other nonprofit environmental groups and organizations to promote the welfare of the Brazos River.

However, their most unique partnership involved Dow Chemical Corporation which FBR joined to fight the expansion of Brazos River Authority power and the perceived diminishment of the rights or water permit holders. While acting in consort to maintain their rights and constrain the expansion of BRA authority, FBR was principally concerned with maintaining ecosystems and environmental flows while Dow was principally interested in maintaining adequate water resources to maintain their business interests. Ultimately Dow chose to work in consort with TCEQ and BRA in the implementation of a new watermaster system—believing that this option best protected their company's economic interests. FBR, by comparison was concerned that this new office could act arbitrarily and function in a way that conflicted with the FBR mission. Consequently, Dow Chemical and FBR sometimes pursued mutual goals but did so independently and based on divergent organizational motives.

FBR efforts were *homegrown* on the banks of the Brazos. They began with concerns among a few landowners up and down the river and eventually grew to become a regional and statewide initiative to protect the Brazos River that held public agencies accountable for fairly administering laws regarding water rights in Texas. In fact, as FBR began to affiliate with other similar grass-roots organization it effectively contributed to the development of a network of local interests willing to challenge lawmakers and state officials involved with every aspect of water rights and management throughout the Brazos watershed.

FBR consistently worked with state agencies responsible for the health of the Brazos River to protect water rights and vouchsafe the ecological health of the river. In so doing they eschewed the pursuit of unrealistic ideological outcomes and instead favored "doable," "pragmatic" "satisficing" outcomes—never allowing the "perfect" outcome to get in the way of "achievable" and "marginally improved" results. In this manner FBR "*satisfied*" and pursued the *communitarian goal of developing a host of "local voices"* who could come together to produce ever-better and ongoing environmental outcomes for the Brazos River system.

FBR also promoted *deliberative democracy* - a political perspective that asserts "political decisions should be the product of fair and reasonable discussion and debate among citizens" (Eagan 2016). Their principal contribution in this regard was their promotion of local, regional and statewide discussions, hearings and debates over the fate of the Brazos River and their ongoing interface with BRA and TCEQ. They likewise developed independent data on the health of the Brazos River and subsequently publicized their findings via community forums and conversations thereby informing and promoting public involvement (Rousiley 2007).

FBR's dedication to the promotion of deliberative interactions between among community interests and state agencies was realized by *engaging a network of "responsibles"* willing to pursue the organization's ecological and property interests on a sustained basis. This two-pronged approach involved identifying and establishing cooperative and collaborative relationships among community stakeholders who valued problem-solving over posturing. Engaging these "responsibles" unavoidably entailed *avoiding* and *if necessary excluding* community interests with no intent of compromising or collaborating—those preferring to "posture," "protest," and ultimately "prevent" collaboration and problem solving.

Conclusion

The FBR collaborative effort, in concert with that of Dow Chemical and other stakeholders, created sustainable stakeholder/public agency relationships to promote the health of the Brazos River. Central to this process was the avoidance of acrimonious relationships that might prevent future cooperation. Likewise, FBR took advantage of Texas's tradition of broadly engaging citizenry prior to enacting legislation to develop a collaborative approach to protecting the Brazos River. This happy convergence produced an exceedingly optimistic perspective on the future of environmental management throughout the Brazos River Basin.

REFERENCES

Bragg, Jay. 2016. Personal Communication, August 19, 2016.

Brazos River Alliance. 2017. "It's Time to Align." Accessed August 4, 2017 https://www.facebook.com/BrazosRiverAlliance/

Brazos River Authority. 2016. "Brazos River." Accessed August 29, 2016 https://www.brazos.org/About-Us/About-the-BRA/About-the-Brazos-River

Buffam, Noelle. (2016) "TCEQ Issues Permit for Brazos River Authority," *KWHI 1280* (Brenham, TX). (August 25), Retrieved from the Worldwide Web October 14, 2016 at http://kwhi.com/tceq-issues-permit-for-brazos-river-authority/

Carter, Rob. 2016. "Water Rights Holders: Brazos River." Brazos River Watermaster Program, Personal Communication (October 13).

Davis, Jess. 2016. "Texas Likely to OK Controversial Water Rights Permit." *Law360.* (January 20), Accessed October 14, 2016 http://www.law360.com/articles/742237/texas-likely-to-ok-controversial-water-rights-permit

Eagan, Jennifer L. 2016. "Deliberative Democracy—Political Theory." *Encyclopedia Britannica.* (May 17), Accessed January 17, 2017 https://www.britannica.com/topic/deliberative-democracy.

Forbes. 2016. "The Ten Fastest Growing States in the U.S.—No. 3 Texas." *Forbes.* Accessed September 29, 2016 http://www.forbes.com/pictures/mhj45mejl/2-district-of-columbia/#76f8f614665e

Friends of the Brazos River (FBR). 2016. "Friends of the Brazos Saving Our River." Accessed October 20, 2016 http://www.friendsofthebrazos.org/slideshow/FBRBooklet.pdf

Houston Chronicle Editorial Staff. 2012. "Editorial: Save the Brazos River." *Houston Chronicle.* (January 24), Accessed August 29, 2016 http://www.chron.com/opinion/editorials/article/Save-the-Brazos-2683985.php

Jones, Kathryn. 2016. "Friends of the Brazos Asks for Help in Water Rights Fight." *Glen Rose Current.* (August 18), Accessed August 17, 2016 http://glenrosecurrent.com/friends-of-the-brazos-asks-for-help-in-water-rights-fight/

Kaiser, Ronald A. 2002. *Handbook of Texas Water Law: Problems and Needs.* College Station, TX: Texas A&M University, Texas Water Resource Institute.

Klare, Michael T. 2016. "The Future of Oil is Here—And it Doesn't Look Pretty." *The Nation.* (March 8), Accessed September 29, 2016 https://www.thenation.com/article/the-future-of-oil-is-here-and-it-doesnt-look-pretty/

Knomea. 2016. "Crude Oil Price Forecast: Long Term 2016 to 2025 | Data and Charts." *Knomea Data Analysis.* (September 13), Accessed September 29, 2016 https://knoema.com/yxptpab/crude-oil-price-forecast-long-term-2016-to-2025-data-and-charts

Koh, Elizabeth. 2013. "Environmental Concerns Rise as Brazos Levels Fall," *The Texas Tribune.* (August 13), Accessed November 16, 2016 https://www.texastribune.org/2013/08/13/environmental-concerns-entangled-fight-over-brazos/

Lowe, Ed. 2016. "Private Conversations and Memorandum." President, Friends of the Brazos.

Malewitz, Jim. 2015. "Water Ruling Cuts State's Power in Droughts." *The Texas Tribune.* (April 2), Accessed August 17, 2016 https://www.texastribune.org/2015/04/02/huge-water-ruling-court-sides-ranchers/

McPhate, Christian and Ashlea Sigman. 2014. "Battling Over the Brazos: Dwindling River and Reservoirs Spark Disputes Over Dam Construction." *Dallas Morning News.* (June 29), Accessed August 17, 2016 http://res.dallasnews.com/interactives/drought/brazos/

Nature Conservancy. 2012. "Dow-TNC Collaboration Analysis Summary Pilot 1: Dow Texas Operations, Freeport, TX Coastal Hazard Mitigation Analysis - Green and Gray Infrastructure: Valuation for Corporate Coastal Hazard Mitigation." Accessed. July 31, 2016 http://www.nature.org/about-us/working-with-companies/companies-we-work-with/dow/freeport-coastal-science-results.pdf

Parker, S. 2005. "Extreme Water Authorities." *Texas Observer.* (January 21), Accessed October 20, 2016 https://www.texasobserver.org/1858-open-forum-extreme-water-authorities/

Patoski, Joe Nick. (2001) "Boone Pickens Wants to Sell You His Water." *Texas Monthly.* (August), Accessed September 8, 2016 http://www.texasmonthly.com/the-culture/boone-pickens-wants-to-sell-you-his-water/

Reddy, Shiela M. W., Robert I. McDonald, Alexander S. Maas, Anthony Rogers, Evan H. Girvetz, Jeffrey North, Jennifer Molnar, Tim Finley, Gena Leathers and Jonathan L. DiMuro. 2015. "Finding Solutions to Water Scarcity: Incorporating Ecosystem Service Values into Business Planning at The Dow Chemical Company's Freeport, TX Facility." *Ecosystem Services.* 12(April): 94-107.

Rousiley, C. M. Maia. 2007. "Deliberative Democracy and Public Sphere Typology." *Estudos em Comunicação.* 1: 69-102

Satija, Neena. 2014. "Appointment of Brazos Watermaster Hotly Contested in East Texas." Texas Tribune. (April 20), Accessed September 13, 2017 https://www.texastribune.org/2014/04/20/brazos-watermaster-hotly-contested/

Sauter, Michael B., Samuel Stebbins and Evan Comen. 2016. "States with the Fastest Growing Economies." *Wall Street Journal.* (June 16), Accessed September 12, 2017 http://247wallst.com/special-report/2016/06/16/states-with-the-fastest-and-slowest-growing-economies-2/

Schalla, Frank E. 2015. "The TCEQ Watermaster Program and Surface Water Management." *LBJ School of Public Affairs Policy Analysis.* (October 7), Accessed October 20, 2016 https://static1.squarespace.com/static/54c15aa8e4b08b9c092063a6/t/56940ac2b204d52491f5b525/1452542661854/Watermasters.pdf

Schutze, Jim. 2012 "Who'll Stop the Rain? Rick Perry's Pals, That's Who." *Dallas Observer.* (January 19), Accessed August 17, 2016 http://www.dallasobserver.com/news/wholl-stop-the-rain-rick-perrys-pals-thats-who-6424418

Smith, J. B. 2016. "Brazos River Authority Close to Winning Long Sought Water Rights Expansion." *Waco Tribune.* (February 5), Accessed August 17, 2016 http://www.wacotrib.com/news/environment/brazos-river-authority-close-to-winning-long-sought-water-rights/article_551ecbde-9c55-5a6f-a33b-f74155fcdddd.html?mode=print

———. 2014. "New Watermaster to Police, Manage Brazos River Usage." *Waco Tribune.* (April 27), Accessed August 17, 2016 http://www.wacotrib.com/news/environment/new-watermaster-to-police-monitor-brazos-river-usage/article_2e9857df-d5e9-5352-b27a-99e2e3e72a0f.html

Texas Commission on Environmental Quality (TCEQ) v. Texas Farm Bureau et al. 2015. Number 13-13-00415-Cv Court of Appeals Thirteenth District of Texas Corpus Christi—Edinburgh.

———. 2016. "Rights to Surface Water in Texas," (March), Accessed August 17, 2016 http://lakesweetwater.com/sw-lake-files/RightsToSurfaceWaterInTexas.pdf

Texas Commission on Environmental Quality (TCEQ). 2008. "The John Graves Scenic Riverway: A Report to the 81st Legislature." TECQ Publication No. SFR-087/08 (December), Accessed October 17, 2016 https://www.tceq.texas.gov/assets/public/comm_exec/pubs/sfr/087_08.pdf

Texas Farm Bureau. 2015. "Court Upholds Texas Private Property Rights." Press Release. (April 2), Accessed August 18, 2016 http://media.texasfarmbureau.org/court-upholds-texas-private-property-rights/

Texas Water Development Board (TWDB). 2004. "The Future of Desalination in Texas -Volume 1." Austin, TX, Accessed August 18, 2016 http://texaswater.tamu.edu/readings/desal/twdbreportondesal.pdf

Thompson, Trish. 2016. "Dow Texas Operations raises $904,000 for United Way of Brazoria County." *Dow Newsletter*. (April 12), Accessed July 24, 2016 http://www.dow.com/locations/texas/freeport/news/2016/20160411c.htm

Tresauge, Matthew. 2012. "Users Fight Over Brazos River Water Rights." *MySA (San Antonio)*. (January 24), Accessed August 17, 2016 http://www.mysanantonio.com/news/local_news/article/Users-fight-over-Brazos-River-water-rights-2682944.php

Trungale Engineering and Science. 2007. "Instream Flow Needs for the Brazos River near Glen Rose, Texas - Instream Flow Analysis Water Availability and Reservoir Operations Alternatives and Implementation Analysis." (July 2), Austin, TX.

Wilde, Gene and Bart Durham. 2007. "Distribution, Status, Habitat Preferences, and Reproductive Ecology of Smalleye Shiner and Sharpnose Shiner in the Brazos River." Texas Parks and Wildlife Final Report E-55. (March 20), Austin, TX, Accessed November 16, 2016 https://tpwd.texas.gov/business/grants/wildlife/section-6/docs/fish/e55_final_report.pdf

Wilder, Forrest. 2012. "Goodbye to the Brazos River?" *Texas Observer*. (January 4), Accessed August 17, 2016 https://www.texasobserver.org/goodbye-to-the-brazos-river/

Wurbs, Ralph A. 2013. *Water Resources Planning, Development and Management*. Rijeka, HR: Intech.

Zaveri, Mihir. 2015. "Customers Hope Watermaster Brings Order to Brazos Watershed." Houston Chronicle. (June 9), Accessed September 13, 2017 http://www.houstonchronicle.com/news/article/Customers-hope-watermaster-brings-order-to-Brazos-6317311.php

CHAPTER 8

The Nature Conservancy and Dow Chemical

CASE STUDY FOUR

Dow Chemical in Texas

Dow Chemical Company is the third largest chemical company in the world (following BASF and Sinopec). Headquartered in Midland, Michigan, Dow produces a variety of products for agriculture, consumers, and so-called performance materials, chemicals, and plastics. The company employs more than 53,000 worldwide and does almost $60 billion in sales annually—principally to industrial customers (Dow Chemical 2015a). Dow's facility in Freeport, Texas began in 1940 when William Dow traveled to this community south of Houston and purchased 800 acres adjacent to Freeport Harbor in Brazoria County (Dow Chemical 2015b).

Soon thereafter the Dow board authorized a new chemical plant to be constructed at the cost of $18 million. The early Freeport facility produced magnesium from seawater—a substance badly needed by the Allies during World War II. Thereafter, the plant produced chlorine, caustic soda and ethylene. Soon a permanent city began to grow around the plant and was named Lake Jackson—a truly "company" town. By 1969 Dow's Freeport facility had grown to more than 3,000 acres and its products were transported by rail and ship worldwide (Dow Texas 2008, 2013; 2015). Today Dow has plants in LaPorte, Texas City, Pasadena, Deer Park, Port LaVaca, Lake Jackson, Freeport and Houston Texas (Dow Chemical 2016).

In 2015, Dow Chemical Corporation worldwide reported $48.78 billion in net sales (Dow Chemical 2015a) and the Freeport facility generated over $1 billion in annual revenues (Manta 2016). Dow Chemical merged with DuPont in December 2015 to create a single entity worth $130 billion (Kaskey 2016). Dow's economic impact upon rural Brazoria County, where the Freeport facility is located, is substantial (Figure 50) annually contributing to $528.7 million in payroll, $80.7 million in pensions, $864.3 million in local purchases, $1.1 million in charitable contributions and $70 million in local taxes. (Dow Texas 2013). Moreover, Dow also contributes to the local community via the United Way (which received $904,000 in 2016) as well as through its Dow Gives program which $2.2 million between 2004 - 2016 (Thompson 2016).

Dow's Pollution History

Dow Chemical has not only contributed mightily to the economy of Brazoria County and the state of Texas, it has quite literally created one of the largest cities in the county and contributes significantly to the county's tax base. That said, these economic contributions have come at a cost—and from the perspective of some in the community—a very steep cost (Cappiello 2005). That cost of course is the cost of air, soil and water pollution.

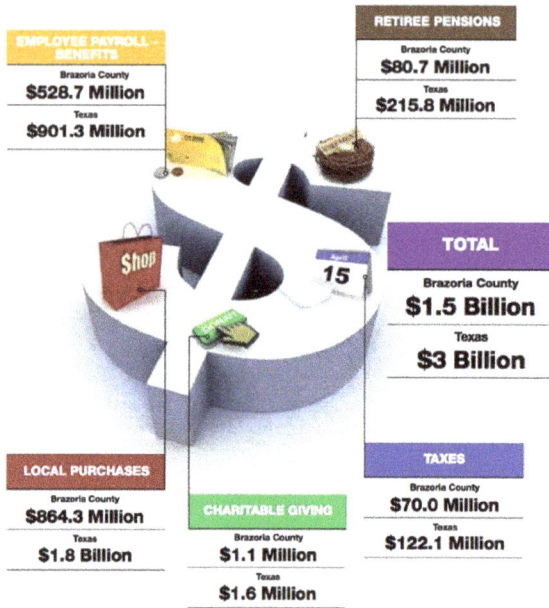

Figure 50: 2012 Economic Impact Dow Texas - Brazoria County
(Source: Dow Texas 2013)

The public counts upon chemical corporations like Dow Chemical to employ the best available technologies to minimize pollution. Given the inherent pollution associated with operating chemical plants Dow's plants worldwide are monitored by national and international agencies and environmental watchdogs to insure they are employing state of the art environmental protection technologies. However, one of the reasons for this ongoing scrutiny is that between 1992 and 1996 Dow Chemical was ranked 48th among the world's top polluters discharging 3,023,495 pounds of toxic pollutants annually (Puchalsky & LaPlante 1998).

Unfortunately, this 1998 statistic is but a small part of Dow's tarnished corporate image. The company's laundry list of environmental problems is extensive to include: (Mattera 2016, Max 2016, SEC 2014, Lappe 2011, Doyle 2004; Schuck 1998)

- 1962-1971 - Manufacturing Agent Orange during the Vietnam War,
- 1984 - Producing defective breast implants (Dow Corning venture),
- 1987 - Receiving repeated complaints of noxious emissions at its Midland, Michigan facility,
- 2002 - Unlawfully discharging polluted water at its Pittsburg, California plant,
- 2007-2008 - Resisting cooperation with the U.S. EPA regarding the extent of the company's Dioxin contamination at its Midland, Michigan plant,

- 2011 - After acquiring Union Carbide, refusing to make restitution to the victims of the Union Carbide's pesticide plant disaster in Bhopal, India seventeen late,
- 2011 - Being fined $207,000 by the Texas Commission on Environmental Quality for various violations involving air emissions and operations at the Freeport facility,
- 2013 - Being fined $100,000 by The Texas Commission on Environmental Quality (TCEQ) for numerous air permit violations at their Freeport facility as well as violations involving the company's wastewater treatment plant (Dow settled paying $67,060 to fund the Houston-Galveston AERCO's Clean Cities / Clean Vehicles program),
- 2014 - Contributing to water shortages along the Brazos River as the largest industrial water user,
- 2016 - Being named the third worst polluter in the nation by the EPA for its The Freeport plant.

Sadly, these prominent controversies do not mark the end of Dow's environmental problems. Per a 2016 report from the Environmental Integrity Project "In 2015, 679 industrial sites in more than 100 Texas counties released more than 34,000 tons of air pollutants during 3,421 incidents of malfunctions and maintenance events, according to industry self-reported data" (Levin et al. 2016). The worst offender of these industries was the Dow Chemical Plant in Freeport Texas which released 15,717 pounds of benzene—a deadly carcinogen—into the atmosphere. Despite Dow's considerable contributions to the Texas economy, Dow Chemical Company and particularly its Freeport facility have a consistently poor track record when it comes to pollution.

Reforming Corporate Image: Sustainability and The Nature Conservancy

Despite its troubled environmental pollution record, in 2011, Dow entered a unique partnership with one of the nation's most prominent environmental organizations— The Nature Conservancy. Its motivation for doing so is not entirely clear. It is obvious that one of the major benefits Dow derives from its association with The Nature Conservancy is that the relationship in part mitigated its otherwise troubling environmental record. In fact, critics wonder whether this environmental initiative with The Nature Conservancy is sincere or it is in fact "greenwashing" (i.e. only superficially embracing environmental sustainability for public appearances) as some of its critics have asserted (Lappe 2011).

To many observers, the partnership between Dow and The Nature Conservancy is about rehabilitating Dow's public image relative to environmental issues (MacDonald 2011). Others regard the partnership as nothing less than a sell-out to "big business" by The Nature Conservancy (Magstadt 2014)—what one critic refers to as "sleeping with the enemy" (Hannibal 2014). Whether factual or not, The Nature Conservancy, which receives 7% of its funding from corporations and 32% from foundations, is often perceived as exchanging environmental endorsements for cash contributions (Beder 2016). Despite these concerns the author gives Dow and The Nature

Conservancy the benefit of the doubt, assuming Dow wants to rehabilitate its corporate image by transforming its industrial practices while the Conservancy uncompromisingly pursues its environmental mission.

3M/3M Foundation	IBM
Alcoa Foundation	International Expeditions
AmazonSmile	Jostens,Inc.
AT&T	JPMorgan Chase & Co.
Avon	Lowe's/Lowe's Charitable and Educational Foundation
Bank of America/ Bank of America Foundation	Microsoft
Barrick Gold Corporation	Mosaic Company
BHP Billiton	Newmont Mining Corporation
BP	Neutrogena
Bunge	Odwalla
Cargill, Inc.	Oracle
Caterpillar/Caterpillar Foundation	Patagonia
Colgate-Palmolive Company	Pentair/ Pentair Foundation
CH2M HILL	PepsiCo Recycle for Nature
Charity Miles	Praxair Inc.
The Coca Cola Company	Quark Expeditions
Delta Air Lines	Rio Tinto
Discovery Channel: North America	SABMiller
Disney	Swiss Re
The Dow Chemical Company	TD Bank
Ecolab/Ecolab Foundation	UPS
FEMSA	Whole Foods Market
General Mills	Xerox/Xerox Foundation
Goldman Sachs	Zig Zag Zoom
Harley-Davidson, Inc./The Harley-Davidson Foundation	Zegrahm Expeditions

Figure 51: Conservancy Corporate Partnerships
(Source: The Nature Conservancy 2016)

In 2011, The Nature Conservancy initiated a collaboration with Dow Chemical demonstrating how "integrating the value of nature into business decisions can lead to better business outcomes and better conservation outcomes" (Nature Conservancy 2015, 4). The Conservancy approached Dow as one of several collaborations designed to break down barriers between the organization and businesses in the interest of better pursuing its conservation mission. The Conservancy has pursued such partnerships for decades recognizing that businesses worldwide exert significant impact upon local, regional and national environmental resources. To date The Conservancy is collaborating with 50 corporations (Figure 51) who realize their conservation efforts and investments serve to "protect business assets, mitigate risk and create opportunities" (The Nature Conservancy 2016).

Peter Kareiva, senior science advisor to The Nature Conservancy and Director of the Institute of the Environment and Sustainability at UCLA has been instrumental in negotiating many of these collaborative environmental partnerships (Karieva 2014). While Kareiva's work in conjunction with private corporations is sometimes debunked as "greenwashing," surveys of corporate leadership have consistently documented the adoption of environmental sustainability practices among top corporations. For instance, the 2014 McKinsey Global Survey Results (Boini & Bové

2014) indicate that from 2010-2014 surveys of corporate leaders believe that sustainability is a top CEO priority (Figure 52).

% of respondents[1]

Sustainability's strategic position on the CEO agenda

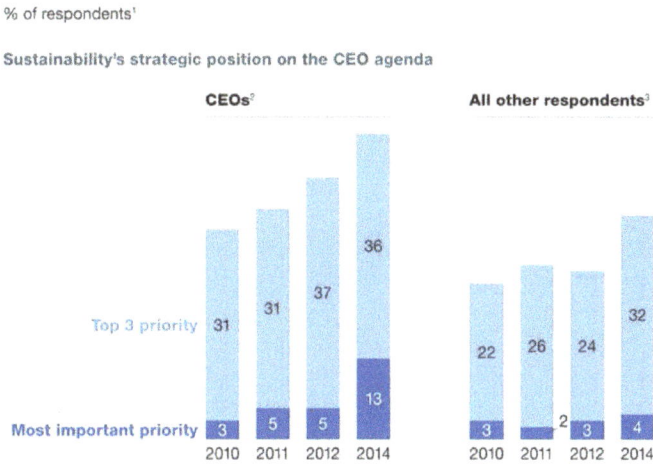

CEOs[2]   All other respondents[3]

Top 3 priority

Most important priority

2010 2011 2012 2014   2010 2011 2012 2014

[1]Respondents who answered "a priority but not a top 3 agenda item," "not a significant agenda item," and "don't know" are not shown.
[2]In 2010, n = 175; in 2011, n = 265; in 2012, n = 364; and in 2014, n = 281. The survey was not run in 2013.
[3]In 2010, n = 1,574; in 2011, n = 2,691; in 2012, n = 3,483; and in 2014, n = 2,623. The survey was not run in 2013.

Figure 52: Sustainability as a Top CEO Priority
(Source: Boini & Bové 2014)

Since their collaboration with The Nature Conservancy began, Dow established an innovative framework designed to aid in identifying, implementing, prioritizing and assigning value to corporate endeavors that promote business and the environment. This framework—known as Dow's 2025 Sustainability Goals—includes seven steps:

1. ***"Leading the Blueprint:*** Dow leads in developing a societal blueprint that integrates public policy solutions, science and technology, and value chain innovation to facilitate the transition to a sustainable planet and society.
2. ***Delivering Breakthrough Innovations:*** Dow delivers breakthrough sustainable chemistry innovations that advance the well-being of humanity.
3. ***Advancing a Circular Economy:*** Dow advances a Circular Economy by delivering solutions to close the resource loops in key markets.
4. ***Valuing Nature:*** Dow applies a business decision process that values nature, which will deliver business value and natural capital value through projects that are good for business and good for ecosystems.
5. ***Increasing Confidence in Chemical Technology:*** Dow increases confidence in the safe use of chemical technology through transparency, dialogue, unprecedented collaboration, research and our own actions.

6. ***Engaging Employees for Impact:*** Dow people worldwide directly apply their passion and expertise to advance the well-being of people and the planet.

7. ***World-Leading Operations Performance***: Dow maintains world-leading operations performance in natural resource efficiency, environment, health and safety" (Dow 2016).

While his framework was designed to improve corporate practice, and enhance the company's environmental image, its principal intent was to begin the process of redefining the culture of the corporation to prepare for a future where economic gain is constrained by environmental limits and social realities. Utilizing Dow's own language, their goal was ambitious as they sought to do nothing short of "redefining the role of business in society" (Dow 2016). In so doing, Dow committed itself to redefining its corporate mission to include (1) "advancing the well-being of humanity by helping lead the transition to a sustainable planet and society and (2) "maximizing economic environmental and social value." Implementing this corporate mission involved three stages to include creating a "footprint," "handprint" and a "blueprint" (Dow 2016).

Dow conceived of the "footprint" stage of implementation as "unlocking the potential of people and science" by harnessing the creativity and passion of people to innovate and generate "value for business, humanity and the environment" (Dow 2016). During this implementation phase Dow pledged to:

1. "Deliver breakthrough innovation to include a six-fold positive impact on sustainable development,
2. Engage employees for impact by seeking to apply employee talents to positively influence the lives of the planet's inhabitants and
3. Engage in world-leading operations performance designed to protect the health and safety of "Dow people and others touched by our supply chain, while maintaining world-leading environmental operations performance" (Dow 2016).

This stage of implementation is clearly dedicated to the reconceptualization of how human resources are employed by the corporation to benefit both the company and the society.

During the "handprint" stage of Dow's sustainability goals shifted from "human" resources to "natural" resources that are all too frequently taken for granted to include valuable services such as clean air and water. Their rationale was simple and straightforward: "it is the right thing to do for people, planet and business" (Dow 2016). In so doing, Dow pledged to deliver a billion dollars' worth of assets to support projects that contribute to good businesses and ecosystems.

Finally, during the "blueprint" stage Dow seeks to foster collaborative relationships across public and private spheres. They do so believing these efforts will produce lasting relationships that will promote sustainable social, economic and environmental outcomes that ultimately enhance the welfare of individuals, the economy and the planet. In pursuing these goals, Dow:

- Funded and directed a collaborative effort to create an inter-disciplinary blueprint for creating a sustainable planet and society,
- Provided leadership to realize a "circular economy" in which waste is incorporated into the development of new designs and delivery of new products and services and
- Through the employment of ongoing dialogue and cooperation enhanced the public's confidence in the safe application of emerging chemical industry technologies (Dow 2016).

Dow Freeport: Assigning Monetary Value to Natural Resources

Dow is investing a substantial sum in promoting its partnership with The Nature Conservancy, donating $7 million toward basic research to develop ecosystem services and directing another $3 million to The Nature Conservancy for consulting services to aid Dow in implementing enhanced ecosystem services (Walsh 2011). As a part of Dow's partnership with The Nature Conservancy, the company selected its Freeport plant as the site for conducting a pilot program to determine ways the plant could economize through implementing environmental reforms. One of the chief goals of the Dow/Nature Conservancy collaboration involves engineering software to assign comparable value to natural resources and man-made assets. To realize this goal, they are piloting a new application, the Ecosystem Services Identification and Inventory (ESII) (McLeod 2015; Max 2014). Dow initiated this partnership with a $10 million contribution from its foundation anticipating that this would help the company realize operationalizing sustainability.

The Ecosystem Services Identification & Inventory (ESII) tool is designed to provide baseline data to quantify the value of nature to Dow and its constituent communities. More specifically, ESII demonstrates linkages between businesses and enables the company to integrate environmental resources throughout its corporate and industrial processes. In so doing, it serves to incorporate nature's value into the corporate production process, not simply as an externality but as a vital productive input. By so doing it serves to incorporate a foundational perspective of the value of ecosystem services across a variety of Dow's units and sites. This allows Dow to incorporate the ecosystem service considerations in a cost benefit scenario that includes corporate and nature benefits and costs. It likewise allows Dow to identify the most promising natural-capital opportunities and pursue them to be best advantage of their business interests while remaining inclusive to the needs of local communities and the surrounding natural environment (Hower 2015)

Since entering their partnership with the Nature Conservancy, DOW has applied this evaluative tool in two pilot settings in West Virginia and Michigan. In West Virginia Dow is working with Union Carbide to redevelop a tract of land adjacent to the Kanawha River from its historical use as a tank storage facility and coal-powered plant into a greenbelt that will serve as a natural filter to rainwater flowing off the surrounding hills and into the river. In this case, ESII tools are being employed to assist planners in determining whether to plant basic sustainable grasses and plants or whether to implemented an enhanced sustainability plan incorporating a mix of native and non-native plants, grasses, shrubs and trees to provide both ecological and aesthetic outcomes. Comparatively in Michigan, Dow pursued restoring a portion of degraded greenbelt at its Midland plant that incorporated "legacy sites" (sites of earlier industrial production activities). Their interest was determining whether to pursue standard brownfield restoration efforts on legacy and brownfield sites, ecological restoration on both sites or ecological restoration on the greenbelt and standard restoration on the brownfield site (ESII Tool 2017).

Nature Conservancy Partnership with Dow Chemical: Forest Restoration

Dow has entered its relationship with the Nature Conservancy with the intent of using the ESII methodology to assess the utility of pursuing a variety of environmental services initiatives. To that end, Dow has prioritized its stewardship initiatives around three projects: (1) Phytoremediation for Groundwater Decontamination in Sarnia, Canada (2) Constructed Wetland for Waste Water Treatment in Seadrift, Texas and air pollution mitigation via reforestation near Freeport, Texas (Dow 2013). Of these three projects, only one—the Seadrift reforestation project (along with a related coastal mitigation project)—is associated with the Dow/Nature Conservancy partnership. The other two projects while laudable have been ongoing and despite their promise, have not been replicated.

The Seadrift forest reforestation project was designed for implementation near the Dow Freeport plant. The goal was to reduce ambient ozone levels in the region surrounding the plant (Kareiva 2014). Ozone, a colorless reactive oxidant associated with atmospheric smog, is produced by the photochemical interaction of sunlight and nitrogen oxides—a process often facilitated by the presence of volatile organic compounds or VOCs. Concentrated ozone exposure can pose serious health problems to include chronic lung disease like emphysema and bronchitis as well as pulmonary bacterial infections. Ozone pollution has long been a problem for the Houston-Galveston metropolitan area in which Brazoria County resides. In fact, given the area's humid Gulf Coast climate, busy shipping port, heavy industrial base and one of the most automobile dependent transportation infrastructures in the nation, this eight-county region has one of the worst smog problems in the nation (Tresaugue 2014).

The VOCs contributing to ozone production are routinely produced by burning carbon based fuels in power plants or through the operation of motor vehicles. Chemical plants, such as the one operated by Dow in Freeport also contribute to the creation of ozone given their production of a variety of VOCs (Figure 53). The ground level ozone levels in the region surrounding the Freeport facility exceed EPA standards (>80 ppb) (Dow 2014). In 1999, Brazoria County, Texas was ranked at 70% among the worst polluted regions in the U.S. relative to ozone pollution and Dow plants within the county ranked 2[nd,] 4th, and 12th as the sources of VOCs and ozone (Scorecard 1999).

Chemical Name	Pounds TRI Release
ETHYLENE	846,467
CHLORINE	39,190
CHLORODIFLUOROMETHANE	37,663
AMMONIA	36,400
DICHLORODIFLUOROMETHANE	14,701
1,1-DICHLORO-1-FLUOROETHANE	5,024
4,4'-ISOPROPYLIDENEDIPHENOL	4,145
N-BUTYL ALCOHOL	3,317
CYCLOHEXANE	1,633
GLYCOL ETHERS	1,462
1,2,4-TRIMETHYLBENZENE	1,461
PHENANTHRENE	1,065
2,3-DICHLOROPROPENE	916
1,2-DICHLOROETHYLENE	868
DICYCLOPENTADIENE	222
DIISOCYANATES	193
BIS(2-CHLORO-1-METHYLETHYL) ETHER	165
PENTACHLOROETHANE	117
HYDROGEN CYANIDE	69
ANTHRACENE	57
TRIETHYLAMINE	29
BROMINE	27
PENTACHLOROBENZENE	14
CUMENE HYDROPEROXIDE	9
COPPER COMPOUNDS	3
N-METHYL-2-PYRROLIDONE	0

Figure 53: Toxic Release Inventory (TRI) Dow Freeport Plant
(Source: Scorecard 2011)

The technological solution to this problem involved either constructing an additional smokestack scrubber—a device that would have to be replaced every two years. The environmental option to accomplish the same outcome involves planting trees which beyond absorbing the ozone, would also capture carbon dioxide, create wildlife habitat and contribute to the natural aesthetics of the area. Moreover, since 75% of the bottomland hardwood forest had been lost during the drought of 2011 after a saline wedge from the Gulf of Mexico worked its way up the Brazos River, reforestation has served to restore a natural resource that would have otherwise been permanently lost (Nature Conservancy 2012).

The rationale for reforestation is based upon scientific research demonstrating trees act as natural filters (Tresaugue 2014). The proposed reforestation approach to ozone abatement was modeled on a proposal by ecologists at the University of Florida, in conjunction with ENVDAT Consulting of Knoxville, Tennessee and Dow Chemical operations staff (Kroeger et al. 2014). These researchers argue that,

> "Reforestation would be cost-competitive because we have already done so much to reduce pollution, especially in Houston, that each additional control will be more expensive. Planting trees can be done at roughly the same cost

as additional technological controls while providing numerous benefits, such as wildlife habitat and improved water quality" (Tresaugue 2014).

Mark Estes, a senior scientist for the Texas Commission on Environmental Quality, agrees that tree planting on an industrial scale (600,000 trees or more) may very well significantly reduce ozone-forming pollution (Tresaugue 2014).

However, not all environmental scientists concur that tree-planting is effective, principally because some tree species emit VOCs and subsequently produce fuel for ozone development. One critic of the approach, Barry LeFer of the University of Houston's Department of Earth and Atmospheric Science commented that while planting trees is always a good idea there is "no guarantee that the trees are cleaning up emissions where we need the reductions " (Tresaugue 2014).

Clearly one of the challenges for Dow and The Nature Conservancy is finding the space to plant trees in the volume required to make a significant difference. Timm Kroeger of the University of Florida who teamed with Dow and The Nature Conservancy to conduct a feasibility study of utilizing trees to reduce ozone levels believes that intensive reforestation in and around Brazoria County southwest of downtown Houston would be an ideal location, in part because it is isolated enough from Houston to reduce the natural VOC emissions of the massive forest (Tresaugue 2014). The Kroeger led study (Kroeger et al. 2014) concluded that planting 1,000 acres with cedar elm, ash, and sugarberry trees may remove 202 tons of nitrous oxides over 30 years. Even so, it is anticipated that adding forests alone would probably be insufficient to bring the Houston area in compliance with EPA smog limits, implying that a truly vast amount of land was needed to achieve deep pollution reduction.

Given these extensive land requirements, the feasibility study focused upon 470,000 acres of land in agricultural use that might more fruitfully be employed for ozone reduction. Unfortunately, the cost of purchasing so much land was prohibitive so The Nature Conservancy and Dow were forced to consider approaching private owners willing to voluntarily reforest a portion of their land or look to public lands for reforestation. Currently, Dow and The Nature Conservancy are still in the exploratory phase of this reforestation effort and are determining whether reforestation efforts can be included in the Texas State Implementation Plan (Dow Chemical 2014).

Coastal Mitigation

Concomitant to Dow's reforestation effort is to protect the fragile Texas coastline from flooding produced by tropical storms and hurricanes. The typical engineering solution to these threats involves constructing levees and seawalls. Comparatively the environmental solution involves restoring marsh, riparian and coastal forests so that they serve as natural buffers in the event of tropical weather. The Dow/ Nature Conservancy collaboration regarding coastal mitigation occurred near the company's Freeport facility which is responsible for more than 20% of Dow's global sales (Reddy, McDonald et al. 2015). The Freeport facility location is low-lying and vulnerable to hurricanes. Its topography consists of a region of coastal marshes, a system of man-made levees (gray infrastructure) and a salt dome (Stratton Ridge) located 12 km inland at 12.46 feet elevation. The salt dome is valuable to Dow's chlorine and caustic plants though the Stratton Ridge salt dome lies beyond the company's levee system along with another large undeveloped parcel (Figure 54).

When faced with issues like coastal flooding most companies pursue engineering solutions (aka gray infrastructure) involving the construction of levees and seawalls. By comparison green infrastructure approaches involve natural habitat restoration. Dow's initial plan is to protect the Stratton Ridge salt dome with a system of levees given the central role salt plays in their industrial production. Green infrastructure is planned in areas not currently protected by levees and an application known as InVEST which provides a coastal protection model to determine how physical and plant habitats influence wave height, water elevation, levee scouring and overtopping and flooding. The InVEST approach models waves riding atop storm surges as previously modeled by others to evaluate cost, benefit and management options (Hopper & Meixler 2016). Considerations are also included regarding recreational use, biodiversity and available carbon resources (Nature Conservancy 2012).

Figure 54: Unprotected Coastal Areas, Dow Freeport
(Source: Nature Conservancy 2012)

Figure 55 illustrates the "green" and "grey" hazard mitigation plan process while Figure 56 presents a method for integrated hazard planning (Boucher et al., 2012) to include assessing the value of coastal habitats and ecosystems to built-environments, evaluating green and gray infrastructure options and ultimately developing a strategy of green/gray infrastructure planning and response for coastal risk management decision making (Boucher et al. 2012). Three infrastructure alternatives (Figure 57) have been incorporated into InVEST to include a "high green" option in which high land below the year 2100 sea level rise (SLR) salt line is either restored or allowed to revert to marshland, a "moderately green" option where limited development and habitat protection/restoration is planned based upon 2040 sea level rise projections, and a "no green" option where all possible development in and around the plant facility is aggressively pursued by the year 2025 (Boucher et al. 2012).

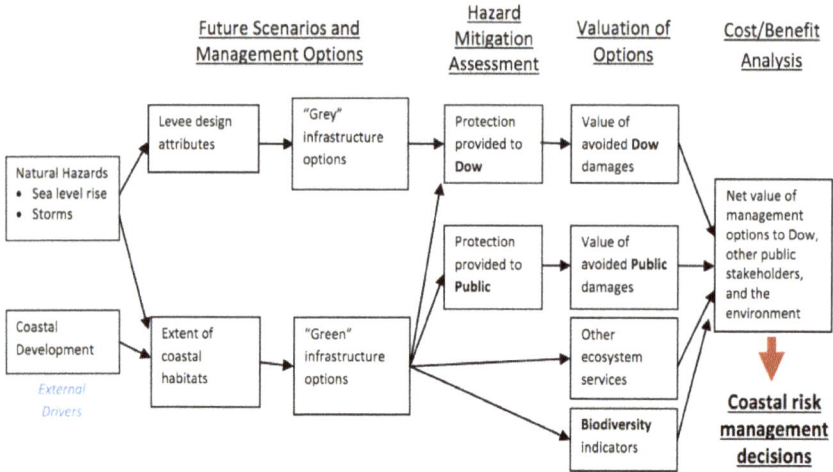

Figure 55: Green & Grey Infrastructure Mitigation Plan
(Source: Nature Conservancy 2012)

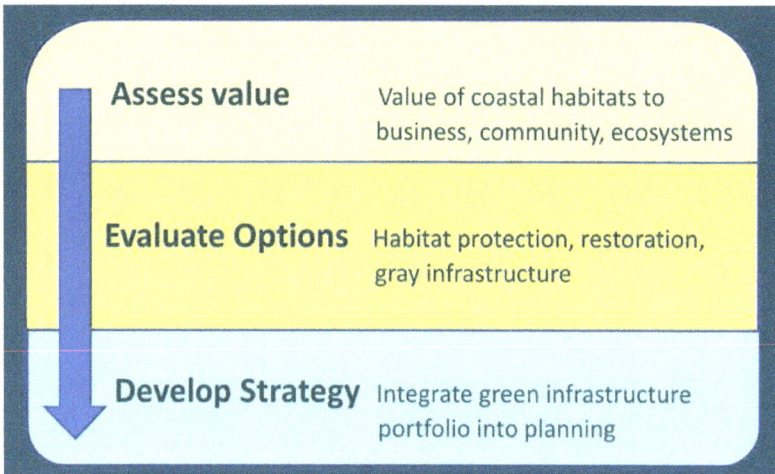

Figure 56: Method for Integrated Hazard Planning
(Source: Boucher et al. 2012)

Figure 57: Alternate Infrastructure Scenarios
(Source: Boucher et al. 2012)

Stakeholders in the Dow / Nature Conservancy Partnership

There are numerous stakeholders involved in this innovative partnership. Among these are the principals Neil Hawkins, Chief sustainability officer for Dow Chemical and Jennifer Molnar, corporate liaison with The Nature Conservancy. Also represented is the Texas Commission on Environmental Quality (TCEQ), the Brazoria County Commission and local environmentalists from Freeport, Texas. Mark Tercek, President and CEO of The Nature Conservancy and Peter Kareiva of the UCLA Institute of the Environment and Sustainability have also played important roles. Based upon Dow Chemical's 2025 future's report, the company plans is to create $1 billion in capital value to the company, in part by including natural capital in capital expenditures or investment decisions (Clancy 2015).

Mark Tercek's principal contribution to the Dow/Nature Conservancy project in Freeport, Texas was his commitment to find models that effectively assign monetary values to natural resources. Tercek instinctively realized that if major industrial polluters such as Dow were to be engaged around more environmentally friendly production processes that it would be necessary to demonstrate an economic value in doing so—thereby engendering a higher level of corporate environmental accountability. Regarding the Dow partnership Tercek comments that,

> "I know there's a lot of skepticism about these corporate initiatives, but for Dow to agree with us philosophically that it relies on nature for business reasons and to begin to put a business value on its natural assets, that's huge" (Wells 2012).

Under Tercek's direction The Nature Conservancy has been encouraging businesses to recognize that "nature is a source for sustainable business value." In partnering with Dow, The Nature Conservancy embarked on an effort to literally "operationalize sustainability" (Max 2014).

From Tercek's perspective, the old rationale for business becoming involved in environmental projects would have involved conservation "for conservation's sake." By comparison, Tercek's rationale for partnering with Dow was "we're doing conservation for business' sake" (Max 2014). In taking over the helm of The Nature Conservancy, Tercek shifted its mission away from narrowly acquiring land for environmental preservation and protection to employing market forces to bolster environmental efforts. As one observer noted, "a preference for financial thinking runs like an underground stream through Tercek's conversation" (Max, 2014). The rationale behind Tercek's investment in Dow is the belief that accurate data trumps illogical rhetoric and can focus goal orientations to achieve sustainable ends. Based upon investments such as the one The Conservancy is making in Dow, Tercek anticipates a future where "impact investments" produce social benefit as well as financial return (Max 2014).

Before assuming his current role as Director of UCLA's Institute of the Environment and Sustainability, Peter Kareiva served as The Nature Conservancy's chief biologist. Upon joining The Nature Conservancy, Tercek found a like-minded ally in Kareiva who had long distinguished himself among environmentalists for his pragmatic approach to environmental problems. Kareiva's approach—known as "new conservation science" recognizes that humans have a rightful place in the natural environment. His philosophy stands in sharp contrast to his ideological opposite - Michael Soulé - who favors a strong demarcation between the built environments of humans and natural ecosystems (Kloor 2015). Unlike Soulé, Kareiva accepts the world as it is rather than demanding ideologically-driven outcomes. While committed to biodiversity, he has grown weary of what he refers to as "doom and gloom" environmentalism—particularly the eco-apocalyptic mindset of activists like Soulé. Kareiva is particularly critical of the degree to which the environmentalist community "is plagued with an astonishing confirmation bias (uncritically interpreting new information in terms of existing theories that does not allow questioning of anything" (Kloor 2015, 73).

Given this perspective, Kareiva established a reputation at The Nature Conservancy as someone who sought to creatively approach environmental problems pragmatically and without preconceptions as well as to engage the public in addressing these problems minus blame or prejudgment. Kareiva asserts that:

> "Forward-looking conservation protects natural habitats where people live and extract resources and works with corporations to find mixes of economic and conservation activities that blend development with a concern for nature" (Kareiva & Marvier 2012, 968).

Kareiva distinguishes himself from many of his environmentalist colleagues and rather than focusimg upon nature's fragility he emphasizes its remarkable resilience. In this way, he conceptualizes human impacts on the environment as both necessary and environmentally tolerable, providing humans don't push environmental resiliency beyond its sustainable limits (Kloor 2015).

Kareiva's most controversial idea, however, is his belief that for conservation to succeed it is necessary to make business a friend and not an enemy. This value opened The Nature Conservancy to partnerships with businesses that historically would have been unthinkable. Mark Tercek's values coincided nicely with Kareiva's making the new CEO and the organization's chief scientist philosophically compatible (Kloor 2015).

Neil Hawkins, Chief Sustainability Officer with Dow Chemical, approaches corporate responsibility as intertwined with social responsibility and environmental sustainability. Hawkins who is the architect of Dow's 2025 Sustainability Goals and the driving force behind Dow's partnership with The Nature Conservancy, believes that "We are citizens of one planet, and this interdependence places an increasing responsibility on each of us to not only take ownership for our actions, but also share in our stewardship for the earth" (Hawkins 2015). Hawkins believes that companies have an obligation to demonstrate stewardship of the planet. Stewardship, from Hawkin's perspective is cooperative involving interdependent relationships with corporate, community, and environmental organizations.

Hawkins takes his company's environmental stewardship mission seriously noting that Dow has "been on a sustainability journey for close to 20 years" to include "environmental health and safety performance, the whole life cycle of our products and delivering products that actually help the world solve major challenges" (Makower 2011). He further asserts "No matter how well it may lead, no one company can achieve long-term sustainability while operating in a silo" (Hawkins 2015). Consequently, Hawkins advocates for companies to adopt a set of sustainable practices to include:

- Providing leadership by "taking the road less traveled" and committing to achieve sustainability goals ahead of competitors,
- Collaborating with groups complement corporate sustainability efforts and share successful practices with other companies,
- Recruiting top leadership talent into the corporation—people capable of and committed to achieving sustainable outcomes,
- Committing to "win" sustainable objectives as surely as the company commits to winning financially by diversifying the definition of corporate success to include people, planet and profit (Hawkins 2015).

Hawkins estimates that by 2015, Dow realized a corporate windfall of $200 million based upon its investments in developing natural capital. Doing so however involved changing its corporate philosophy - acknowledging that a "one-to-one relationship exists between corporate revenue and environmental destruction. Rendering this into a sustainable relationship mandated a delicate balance between fiscal and environmental sustainability—which in effect necessitates asking "how much" sustainability can be realized "when" over what "time-frame" and at what cost.

Hawkins, recipient of Harvard's Roy Family Award for Environmental Partnership for his innovative corporate partnership with The Nature Conservancy, shares Mark Tercek's passion for putting a monetary value on natural resources in the interest of making "the economics of ecological systems work hand-in-glove with business decision-making" (Harvard 2013; Russell 2013). Even though the Dow/Nature Conservancy partnership involves "odd bedfellows," it has been successful despite the divergence of corporate environmental philosophies. Nevertheless, The Nature Conservancy under Tercek has demonstrated a willingness to be "ruthlessly pragmatic" in its commitment to partner with industry for environmental goals while Dow has demonstrated a commitment under Hawkins to become a corporate sustainability leader, despite its checkered environmental past (Russell 2013).

Beyond the obvious stakeholders there are numerous other former Dow Chemical employees (mostly retirees) who continue to contribute significantly to environmental sustainability in the Brazoria County. Some are very visible such as Carolyn H. Johnson, a board member for the Brazoria River Authority and Carol Jones, Director of Gulf Coast Bird Observatory. Others are less evident but very influential to include Bill Bennett, Professor of Process Technology and Chemistry at Brazosport College in Lake Jackson, Texas and David Plunkett, a volunteer at Friends of Brazoria Wildlife Refuge where he serves with several other retired Dow employees. Many of these retirees were involved in earlier stages of Dow's sustainability efforts and in retirement serve on one or more of the advisory boards Dow utilizes to involve the public in its environmental efforts.

The Texas Commission on Environmental Quality (TCEQ 2013; 2009) is also an important stakeholder. Its statutory role involves protecting the state's "public health and natural resources consistent with sustainable economic development." Consequently, TCEQ plays an oversight role for Dow Chemical in Freeport, Texas and is a stakeholder in seeing Dow's Partnership with The Nature Conservancy yield fruitful results. However, as a stakeholder it assumes a "carrot and stick" approach like when it awarded its 2013 Environmental Excellence award to Dow after having historically fined the company in 2009 for air pollution violations at its Freeport facility (TCEQ 2013).

While no identifiable Brazoria County environmental organization have commented on Dow's sustainability efforts and its partnership with The Nature Conservancy, Dow was recognized in 2015 by the Sustainable Accounting Standards Board for having reduced overall industrial waste by 17% between 2005 and 2010 having managed 97% of its toxic recovery inventory (TRI) wastes via recycling or energy recovery processes (SASB 2015). Comparatively, Dow received scathing criticism in 2014 from the Environment America Research and Policy Center in Boston, Massachusetts for its pollution practices along the lower Brazos River (Inglis 2014). This organization roundly criticized Dow for leading the nation in 2012 as an industrial polluter - having released 33,474,505 toxicity weighted pounds of pollutants into the Brazos. To get a feel for just how immense that amount of pollutants is, the second highest polluting company (Dow Chemical, Louisiana) dumped 1,876,479 toxicity weighted pounds into the Mississippi at its Plaquemine plant (Inglis 2014).

Luke Metzger, Director of Environment Texas, has been particularly critical of Dow's ongoing environmental record (Metzger 2014) and characterizes the Dow/Nature Conservancy partnership as "classic greenwashing" meant to divert attention from Dow's ongoing pollution practices (Metzger 2016a). Metzger points to

Dow's Freeport plant's reputation as being the worst industrial polluter in the Houston area and one of the worst in the nation releasing 1.3 million pound of pollutants in 2015 to include 15,717 pounds of benzene into the atmosphere. In fact, during a single plant malfunction on February 2, 2015 the Freeport facility released 1,407 pounds of benzene over a 13-hour interval despite that the plant's state permit allows no more than 339 pounds (Metzger 2016b). Air Alliance Houston is likewise critical of Dow for its contribution to regional air pollution. Most recently these organizations protested flaring toxic gases at the Freeport facility which released significant amounts of more than a dozen toxic pollutants (Figure 58) (Shelly 2016).

Source 1: Elevated Flare , EPN number OC6F1

Contaminant	Authorization	Limit	Amount Released
1,3-BUTADIENE	#20432	0.01 LBS/HR	150.0 lbs (est.)
Acetylene	#20432	0.01 LBS/HR	150.0 lbs (est.)
Benzene	#20432	0.01 LBS/HR	150.0 lbs (est.)
Butane	#20432	0.01 LBS/HR	300.0 lbs (est.)
Butene	#20432	0.01 LBS/HR	300.0 lbs (est.)
Carbon Monoxide	#20432	0.06 LBS/HR	47000.0 lbs (est.)
Ethane	#20432	0.01 LBS/HR	15000.0 lbs (est.)
Ethylene (gaseous)	#20432	0.01 LBS/HR	41000.0 lbs (est.)
Hydrogen	#20432	0.01 LBS/HR	2200.0 lbs (est.)
Methane	#20432	0.01 LBS/HR	8200.0 lbs (est.)
Nitrogen Oxides	#20432	0.01 LBS/HR	7000.0 lbs (est.)
Propylene	#20432	0.01 LBS/HR	300.0 lbs (est.)

Source 4: Ground Flare , EPN number OC6F1000

Contaminant	Authorization	Limit	Amount Released
1,3-BUTADIENE	#20432	24.58 LBS/HR	150.0 lbs (est.)
1-Butene	#20432	24.58 LBS/HR	300.0 lbs (est.)
Acetylene	#20432	24.58 LBS/HR	150.0 lbs (est.)
Benzene	#20432	24.58 LBS/HR	150.0 lbs (est.)
Butane	#20432	24.58 LBS/HR	300.0 lbs (est.)
Carbon Monoxide	#20432	91.17 LBS/HR	47000.0 lbs (est.)
Ethane	#20432	24.58 LBS/HR	15000.0 lbs (est.)
Ethylene (gaseous)	#20432	24.58 LBS/HR	41000.0 lbs (est.)
Hydrogen	#20432	24.58 LBS/HR	2200.0 lbs (est.)
Methane	#20432	24.58 LBS/HR	8200.0 lbs (est.)
Nitrogen Oxides	#20432	17.53 LBS/HR	7000.0 lbs (est.)
Propylene	#20432	24.58 LBS/HR	300.0 lbs (est.)

Figure 58: Dow June 15, 2016 Flaring Event Pollution Release
(Source: Shelly 2016)

The Farm and Ranch Freedom Alliance also took issue with Dow and its Freeport facility for producing the 2, 4-D herbicide, one of the oldest and most widely used herbicides in the world that targets broadleaf weeds while leaving grasses and cereals intact (Farm & Ranch Freedom Alliance 2014). Dow also produces genetically modified organisms (GMOs) that are resistant to 2, 4-D herbicides. Joining the Farm and Ranch Freedom Alliance in their opposition to the use of this herbicide and the production or herbicide resistant GMOs is the Environmental Health Fund (EHF) and the Pesticide Action Network of North America (PANNA) (Spear 2012). These two organizations have taken the lead in issuing statements and press releases critical of Dow and its herbicide / GMO seed production activities and have also linked with a group of like-minded environmental organizations to include Beyond Pesticides, Organic Consumers Association, ETC Group, Union of Concerned Scientists and Friends of the Earth (Spear 2012).

Of course, Dow Chemical has a long standing environmental adversary in the form of Greenpeace who published an influential book on Dioxin pollution in 1994 entitled *Dow Brand Dioxin: Dow Makes You Poison Great Things* (Weinberg 1994). Greenpeace remains skeptical of Dow despite its newfound partnership with The Nature Conservancy. Per Greenpeace legislative director, Rick Hind,

> "Companies like Dow have a lot of money to do this kind of PR, and they do it because it works." Yet from Hind's perspective these efforts are inadequate since they fail to "address the lion's share of contamination that they're responsible for" (Moodie 2015).

Ecopragmatic Principles in the Dow/Nature Conservancy Partnership

The Dow Chemical/Nature Conservancy partnership embodies numerous ecopragmatic principles. The collaboration is a striking example of *collaboration among strange bedfellows* as one of the world's most notorious polluters teams with one of the world's most prestigious and effective environmental organizations. What concerns most outsiders witnessing this partnership is to what degree will this partnership result in significant environmental improvements in Dow's operations, or is this partnership simply good public relations for the corporation.

As has been discussed, Dow Chemical is an international petrochemical conglomerate with a very checkered history of environmental pollution as well as a problematic history relative to human health and well-being in and around its chemical plants. In fact, it is hard to imagine a major corporation more in need of a better public reputation regarding its human and environmental health practices. By comparison the Nature Conservancy is a large international NGO (non-governmental organization) that has historically made inroads in "conservation" (as compared to environmentalism) precisely but its willingness to partner with polluters to improve their environmental practices. Consequently, from the Nature Conservancy's perspective their partnership with Dow is not unusual.

By comparison, from the perspective of the petro chemical industry such a partnership is quite unique and perhaps unintuitive. Cynics might be tempted to look at this relationship as an example of "greenwash"—presenting one's interests as if one is committed to environmental issues when in fact environmental efforts are meant to be token and cosmetic. Likewise, they might be tempted to criticize the Nature Conservancy for "selling out" to corporate interests and not remaining true to their environmental mission. Worse still, some might accuse this NGO of being "used" and "played" by big oil.

However, when one considers the nature of the relationship that these two organizations have established together it seems clear that while Dow efforts are incremental and not hugely capitalized, their commitment to EII signals a serious intent to capitalize the value of environmental services in the products they produce. This approach which has been prioritized within their partnership with the Nature Conservancy seems to portend a long-term commitment to doing their business in a new way. That said, it would be naïve to expect that Dow won't continue to pollute - indeed it is hard to imagine how they can produce their products and not do so. Nevertheless, their innovations to date suggests that Dow appears committed to a future where they seek to be increasingly productive as a corporation but with a minimal of environmental externalities.

Arguably, this unusual partnership also exemplifies the *application of satisficing communitarianism*. Implicit in this Dow/Nature Conservancy partnership is a pragmatic approach to solving problems that doesn't allow the "ideal" outcome to become a deterrent to options that marginally improve their environmental track record. This approach—known as satisficing—appears to be occurring in an inclusive fashion incorporating concerns from local public officials, citizen's groups, former employees and other state and local environmental advocacy groups. This renders Dow's satisficing business model communitarian in orientation allowing for corporate planning to more predictably move in concert to local and regional needs.

Dow Chemical and The Nature Conservancy have also *engaged a network of "responsibles"* within their partnership. They have done so in the interest of pursuing several strategic corporate, economic and environmental objectives in conjunction with local officials, organizations and other non-regional expertise. Some of these "responsibles" include:

- The Nature Conservancy
- The Friends of the Brazos River,
- The Houston-Galveston Area Council of Governments (regarding the Regional Air Quality Planning Advisory Committee) (HGAC 2016),
- The Michigan State University Center for Sustainable Packaging and the Ocean Conservancy (Wooster 2016),
- The Port of Freeport, Texas (Port Freeport 2015),
- Citizens for Clean Air/Clean Water, Brazoria County, Texas,
- Sierra Club Houston Group,
- Water Texas,
- Public and environmental health programs as the University of Texas Health Science Center in Houston and the University of Texas Medical Branch in Galveston (USOTA 1990),
- Brazosport College;
- Sea Center Texas (a fish hatchery and environmental education center).

Dow has also dedicated itself to *maintaining relationships with organizations that are typically their detractors*. Given Dow's extensive record of pollution one would expect their relationships with environmental groups to be minimal. However, that is not the case. Beyond the obvious example of their relationship with The Nature

Conservancy, Dow has additionally maintained functional and pragmatic working relationships with Water Texas (Barer 2013), Friends of the Brazos River (Glen Rose Current 2014), the Wildlife Habitat Council (Keller 2016), and Texas Audubon (Reddy, Guannel et al. 2015). Although the likely reason Dow cooperates with these groups is in the interest of improving their marketing optics, their relationship with the Nature Conservancy and their investment in EII tends to lend credence to their claim that Dow is not just about producing petroleum products and making money for stockholders. They are also interested in achieving a better balance between their corporate and environmental activities that will help them be profitable as well as role models for local sustainable environmental stewardship and investment.

Dow's environmental commitment is grounded in what it refers to as "circular economics." Circular economics is a model that relies upon extending the employment of natural resources over the longest possible period in the interest of extracting maximum value while creating minimal pollution. This approach requires a commitment to sustainably recovering, extending and regenerating products and materials (Ellen MacArthur Foundation 2017) (See Figure 59). Realizing this goal necessitates a high degree of coordination and communication between the range of business and community stakeholders involved in the productive process. In the absence of a wide network of communication and cooperation it would be impossible for Dow to efficiently and effectively realize the benefits of circular economics (Ellen MacArthur Foundation 2015). Having committed itself to this economic philosophy Dow joined a group of corporations known as the "Circular Economy 100" (Foundation for Circular Economy 2015) sponsored by the Ellen MacArthur Foundation. By embracing the principle of circular economics Dow has endeavored to integrate EII into its economic model and in so doing has expanded its range of stakeholders beyond those narrowly involved in its productive process to additionally include environmental, governmental and civic stakeholders (Barney 2016). This commitment to circular economics and EII illustrates a philosophical confluence between the corporation's environmental and economic interests.

As Dow and The Nature Conservancy pursued "satisficing" approaches to problem solving they never let the "perfect" become an obstacle to realizing a "good" option. This perspective *avoids narrow "either-or" thinking and instead illustrates a "both- and" approach* where more than one goal can be pursued simultaneously to include tradeoff and compromises as necessary. The Nature Conservancy incorporates this perspective whenever it partners with corporations like Dow, knowing full well that such partnerships will not eliminate pollution but rather minimize it. In like manner Dow seeks to realize its economic agenda on behalf of its customers and shareholders but seeks to do so in a way that minimizes negative outcomes. Neither

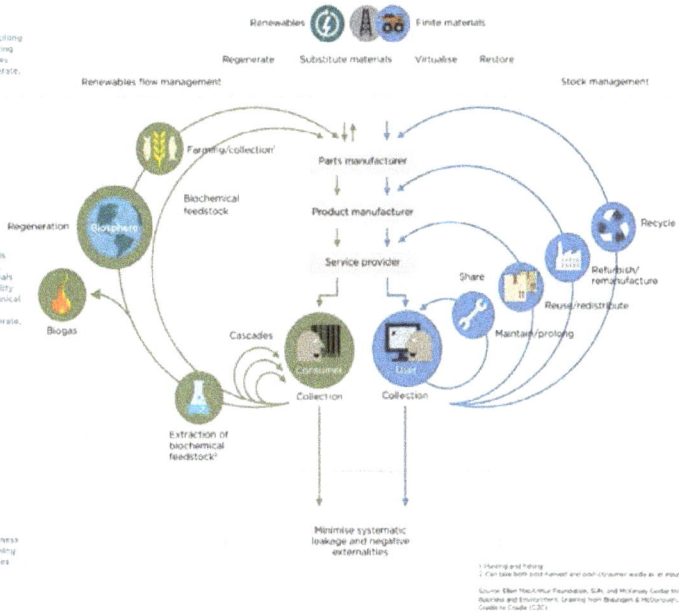

Figure 59: Circular Economy Overview
(Source: Ellen MacArthur Foundation 2017)

Neither Dow nor the Nature Conservancy approaches their partnership with the "either-or" perspective of "polluting versus not polluting" or "being economically productive or nonproductive." Rather, each approaches one another looking for tradeoffs between economic productivity and environmental conservation.

As illustrated throughout this case study, Dow Chemical *invests heavily in developing science based approaches to promote environmental health and safety.* Dow does so by investing in research, development and consultation to include:

- **Environmental Regulatory Management** - Regulatory expertise on EH&S, and implementation support to Dow sites and businesses, development of relationships with external research organizations (governmental and academic); utilizing the expertise in Dow's Epidemiology Expertise Center to conducts product safety studies.
- **Environmental Operations** - Technical expertise regarding air emissions, wastewater management and waste management through permit implementation and reporting to improve environmental compliance.
- **Epidemiology** - Technical expertise regarding health-related issues in consultation with corporate and external research organizations to ensure product safety.

- **Industrial Hygiene** - Technical expertise regarding exposure assessment to Dow businesses and their customers to include consultation.
- **Life Cycle Assessment** - Technical assistance for business leaders in employing Dow's Life Cycle Assessments (LCA) and their related sustainable chemistry concept which promotes life cycle thinking.
- **Occupational Health** - Technical assistance and consultation on occupational health and safety.
- **Product Sustainability** - Technical assistance and consultation from Dow's Product Sustainability Team to businesses to improve their risk management practices.
- **Toxicology** - Technical assistance from Dow's Toxicology Expertise Center and Research Laboratory to conduct laboratory-based studies regarding human and environmental health, regulatory and product safety (Dow 2017).

CONCLUSION

Although Dow's partnership with the Nature Conservancy could conceivably be discounted as "greenwash" and the role of the Nature Conservancy regarded as "diluted environmentalism," this partnership represents a pragmatic, mutually beneficial effort to meet the petro-chemical demands of the nation and the world while simultaneously mitigating environmental pollution. Such compromising approaches satisfy neither the hardcore environmentalist nor the hardcore capitalist. Even so, capitalists and environmentalists don't exist in ideal worlds where the realization of one set of goals (environmental sustainability for instance) can be realized without costs being imposed elsewhere (i.e. economic sustainability). The hard truth of conversations between economic and environmental interests is that there are no ideal solutions and there is no "free lunch."

Inevitably conversations such as those between Dow and the Nature Conservancy must embrace the reality that all efforts toward a more sustainable world require economic and lifestyle tradeoffs. To the credit of Dow Chemical and the Nature Conservancy, both recognize this reality and have embraced it by becoming ongoing partners dedicated to incrementally contributing to environmental sustainability while simultaneously responding to economic demand for new and innovative petrochemical products and services. Consequently, rather than criticize or discount the value of their unique relationship, the realistic and pragmatic environmentalist or conservationist might rather regard these two strange bedfellows as heralds of things to come and a sustainable future worth embracing.

REFERENCES

Barer, David. 2013. "Major Water Campaign Water Texas PAC Raises Nearly $1 Million." *Dallas Morning News.* (October 3), Accessed April 17, 2017 https://www.dallasnews.com/news/politics/2013/10/08/major-water-campaign-water-texas-pac-raises-nearly-1-million

Barney, Craig. 2016. "Dow Doubles Down on Sustainability." *Good360.* (July 18), Accessed April 17, 2017 https://good360.org/dow-doubles-down-on-sustainability/

Beder, Sharon. 2014. "Business-Managed Environment: The Nature Conservancy TNC." *Business-Managed Democracy.* Accessed August 14, 2016 http://www.herinst.org/BusinessManaged Democracy/environment/environmentalists/TNC.html

Boini, Shiela and Anne Titia Bové. 2014. "Sustainability's Strategic Worth: McKinsey Global Survey Results." *McKinsey and Company Survey.* (July), Accessed July 24, 2016 a http://www.mckinsey.com/business-functions/sustainability-and-resource-productivity/our-insights/sustainabilitys-strategic-worth-mckinsey-global-survey-results

Boucher, Tim; Sheila Walsh, Jorge Brenner, Rob Griffin, Greg Guannel, Ann Guerry and Jen Molnar. 2012. "Green and Gray Infrastructure: A Spatial Framework for Considering Impacts—The Nature Conservancy Dow Collaboration." The Nature Conservancy and the National Capital Project, Accessed July 31, 2016 https://conference.ifas.ufl.edu/aces12/presentations/2%20Tuesday/2%20Key%20West-Palm%20Beach/Session%202B/YES/0510%20Boucher.pdf

Cappiello, Dana. 2005. "Dow Chemical Brought Growth, Regrets to Freeport." *Houston Chronicle.* (January 1), Accessed July 24, 2016 http://www.chron.com/news/article/Dow-Chemical-brought-growth-regrets-to-Freeport-1922627.php

Clancy, Heather. 2015. "Dow's Plan to Bank $1 Billion on Natural Capital by 2025." *GreenBiz.* (April 15), Accessed August 3, 2016 https://www.greenbiz.com/article/dow-chemical-thinks-it-can-generate-1-billion-valuing-nature

Dow Chemical. 2017. "Environmental Health and Safety." Accessed April 17, 2017 http://www.dow.com/en-us/careers/career-areas/eh-s-and-sustainability#

———. 2016. "2025 Sustainability Framework." Accessed July 24, 2016 http://www.dow.com/en-us/science-and-sustainability/2025-sustainability-goals/valuing-nature

———. 2015a. "2015 Annual Report." Accessed July 24, 2016 http://storage.dow.com.edgesuite.net/dow.com/investors/2015_Dow_Chemical_Annual_Report.pdf

———. 2015b. "Dow Sustainability: Valuing Ecosystems—2013-2014 Conservation Report." Accessed July 29, 2016 http://www.dow.com/-/media/dow/business-units/dow-us/pdf/valuing-ecosystems-2013-2014.ashx?la=en-us

———. 2014. "The Nature Conservancy and Dow: 2014 Annual Progress Report." Accessed July 29, 2016 http://www.nature.org/about-us/working-with-companies/companies-we-work-with/dow/

———. 2013. "Green Infrastructure Case Studies." (June), Accessed August 3, 2016 http://www.nature.org/about-us/working-with-companies/case-studies-for-green-infrastructure.pdf

Dow Texas. 2015. "75 Years Dow Texas Operations." *Impact.* (Quarterly Publication Dow Chemical Texas), Accessed July 24, 2016 http://www.dow.com/locations/texas/freeport/pdf/impact/75thAnniversary_Texas_final.pdf

———. 2013. "Dow's 2012 Economic Impact in Texas and Brazoria County." Accessed July 24, 2016 http://www.dow.com/locations/texas/freeport/pdf/impact/Impact-Summer_2013.pdf

———. 2008. "Dow's Texas Operations Receives International Habitat Conservation Award." Accessed April 17, 2017 http://www.csrwire.com/press_releases/ 25986-Dow-s-Texas-Operations-Receives-International-Habitat-Conservation-Award

Doyle, Jack. 2004. *Trespass Against Us: Dow Chemical and the Toxic Century.* Monroe: Common Courage Press.

Ellen MacArthur Foundation. 2017. "Circular Economy Overview." Accessed April 17, 2017 https://www.ellenmacarthurfoundation.org/circular-economy/overview/concept

———. 2015. *Towards a Circular Economy: Business Rationale for an Accelerated Transition.* Crowes: Ellen MacArthur Foundation.

ESII Tool. 2017. "Case Studies." Accessed April 13, 2017 http://www.esiitool.com/case-studies/

Farm and Ranch Freedom Alliance. 2014. "Save Our Farmers—Tell Congress to Oppose New Use of Toxic Herbicide." *Action Alert.* Accessed August 17, 2016 http://farmandranchfreedom.org/alert-tell-congress-to-oppose-new-use-of-herbicide/

Foundation for Circular Economy. 2015. "CE100 - A Global Circular Economy Innovation Platform." Budapest, Hungary, Accessed April 17, 2017 http://circularfoundation.org/en/ce100-global-circular-economy-innovation-platform

Glen Rose Current. 2014. "Friends of the Brazos Ask for Help in Water Rights Fight." *Glen Rose Current.* (April 20), Accessed April 17, 2017 http://glenrosecurrent.com/friends-of-the-brazos-asks-for-help-in- water-rights-fight/

Hannibal, Mary Ellen. 2015. "Sleeping with the Enemy." *Huffington Post.* (June 2), Accessed August 14, 2016 at http://www.huffingtonpost.com/mary-ellen-hannibal/sleeping-with-the-enemy_1_b_5423950.html

Harvard Kennedy School Communications. 2013. "Dow Chemical—Nature Conservancy Collaboration Honored." *Harvard Gazette.* (October 3), Accessed August 14, 2016 http://news.harvard.edu/gazette/story/2013/10/dow-chemical-nature-conservancy-collaboration-honored/

Hawkins, Neil. 2015. "Six Habits of Leading Sustainable Enterprises." *Ensia.* (August 27). Accessed August 3, 2016 http://ensia.com/voices/six-habits-of-leading-sustainable-enterprises/

Hopper, Thomas and Maria S. Meixler. 2016. "Modeling Coastal Vulnerability through Space and Time." *Plos One.* (October 12), Accessed September 17, 2017 http://journals.plos.org/plosone/article?id=10.1371/journal.pone.0163495

Houston-Galveston Area Council of Government (HGAC). 2016. "Regional Air Quality Planning Advisory Committee." (November 1), Accessed April 17, 2017 http://www.h-gac.com/board-of-directors/advisory-committees/regional-air-quality-planning-advisory-committee/documents/2017/2017-01-26/ITEM_1b_RAQPAC_Meeting_Minutes_11-17-2016.pdf

Hower, Mike. 2015. "Dow, TNC Building Tool to Help Companies Better Understand Value of Natural Capital." *Sustainable Brands.* (January 26), Accessed April 13, 2017 http://edwardwimberley.com/courses/80458/hower.pdf

Inglis, Jeff, Tony Dutzik and John Rumpler. 2014. *Wasting Our Waterways: Toxic Industrial Pollution and Restoring the Promise of the Clean Water Act.* Boston, MA: Environment America Research and Policy Center (Distributed by Environment Texas), Accessed August 17, 2016 http://environmenttexascenter.org/sites/environment/files/reports/wastingwaterways.pdf

Kareiva, Peter. 2014. "Peter Kareiva on Why the Ozone-Reforestation Study is Important." *Cool Green Science.* (September 9), Accessed July 24, 2016 http://blog.nature.org/science/2014/09/09/kareiva-pnas-forest-ozone-dow-epa/#

Kareiva, Peter and Michelle Marvier. 2012. "What is Conservation Science," *Bioscience.* 62(11): 962-969.

Kaskey, Jack. 2016. "Dow-DuPont Shareholders Approve $59 Billion Merger of Equals." *Crains Detroit Business.* (July 20), Accessed July 24, 2016 http://www.crainsdetroit.com/article/20160720/NEWS01/160729994/dow-dupont-shareholders-approve-59-billion-merger-of-equals

Keller, Monica. 2016. "New White Paper Examines Opportunities for the Corporate Campus to Benefit Biodiversity, Employees and Communities." *Wildlife Habitat.* Accessed April 17, 2017 http://www.wildlifehc.org/new-white-paper-examines-opportunities-for-the-corporate-campus-to-benefit-biodiversity-employees-and-communities/

Kloor, Keith. 2015. "The Battle for the Soul of Conservation Science." *Issues in Science and Technology.* 31(2): 74-79.

Kroeger, Timm; Francisco J. Escobedo, Jose L. Hernandez, Sebastian Varela, Sonia Delphin, Jonathan R. B. Fisher and Janice Waldron. 2014. "Reforestation as a Novel Abatement and Compliance Measure for Ground-Level Ozone." *PNAS.* (September 8), EA4204-EA4213. Accessed September 17 http://edwardwimberley.com/courses/10199/kroeger.pdf

Lappe, Anna. 201.) "What Dow Doesn't Want You to Know About Your Water (Video)," *Grist.* (June 9), Accessed Worldwide Web July 24, 2016 at http://grist.org/pollution/2011-06-08-what-dow-chemical-doesnt-want-you-to-know-about-your-water/

Levin, Ilan, Kira Burkhart, Luke Metzger and Sara Smith. 2016. *Breakdowns in Air Quality: Air Pollution from Industrial Malfunctions and Maintenance in Texas.* Washington: Environmental Integrity Project.

MacDonald, Christine. 2011. "Green or Greenwashing?—Dow Chemical's $10 Million Plan to Value Nature." *E—The Environmental Magazine.* (March 7), Accessed August 14, 2016 at http://www.emagazine.com/blog/green-of-greenwashing

Magstadt, Thomas. 2014. "Cover-Up: The Nature Conservancy Goes Corporate." *Reader Supported News*. (May 23), Accessed August 14, 2016 http://readersupportednews.org/pm-section/27-27/23829-coverup-the-nature-conservancy-goes-corporate

Makower, Joel. 2011. "Two Steps Forward: Why Dow is Putting Nature on the Balance Sheet." *Green.Biz*. (January 24), Accessed August 14, 2016 https://www.greenbiz.com/blog/2011/01/24/why-dow-chemical-putting-nature-balance-sheet

Manta. 2016. "Online Visibility Report: Dow Chemical, Freeport, TX." Accessed July 24, 2016 http://www.manta.com/c/mmc3lj6/dow-chemical-co

Mattera, Philip. 2016. "Dow Chemical Corporate Rap Sheet." The Corporate Research Project. New York, NY., Accessed July 24, 2016 at http://www.corp-research.org/dowchemical

Max, D.T. 2014. "Green is Good: The Nature Conservancy Wants to Convince Big Business to Save the Environment." *The New Yorker*. (May12), Accessed July 24, 2016 http://www.newyorker.com/magazine/2014/05/12/green-is-good

McLeod, Ben. 2015. "Building an Ecosystems Software Solution for Dow and The Nature Conservancy." *The Gartrell Group*. Accessed August 14, 2016 http://www.gartrellgroup.com/building-ecosystem-services-software-solution/

Metzger, Luke. 2016a. "Personal Communication," August 18, 2016.

———. 2016b. "Texas Breakdown: 68 Million Pounds of Pollution Released During Industrial Malfunctions and Maintenance Last Year - New Report Ranks Worst Polluters and Regions." *Environment Texas Press Release*. (April 27), Accessed August 17, 2016 http://environmenttexas.org/news/txe/texas-breakdown-68-million-pounds-pollution-released-during-industrial-malfunctions-and

Metzger, Luke. 2014. "Over 16 Million Pounds of Toxic Chemicals Dumped into Texas Waterways." *Environment Texas Press Release*. (June 19), Accessed August 17, 2016 http://environmenttexas.org/news/txe/over-16-million-pounds-toxic-chemicals-dumped-texas%E2%80%99-waterways

Moodie, Allison. 2015. "Dow Chemical Aims to 'Redefine the Role of Business in Society." *The Guardian*. (May 21), Accessed August 17, 2016 t https://www.theguardian.com/sustainable-business/2015/may/21/dow-chemical-epa-sustainable-business-the-nature-conservancy

Nature Conservancy. 2016. "Working with Companies: Making Better Business Decisions for Nature" Accessed July 24, 2016 http://www.nature.org/about-us/working-with-companies/index.htm

———. 2015. "The Nature Conservancy & Dow 2015 Annual Report." Accessed May 7, 2015 http://www.dow.com/en-us/science-and-sustainability/collaborations/nature-conservancy/

———. 2012. "Dow-TNC Collaboration Analysis Summary Pilot 1: Dow Texas Operations, Freeport, TX Coastal Hazard Mitigation Analysis - Green and Gray Infrastructure: Valuation for Corporate Coastal Hazard Mitigation." Accessed July 31, 2016 http://www.nature.org/about-us/working-with-companies/companies-we-work-with/dow/freeport-coastal-science-results.pdf

Port Freeport. 2015. "Port Freeport—The Coast is Clear." Port of Freeport, Freeport, Texas, Accessed April 17, 2017 https://www.h-gac.com/taq/transportation-committees/TAC/2015/11-nov/docs/ITEM-11-Port-of-Freeport-%20M-Wilson.pdf

Puchalsky, Richard and Allison LaPlante. 1998. *Troubled Waters: A Report on Toxic Releases into America's Waterways*. Boston: U.S. Public Interest Research Group.

Reddy, Shiela M. W., Robert I. McDonald, Alexander S. Maas, Anthony Rogers, Evan H. Girvetz, Jeffrey North, Jennifer Molnar; Tim Finley, Gena Leathers and Jonathan L. DiMuro. 2015. "Finding Solutions to Water Scarcity: Incorporating Ecosystem Service Values into Business Planning at the Dow Chemical Company's Freeport, TX Facility." *Ecosystem Services*. 12(April): 94-107.

Reddy, Sheila M.W., Gregory Guannel, Robert Griffin, Joe Faries, Timothy Boucher, Timothy Thompson, Michael Thompson, Jorge Brenner, Joey Bernhardt, Gregory Verutes, Spencer A. Wood, Jessica A. Silver, Jodie Toft, Anthony Rogers, Alexander Maas, Anne Guery, Jennifer Molnar and Jonothan L. DiMuro. 2015. "Assessment Method and Application to a Business Decision," *Integrated Environmental Assessment Management*. 12(2): 328-344.

Russell, Christine. 2013. "Putting a Price on Nature." Belfer Center for Science and International Affairs, Harvard University, Cambridge, MA, Accessed August 3, 2016 http://www.belfercenter.org/publication/putting-price-nature-0

Schuck, Peter. 1998. *Agent Orange on Trial: Mass Toxic Disasters in the Courts*. Cambridge: Belknap Press.

Scorecard. 2011. "Pollution Locator: Toxic Chemical Releases, Releases to Air: TRI Chemicals Lacking Exposure Data." Dow Chemical Company, Freeport Facility, Freeport TX, Accessed July 24, 2016 http://scorecard.goodguide.com/env-releases/facility-safety-detail.tcl?release=air&type=exp&tri_id=77541THDWCBUILD

———. 1999. "Pollution Locator: Brazoria County Texas." Accessed July 29, 2016 http://scorecard.goodguide.com/env-releases/cap/rank-facilities-in-county.tcl?how_many=25&pollutant=voc_osd&fips_state_code=48&fips_county_code=48039

SEC (United States Securities and Exchange Commission). 2014. "Form 10-K: Dow Chemical." (December 31), Accessed August 20, 2016 https://www.sec.gov/Archives/edgar/data/29915/000002991515000011/dow201410k.htm

Shelly, Adrian. 2016. "Planned Pollution: Dow Chemical and Mallet CO2." *Air Current News*. (May 25), Accessed September 18, 2017 http://airalliancehouston.org/news/planned-pollution-dow-chemical-and-mallet-co2/

Sustainable Accounting Standards Board (SASB). 2015. "Industry Brief: Chemicals." (March), Accessed August 17, 2016 http://www.sasb.org/wp-content/uploads/2015/03/RT0101_Chemicals_Brief.pdf

Spear, Stefanie. 2012. "USDA Receives Overwhelming Opposition Against Approval of 2, D-4 Resistant Corn." *EcoWatch*. (April 27), Accessed September 18, 2017 https://www.ecowatch.com/usda-receives-overwhelming-opposition-against-approval-of-2-4-d-resist-1881611739.html

Texas Commission on Environmental Quality (TCEQ). 2013. "Texas Environmental Excellence Awards 2013." Accessed August 3, 2016 https://www.tceq.texas.gov/publications/pd/020/2013-NaturalOutlook/texas-environmental-excellence-awards-2013/#water

———. 2009. "Rights to Surface Water in Texas." (March), Accessed August 17, 2016 http://lakesweetwater.com/sw-lake-files/RightsToSurfaceWaterInTexas.pdf

Thompson, Trish. 2016. "Dow Texas Operations raises $904,000 for United Way of Brazoria County." *Dow Chemical Newsletter*. (April 12), Accessed July 24, 2016 http://edwardwimberley.com/courses/80458/DowTxOps.pdf

Tresauge, Matthew. 2014. "Planting Trees Could Be a Weapon in The Battle Against Smog." *Houston Chronicle*. (September 12), Accessed August 1, 2016 http://www.houstonchronicle.com/news/science-environment/article/Planting-trees-could-be-a-weapon-in-the-battle-5752142.php

U.S. Congress Office of Technology Assessment (USOTA). 1990. *Genetic Monitoring in the Workplace*. OTA-BA-455, (October), Washington: U.S. Government Printing Office.

Walsh, Bryan. 2011. "Nature: A Major Company Puts a Value on the Environment." *Time*. (January 24), Accessed August 14, 2016 http://science.time.com/2011/01/24/nature-a-major-company-puts-a-value-on-the-environment/

Weinberg, Jack. 1994. *Dow Brand Dioxin: Dow Makes You Poison Great Things*. Washington: Greenpeace.

Wells, Ken. 2012. "Tree-Hitter Tercek Channels Goldman at Nature Conservancy." *Bloomberg Reports*. (May 31), Accessed August 14, 2016 at http://www.bloomberg.com/news/articles/2012-05-31/tree-hitter-tercek-channels-goldman-at-nature-conservancy

Wooster, Jeff. 2016. "Circular Economy: Our Perspective and Driving Action." Dow Chemical, Houston Texas, Accessed April 17 https://www.h-gac.com/community/recycling/workshops/documents/2016-09-08DowChemicalPresentation-JeffWooster.pdf

CHAPTER 9

Bone Valley: Phosphate Mining along Florida's Peace River

BACKGROUNDER FOR CASE STUDY FIVE

Phosphate Basics

The important role that phosphorus plays for animal and plant growth was first discovered in the early 19th century. Phosphorous is a key component of a plant's nucleic acid configuration and serves to regulate protein synthesis by transferring energy. Phosphorus is organically available to plants through animal manure and crushed bone material. As a mineral phosphate is found in "rock" and "pebble" formations and is transformed into plant fertilizer by crushing the rock and processing the phosphate first with sulfuric acid to create phosphoric acid and then with ammonia to create phosphate $[PO_4]^3$.

The phosphorus cycle encompasses the uptake, transmission and output of phosphorus throughout the life cycle of plants and animals. When phosphate is introduced as a fertilizer it is taken up in plants and then returned to the soil as manure (as plant material is consumed by animals) and as plant debris that is absorbed into the soil Much of the phosphorus leaches into surface and aquifer water systems and someworks its way down into the lower regions of the soil where the phosphate is mineralized in rock or pebble formations (Figure 60) (Busman et al. 2009).

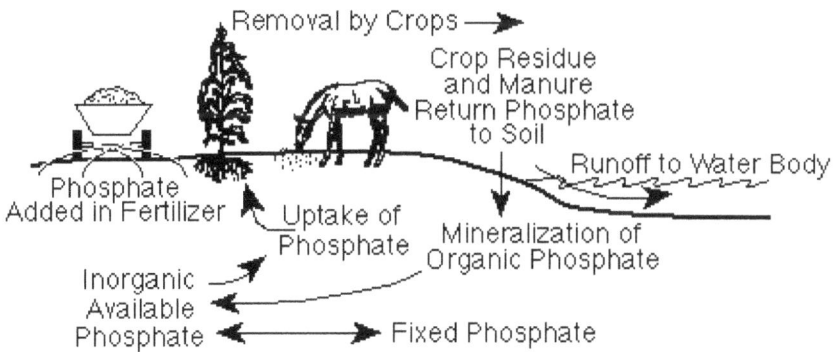

Figure 60: The Phosphorus Cycle
(Source: Busman et al. 2009)

Phosphate in Florida exists as phosphate rock (in north Florida) and in pebbles embedded in sand and clay (known as matrix) in central and south Florida. Phosphate was probably introduced into the Florida peninsula at a time when the region was covered with seawater and phosphorus solidified and sank to the bottom (precipitation). As such it became a component of the ocean's sedimentary layer sitting atop the calcified remnants of ancient marine reef formations - limestone. As the planet's climate changed and the seas receded the Florida peninsula began to emerge and these sediment levels rose to the surface. Eventually rivers and streams coursed across the now elevated sea floor and animal waste and natural phosphorus deposits were washed into coastal lagoons forming deposits of sand, clay and phosphate as well as the bone remnants of land animals and marine creatures. It is from these processes that Florida's richest phosphate deposit—The Bone Valley Formation—was created (FIPR 2017a).

Florida's Phosphate Resources

Much of the Florida peninsula is covered with a clay, sand and phosphate matrix some 12 to 15 feet deep and lying beneath 15 to 30 feet of a parfait of soil levels loosely referred to in the phosphate industry as "overburden." While phosphate resources are found in various areas across Florida to include Hamilton, Columbia, Suwannee and Alachua Counties, the richest reserves are found in the Bone Valley formation stretching beneath Hillsborough, Polk, Hardee, Manatee and DeSoto Counties. The oldest "rock" phosphate mines are found in North Florida in and around Hamilton and Alachua Counties. In central Florida, the oldest mining operations processed "pebble" phosphate embedded in the sand and clay of the Peace River bottom and shores around the turn of the 20th century. Today, mining in central Florida has shifted to areas adjacent to the Peace River where very large open pit mines are dug with enormous electric bulldozers (ManaSota-88 2008).

This extremely rich central Florida phosphate reserve has been mined since the turn of the 20th century and is likely to be mined for many more years before the last of the readily available phosphate resources are depleted. Phosphate could be mined most economically in the upper reaches of the Bone Valley formation principally because the "matrix" (that substrate of clay and sand in which phosphate pebbles are embedded) has only three components: clay, sand and phosphate mineral. However, the further south and west mining occurs the greater the expense incurred in separating the phosphate pebbles from the clay and sand matrix. The principal factor contributing to this additional expense is the presence of "dolomite" (MgO) that requires an additional screening process in processing the matrix material (FIPR 2017b).

Historically, as phosphate resources were recovered and mines moved southwestward down the Florida peninsula, the mined land was left despoiled and in many cases the water table in the aquifer became depleted. Thus, the legacy of phosphate mining in Polk and other counties on the northern edge of the Bone Valley formation entailed despoiled land, depleted aquifers and huge gypsum ($CaSO. 2H_2O$) mounds. These waste mounds pose low level radiation risks to surrounding residents via water, air and soil (Pittman 2017).

Mining and Processing Phosphate Pebbles

Phosphate mining entails using a large electric dredge to remove 15-50 feet of soil to reveal a matrix of clay, sand and phosphate pebbles some 10-20 feet thick. The dredge tosses this matrix to one side and the soil overburden to another pile where it is left until the land is reclaimed. In Florida, the soil is layered like an ice cream parfait into what are called soil horizons (Figure 61). These various layers differ in their composition of sand, clay and organic matter and taken together serve to make the soil permeable, hold moisture and allow for plant growth.

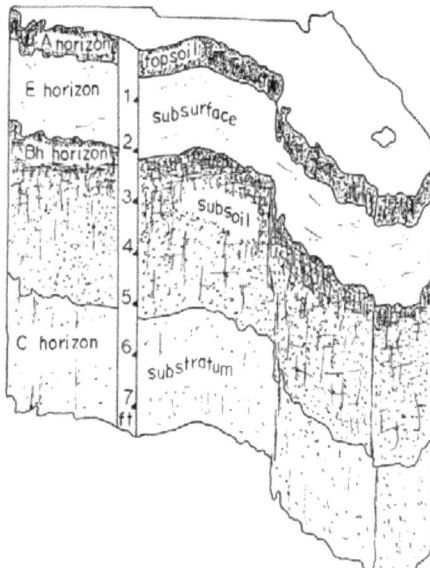

Figure 61: Florida Soil Horizons
(Source: IFAS 1993)

Soil horizon O is a layer of organic matter lying atop the topsoil. Horizon A lies beneath Horizon O and is known as "the zone of leaching" where organic material and minerals from the surface leach downward in and around plant root systems to the lower soil strata. Horizon A consists of a layer of coarse topsoil containing root systems, micro-organisms, humidified organic matter, insects and earthworms. Along with Horizon O the topsoil serves to hold moisture near the soil surface. E Horizon is a pale mineral horizon located beneath the topsoil that in Florida is found primarily in forested areas and lies beneath the O and A horizons. Horizon B is a subsoil layer through which rain water has percolated and leached surface material. This horizon may appear brighter in color than Horizon A (Schuster 2012; IFAS 1993).

The bulk of the soil in the Peace River basin is classified as "Myakka Sand" and within that sand Horizon B is additionally classified as "Bh" signifying that this subsoil consists of alluvial accumulations of organic matter—namely organic matter distributed by the flowing water. The deepest soil layer is the C Horizon which is referred to as the soil substratum. Horizon C consists of some clay, sand, weathered sediments and disintegrated mineral particles. This is the layer in the Bone Valley formation where phosphate pebbles are found in a clay/sand matrix (Schuster 2012; IFAS 1993).

The "overburden" material dredged in phosphate mines consists of a mixture of all soil horizons. Consequently, when it is returned to the land during reclamation it no longer has its previous soil layers which means that this reclaimed soil will not function to drain water or support plant life in the same manner as the original "layered" soil. To compensate for this reclamation after mining typically puts the overburden mixed with sand into the open mine, adds a layer of topsoil dug from another site and, contours the site to function as a hydrologic system and plants native shrubs, grasses and trees in the topsoil. Consequently, what began prior mining as a multi-layer soil matrix (Horizons O, A, E, B and C) is reclaimed as a two-layer soil (a shallow layer of topsoil atop a deep layer of overburden) (Peterson 2011; Blanchard 2010)

Comparatively the phosphate matrix of clay, sand and phosphate pebbles is blasted with powerful water cannons. This liquefies the phosphate matrix which is then pumped to a processing plant where the matrix undergoes a beneficiation process. Beneficiation is achieved by applying a variety of physical process to separate the clay and sand from the phosphate pebbles. Sand that is separated from the clay and phosphate is returned to the mine site to be reclaimed with the overburden when the mine is closed (Peterson 2011; Blanchard 2010).

The separated clays—known as phosphate clays—are placed in a settling pond where the clay particles eventually migrate to the bottom. Water from these ponds is recycled for use by the water cannons throughout other parts of the phosphate processing. Eventually the ponds are dried up (de-watered) and the clays allowed to harden. Clay settling ponds are ultimately reclaimed—sometimes for agriculture or forest reserves. Though plants can grow on the upper layer of these de-watered and reclaimed clay phosphates, the lower clay layers remain wet and plastic for many years and are therefore unsuitable for home or commercial development sites. These ponds account for fully 40% of all reclaimed phosphate land in Florida (Peterson 2011; Blanchard 2010).

The phosphate pebbles are immersed in sulfuric acid to produce phosphoric acid. This process produces a byproduct—phosphate gypsum ($CaSO_4 2H_2O$)—which is mildly radioactive. The phosphoric acid is then treated with ammonia to create phosphate that is sent by rail to the Port of Tampa where it is shipped throughout the U.S. and internationally. Phosphoric acid is also marketed as a mine product and it too is shipped by rail for use in a variety of industrial capacities (Peterson 2011; Blanchard 2010).

Phosphate mining in the Bone Valley formation began around 1880 along the Peace River with mining phosphate pebbles in the river. Thereafter rock phosphate mining dominated to mine deposits in several north Florida counties to include Alachua, Citrus, Columbia, Dixie, Gilchrist, Hamilton, Hernando, Lafayette, Levy, Marion, Sumter and Taylor Counties. In 1900 rich pebble phosphate deposits were discovered in Polk County Florida. By 1923 electric draglines were employed to mine the phosphate matrix and open pit mines emerged throughout the upper reaches of the Peace River basin—particularly in Polk County. These large mines employed powerful water cannons to slurry the phosphate matrix for processing. This process utilized millions of gallons of water daily that was pumped from the underground aquifer.

Phosphate Mining and the Environment: The Polk County Experience

The richest land-based deposits of pebble phosphate have historically been mined along the upper reaches of the Peace River basin in Polk County. Phosphate mining in Polk County began on the Peace River near Fort Meade and continued throughout the late 1800's until extraction costs became prohibitive. Beginning in 1890 and continuing through the 1940's, Polk County mining centered around Bartow and Fort Meade. By the 1950s mining spread to Homeland, Clear Springs and near Kissengen Springs in the 1960s. During this period the state allowed mining to proceed without mandating land reclamation (Metz & Lewelling 2009).

The hydrology of the Upper Peace River basin has been significantly altered since the turn of the 20th century by phosphate mining, agriculture and dramatic increases in groundwater use. Figures 62 and 63 illustrate the degree of riparian change between 1850 and 1985. Changes in drainage significantly altered groundwater flow patterns and reduced streamflow across the Upper Peace River basin. The most significant impact of mining water use is the degree to which the "potentiometric surfaces" (the level to which water will rise in tightly cased wells) (USGS 2016) in the intermediate and Upper Floridan aquifers underlying the Peace River have lowered causing water to flow downward into the aquifer system rather down the riverbed. These changes produced a marked decline in river flow and volume in the uppermost reaches of the Peace River (Metz & Lewelling 2009).

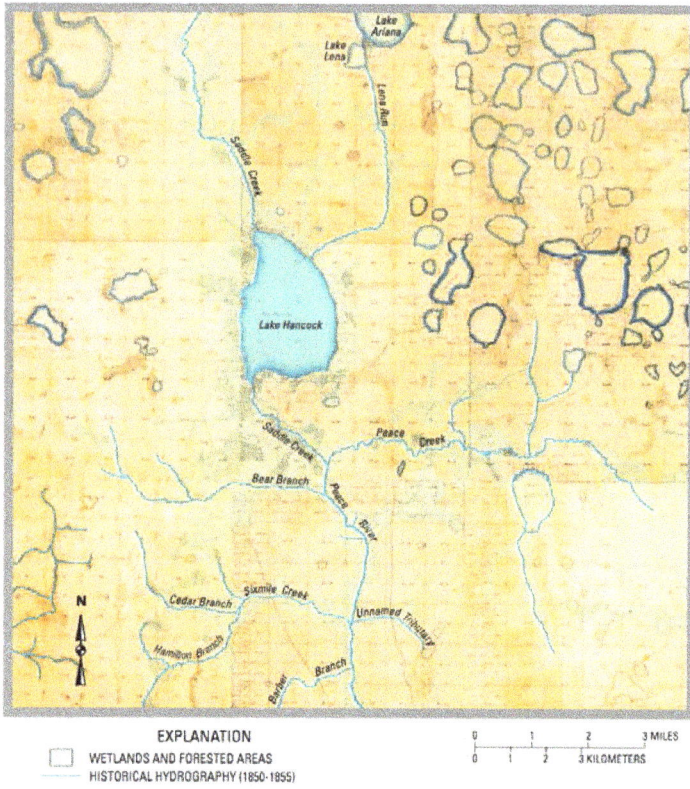

Figure 62: Upper Peace River Hydrography 1850-1855
(Source: Metz & Lewelling 2009, 12)

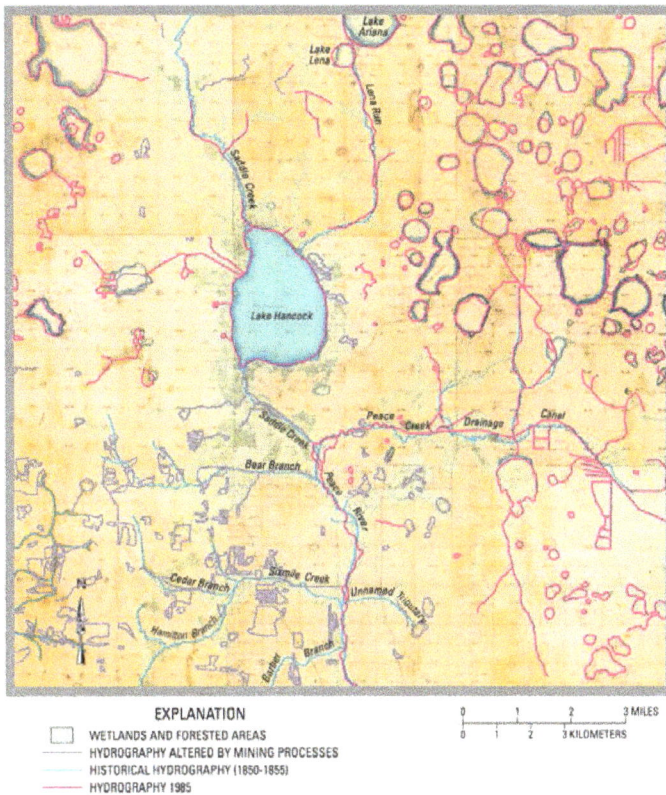

Figure 63: 1850-55; 1985 Upper Peace Hydrography
(Source: Metz & Lewelling 2009, 13)

As the water table within the intermediate and Upper Floridan aquifer fell and river waters receded, sink holes and other surface karst formations appeared through which groundwater flowed underground. This karst limestone substrate is subject to natural erosion when exposed to low levels of carbonic acid found in rainwater. In fact, this is how karst formations become aquifers in the first place - as carbonic acid erodes holes and fissures in the limestone where water is stored much like a stone sponge. During the 1950's this natural acidification was accentuated when many of the outflows in the upper basin became contaminated with mine acid. This contamination served to further erode the karst aquifer resulting in more sinkholes further exacerbating the extent to which surface waters were syphoned downward into the aquifer system below (Lanquist 1955).

Compared to predevelopment levels, the Upper Peace River basin groundwater levels declined an average 50 feet by 2009. Historical water records suggest the decline began in 1930 after draglines and water cannons were introduced to mine phosphate. The extent of groundwater decline eventually resulted in the cessation of spring flow to Kissengen Springs by 1950 (a magnitude two springs located near

Bartow) as well drying up numerous other minor springs throughout the upper reaches of the basin and numerous artisan wells (Metz & Lewelling 2009; Hutchinson 1978; Stewart 1966; Peek 1951).

The demise of Kissengen Springs is emblematic of this era in phosphate mining when mine operators pumped enormous amounts of water from the underlying aquifer system. The decline of Kissengen Springs was linked to a nearby phosphate mine that installed a 24-inch diameter well near the spring head and pumping 75 million gallons of water daily from the aquifer beneath. Prior to the installation of the well-head and the opening of the mine Kissengen Springs generated 20 million gallons of water daily. By 1950, Kissengen Springs completely ceased to flow (Martin 2008).

Phosphate production in the upper basin peaked in the 1970s when some 270 million gallons daily was pumped from the underlying aquifers (Spechler & Kroening 2007). In fact, by 1970 Florida's phosphate industry withdrew 3,475 gallons of water for ever ton of phosphate produced. In 1975 the Florida legislature imposed pumping restrictions on the industry. Consequently, by 1990 the industry was pumping 1,200 gallons of water per ton of phosphate produced and by 2011 had reduced pumping to 600 gallons per ton (Barnett 2011). While groundwater use by the industry has dramatically declined the industry still uses a great deal of groundwater. Today the Mosaic Company is permitted to pump 70-99 million gallons of water daily from the area's aquifers (Pittman 2013).

The 1975 Mandatory Mine Reclamation Act and Reclamation

Beginning in 1975, the Florida legislature began the process of addressing the serious environmental issues associated with phosphate mining. These issues included among others:

- Groundwater Depletion,
- Diminished streamflow,
- Aquifer and stream acidification and pollution,
- Soil erosion and sedimentation,
- Ground subsidence,
- Gypsum related environmental issues;
- Post-mining land reclamation (Metz & Lewelling 2009)

To address these issues, the state legislature enacted the Mandatory Mine Reclamation Act. This act proscribed a set of state guidelines for land reclamation after mining was completed. Central to these regulations is the notion that phosphate mining is a "temporary" land use despite that it produces virtually permanent changes in the landscape after the phosphate pebbles have been mined (ManaSota-88 2017).

The reclamation provisions of the Mandatory Mine Reclamation Act are embodied in Section XVIII of the Florida State Statutes and legally define "reclamation" in the following fashion:

"378.207   Reclamation criteria and standards.

(1)   The department, by rule, shall adopt statewide criteria and standards for reclamation. Such rules shall recognize that surface mining takes place in diverse areas where the geologic, topographic, and edaphic conditions are different, and that reclamation operations and the specifications therefor may vary accordingly. The rules, recognizing technological limitations and economic considerations, shall require the return of the natural function of wetlands or a particular habitat or condition to that in existence prior to mining.

(2)   The criteria and standards shall govern performance of reclamation and not the methodology to be used to achieve compliance with the reclamation obligation or the manner in which mining and associated activities are conducted" (FSS 2012).

Today, the specific reclamation requirements for mined land are determined by the Florida Department of Environmental Protection (FDEP) and these requirements vary with the terrain in which the mining occurs. Moreover, reclamation requirements incorporate the cost of reclamation (versus the value of the mineral being mined) as well as limitations in reclamation technology. To that end FDEP protocol reads as follows:

"Mine operators are required to provide the Department with a conceptual reclamation plan. Part of our extensive evaluations in reclamation design includes analysis of water quantity impacts, consideration of best available technology, and focusing on preservation of wildlife habitat and resources. Reclamation standards for phosphate lands include contouring to safe slopes, providing for acceptable water quality and quantity, revegetation, and the return of wetlands to pre-mining type, nature, function, and acreage" (FDEP 2017).

FDEP standards conform to state regulatory guidelines by principally focusing upon what is on top of the soil (contours, vegetation, water, wetlands) but fail to address either in law or practice the productivity of the soil itself. Arguably sustainable land use is linked to the creation and maintenance of sustainable soils (Kruse 2007). To date the statutes have not mandated any pre- post-mining comparisons of land productivity before and after mining consequently there has never been a process whereby citizens in impacted counties could determine prior to the commencement of mining the tradeoffs between near-term economic gain versus long-term economic and environmental sustainability. Instead mining companies persuade local citizens to allow mining based on short-term economic outcomes and comparatively neglect looking at post mining environmental and economic sustainability. They talk about the benefits of mining in terms of employment and economic growth "as if" the mines and the company payroll will be in the community in perpetuity.

Despite the short-term economic effect in which a given mining company makes a significant economic contribution to a local economy for 15, 20 or 50 years, ultimately the mining company will deplete the natural resource—in this case phosphate—and will depart, leaving the local economy to redefine itself in some new fashion. When dealing with a depletable resource such as phosphate this is to be expected. After all, the company's goal is very straightforward—find the phosphate matrix, mine the phosphate, process and sell it and eventually move on to a new site.

This process produces a cycle of local economic boom and bust that has been an historical reality for virtually every community whose economy was principally derived from extracting nonrenewable minerals and resources (O'Leary & Boettner 2011; Doukas, Cretney & Vadgama 2008). In virtually every instance, mining communities will eventually experience a dramatic decline in employment and with it deteriorating economic affluence, and increased poverty, social stress, outward population migration, and degraded ecosystems. These inevitable outcomes are only mitigated in the rare cases where community leaders recognize the temporary nature of extracting natural resources at the outset and plan for a post-extraction economy and community (Stacey et al. 2010; Doukas, Cretney & Vadgama 2008). In Florida, planning for post mining communities, environments and economies has never been a priority of phosphate mining companies even though the lifecycle of mining ensures that mines will eventually close, mining companies will depart and communities and environments will be depleted. However, in other parts of the world economic, social and environmental planning for post-mining communities and economies is being approached in a proactive manner, engaging a broad network of stakeholders to achieve a smooth transition from mining to post-extraction local economies (DeBeers 2016; 2010).

If such a proactive approach were pursued in Florida, then one might reasonably expect that the state and mining companies would adopt a reclamation standard that requires future soil productivity to be comparable to past soil productivity levels. The adoption of such a standard would serve to ease the boom and bust cycle by allowing communities to return to an economic base comparable to the one they experienced prior to the entrance of the mining companies. Within this reclamation paradigm the productivity of land (for instance the productive capacity of a citrus grove, pasture or agricultural field) would be determined prospectively and subsequent reclamation standards would be benchmarked against the productivity of the soil prior to mining. Successful reclamation, therefore, would be achieved when the land was restored to a comparable level of productivity to that realized prior to mining. If this standard were employed, then communities could anticipate more resources would be invested in removing soil and returning it in ways to maximize soil productivity. Currently Florida's reclamation statutes relieve companies of this burden and unwittingly serve to set up mining communities for periods of economic booms and busts.

Given the language of the Florida Statute, mining companies are relieved of this "higher standard" since the statute considers issues of cost and technology but not prospective environmental and economic sustainability standards. The statutory provisions acknowledge the reality that phosphate companies are impacted by market competition consequently they have strong incentives to contain production costs to generate a profit. However, despite what companies may say to the contrary their principal commitment is to their company's bottom line and not to environmental restoration or community economic and social sustainability. Where they adopt such standards, they are typically compelled to do so (Zorilla et al. 2009).

Current FDEP reclamation requirements that involve a return of the mined land to a "natural state" necessarily entail a lesser environmental and economic productivity standard than would be the case if for instance a highly productive citrus grove is sacrificed for mining and must be restored after phosphate extraction to a comparably productive state. Reclamation guidelines that focus primarily upon restoring the land to its natural state in terms of the composition of the topsoil and the native species that grow upon that topsoil are obviously less costly and less involved to produce than is a standard that (a) requires the soil be returned—layer by layer (or horizon by horizon) to essentially the form it assumed prior to mining and (b) requires that the productivity of that soil remain consistent relative to what it historically produced (e.g. hay, beef, dairy products, citrus, vegetables etc.) and be as productive after mining as it was before. Such a standard, while environmentally desirous is not employed simply because it is not politically perceived as being economically pragmatic - imposing a burden so significant that the cost of phosphate extraction becomes prohibitive unless and until demand for the mineral are so high that it can be profitably be extracted and the land restored to essentially it original state.

Simply put that means that reclamation of land after phosphate mining—while legally considered a "temporary" land use—essentially results in substantive and permanent changes in the composition of the soil and its productivity. It is this "reality" that engenders concern and opposition to phosphate mining in Florida. Exemplary of this issue of comparative land value and productivity prior to and following phosphate mining is the debate that went on in Hardee County in 2003 regarding long-term land valuation.

The Hardee County Experience

In 2008, governmental leaders—cognizant of the mining related environmental issues that had historically befallen neighboring Polk County—were confronted with issues of short-term versus long-term economic and environmental costs and benefits associated with phosphate mining in Hardee County, Florida. Their county boundary abutted Polk County to the north and even a casual examination of the land and water resources in that neighboring county—especially the vast expanse of mined land that had been mined prior to the state's mandatory reclamation laws in 1975 and never restored—were ever-present sobering reminders of the environmental consequences of phosphate mining. Figure 64 illustrates the extensive land and water resources that had been employed for phosphate mining in western Polk County. Community leaders who had witnessed the environmental issues associated with mining in Polk County expressed their reservations about expanding phosphate mining into Hardee county.

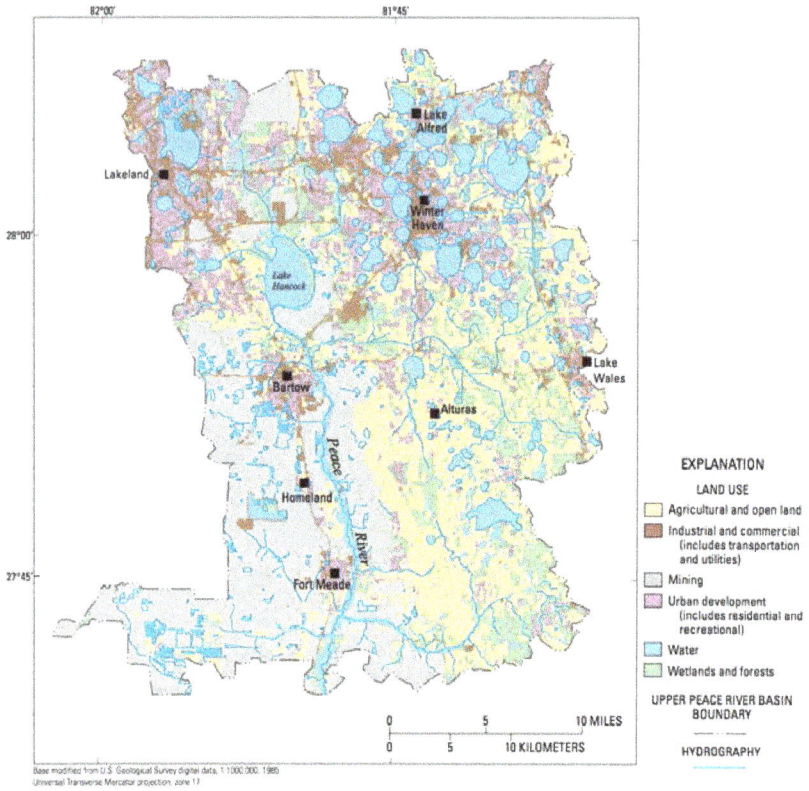

Figure 64: Land Use in the Upper Peace River Basin, 1985
(Metz & Lewellling 2009, 14)

The leading voice expressing these concerns at the time was the Chair of the Hardee County Board of County Commissioners William Lambert Jr. During hearings regarding the expansion of mining Lambert made this assertion: "If Hardee County is to effectively survive the impact of mining, the dragline must be held in check and not allowed to dominate the political and socio-economic infrastructure." More specifically Lambert and fellow commissioner Walter Oliff, Jr. questioned whether reclaimed mine land would ever be suitable for agricultural, commercial, and residential uses. Alluding to the environmental landscape in neighboring Polk County following mining Lambert and Ollif's conclusion was that land reclamation after mining was akin to "dumping sand in a flowerpot - You could put all the fertilizer in the world on it, and nothing would grow" (Bouffard 2003).

Despite the concerns of these two County Commissioners, Hardee County eventually permitted Mosaic Company to mine in the county and imposed the following reclamation requirements consistent with Florida Statute to include "(a) conducting wildlife pre-clearing surveys, (b) constructing the perimeter "ditch and berm" systems, to protect adjacent property boundaries and wetlands, (c) installing the necessary piping, pumps and mine infrastructure, (d) clearing the land, (e) excavating the ore matrix, (f) backfilling the mined land with residual sand and clay from the mined area, (g) grading and contouring the mined areas to achieve the post-reclamation contours and , (h) revegetating the land to achieve the post-reclamation vegetative conditions (Hardee Resolution No. 8-19 2008) (Hardee County Board of Commissioners 2008).

A Higher Reclamation Standard

The concerns of commissioners Lambert and Oliff expressed at the outset of IMC Phosphate's application to expand mine operation in Hardee County were ultimately ignored in the 2008 adoption of county reclamation standards for the Mosaic Company who had acquired IMC Phosphate in the interim. In 2008 well-regarded ecological engineer Kevin Erwin conducted a survey of reclaimed land in and around Hardee County's Ona Mine. Concerns regarding the adequacy of reclamation expressed by members of the Hardee County Commission in 2003 were reiterated more explicitly in his post-reclamation report. Accordingly, Erwin concluded that:

> "The strip mining process causes complete alterations of soils, ground and surface water hydrology and regional landscapes that are not typical of other wetland construction projects. Strip mining's complete disturbance of the land from the surface down forty-five feet or more represents a significant challenge for successful reclamation of mined lands where replacing the type, nature, and function of disturbed habitats is required by law. This challenge is much greater than attaining successful restoration or enhancement of habitats on unmined lands" (Erwin 2008, 1).

Erwin continues by distinguishing the plants community growing on top of the reclaimed soil and the long-term sustainability of the soil itself observing that:

> "After mining, IMC does not attempt to reclaim the near surface physiology of reclaimed soils nor does the company restore the natural slopes contours and micro-topography of the unmined landscape. Without soil, habitat restoration is destined to fail. In addition the natural relationship between the soil and water table elevations does not exist in IMC reclamation sites. IMC's need to strip, segregate, relocate, and protect/stockpile the native soils A, Band C horizons during mining and properly relocate/contour these soils after mining during reclamation. This will cost substantially more than what they've budgeted, but the results will be substantially better" (Erwin 2008, 3).

Erwin's point is that when the dragline removes the upper layers of earth to expose the "matrix" of clay and sand where the phosphate pebbles may be recovered, that they simply pile the excavated earth in large mounds where various layers (horizons) of soil are intermixed. This excavated material is referred to as "overburden" and is simply returned to the pit along with reclaimed sand and topped with topsoil recovered elsewhere and transported to the reclamation site.

This IMC approach is consistent with reclamation language in the Florida State Statutes which says "The rules, recognizing technological limitations and economic considerations, shall require the return of the natural function of wetlands or a particular habitat or condition to that in existence prior to mining" (FSS XVIII, 378.207). IMC employed this approach based upon economic and technological considerations. Erwin argues that ideally IMC Phosphate should:

> "strip, segregate, relocate, and protect/stockpile the native soils A, Band C horizons during mining and properly relocate/contour these soils after mining during reclamation. This will cost substantially more than what they've budgeted, but the results will be substantially better" (Erwin 2008, 3).

Admittedly, Erwin's standard, while more likely to achieve a more authentic reclamation outcome, is economically challenging to the extent that employing such a process would entail developing new and innovative mining technology and would dramatically increase the company's mining expenses resulting in diminished corporate profitably. Simply stated, mining and reclaiming land along the lines Kevin Erwin and other environmental groups advocate would likely render phosphate mining in Florida unprofitable for the foreseeable future. The net effect would arguably be good for Florida's environment but would constitute a significant economic loss for Florida and particularly for central Florida and the Port of Tampa whose revenue is significantly tied to phosphate shipping.

Phosphate products dominate the bulk tonnage shipped from the Port of Tampa (Figure 65). In 2016, phosphate and limestone shipments totaled 9,531,072 tons representing 70% of the dry bulk cargo shipped out of the port that year and 26% of the total bulk cargo shipped out of Tampa. This rate has remained relatively consistent over the last six years with phosphate and limestone tonnage representing 67% of dry bulk cargo shipments and 26% of total bulk shipping (Port of Tampa 2017).

Commodity	FY16	FY15	FY14	FY13	FY12	FY11
DRY BULK CARGO	NET TONS	NET TONS	NET TONS	NET TONS	NET TONS	NET TONS
CEMENT, BULK	371,630	216,210	131,736	189,547	84,564	105,072
CITRUS PELLETS	8,836	59,736	94,431	135,587	229,459	329,736
COAL	1,561,180	2,499,783	2,724,860	2,237,293	2,112,690	2,391,164
GRANITE ROCK, BULK	602,352	583,768	653,167	734,132	853,643	1,023,928
LIMESTONE	2,155,552	2,267,885	1,838,451	1,414,676	924,475	657,836
PHOSPHATE, ROCK/CHEMICAL	7,375,520	7,940,144	7,892,975	7,257,835	6,801,342	6,637,364
Other Dry Bulk Commodities	1,552,352	1,106,474	1,112,115	1,022,035	864,699	1,015,803
Total Dry Bulk Cargo:	13,618,586	14,674,000	14,447,735	12,991,105	11,870,872	12,160,903
% change from previous year	-7.2%	1.6%	11.21%	9.44%	-2.38%	-16.13%
LIQUID BULK CARGO						
AMMONIA, ANHYDROUS	1,419,842	1,695,115	1,827,227	1,830,800	1,835,289	2,057,586
CONCENTRATE, CITRUS BULK	83,260	103,371	88,384	178,574	84,586	46,938
PETROLEUM PRODUCTS	17,678,990	16,418,704	15,528,358	15,553,789	15,536,175	15,437,617
SULPHUR, LIQUID	3,342,409	3,038,664	2,994,374	3,026,081	3,096,972	3,281,495
SULPHURIC ACID	63,441	64,782	12,402	53,425	88,470	96,033
Other Liquid Bulk Commodities	233,618	206,931	142,779	212,468	153,554	150,188
Total Liquid Bulk Cargo:	22,821,560	21,527,567	20,593,524	20,855,137	20,795,046	21,069,857
% change from previous year	6.01%	4.54%	-1.25%	0.29%	-1.30%	-2.17%
TOTAL BULK CARGO:	36,440,146	36,201,567	35,041,259	33,846,242	32,665,918	33,230,760
% change from previous year	0.66%	3.31%	3.53%	3.61%	-1.70%	-7.78%

Figure 65: Phosphate / Limestone Shipments, Port of Tampa
(Source: Port of Tampa 2017)

International Phosphate Supply and Demand and U.S. Production

The Food and Agriculture Organization of the United Nations (FAO) predicts international demand for phosphate fertilizers will increase through 2019 (Figure 66). Since accessible phosphate reserves have been depleted the richest remaining reserves are found among the world's most unstable nations (Figure 67). These international trends are important when considering U.S. phosphate reserves.

	2014[1]	2015	2016	2017	2018	2019	CAGR (%)
WORLD	41 875	42 113	42 865	43 785	44 652	45 527	1.97
AFRICA	1 510	1 539	1 579	1 626	1 675	1 727	2.93
North Africa	613	613	620	629	642	658	1.77
Sub-Saharan Africa	897	925	959	997	1 033	1 069	3.68
AMERICAS	11 822	11 623	11 933	12 308	12 646	12 973	2.79
North America	4 948	4 822	4 903	4 942	4 992	5 032	1.07
Latin America & Caribbean	6 874	6 801	7 030	7 366	7 653	7 941	3.95
ASIA	23 397	23 805	24 161	24 576	24 986	25 417	1.65
West Asia	1 015	1 045	1 076	1 120	1 161	1 211	3.76
South Asia	7 590	7 967	8 220	8 528	8 843	9 166	3.57
East Asia	14 792	14 794	14 866	14 928	14 981	15 040	0.41
EUROPE	3 752	3 825	3 896	3 959	4 019	4 072	1.58
Central Europe	749	766	793	821	850	875	3.38
West Europe	1 894	1 881	1 887	1 883	1 875	1 864	-0.23
East Europe & Central Asia	1 109	1 178	1 216	1 255	1 294	1 333	3.14
OCEANIA	1 395	1 322	1 295	1 316	1 327	1 338	0.30

[1] = Estimated consumption; CAGR = Compound annual growth rate 2015 to 2019.

Figure 66: International Phosphate Demand Through 2019
(Source: FAO 2015)

	Mine production		Reserves[4]
	2013	2014°	
United States	31,200	27,100	1,100,000
Algeria	1,500	1,500	2,200,000
Australia	2,600	2,600	1,030,000
Brazil	6,000	6,750	270,000
Canada	400	--	76,000
China[5]	108,000	100,000	3,700,000
Egypt	6,500	6,000	715,000
India	1,270	2,100	35,000
Iraq	250	250	430,000
Israel	3,500	3,600	130,000
Jordan	5,400	6,000	1,300,000
Kazakhstan	1,600	1,600	260,000
Mexico	1,760	1,700	30,000
Morocco and Western Sahara	26,400	30,000	50,000,000
Peru	2,580	2,600	820,000
Russia	10,000	10,000	1,300,000
Saudi Arabia	3,000	3,000	211,000
Senegal	800	700	50,000
South Africa	2,300	2,200	1,500,000
Syria	500	1,000	1,800,000
Togo	1,110	1,200	30,000
Tunisia	3,500	5,000	100,000
Vietnam	2,370	2,400	30,000
Other countries	2,580	2,600	300,000
World total (rounded)	225,000	220,000	67,000,000

Figure 67: Worldwide Phosphate Reserves & Production
(Source: USGS, 2015)

Although Florida is the leading producer of phosphate in the United States the world's leader in phosphate reserves is Morocco and the Western Sahara and the largest producer of phosphate is China—both nations who are not constrained in production with American styled environmental regulations (White 2015; Kewei et al. 2014). Likewise, while the United States (and Florida) are major phosphate producers on an international scale producing approximately 12% of the world's phosphate reserves, U.S. phosphate production is dwarfed by production in China and West Africa. This awareness underscores what is at stake if federal, state and local environmental regulations serve to increase the costs of mining phosphate in the U.S. If companies like Mosaic can carry their operations overseas and profitably mine phosphate at a lower cost with fewer environmental regulations, then the economic impact upon phosphate producers like Florida could be significant. State and federal regulators are certainly cognizant of the economic consequences that would befall them if mining reclamation standards which preserve the environment serve to make U.S. phosphate uncompetitive in international phosphate markets. Such considerations tend to influence state, local and federal governments regarding just how much regulation can be imposed before regulations drive phosphate producers overseas where Mosaic already operates mines in Asia, South America and Australia.

Phosphate Costs, Externalities and Consequences:

Regulatory costs are just some of the costs that go into the price of phosphate fertilizer. Such production costs are born by phosphate companies such as Mosaic and include expenditures for labor, energy, technology, health care, lobbying, accounting, public relations, raw materials, land acquisition and more. Each company budgets how much of each input at what cost the company can afford to generate a profit margin. Beyond these "production costs" there are also user costs (as illustrated in

Figure 68). User costs begin with the wholesale cost of fertilizer produced by companies like Mosaic that reflect total production costs plus profit margin. Thereafter retailer costs are included incorporating transportation, marketing, human resources, regulation and taxes. Thereafter the end-user (farmer) incurs expenses to include shipping, port transfer, duties, overland transportation etc. These are typically the costs that determine how much the farmer must pay for phosphate fertilizer. However, the ultimate cost typically fails to include other hidden costs associated with the production of the fertilizer and its use. These hidden costs are referred to as "externalities" and include environmental wastes like gypsum, phosphate clays, and water, air and soil pollution (Cordell & White 2014).

Externalities also include hidden costs associated with the destruction of riparian systems and wetlands, the loss of fertile soil, habitat loss and conditions unconducive to the sustainable growth of wild plant and animal species. As numerous as these externalities are there are many more of concern to include energy use in producing and using phosphate fertilizer, stream eutrophication, overproduction of beef, pork and chicken with all the impacts these agribusinesses have upon climate. There are also issues of human rights, governmental/regulatory corruption and economic justice among those in Morocco and West Africa who mine and produce phosphate products (Cordell & White 2014).

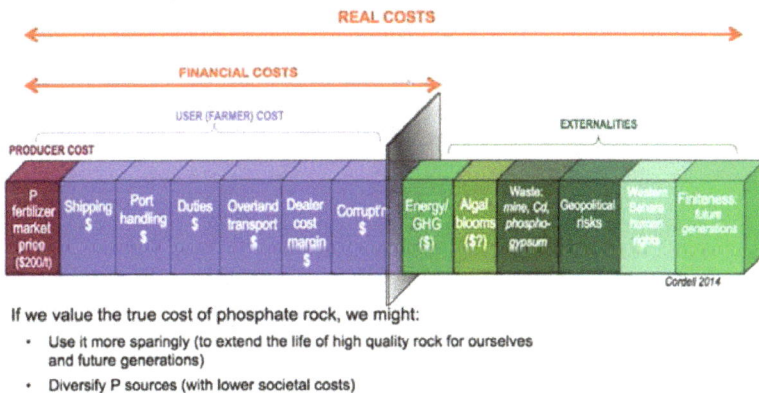

If we value the true cost of phosphate rock, we might:
- Use it more sparingly (to extend the life of high quality rock for ourselves and future generations)
- Diversify P sources (with lower societal costs)

Figure 68: The Real Cost of Phosphate
(Source: Cordell & White, 2014)

Additionally, there is a risk to the world's population that has become increasingly dependent upon readily available and comparatively cheap food produced with phosphate fertilizer. Phosphate as a resource is available but not unlimited in rock and pebble form. Since the most available phosphate has already been mined, future fertilizer costs will go up as the cost of production / regulation increases and eventually many in the world who have become dependent upon fertilizer to produce crops to feed hungry mouths may discover that they can't afford rising fertilizer costs, resulting in a geopolitical destabilization, famine and conflict (Kasprak 2016; Cordell & White 2014; von Horn & Sartorious 2009).

To date, each pound of fertilizer reflects production, retail and user costs plus profit margins. If externalities were included the cost of fertilizer and food would precipitously increase and famine would soon follow. This is of course a worst-case scenario and is not likely to happen since phosphate producers, farmers, food retailers, farm implement companies etc. work together to insure governmental officials don't disrupt food prices with overly strict regulation. While governmental action and influence are largely effective in prioritizing economic growth and food production and sales the environmental costs of phosphate-driven farming will not indefinitely go unpaid. Easily mined and inexpensive phosphate is becoming scarce and new phosphate production sites entail larger financial investments that are ultimately reflected in the cost of fertilizer and food to users.

From a narrowly economic perspective phosphate scarcity is good to the degree that it produces higher prices and creates incentives for end-users to more judiciously use fertilizer. Such efficient farm practice will help the farmer generate a profit and will protect the environment from phosphate pollution while insuring phosphate resources for future generations. However, such price increases, even with improved farming practices, will ultimately drive up food prices that many nations will have trouble affording—resulting in inequitable food supply, food shortages and sociopolitical and economic disruption.

Such are the economic constraints associated with phosphate production and use. Ultimately governments decide how much industry regulation their economies can afford. The world's most affluent nations like the United States, Canada, the United Kingdom and much or Europe have chosen to "afford" a significant degree of environmental regulation pertaining to the phosphate industry that promotes food production and the phosphate industry (producers and suppliers). However, they do so by regulating not based upon what a sustainable environment demands, but rather upon the basis of what the political economy can afford.

This same rationale is employed worldwide. Each nation decides how much it wants to spend upon externalities associated with phosphate fertilizer production and use. Likewise, organizations such as the United Nations and its Food and Agriculture Organization (FAO) attempt to address environmental and economic issues via negotiation and treaty agreements based upon a balance of environmental and political-economic factors. Ultimately environmental regulations that are supported by the UN are those that address an admixture of diplomatic, economic, military, health, and stability concerns. These alliances, treaties, bills and statutes are never intended to address "ideal" environmental outcomes but rather focus upon how "affordable" outcomes are prioritized. Such is the state of the policy environment in Florida and worldwide regarding phosphate mining, farming and environmental protection. Ultimately the salient issue is never "how much regulation does the environment demand?" or even "what are the best practices?" Instead the salient issue applicable to environmentally regulating the phosphate industry is "how much regulation can we afford—at this point in history?"

The Bone Valley Formation

In Florida, the bulk of the state's political, environmental and economic concerns regarding the phosphate industry are centered in central to southwest Florida in what is known as the Bone Valley formation (also known as the Peace River Formation). This region contains one of the richest pebble phosphate deposits in the world. The

Bone Valley Formation extends from roughly around Plant City and Lakeland Florida in Central Florida down through Polk and Hardee Counties ending in southwest DeSoto County near the Myakka River (Figure 69) (Matson 1915). The formation extends along both banks of the Peace River (Figure 70) stretching from near Lakeland south to Charlotte Harbor on the west coast of Florida. The Peace River is one of Florida's longest tributaries extending 106 miles and encompassing a drainage basin of some 1,367 square miles. It is also one of Florida's most altered streams with more than 63% of its watershed having been altered from its native state. Half of the total watershed area has been altered by agriculture and phosphate mining (SWFWMD 2001; 2004).

The Bone Valley formation is roughly situated within the Peace River and its tributaries and cuts through three largely rural counties. The headwaters of the river lie in and around the city of Lakeland encompassing some 651,300 people within its metropolitan boundaries (Forbes 2016). Beyond the metro Lakeland area Polk County is largely rural including communities like Bartow Lake Wales, Fort Meade, Mulberry, Frostproof, Winter Haven and Auburndale. In fact, the county's jurisdiction stretches from just outside the metropolitan Tampa area to the borders of Orange County and Orlando. Of these communities, Bartow, Mulberry, Fort Meade and Bowling Green lie within the Peace River Valley - all involved in phosphate mining.

Figure 69: Bone Valley Formation
(Source: Manatee County, FL 2016)

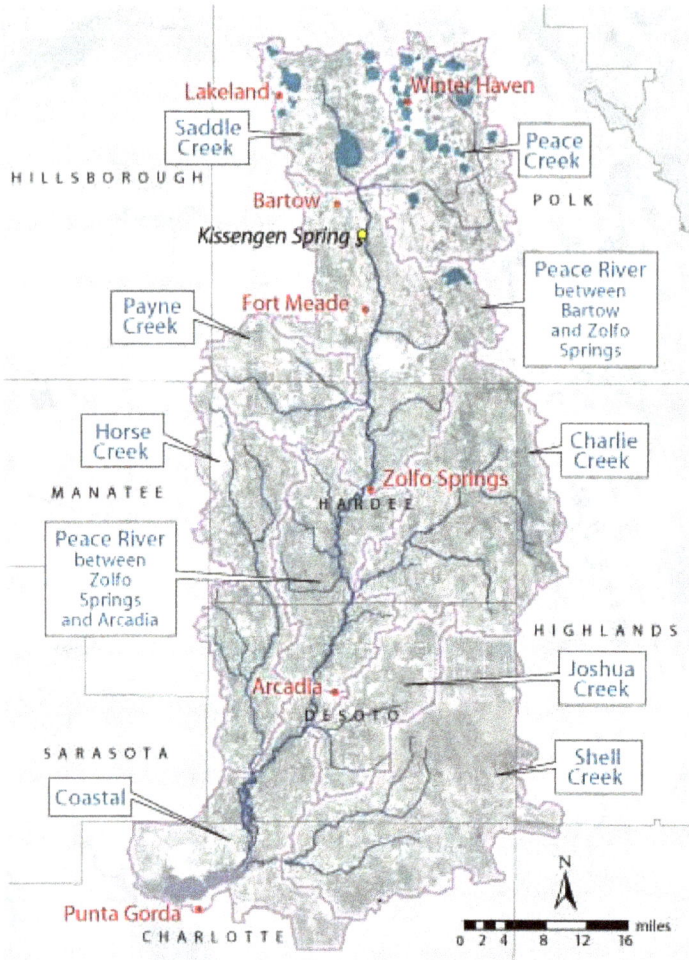

Figure 70: Peace River Basin.
(Source: SWFWMD 2017)

Based upon 2015 data compiled by the Florida Legislature, Polk county only employed 2.5% (Figure 71) of its population in natural resources and mining—with the bulk of that employment situated in Bartow and Mulberry where Mosaic operates their phosphate production facilities. However, that employment figure is misleading since Polk County was the first part of the Bone Valley formation to be intensively mined—as was portions of adjacent Hillsborough County. Mining began in Polk County near Mulberry in 1893 (FIPR 2017b) and continued until 2013 when the last operational mine closed (Sussingham 2013).

Average Annual Employment, % of All Industries, 2015	Polk County	Florida
All industries	203,802	8,039,635
Natural Resource & Mining	2.5%	1.0%
Construction	5.3%	5.4%
Manufacturing	8.0%	4.3%
Trade, Transportation and Utilities	24.4%	20.9%
Information	0.8%	1.7%
Financial Activities	5.7%	6.6%
Professional & Business Services	12.2%	15.2%
Education & Health Services	14.8%	14.7%
Leisure and Hospitality	10.7%	14.1%
Other Services	2.4%	3.3%
Government	13.2%	12.9%

Average Annual Employment, % of All Industries, 2015	DeSoto County	Florida
All industries	8,334	8,039,635
Natural Resource & Mining	13.4%	1.0%
Construction	5.1%	5.4%
Manufacturing	3.2%	4.3%
Trade, Transportation and Utilities	26.8%	20.9%
Information	NA	1.7%
Financial Activities	2.5%	6.6%
Professional & Business Services	4.9%	15.2%
Education & Health Services	9.4%	14.7%
Leisure and Hospitality	8.1%	14.1%
Other Services	NA	3.3%
Government	24.8%	12.9%

Average Annual Employment, % of All Industries, 2015	Hardee County	Florida
All industries	7,392	8,039,635
Natural Resource & Mining	27.7%	1.0%
Construction	3.1%	5.4%
Manufacturing	3.9%	4.3%
Trade, Transportation and Utilities	14.4%	20.9%
Information	NA	1.7%
Financial Activities	3.5%	6.6%
Professional & Business Services	3.7%	15.2%
Education & Health Services	12.8%	14.7%
Leisure and Hospitality	7.4%	14.1%
Other Services	NA	3.3%
Government	22.0%	12.9%

Figure 71: Employment by Industry—Polk, DeSoto & Hardee Counties
(Source: OEDR 2015)

As phosphate resources were depleted within Polk County, phosphate companies began a southwestward push into Hillsborough, Hardee, Manatee, Sarasota and DeSoto Counties. In 2008 Mosaic was granted permission by the Hillsborough County Commission to mine a square mile area in the southeastern corner of the county (Vander Velde 2008). In 2013, Mosaic purchased the holdings of CF Industries in Hardee County (Hughlett 2013) where phosphate mining had been underway since 1975 (CF Industries 2008). Today, Hardee County is where the bulk of "pebble" phosphate is mined. In fact, Mosaic is looking to expand its phosphate mining operation by opening the new Ona Mine and expanding its South Pasture Mine by 7,500 acres (Pugh 2017). Given these mining expansions employment in "natural resources and mining" involves some 27% of the workforce in 2015 and can be expected to further increase in 2017 and thereafter.

Mosaic also acquired phosphate resources in Manatee County where the county commission recently agreed for the company to expand their Wingate mine. Phosphate has been mined in Eastern Manatee County since 1981. Currently some 17,000 acres have been mined by Mosaic (Manatee County Commissioners 2016). They are looking to add an additional 3,600 acres to their Wingate Creek Mine though their efforts are meeting with opposition within Manatee County.

Neighboring Sarasota County has a comparatively small phosphate reserve on its eastern boundary along the Big Slough Watershed (Sarasota County 2016). To date Sarasota County has resisted allowing phosphate mines to operate within their jurisdiction in part because of the presence of housing developments that sit atop phosphate reserves as well as out of concern for protecting the county's wetland resources. In fact, the Sarasota County legislative delegation took a strong stand against phosphate mining in 2017 when they argued to:

- Oppose "modifications to Florida phosphate mining statutes that would erode protection of water resources within the Myakka or Peace River basins,"
- Support a Florida Department of Environmental Protection (FDEP) initiative to develop a single mining/reclamation process to achieve a more comprehensive and protective program that would combine the state's Comprehensive Reclamation Plan and the Environmental Resource Permit into a single permit process, and
- Support FDEP's call for a cumulative impact analysis of the impacts of phosphate mining on the Peace and Myakka River watersheds (Sarasota County 2017)

By comparison, DeSoto County welcomed Mosaic to mine the last of the Bone Valley reserves in their county's northwestern corner near the Myakka River in Manatee and Sarasota Counties. In 2014 the County Commission approved a "Generalized Phosphate Mining Overlay Designation" (found in the county's comprehensive plan) (DeSoto County Board of Commissioners, 2017) to govern phosphate mining in the county. They did so in part because mining had historically occurred in an area west of highway U.S. 17—a north-south corridor dissecting the county. Although active mining had not occurred for more than a decade, the County Commissioners anticipated that eventually mining would resume to extract the last phosphate resources in the Bone Valley Formation (DeSoto County Board of Commissioners, 2016; 2014).

Mosaic anticipates opening the 18,000-acre DeSoto Mine and is awaiting approval from the Florida Department of Environmental Protection, the Southwest Florida Water Management District, the U.S. Army Corps of Engineers and the federal EPA. Currently the land to be mined in DeSoto County is dedicated to agriculture (62%), rangeland (4%), upland Forests (11%), ponds and streams (.7%), wetlands (22%) and to public utilities (.3%) (Mosaic DeSoto 2017). Mosaic officials claim when the land is restored it will be returned to a "natural state" meaning there will be no comparative productivity assessment of the land on the site prior to and following mining. The absence of this environmental and economic assessment prompted the Florida Sierra Club, ManaSota 88, and People for Protecting the Peace River to oppose this last mine in the Bone Valley Formation (Murdoch 2016).

Mosaic in DeSoto and Beyond

As mining commenced in 1881 along northern Bone Valley Formation, so it will end in DeSoto County with extraction of the last pebble phosphate. Paradoxically, mining for pebble phosphate commenced in the Peace River near Arcadia in 1888 with Arcadia Phosphate Company (Millar 1891) followed by the Peace River Phosphate Company and the DeSoto Phosphate Company in 1889 (Wyatt 1892). When the cost of recovering river pebble phosphate became prohibitively expensive mining in the county disappeared. Now as the upper Bone Valley Formation is being depleted Mosaic is pursuing the southernmost reserves.

In 2012, Mosaic commenced working with the county, FDEP, SWFWMD, and the U.S. Corps of Engineers to open the DeSoto Mine along the western county line. While mining has not commenced and opposition groups continue to litigate the county commissioners remain committed to mining as reflected in their 2040 Long Range Planning Map (Figure 72). The chapter to follow explores the dynamics of the effort to introduce phosphate mining into this last county.

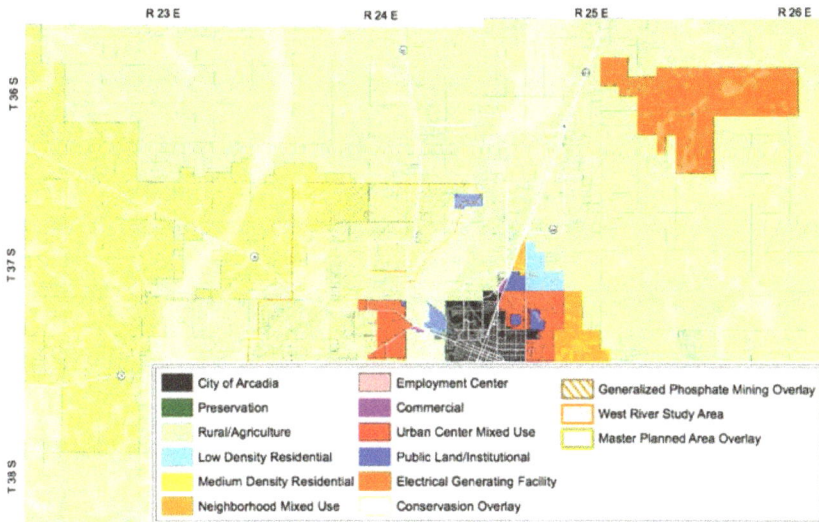

Figure 72: Western DeSoto County 2040 Future Land Use Map
(Source: DeSoto BCC 2017)

This final chapter will profile the Mosaic company and its approach to public relations, mining and reclamation and will look at the county government and its response to Mosaic's interest in their county. It will likewise consider the implications of the DeSoto mine upon the Myakka River and neighboring counties. Organizations opposed to the mine will also be profiled, particularly the Florida Sierra Club, ManaSota-88, and People for Protecting the Peace River. The comparative absence of cooperative environmental partnerships involving Mosaic and other organizations and groups will be explored as will the impact of mining upon downstream neighbors in Charlotte County since ultimately what happens upriver in the Peace River Basin impacts the health of the lower Peace River and Charlotte Harbor. Unfortunately, this final case study will not illustrate productive partnering between Mosaic and any environmental group situated within the Peace River Basin. The reasons for the absence of such relationships will be explored and explained. This case study will however make concrete suggestions how changes in law, regulations and practices might promote such partnerships in the future.

REFERENCES

Barnett, Cynthia. 2011. "Hope Lives, Even as Marker Notes Polk's Kissengen Springs, Dry Since 1950." *Tampa Bay Times*. (September 24), Accessed June 23, 2017 http://www.tampabay.com/news/perspective/hope-lives-even-as-marker-notes-polks-kissengen-springs-dry-since-1950/1193065

Blanchard, Greg. 2010. "Phosphate Mining Overview." Manatee County Florida Division of Environmental Services, Accessed June 22, 2017 https://www.mymanatee.org/home/government/departments/parks-and-recreation/natural-resources/environmental-protection/mining-services/phosphate-mining-overview.html

Bouffard, Kevin. 2003. "Two Sides in Dispute Over Mining's Impact on Land Use." *Lakeland Ledger*. (January 6), Accessed June 23, 2017 http://www.theledger.com/article/LK/20030106/News/608090597/LL/

Busman, Lowell, John Lamb, Gyles Randall, George Rehm and Michael Schmitt. 2009. "The Nature of Phosphorus in Soils." *Nutrient Management*. University of Minnesota Extension, Accessed June 23, 2017 at https://www.extension.umn.edu/agriculture/nutrientmanagement/phosphorus/the-nature-of-phosphorus/

CF Industries Holdings. 2008. "Annual Report." Accessed June 17, 2017 https://www.cfindustries.com/globalassets/cfindustries/media/documents/reports/annual-reports/ar2008.pdf

Cordell, Dana and Stuart White, Stuart. 2014. "Life's Bottleneck: Sustaining the World's Phosphorus for a Food Secure Future." *Annual Review of Environmental Resources*. 39: 161-188.

DeBeers Group of Companies (DeBeers). 2016. *Building Forever—Report to Society 2016*. DeBeers Group, London, UK, Accessed September 17, 2017 file:///Users/edwardwimberley/Documentz/DeBeers_RTS_2016.pdf

———. 2010. *Living Up to Diamonds—Report to Society 2010, Full Report*. DeBeers Group, London, UK, Accessed September 18, 2017 http://www.angloamerican.com/~/media/Files/A/Anglo-American-PLC-V2/investors/reports/csreports/2011br/de-beers2010-reporttosociety.pdf

———. 2017. "DeSoto County 2430 Future Land Use Map." Accessed June 26, 2017 http://DeSotobocc.com/images/planning_zoning/INTERIM_2040_FLU_MAP_with_Phosphate_Overlay.pdf

———. 2016. "DeSoto County 2040 Comprehensive Plan." (May 28), Accessed June 17, 2017 http://DeSotobocc.com/images/planning_zoning/2040_Comprehensive_Plan_Volume_1__Goals_Objectives_Policies.pdf

———. 2014. "July 22, 2014 Public Hearing." Accessed June 17, 2017 http://www.ordinancewatch.com/files/82613/LocalGovernment101782.pdf

Doukas, Alex, Alison Cretney and Jaisel Vadgam. 2008. "Boom to Bust: Social and Cultural Impacts of the Mining Cycle." *After the Gold Rush CA*. (February), A Publication of Pembina Institute, Calgary, CA. Accessed June 23, 2017 https://www.pembina.org/reports/boombust-final.pdf

El-Shall, Hassan and Michael Bogan. 1994. "Characterization of Future Phosphate Resources." Florida Industrial and Phosphate Research Institute (FIPR) Contract No. 89-02-082R." Accessed June 23, 2017 http://fipr.state.fl.us/wp-content/uploads/2014/12/02-082-105Final.pdf

Erwin, Kevin. 2008. "IMC's Strip Mining of the Peace River Basin: The Cost of Reclamation, the Price of Failure." Ecological Consultant Report on the IMC Ona Mine in Hardee County, Florida, Accessed June 23, 2017 http://www.ourphosphaterisk.com/downloads/Kevin%20Erwin%20Reclamation.pdf

Florida Department of Environmental Protection (FDEP). 2017. "Phosphate Mines." Accessed June 23, 2017 http://www.dep.state.fl.us/water/mines/manpho.htm

Florida Industrial and Phosphate Research Institute (FIPR). 2017a. "Phosphate Primer: How Phosphate Was Formed." Bartow, FL: Accessed June 23, 2017 http://www.fipr.state.fl.us/about-us/phosphate-primer/phosphate-and-how-florida-was-formed/

———. 2017b. "Timeline of Phosphate Communities." Bartow, FL: Florida Industrial and Phosphate Research Institute, Accessed June 17, 2017 http://www.fipr.state.fl.us/about-us/phosphate-primer/timeline-of-phosphate-communities/

Florida State Statutes (FSS). 2012. Title XXVIII - Natural Resources: Conservation, Reclamation and Use), Chapter 378 Section 207.

Food and Agriculture Organization of the United Nations (FAO). 2015. "World Fertilizer Trends and Outlook." UN Rome Headquarters Report, Accessed June 23, 2017 http://www.fao.org/3/a-i4324e.pdf

Forbes. 2016. "2016 Ranking: Lakeland Florida." Accessed June 21, 2017 https://www.forbes.com/places/fl/lakeland/

Hardee County Board of Commissioners. 2008. Hardee County Resolution No. 08-19. (September 18), Wauchula, FL. Accessed September 20, 2017 http://hardeebusiness.com/archive/public_records/Contracts_Appraisals/Mosaic_Agreement_signed_copy.pdf

Hughlett, Mike. 2013. "Mosaic Buys Florida Phosphate Business for $1.4 Billion." *Tampa Star-Tribune*. (October 29), Accessed June 17, 2017 http://www.startribune.com/mosaic-buys-florida-phosphate-business-for-1-4-billion/229532511/

Hutchinson, C.B. 1978. *Appraisal of Shallow Ground-Water Resources and Management Alternatives in The Upper Peace and Eastern Alafia River Basins, Florida*. Washington: U.S. Geological Survey Water-Resources Investigations Report.

Institute of Food and Agricultural Science (IFAS). 1993. "Myakka Fine Sand." University of Florida, Gainesville, FL, Accessed June 22, 2017 at https://soils.ifas.ufl.edu/media/soilsifasufledu/sws-main-site/pdf/about/Myakka-Fl-State-Soil.pdf

Kasprak, Alex. 2016. "The Desert Rock that Feeds the World." *The Atlantic*. (November 29), Accessed June 23, 2017 https://www.theatlantic.com/science/archive/2016/11/the-desert-rock-that-feeds-the-world/508853/

Kewei, Hu, Yang Mingzhu, Ren Shizheng, Feng Jia, Hu Kewe and Adina Matisoff. 2014. "China's Mining Industry at Home and Overseas: Development, Impacts and Regulation." *Bulletin of The Climate and Finance Policy Centre*. Greenovation Hub, Beijing, China Accessed June 23, 2017 http://www.ghub.org/cfc_en/wp-content/uploads/sites/2/2014/11/China-Mining-at-Home-and-Overseas_Main-report2_EN.pdf

Kruse, John S. 2007. "Framework for Sustainable Soil Management Literature Review and Synthesis." *Soil and Water Conservation Society Publication 2007-001*, Accessed June 23, 2017 http://www.swcs.org/documents/filelibrary/BeyondTwhitepaper3_1F1A3606C7D63.pdf

Lanquist, E. 1955. *Peace and Alafia River Stream Sanitation Studies*. Tallahassee: Florida State Board of Health, Supplement I to vol. 2.

Manatee County Commissioners. 2016. "Mining Services." Accessed June 22, 2017 https://www.mymanatee.org/home/government/departments/parks-and-recreation/natural-resources/environmental-protection/mining-services.html

Manatee County, Florida 2016. "Map of the Bone Valley Formation." Accessed June 17, 2017 https://www.mymanatee.org/dms/departments/natural-resources/environmental-protection/documents/mining-map-bone-valley-formation/Bone%20Valley%20Formation.pdf

Martin, Greg. 2008. "Kissengen Springs Among the Lost Resources." *Charlotte Sun-Herald.* (May 18), Accessed June 23, 2017 http://itech.fgcu.edu/faculty/ndemers/mining/kissengen%20Springs%20may%202008.htm

Matson, George Charlton. 1915. *The Phosphate Deposits of Florida.* Washington: U.S. Government Printing Office.

Metz, P.A. and B. R. Lewelling. 2009. "Streamflow Losses in a Karst Region of the Upper Peace River, Polk County, Florida." Scientific Investigation Report 2009-5140, U.S. Department of Interior, U.S. Geological Survey (USGS), Reston, VA, Accessed June 24, 2017 https://pubs.usgs.gov/sir/2009/5140/pdf/sir2009-5140.pdf

Millar, C. C. Hoyer. 1891. *The Phosphate Fields of Florida—A Pamphlet.* London: Eden, Fisher and Company.

Mosaic DeSoto. 2017. "Mosaic in DeSoto: Just the Facts." Accessed June 17, 2017, http://mosaicinDeSoto.com/DeSoto-project/just-the-facts/

Murdoch, Zach. 2016. "Phosphate Industry Has a Large Footprint in Florida." *Sarasota Herald-Tribune.* (December 20), Accessed June 17, 2017 http://www.heraldtribune.com/news/20161220/area-environmental-groups-target-mining-permits

Office of Economic and Demographic Research (OEDR). 2015. "County Profiles." Florida Legislature, Tallahassee, FL.

O'Leary, Sean and Ted Boettner. 2011. *Booms and Busts: The Impact of West Virginia's Energy Economy.* Charleston: West Virginia Center on Budget and Policy.

ManaSota-88. 2008. "Our Phosphate Risk - History of Phosphate in Florida." Accessed June 17 at http://www.ourphosphaterisk.com/

Peek, H.M. 1951. "Cessation of flow of Kissengen Spring in Polk County, Florida." In *Water Resource Studies.* Tallahassee: Geological Survey Report of Investigations 7, 73-82.

Peterson, Mark. 2011. "Phosphate Mining in the Bone Valley." U.S. Army Corps of Engineers, (January 14), Accessed June 14, 2017 http://myakkarivermanagement.org/Minutes/011411Attachments/COE%20Phosphate%20in%20the%20Bone%20Valley.pdf

Pittman, Craig. 2017. "The Clock is Ticking on Florida's Mountains of Hazardous Waste." *Sarasota Magazine.* (April 26), Accessed June 23, 2017 https://www.sarasotamagazine.com/articles/2017/4/26/florida-phosphate

———. 2013. "Phosphate Giant Mosaic Pumps from Florida's Aquifer to Dilute its Pollution." *Tampa Bay Times.* (July 20), Accessed June 23, 2017 http://www.tampabay.com/news/environment/water/phosphate-giant-mosaic-pumps-from-floridas-aquifer-to-dilute-its-pollution/2132394

Port of Tampa. 2017. "Total Port Statistics." Accessed September 18, 2017 https://frontrunner-bucket.s3.amazonaws.com/C57DE5CE-5056-907D-8D5E-C3857E5E3E70.pdf

Pugh, Tony. 2017. "I Don't Know and I'm Scared to Death." *McClatchy D.C. Bureau.* (January 21), Accessed June 17, 2017 http://edwardwimberley.com/courses/10199/Pugh.pdf

Sarasota County, FL. 2017. "2017 Legislative Priorities." Accessed June 17, 2017 https://www.scgov.net/LegislativePriorities/Documents/2017%20State%20Legislative%20Priorities.pdf

———. 2016. "Comprehensive Plan." Accessed June 17, 2017 https://www.scgov.net/CompPlanUpdate/Documents/Sarasota%20County%20Comprehensive%20Plan%20-%20Volume%202%20-%20Accepted%2010252016.pdf

Schuster, Joseph M. 2012. *Basics Soils Training Program Manual.* Tallahassee: Florida Department of Health.

Southwest Florida Water Management District (SWFWMD). 2017. "Peace River Basin." Accessed June 23, 2017 http://www.swfwmd.state.fl.us/waterman/peaceriver/images/map.jpg

———. 2004. "Peace River Comprehensive Water Management Plan: 2001." Accessed June 14, 2017 http://www.swfwmd.state.fl.us/documents/plans/cwm/cwm-peaceriverpart2.pdf

———. 2001. "Background Information on the Peace River Basin." Accessed June 14, 2017 https://www.swfwmd.state.fl.us/waterman/peaceriver/files/peace_background.pdf

Spechler, R.M., and S. E. Kroening. 2007. *Hydrology of Polk County, Florida.* Washington: U.S. Geological Survey Scientific Investigations Report, 2006-5320.

Stacey, J., A. Naude, M. Hermanus and P. Frankel. 2010. "The Socio-Economic Aspects of Mine Closure and Sustainable Development: Literature Overview and Lessons for the Socio-Economic Aspects of Closure—Report 1." *The Journal of the Southern African Institute of Mining and Metallurgy.* 110(July): 379-394.

Stewart, H.G. Jr. 1966 *Groundwater Resources of Polk County, Florida*: Tallahassee: Geological Survey Report of Investigations 44.

Sussingham, Robin. 2013 "End of an Era: Last Phosphate Mine in Polk County to Close." *WUSF News.* (October 9), Accessed June 22, 2017 http://wusfnews.wusf.usf.edu/post/end-era-last-phosphate-mine-polk-county-close#stream/0

U.S. Geological Survey (USGS). 2016. "Groundwater." Accessed June 26, 2017 https://pubs.usgs.gov/gip/gw/gwgip.pdf

———. 2015. "Mineral Commodity Summaries 2015." Accessed June 23, 2017 https://minerals.usgs.gov/minerals/pubs/commodity/phosphate_rock/mcs-2015-phosp.pdf

Vander Velde, Jessica. 2008. "Phosphate Miner's Win is Big Drag for Some." *Tampa Bay Times.* (March 13), Accrssed June 17, 2017 http://www.tampabay.com/news/growth/phosphate-miners-win-is-big-drag-for-some/414852

von Horn, J. and C. Sartorius. 2009. "Impact of Supply and Demand on the Price Development of Phosphate (Fertilizer)." in *International Conference on Nutrient Recovery from Wastewater Streams.* ed. by Ken Ashley, Don Mavinic and Fred Koch. London: IWA Publications. 45–54.

White, Natasha. 2015. "Toxic Shadow: Phosphate Miners in Morocco Fear They Pay a High Price." *The Guardian.* (January 16), Accessed June 23, 2017 http://www.theguardian.com/global-development/2015/dec/16/toxic-shadow-phosphate-miners-morocco-fear-they-pay-high-price

Wyatt, Francis. 1892. *The Phosphates of America - Where and How They Occur; How They Are Mined; And What They Cost.* New York: The Scientific Publishing Company.

Zorilla, Carlos, Arden Buck, Paula Palmer and David Pellow. 2009. *Protecting Your Community Against Mining Companies and Other Extractive Industries—A Guide for Community Organizers.* Englewood Cliffs: Global Response Partners.

CHAPTER 10

Peace in the Valley? Phosphate's Last Stand

CASE STUDY FIVE

The Last Hurrah

Every other case study in this text involves cooperative partnerships between would-be adversaries to tackle common environmental problems at the local and regional level. This final case study, breaks that mold and instead presents an example of the conditions in which local environmental partnership fail to materialize. The rationale for including a case like this is unfortunately very straightforward. There are many, many counties and regions of the U.S. that are so impoverished, rural and isolated that it is unlikely that any local sustained effort can be expected to emerge in the face of external pressure upon local environments. These conditions underscore why national and international environmental organizations like the Sierra Club are so vital.

At the outset, this book discussed five ecopragmatic principles (partnership among "strange bedfellow," home-grown imitative, satisficing communitarianism, deliberative democracy, and promoting free-market alternatives) and emphasized the goal of avoiding "either-or" mindsets in favor of "both-and" mentalities when solving local environmental problems. The intent of employing these principles and adopting a fresh mindset toward problem-solving was to avoid victimization and Balkanization among local environmental policy stakeholders and to replace alienation with productive partnerships. While such principles and intent are laudable there are situations in which it is virtually impossible to avoid adversarial relationships among local stakeholders involving environmental issues. This final case study is a testament to such conditions and is included in this text as acknowledgement that cooperation and partnership is not always possible and to illustrate the conditions within which ecopragmatism is not an alternative.

Despite the importance of these large advocacy organizations, whenever possible we believe that local efforts can be most productive and effective in protecting local ecosystems—especially when they network with larger organizations. The key importance of these local organizations is that they force local political, economic and environmental dialogue about what is good for the community and the environment and their presence—especially when networked nationally and internationally—serves to protect the environment from ready exploitation by powerful economic interests. Moreover, because these groups and well situated and integrated into local communities, their presence creates incentives for corporate interests to form fruitful partnerships in the interest of pursuing environmental and economic goals.

Comparatively, in their absence corporate interests are given a great deal more latitude.

DeSoto County, Florida is representative of one of those rural and poor counties lacking any organized local environmental advocacy. They sit atop huge wealth in the form of pebble phosphate deposits that in theory are protected by state, federal and local laws and regulations. However in reality, the regulatory environment in the state and region have largely failed to prevent extensive environmental damage to the land and water in central Florida at the hands of phosphate production companies.

DeSoto County constitutes the very last rich phosphate deposit in the region and mining this final deposit has become the highest priority for the state's lone phosphate mine operator, the Mosaic Company. As Mosaic pursues a mining permit the county finds itself at risk to significant environmental damage if the regulatory failures of the past are repeated. If the regulatory process fails the sources of that failure will involve multiple agencies that extend beyond the county line to the distant halls of Congress, the Florida Legislature and into corporate boardrooms operating beyond the prying eyes of investigative authors and journalists. In cases like these—involving impoverished rural areas lacking indigenous organized environmental advocacy—cooperative partnerships are infeasible - meaning that only adversarial relationships can exist between corporate polluters and environmental advocates. Ideally such confrontations are to be avoided in favor of negotiation and cooperation. However, in places like DeSoto where little to no organized local environmental advocacy is forthcoming, confrontation and adversarial relationships are inevitable and necessary. What ultimately is at stake in such settings is a seemingly unavoidable conflict between economic and environmental needs producing outcomes that almost never fully satisfy anyone.

Boom and Bust in Bone Valley: Historic Florida Phosphate Communities

The story unfolding in DeSoto County Florida and its county seat Arcadia is a familiar one retold repeatedly across America, where mineral and or energy resources are discovered that are sorely needed by a much larger economic world. Property owners with these resources lying beneath their land are presented with a once in a lifetime opportunity to "strike it rich" while surrounding communities are given the opportunity to prosper to a degree well beyond what their historical economics could ever offer. In most cases a pattern of high unemployment and low wages are reversed and local and regional economies "boom" with the influx of new money and jobs. It doesn't take long before this newly acquired affluence begins to feel familiar and citizens and community leaders find themselves lulled into a sense that the good times will just keep on rolling on—but they never do. Historically in community after community that blossoms economically from the extraction of minerals, energy or any other "non-renewable" resources, "booms" are eventually followed by "busts" and communities are seldom prepared for that transition (Thomas & Thomas 2017; Meyer 2017; Raguse 2016: Wynne 2010; Levi 2007; Ringholz 2003; Powers 1996; Bartlett 1987).

Cycles of "boom and bust" are particularly prevalent in communities built around the phosphate industry. Four communities within Florida are particularly illustrative of the "boom and bust" cycle: Dunnellon in Marion County, Floral City in Citrus County, Fort Meade in Polk County and Arcadia in DeSoto County. The historical experiences of these communities provide a valuable context for understanding what the future may hold for modern day DeSoto County when eventually phosphate plays out and Mosaic packs up and leaves.

Dunnellon

Consider the case of Dunnellon, Florida for instance. Dunnellon is a town in western Marion County, Florida born out of the discovery of phosphate rock reserves by Albertus Vogt in 1889. The discovery brought a decade long era of wealth to this small community. It also brought a long era of lawlessness and carnal excess that earned the town a large degree of undesirable notoriety. Dunnellon in its heyday had it all: saloons, honky-tonk pianos, gamblers, hustlers, con-men (and women) and criminals. Since mining companies had a habit of paying their workers every Friday afternoon, virtually every weekend in Dunnellon was a drunken and often lawless occasion. Indeed, those locals who could not get out of town over these weekends often chose to bolt their doors and stay inside until the revelry ended. These wild and wooly weekends, along with vast wealth and power, were the accoutrements of being the largest phosphate producer in the world (Burnett 1972).

At the time of Vogt's discovery, Dunnellon was a relatively new community founded as a health resort along the banks of the Rainbow River in 1887 by Ocala banker John F. Dunn. Upon discovering the phosphate rock on his property, Vogt went to Dunn for financing and together they purchased several thousand acres of land, secured a partnership of investors to include John Inglis and the Teague brothers from Ocala (Frank and Samuel) and within a matter of months formed the Dunnellon Phosphate Company. Once organized, the company included $1,200,000 in capital and controlled some 90,000 acres of land. A year later Dunnellon was surrounded by no less than 41 mining operations producing so much phosphate that the Dunnellon Phosphate Company could afford to build a dock and a shipping port (Port Inglis) at the mouth of the Withlacoochee river to ship rock to markets worldwide (Burnett 1972).

Prior to the discovery of phosphate, western Marion county had been quite impoverished as natives of the area (called "crackers"), struggled to eke out a living in the sandy scrub. However, with the discovery of phosphate erstwhile poor dirt farmers found themselves transformed overnight into people of substance and even prominence. Some locals sold their land to mining companies while others leased the property's mineral rights thereby allowing them to stay on their land and reap the rewards of phosphate rock while vouchsafing the discretion to dispose of the property later (Burnett 1972).

Community growth was so dramatic following the phosphate discovery that businesses struggled to keep up with demand and frequently found themselves selling their wares faster than they could restock the shelves. Likewise, as the town grew so did the need for better government—especially law enforcement. Unfortunately, effective government services (whether law enforcement, public services or tax collection) also foundered, and their absence engendered additional lawlessness, unhygienic conditions and vigilantism (Burnett 1972).

One major difficulty Florida mine operators encountered in the late nineteenth and early twentieth century was the scarcity of labor resources. An enormous labor force was required since early rock phosphate mining was done with a pick and a shovel. These "shovel and pick" miners would be deployed in large work gangs to recover the phosphate ore. Later they would be replaced with enormous steam shovels capable of mining much more ore over a much shorter period. Consequently, labor shortages were more of an issue early in Florida's phosphate history than it would prove to be later given advancements in technology (Matson 1915).

An essay pertaining to labor practices in phosphate mining published in 1892, claimed that in Florida the only local labor available to the mine operator was the indigenous "cracker" who was described as "naturally intelligent," though "indolent" and "independent in their views"—rendering them useful for little more than "cutting cord wood" (Millar 1892, 109). The scarcity of local labor resources and the questionable worth of "cracker" labor necessitated the importation of so-called "coloured gangs from Georgia and Alabama" who were housed in work camps and treated as virtual prisoners by their overseers. These conscripted work gangs were augmented by convict labor when available at a per diem pay of $1 daily (Millar 1892, 110). Needless to say, the overwhelming majority of laborers recruited and conscripted for work in the phosphate mines were African American (Burnett 1972). By comparison skilled labor such as engineers and surveyors were more likely to be white and were readily recruited from northern states and paid $50-$75 monthly (Millar 1892, 110).

As new mines opened around Dunnellon hundreds of these imported workers began to pour into Marion county and as their numbers swelled so did the number of labor camps for conscripts and prisoners. Skilled workers on the other hand contributed to the local demand for homes. Ultimately, so many homes were being built that the community opened a timber company and mill just to keep up with demand. At the height of the phosphate boom banks, law offices and land companies were constantly being formed—as were companies to procure labor for the phosphate mines. A rail spur was built by the Silver Springs, Ocala and Gulf Railroad between Ocala and Dunnellon that ultimately extended to Port Inglis on the Gulf of Mexico. This rail was employed to import labor and ship phosphate from the mines to port for shipping (Cook 2010; Burnett 1972; Millar 1892).

Sanitation was also a major problem for Dunnellon during the phosphate boom particularly when torrential rains flooded the streets, carrying with it animal manure and human waste. Indeed, it was these conditions that resulted in a smallpox epidemic in 1899. Ironically, although the community possessed the wealth to improve the safety, sanitation and aesthetics of the community, those in power chose to forgo these expenditures in the interest of further enriching themselves (Burnett 1972).

Dunnellon's boom period, while lasting for a decade, ultimately ended. The community's demise was gradual beginning with the discovery of large deposits of phosphate pebbles in Hillsborough and Polk Counties that could be more easily mined than the rock phosphate being extracted in Marion County. It was during this period that phosphate rock reserves throughout Marion County were being steadily depleted leading investors further south into the Bone Valley Formation of central and Southwest Florida. Dunnellon's economy was also impacted by the Panic of 1897 which wiped out the assets of many phosphate investors, reduced demand for phosphate that in turn produced a glut of phosphate on the market, and eventually diminished the price of phosphate to the point where many mine companies simply could not continue producing the mineral. However, the final "nail in the coffin" for Dunnellon was the outbreak of World War I which diverted labor to the war effort, diminished international demand for phosphate and forestalled foreign investment (Cook, 2011; Burnett, 1972).

Floral City

A similar pattern occurred to the south of Dunnellon in Citrus County's Floral City. Rock phosphate deposits were discovered near Floral City in 1889 soon after similar deposits were found in Marion County near Dunnellon. This discovery marked an era in the early twentieth century in which rock phosphate mining produced much wealth in West, North and North-Central Florida. The timing of the discovery near Floral City proved to be fortuitous since it was followed by "The Great Freeze of 1894 and 1895" that decimated the region's citrus groves and derailed the local economy. The discovery of phosphate reserves not only employed local workers and sustained the local economy, it also resulted in a huge influx of people and money into the community throughout the 1890's. At the height of the phosphate boom nearly a dozen mines were operating around Floral City. (Citrus County Historical Society 2017; Floral City Heritage Council 2017).

Mining was done manually and employed a sizeable workforce. The recruitment of workers from across the lower South and beyond eventually produced a community twice as large as Miami, swelling to as many as 10,000 people. As it happened, 96% of these new workers were African-American resulting in Floral city having one of the largest African-American communities in Florida. Later, draglines replaced manual laborers and the mines around Floral City became much more productive and required much less physical labor (Floral City Heritage Council 2017).

Ultimately, the infusion of wealth and workers into Floral City served to transform the community into a "wild west" town where all the excesses of the burgeoning community were on full display (Citrus County Historical Society 2017). The community became extremely affluent with banks and businesses abounding as well as a hotel, cafes, saloons and comfortable homes cropping up throughout Floral City. The money also attracted speculators and investors and throughout the early twentieth century many fortunes were made and squandered in the community (Floral City Heritage Council 2017).

The bulk of the phosphate produced in Citrus County at the time was exported overseas. With the outbreak of WWI European markets for American phosphate dried up. As demand fell, so did local fortunes. Workers were laid off, and many moved on in search of greener pastures. Ultimately, the outbreak of WWI ushered in the demise of phosphate mining in the Floral City area and a community that had one time experienced dramatic growth and untold wealth devolved into a sleepy agricultural town principally driven by farming, ranching and citrus production (Floral City Heritage Council 2017; Ritchie, Peters & Ritchie 2012).

Fort Meade

To the north of DeSoto County, Polk County's Fort Meade also went through several cycles of boom and bust related to phosphate (Brown 1995). Fort Meade is the oldest town in the interior of South Florida founded in 1855. By 1886 phosphate deposits were found in the Peace River near Fort Meade and by 1890 the phosphate boom began with the introduction of the Virginia-Florida Phosphate Company. Unfortunately, the community's economic high times only lasted four years and ended in 1894 following an international economic depression—the "Panic of 1893." This economic downturn hit England particularly hard and it had principally been English investors who underwrote the bulk of Polk County's early phosphate mining (Brown, Jr. 2001).

Fort Meade's local economy remained depressed for four years before rebounding modestly in 1897 with a 29% rebound and in 1899 with a 47% rebound in phosphate production (Brown, Jr. 2001, 194). Most of the phosphate mined in the vicinity of Fort Meade during this period came from the Tiger Bay mine. However, by 1899 the bulk of phosphate mining and processing moved from Fort Meade and Bartow westward to the community of Mulberry - which by 1904 employed 800 to 1,000 workers in phosphate mining and processing (Brown, Jr. 2001 195).

Meanwhile, back in Fort Meade surprise and disappointment gave way to the pursuit of other avenues of economic gain to replace some of the wealth that had dissipated with the Panic of 1893 and the emergence of Mulberry as a major center of the phosphate industry in Polk County. Fortunately, the region around Fort Meade offered other economic opportunities to include growing tobacco, planting citrus orchards, timbering, turpentine production and cattle ranching. Locals pursued each of these alternatives over the years so that by the early 20th century Fort Meade, while not enjoying the extreme wealth it had experienced during the heart of the phosphate boom, enjoyed a modest diversified economy based upon phosphate mining, timbering and turpentine, ranching, farming and citrus production (Brown, Jr. 2001, 196-197).

By the time Fort Meade's economy began to stabilize during the early 1900's, phosphate production had moved out of the river bed of the Peace River and into land based mining. Economic considerations drove this transition since it was much more expensive by 1904 to mine phosphate pebbles in the river than it was to mine buried pebbles in the land. The Tiger Bay mine near Fort Meade opened around this time and included a railroad spur to transport the mined phosphate for processing and to market. In 1907, Fort Meade became the home of Charleston Mining and Manufacturing Company's state of the art phosphate processing plant which employed some 175 workers and processed 100,000 tons of phosphate annually. The following year B.H. Brewster of Baugh and Sons of Baltimore (one of the nation's largest fertilizer retailers) began excavation of the Brewster mine ten miles west of Fort Meade (Brown, Jr. 2001, 213).

The outbreak of World War I (WWI) in 1914 marked another period of decline in Florida's phosphate industry—a decline that would persist through 1918. So severe was this decline, that phosphate prices would not return to pre-WWI levels until 1920 marking a six-year slump in phosphate prices (Brown, Jr. 2001, 241). One of the legacies of phosphate mining in Polk County prior to the war was the development of an extensive infrastructure of rail lines and paved roads. In fact, after WWI, Polk County, Florida stood out as one of the few areas in the U.S. with a paved road system intersected with railroad lines (Brown, Jr. 2001, 257). This infrastructure in part allowed the phosphate industry to rebound and by 1919 phosphate plants like Charleston Mining and Manufacturing Company's Fort Meade Plant began to gradually increase their production capacity (Brown, Jr. 2001, 261).

Unfortunately, during the post war period the phosphate industry was confronted with yet another challenge—the labor movement and the rise of unionization. In 1919 1,800 of Polk County's phosphate miners—organized via the International Union of Mine, Mill and Smelter Workers went on strike (Brown, Jr. 2001, 261-262). Since Fort Meade was an important center for phosphate mining and processing in southern Polk County much of the labor unrest occurred in and around their community.

Mine operators such as those operating the Tiger Bay mine west of Fort Meade responded to the labor strike by hiring substitute workers called "scabs" which infuriated strikers ultimately leading to acts of violence. Polk County Sheriff John Logan, who associated the striking workers with "Soviet Bolsheviks," responded by organizing the county home guard (effectively deputizing a small police force) to protect Tiger Bay and other mines across Polk County. The sheriff's actions were widely criticized as being high handed and demonstrating favoritism toward the phosphate mine owners. Ultimately, Sheriff Logan's actions served to exacerbate tension between the phosphate miners and their employers countywide. Mine owner organized a vigilante group called the "Law and Order League" to deal with recalcitrant miners and support the efforts of Sheriff Logan. Miners in turn resisted and tensions remained quite high until Logan left office in 1924 having served 16 years, making him the longest serving sheriff in Polk County history (FloridaGenWeb.org 2017).

By 1925 Polk County produced 45% of the world's phosphate and the technology accompanying phosphate mining had improved to the point where mine operators could recover 92% or more of the phosphate pebbles embedded in the sand and clay phosphate matrix. These developments in technology allowed for the "re-mining" of vast tracts of land across Polk County and surrounding Fort Meade to recover heretofore unrecoverable phosphate mineral. The employment of this technology coupled with the now persistent demand for phosphate internationally was significant enough to sustain phosphate towns like Fort Meade through a prolonged period of economic decline that began in 1925 with the Florida Land Bust (when real estate prices plummeted statewide) (White, 2009) and continued from 1929-1941 with the Great Depression (Brown, Jr. 2005).

World War II brought the U.S. out of the Great Depression and signaled the beginning for a tremendous boom in the phosphate industry as production was disrupted overseas therefore bringing the price of U.S. phosphate to a premium. By 1941 the world's demand for phosphate reached an all-time high and Florida was producing 82% of that demand. International demand for phosphate continued to grow after the war with the introduction of modern farming techniques worldwide and the increasingly widespread use of fertilizer to more productively feed the hungry of the world. Demand for phosphate continued to grow throughout the fifties and sixties and by 1963 Florida was producing 86% of U.S. phosphate resources and supplying 30% of the world's demand. The 1960's also ushered in the era of large phosphate conglomerates that acquired smaller mining and production companies and introduced newer and more sophisticated mining technologies. Between 1963 and 1967 these large companies had not only largely consolidated their control over phosphate mining, production and distribution, they actually tripled the industry's productive capacity (Dewey 2008, 348).

The post WWII phosphate boom was good for Fort Meade. By 1967, one of the emerging phosphate conglomerates—CF Industries—opened a land mine opened near Fort Meade and another international conglomerate (IMC Phosphate) took over the Fort Meade Mine. Today the city is recognized as one of the leading phosphate producing communities in Florida (USGS 1985; Barnett 2008). It persists as an example of a resilient community having weathered various booms and busts. It remains to be seen whether this community will weather its greatest challenge—the day the last of the phosphate is mined from its underground reserves and the local phosphate mines are forever closed.

Arcadia

Arcadia, Florida has been the county seat of DeSoto County since 1888, eighteen months after the county was carved out of Manatee County. Arcadia was selected over the original site at Pine Level in part because the Florida Southern Railroad had completed a rail line to Arcadia which at the time stood at the southern end of the railroad line. The presence of the railroad favored settlement in this town sitting high on the banks of the Peace River as well as providing a link for shipping local products northward and westward to the Tampa. In 1892 Henry Plant acquired the railroad line adding it to his extensive network. Following Plant's death, the railroad became part of the Atlantic Coastline Railroad which was eventually connected in 1907 to a spur from Arcadia to Charlotte Harbor. Initially the rail line shipped timber since yellow pine grew densely along the banks of the Peace River. Later the line transported phosphate along the river to Charlotte Harbor to be shipped from the deep-water port of Boca Grande to Tampa and beyond. (DeSoto County Historical Society 2017).

Like other communities throughout central Florida, Arcadia experienced a series of booms and bust, some related to broader economic crises, some related to changes in local industry and in one case due to a devastating fire. In 1905 a fire broke out in downtown Arcadia which destroyed most of the downtown area. The fire was devastating to the local economy and contributed to a temporary setback in the local economy—an economic "bust" that was reversed when the downtown was recreated using brick and concrete block construction. However, another "boom and bust" cycle came later involving the mining of phosphate from the Peace River (DeSoto County Historical Society 2017).

Phosphate came to DeSoto County and Arcadia in 1881 when U.S. Army Corps of Engineer Captain Francis J. LeBaron discovered pebble phosphate in the Peace River. LeBaron was surveying the river in accord with Congressional legislation to plan a cross-Florida barge canal that would connect the St. Johns river to be Peace

River. Had he not been on this mission directed from the Congress he might never have realized that beneath the banks and bottom of the river was a vast matrix of bones and phosphate pebbles (Ware 1984; Burnett 1979). Five years later in 1886, John C. Jones and Captain W.R. McKee of Orlando took a hunting trip south along the Peace River where they discovered high grade phosphate pebbles along the banks of the river. As the story goes, Jones and McKee were in the processing of tying up his boat along the banks of the Peace River when they realized the branch they were tying into was the exposed tusk of a prehistoric mastodon. Their discovery occurred along a stretch of river between Fort Meade and Charlotte Harbor. The two hunters turned phosphate prospectors kept their find quiet and purchased as much land as they could along the river. To mask their deception the pair devised a narrative explaining that they desired to purchase the land to extract tannic acid from the roots of the palmetto palm growing densely along the river banks and once they had harvested these resources they would sell the land back to their original owners for a pittance. Ultimately Jones and McKee purchased 43 miles of riverfront property using this deception (FIPR 2017).

Thus began "river pebble mining" along the Peace River. In 1888 the Arcadia Phosphate Mining Company was formed and began mining operations along what is now known as the Bone Valley Formation. Arcadia Phosphate's efforts were productive and they successfully shipped their first load of processed ore a year ahead of their competitor the Peace River Phosphate Company. The Peace River Phosphate Company and DeSoto Phosphate Company were incorporated a year after Arcadia Phosphate Mining Company. The discovery of phosphate along this stretch of the Peace River generated interest nationwide and prospectors began to descend on the Peace River valley sharply inflating the cost of land throughout the region. Ultimately the three phosphate mining companies established between 1888 and 1889 would be accompanied by 10 more mining companies (FIPR 2017; Burnett 1979).

As had been the case in other mining areas across Florida, early mining efforts employed vast labor forces using picks, axes and shovels. These workers were replaced with steam dredges that could process 40 tons of pebbles daily. Soon land based phosphate pebble mining proved to be more cost effective than mining for river pebbles so phosphate mining efforts moved off the river and on to dry land by around 1908. Up until the late 1890's timber had also figured hugely in the DeSoto County economy as logs were girdled, cut and floated downstream on the river. However, with the advent of phosphate mining the riverbanks became despoiled of timber. Barges were employed to ship the timber downstream to Charlotte Harbor. Dredge barges pumped phosphate pebbles from the riverbed while other dredges worked the river banks. So intensely was the river and its environs mined that loggers all but quit using the river as a means of transport. Once adequate rail service arrived along the banks of the river with the addition of the Charlotte Harbor spur the river was abandoned as a means of transporting phosphate. Sadly, the legacy of the mining along the Peace River was the destruction of the riparian ecosystem, stripping of the forest landscape along the river banks and the littering of the river bottom with logs and sunken phosphate barges (Ware 1984; Burnett 1979).

During the peak of river pebble dredging and mining along the Peace River, Polk County's phosphate resources were comparatively ignored. In fact, these reserves were meagerly explored for almost 15 years while hard rock phosphate was mined to the north in Hamilton, Alachua, Marion and Citrus counties. During that time, however savvy speculators quietly purchased as much land as possible throughout Polk County and across central Florida. By 1890 two phosphate mines opened in Polk County - the Florida Phosphate Company in Phosphoria and the Pharr Phosphate Company in Pebbledale. In 1891 Pharr Phosphate shipped the first load of land pebble phosphate to market. By 1893 river pebble phosphate mining had peaked and by 1908 the comparative expense of river pebble phosphate recovery versus land pebble mining drove river mining production out of business as miners and speculators left the lower and middle stretches of the Peace River and focused upon land mining in Polk County's upper Bone Valley Formation (FIPR 2017).

Pebble phosphate mining contributed to Arcadia's growth and prosperity through 1908 when river mining ceased in favor of land pebble mining in Polk County (Mahler 2014). Thereafter, the DeSoto County economy returned to an agricultural base involving cattle ranching, citrus production and some farming. Phosphate mining seemingly disappeared from the DeSoto County economy permanently—that is until it reappeared in the form of Mosaic Phosphate more than a century later.

Mosaic in DeSoto: The Return of Phosphate

A hundred years is a long time and it would be more than a little unrealistic for anyone in DeSoto County to remember the end of river pebble phosphate in the Peace River. Certainly, nobody was alive who survived those years and time can erase a lot—particularly the environmental harm visited upon the banks and bottom of the riverbed by phosphate mining a lifetime ago. Realistically speaking, who would expect 21st century DeSoto residents to have learned from forgotten experiences from yesteryear?

Even so, when the prospect of phosphate mining finally returned to DeSoto County a casual observer might be forgiven for wondering whether county officials and residents had not seen the environmental devastation to the north in Polk county to include stripped land, befouled water, towering gypsum stacks and river pollution and were not a least a bit wary of introducing phosphate mining into their community. In fact, it is hard to understand how a DeSoto County resident could not be aware of all the environmental havoc that that been caused by phosphate mining. After all, the main routes in and out of the county on the way to destinations north of Arcadia cut right through the heart of phosphate country. Conceivably anyone traveling north out of the county could not help but see what phosphate mining had done to DeSoto's neighbor to the north. Consequently, it is hard not to inquire as to how community leaders in DeSoto County could have not known what they were about to get into when Mosaic Phosphate came knocking on their door.

One could only wonder whether old-timers in DeSoto County remembered all the phosphate ghost towns in Polk county and had failed to relay these stories to younger generations—stories about places like Agricola, Brewster, Bereah, Bonnie,, Crum, Fuller Heights, Greenbay, Green Pond, Lake Noralyn, Midland, Nichols, Pembroke, Pebbledale, Phosphoria, and Pierce (Pike 2017). Whether they relayed these stories or not, it would seem this historical lore was simply forgotten or ignored. Nevertheless, it is difficult believe that DeSoto County residents were completely oblivious to their existence since the "bones" of these communities and their history remain in the form of dilapidated processing plants, abandoned streets and buildings and strip mines. Likewise, one could only wonder if county and civic leaders had ever ventured around Fort Meade where the city limits are physically confined from growing—even if there was an economic stimulus for doing so—because the surrounding terrain is mined to resemble a "moonscape" (Quinones 2011).

Given the long-established history of boom and bust in the phosphate industry and since there were so many examples of this phenomenon situated in communities present and past and proximally near DeSoto County, one can't help but wonder why more opposition to mining did not emerge in the county. The most plausible explanation for acquiescing to the opportunity to mine phosphate in DeSoto County was likely three-fold: (1) the local economy needed the money, (2) the mine would lie West of Arcadia, mostly beyond eyesight and in "somebody else's back yard," and (3) the state would require the mining company to restore the land after they extracted the phosphate. Based upon these assumptions it is understandable why community leaders might have been comfortable ignoring evidence to the north that phosphate mining—though defined by state law as "temporary" land use—was hugely and permanently destructive of land water and community. There was however a fourth reason why many in DeSoto County ultimately embraced phosphate mining and that had to do with the tremendous public relations campaign launched by Mosaic International—the county's would-be mining conglomerate—to win over the hearts and minds of DeSoto County citizens.

Mosaic International is the world's largest producer and marketer of phosphate and potash. The company produces some 12% of the world's phosphate and 40% of all phosphate mined in the United States. As of 2016 Mosaic International produced 7.6 million tons of phosphate (Mosaic International 2017). In 2011 Mosaic began the process of opening its southernmost mine in western DeSoto County. A year later they opened their DeSoto office in Arcadia and began the process of convincing the people and the leadership of the county that the opening of a phosphate mine in the western end of the county would be good for DeSoto and Arcadia (Mosaic in Desoto 2017). Since 2012, Mosaic has been extensively involved with public relations, politicking, and regulatory review while defending itself in a lawsuit, dealing with opposition from local and national environmental organizations and committing the corporation to contribute three million dollars toward the construction of a brand-new rodeo arena (to be called Mosaic Arena) in a community famous in Southwest Florida for its cowboy traditions (Hirsch 2016; Logan 2016).

The company's public relations strategy is straightforward and one they have repeated in community after community. First set up a local office in the county or community to be mined—ideally choosing an older home that they restore to give the company a "homey" face in the community. Thereafter, hire local people to work for the company so that community members can associate familiar faces and names with the company's brand. Lobby and politic local elected officials as well as state officials and legislators in Tallahassee to garner support and curry favor. Engage in local philanthropy like funding a rodeo arena can likewise prove to be a very effective way to win local support for phosphate mining in cowboy country. Local corporate efforts also include educating the public to understand that phosphate mining will benefit the community and that any environmental damage produced by mining will be completely mitigated so that the post- mining site is environmentally restored and sustainable.

Perhaps the most important part of Mosaic's local approach to soliciting community support is to suggest that their company is fully committed to their "operating communities," assuring these communities that the company is there for the long-haul. Accordingly, Mosaic's public posture on this issue assures their "partners" that:

> "Mosaic is an important driver of economic activity in each of our operating communities. We strive to be a thoughtful and engaged neighbor, using our financial resources, expertise and innovative spirit to demonstrate our shared commitment to good corporate citizenship" (Mosaic International 2017)

This commitment is reflected in local hiring strategies, where they choose to situate their local headquarters, and what local causes and charities they support.

While never explicitly saying so, the company approaches their operating communities *as if* they are going to be economic contributors to the community "forever." In fact, Mosaic representatives fully realize their community commitments are time-limited and that one day, when phosphate has played out, they will fold-up and move. Mosaic spokespeople acknowledge this reality when they address environmental issues in phosphate mining by referring to mining as "temporary land use."

In truth, there appears to be no corporate strategy to fool or mislead communities regarding their intent. As a matter of fact, the temporary nature of mining and its implications for the community's long-term prosperity and sustainability is a reality that virtually every stakeholder in the community is aware of—if for no other reason because the environmental and economic impacts of phosphate mining is so readily visible in counties to their north where the economic and environmental ramifications of mining are demonstrable and compelling. Nevertheless, for many DeSoto County residents the benefits of mining are so alluring—particularly given the county's economic needs—that it becomes very easy to overstate and overestimate the benefits of mining and underestimate and understate the long term economic and environmental consequences of phosphate mining.

The Loyal Opposition and the Ona Mine:

Not everyone in DeSoto County forgot the history of phosphate mining in the Bone Valley Formation or ignored the obvious environmental impacts of mining in Hillsborough, Hardee and Polk Counties. One group of local citizens organized to resist the introduction of phosphate mining in western DeSoto County. They organized themselves into a non-profit organization aptly named People for Protecting Peace River. This group consists of DeSoto and Hardee county residents and is led by Dennis Mader. Mader has been instrumental in coordinating his organization's efforts with two other influential environmental organizations—Manasota 88 (a group based out of Manatee and Sarasota Counties), Earthjustice and the Florida Sierra Club. Together these nonprofit environmental advocacy groups have taken on the largest phosphate mining operation in Florida—the Mosaic Company. Their strategy is straightforward: use the courts and state and federal regulatory systems to consistently oppose the expansion of any additional phosphate mining in the Bone Valley Formation principally on environmental grounds.

As the leader for People Protecting Peace River, Mader is a veteran when it comes to litigating to limit phosphate mining in Florida. In 2003 he litigated Mosaic's predecessor by filing a lawsuit against IMC Phosphate Company and the Florida Department of Environmental Protection (FDEP) regarding the excavation of a new mine in Ona (Mader's home of residence). The proposed mine would have encompassed 22,483 acres of which 18,776 acres would have been "disturbed' and 16,842 acres mined (Mosaic Hardee 2017). Mader and other litigants opposed the mine citing that it would "destroy or displace fish and wildlife including numerous threatened or endangered species" as well as destroy "wildlife nesting, resting and forage habitat" and diminish "wildlife corridors and migratory pathways" (Mader v. IMC Phosphate 2003).

At the time, IMC was seeking a variance to develop the new Ona mine, Mader's lawsuit was joined by a sizeable number of Charlotte County petitioners. Ultimately these litigants forced an FDEP evidentiary review of IMC's proposal which in turn prompted IMC to withdraw their request for a variance. Consequently, Mader's initial challenge to IMC proved successful in at least temporarily forestalling the excavation of the Ona mine (Graettinger v. IMC Phosphate 2003). Unfortunately, however, FDEP approved IMC Phosphate's request to expand their Ona mine a year later. Mader—now head of Hardee Citizens Against Pollution—rejoined the environmental petitioners from Charlotte County to continue opposition to the mine expansion.

Fortuitously, this drama caught the attention of a prominent national environmental organization—American Rivers—who added the Peace River to a list of the nation's 10 most endangered rivers (American Rivers 2004). Ranked eighth among the nation's most endangered rivers, American Rivers identified the principal threat to the river unequivocally—phosphate mining. From the magazine's perspective, FDEP and the Southwest Florida Water Management District must prohibit further mining along the Peace River noting that "More than 180,000 acres have been mined in the Peace River watershed already, and mining corporations are now seeking permits for another 100,000 acres—an expansion of more than 50 percent" (American Rivers 2004, 28).

The principal focus of the American River's concern was the phosphate clay settling ponds. These ponds are formed when slurried phosphate clay and sand are deposited in containment ponds after the process of washing and flotation of the phosphate ore has been completed. The solid content of the clays are relatively low - averaging three to five percent. When fully saturated phosphate clay wastes are generally impermeable, extremely plastic and poorly consolidated. These clays remain highly compressible even decades after being de-watered in the settling ponds and are not sound weight bearing foundations due to their low shear strength. Although such clay soils have been used to a limited degree for agricultural production once they have become sufficiently dry, they are generally unsuitable for building and construction due to their compressibility (Ericson, Moore & Madrid 1993, 1189).

Phosphate clays are a significant portion of the waste produced in phosphate mining and comprise at least 40% of all mined sites. Accordingly, American Rivers warned that:

> "Some of these ponds can measure thousands of acres. Rain is trapped in these massive clay-laden ponds rather than soaking into the soil to replenish underlying aquifers. This reduces flows in the Peace River. Since the 1960s, the average annual flow of the middle Peace River has declined from 1,350 cubic feet per second (cfs) to 800 cfs. Most of this flow reduction is due to phosphate mining. Each holding pond is a potential time bomb that threatens water quality, public health, wildlife and the regional economy. Dams restraining the ponds have burst or over- flowed, sending a slurry of clay, containing uranium and radium, into the river, and coating the riverbed for many miles with a toxic clay slime that suffocates flora and fauna" (American Rivers 2004, p. 28).

Litigation in opposition to the Ona mine persisted for years, consolidating regional antagonism to additional phosphate mining up and down the Peace River basin. In 2009, the Florida District Court of Appeals upheld FDEP's decision to issue a mining permit. Resistance to the mine, however prevented Mosaic (who acquired IMC in 2008) from proceeding with the excavation. By 2016 the project was still awaiting final approval by the US Army Corps of Engineers (Clean Water Act Section 404 DA permit) and the Hardee County Commission regarding approval of a Mining Major Special Exception (MMSE) and Master Mining and Reclamation Plan (MMRP). Mosaic was also awaiting approval from FDEP for an Industrial Wastewater Facility Permit and additional permits for NPDES outfall locations. The protracted nature of the permitting process—involving local, state and federal regulatory rulings—has been extended and exacerbated at every juncture by the willingness of groups like Manasota-88 and People Protecting Peace River to resist, thwart and delay the permitting process for as long as possible—perhaps to the point where Mosaic decides the costs are just too great and moves on.

While multiple environmental groups have been playing the role of "David" hoping to eventually slay their Mosaic phosphate behemoth ("Goliath") the stark reality is that Mosaic is in it for the long haul. Mosaic remains undeterred in the face of environmental opposition - determined to extend mining as far south into the Bone Valley as possible despite the dogged opposition of groups like Manasota-88 and People for Protecting Peace River (Stockfisch 2015). In truth, this corporation has time and vast resources on its side. It also has the advantage of operating in a region of Florida that tourists and Florida citizens rarely see.

In fact, the only real chance environmental groups have to halt the seeming inevitable creep of phosphate mining deep into DeSoto County iso to make their case visible in the media and to the public residing outside of the Peace River basin. Exposes such as those launched by American Rivers and featured stories in the *Tampa Bay Times* and *Sarasota Magazine* have proved hugely influential—as have stories such as the one in 2017 involving the sinkhole in one of Mosaic's retaining ponds that leaked thousands of gallons of radioactive waste into the underlying aquifer. These stories, along with the national coverage they garnered, are the tools which opposition groups seek to employ to convince the public that phosphate mining is too environmentally harmful to be allowed. These groups litigate, protest and advocate against phosphate mining in the hope that they will ultimately influence public opinion to such an extent that legislators and regulators are absolutely compelled by public opinion to act on behalf of environmental interests and in opposition to the phosphate companies.

The DeSoto Mine

The final battleground in the "David and Goliath" struggle between environmentalists and Mosaic will be played out in western DeSoto County. The proposed DeSoto Mine lies at the western boundary of DeSoto County adjacent to the Myakka River and Manatee County and just below Hardee County (Figure 73). Upon completion, the DeSoto Mine will be situated on 18,287 acres and will disturb 11,403 acres. Beyond this initial development, another 13,948 acres are "eligible" for mining—meaning additional land may be mined later. The actual DeSoto Mine is expected to require 4,778 acres. Mosaic acquired ownership of its 18,000-acre tract in 2004 (Mosaic in DeSoto 2016).

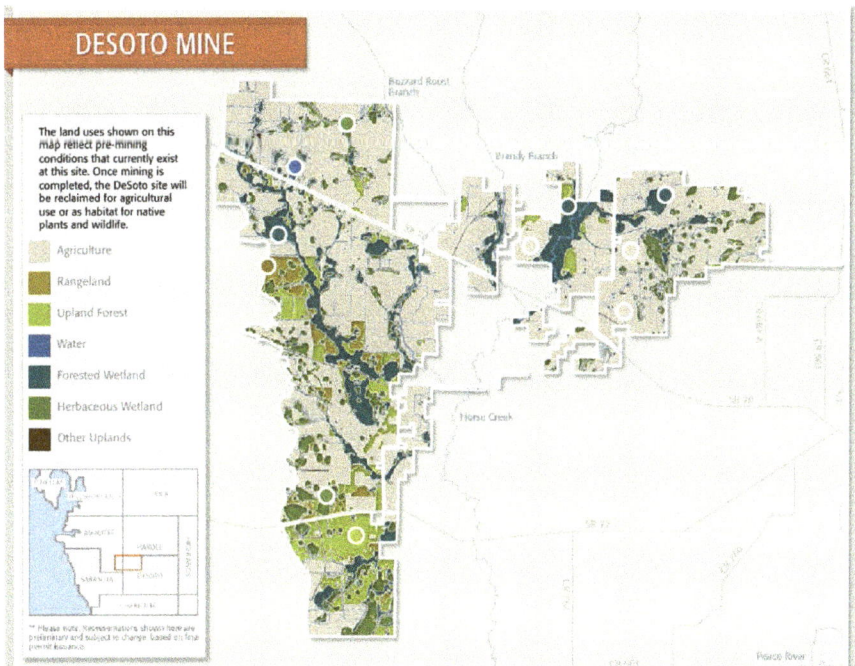

Figure 73: Proposed DeSoto Mine, DeSoto County, Florida
(Source: Mosaic in DeSoto 2017)

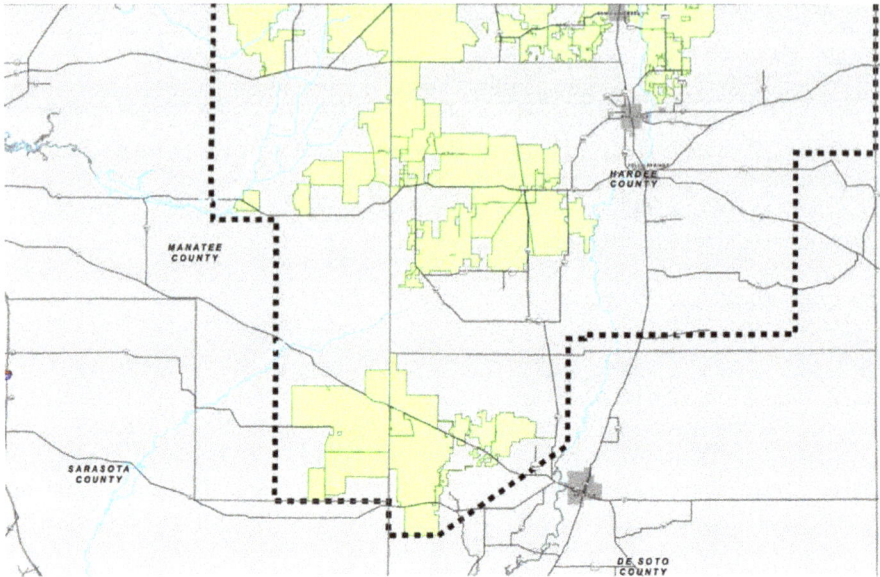

Figure 74: Final Mine Tract in Hardee, Manatee & Desoto Counties
(Source: Demers 2016)

The DeSoto mine is situated within a much larger tract that spans Hardee County to the north and Manatee County to the east (Figure 74). In this map, the dotted line indicates the region within which Mosaic might pursue phosphate mining while the green shaded tracts identify land that has been acquired by Mosaic. The Hardee County portion of proposed mining area lies southwest of Fort Meade while the Manatee County are lies west of the DeSoto/Manatee county line and east of the Myakka River (Demers 2016). This tri-county tract encompasses some 50,000 acres of ecosystems environmental advocates claim serves as habitat for a variety of endangered and threatened species. They fear that once the phosphate in this tract has been mined that the area will be burdened with another 50 million tons of phosphor-gypsum that will pose an environmental hazard to the region for generations to come (Kinane 2016).

Having committed to mine this tri-county tract, in 2012, Mosaic signaled its intention to pursue a mine permit in DeSoto County by opening an office in the county seat, Arcadia. The company selected for its headquarters the historic Hollingsworth House and fully restored it to provide an inviting and symbolic corporate community presence. This approach is consistent with their approach in Hardee County where Mosaic purchased an historic 1910 craftsman home on Main Street and refurbished it as their Hardee headquarters. The acquisition of such space communicates that Mosaic is established locally and visitors to their county offices are welcomed into a hospitable "home" environment.

When Mosaic opened its DeSoto office to pursue a mine permit, they embarked on a protracted permitting process that would eventually encounter opposition.

Mosaic acknowledged the reality of mine opposition as it published its "Mosaic in Desoto" website (Mosaic in DeSoto 2016). The company enumerates multiple agencies involved in permitting (Figure 75) and ongoing litigation that also extends the process. Accordingly, they observe that:

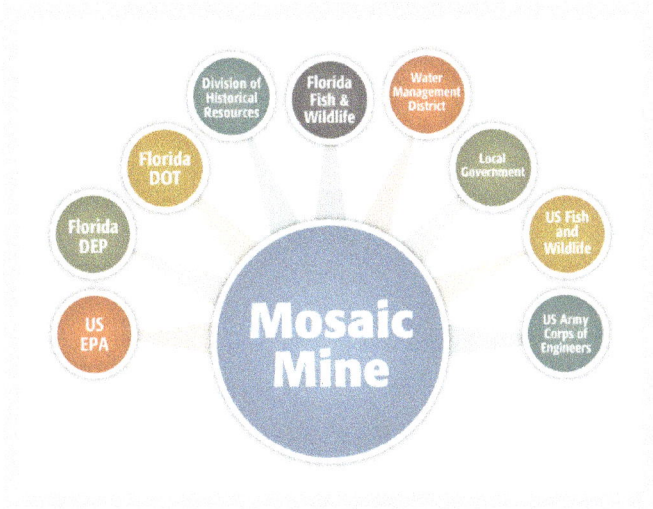

Figure 75: Permitting Agencies for Mine Approval
(Source: Mosaic in Desoto 2012)

"The most recent new phosphate mine operation to be successfully permitted in Florida opened in 1995. In recent years, permitting efforts focused on extensions to existing mine operations. Extension permits have taken an average of 5-7 years to work through the regulatory process. Litigation brought by various interest groups has, at times, added an additional 1-2 years to the permitting process. When compared to peer nations with comparable natural resources, mine permitting in the United States is a much longer process. In a 2011 study of mining industries in 25 resource rich countries, Behre Dolbear, a global mineral industry advisory firm, ranked the United States as the worst country for delays in the mine permitting process" (Mosaic in Desoto 2017).

Opposition to mining the 50,000-acre tri-county tract publicly emerged in January, 2017 at a county commission meeting in Manatee County when Mosaic came before the commission to make their case for expanding their mine operation at their East Wingate mine as well as mining the proposed new Ona and DeSoto mines. The meeting was well attended and many citizens expressed their opposition to the additional mining both during and prior to the meeting (Aronson & Morse 2017; Morse 2017). Mosaic representatives anticipated this opposition and had initiated a public relations effort to reassure citizens of the tri-county area. Prior to the meeting with the commissioners Mosaic established corporate offices in each county and created county-specific websites –DeSoto (Mosaic in DeSoto 2017), Manatee (Mosaic in Manatee 2017) and Hardee Counties (Mosaic in Hardee 2017). The company uses these websites to distribute information about the proposed mines (Wingate East in Manatee, DeSoto Mine in DeSoto, and South Fort Meade and South Pasture mines Hardee Counties) as well as to communicate information to residents about the Mosaic company.

On each of those websites, Mosaic addresses the issue of opposition to mining. As a matter of corporate policy, they attempt to anticipate and stay in front of opposition groups in part by publicly acknowledging that people may oppose mining because they are "opposed to mining or the temporary environmental impacts associated with extracting the ore," or because they "do not trust the industry to meet our environmental commitments." Mosaic readily acknowledges that "environmental issues associated with earlier phosphate mining operations have bred skepticism among opponents" (Mosaic in DeSoto 2017). Throughout their many public relations efforts Mosaic urges opponents to give them a chance and discover the company's commitment to full reclamation and environmental restoration.

Unfortunately, Mosaic's efforts are undercut not only by the ongoing environmental legacy of phosphate mining throughout north and central Florida, but also on the basis of more recent incidents like the New Wales sinkhole event that dumped millions of gallons or polluted water into the aquifer (Chow 2016) or the necessity of a coalition of environmental groups suing the corporation to force a solution to the ongoing pollution issues associated with the huge gypsum stacks dotting the central Florida landscape (Pittman 2015). Perhaps the greatest obstacle for Mosaic is skepticism regarding the extent to which their rhetoric matches their performance.

Kevin Erwin is exemplary of Mosaic's environmental skeptics. Based upon his extensive evaluations of Florida mine reclamation sites, Erwin questions the accuracy of Mosaic's claims that the company engages in environmentally sustainable reclamation. Instead he argues that phosphate companies consistently fail to reclaim mined land to a state that is anywhere nearly as functional as the site was prior to mining. As noted earlier, his principal criticism is the way the land is restored using overburden and sand fails to create a sustainable soil system to support plants and maintain moisture over the long term (Erwin 2008; 2006; Manfuso 2004).

Economist Richard Weisskoff of the University of Miami is also skeptical. He challenges Mosaic's claims that strip mining land for phosphate increases employment and maximizes wealth beyond what other land use alternatives. In Manatee County Weisskoff challenged these assumptions and concluded that phosphate mining is not necessarily the most productive use of land over the long run—and may indeed be less productive than agricultural uses. Weisskoff has also challenged Mosaic's assertion that phosphate mining increases local employment by pointing out that the mechanization of phosphate mining requires fewer workers than before and may not employ as many workers as agriculture or the building trades (Weisskoff 2016; 2012).

Municipality County	Decennial Census Population Counts					Percentage Change				entire period	last 30 yrs
	1970 [1]	1980 [2]	1990 [3]	2000 [4]	2010 [5]	1970-1980 [6]	1980-1990 [7]	1990-2000 [8]	2000-2010 [9]	1970-2010 [10]	1990-2010 [11]
1 Polk County Total	227,222	321,652	405,382	483,924	602,095	41.6%	26.0%	19.4%	24.4%	165.0%	48.5%
2 Bartow Polk	12,891	14,780	14,716	15,340	17,298	14.7%	-0.4%	4.2%	12.8%	34.2%	17.5%
3 Fort Meade Polk	4,374	5,546	4,993	5,691	5,626	26.8%	-10.0%	14.0%	-1.1%	28.6%	12.7%
4 Mulberry Polk	2,701	2,932	2,988	3,230	3,817	8.6%	1.9%	8.1%	18.2%	41.3%	27.7%
5 13 other Polk municipalites	93,079	108,323	140,562	156,866	199,707	16.4%	29.8%	11.6%	27.3%	114.6%	42.1%
6 Rest of Coun Polk	207,256	298,394	382,685	459,663	575,354	44.0%	28.2%	20.1%	25.2%	177.6%	50.3%
7 Hardee Cor Total	14,889	19,379	19,499	26,938	27,731	30.2%	0.6%	38.2%	2.9%	86.3%	42.2%
8 Bowling Gre Hardee	1,357	2,310	1,836	2,892	2,930	70.2%	-20.5%	57.5%	1.3%	115.9%	59.6%
9 2 other Hardee municipalities'	4,124	4,481	4,462	6,009	6,828	8.7%	-0.4%	34.7%	13.6%	65.6%	53.0%

Figure 76: Employment Rates in Phosphate Towns
(Source: Weisskoff, 2016; BEBR, 2016)

Weisskoff also evaluated phosphate communities to determine if overall community employment levels have improved over a 50-year period. Based upon federal demographic data, he concluded that when 21st century employment rates in phosphate communities (like Bartow, Fort Meade and Mulberry) are compared to each community's 50-year employment rates (Figure 76) that 21st century rates lag far behind long-term historical rates—lagging 12.8% for Bartow, 29.7% for Fort Meade and 23.1% for Mulberry (Weisskoff 2016).

Skepticism such as that voiced by Kevin Erwin and Richard Weisskoff is most visibly embodied among the various environmental groups that have organized to stop phosphate mining in Manatee, Hardee and Desoto Counties. These organizations include People for Protecting Peace River (Hardee County), the Florida Sierra Club (Pinellas County), Manasota-88 (Manatee and Sarasota County), Suncoast Waterkeepers (Sarasota County) and the Center for Biological Diversity (Pinellas County). This informal coalition of environmental advocacy groups filed a lawsuit in 2016, suing U.S. the Fish and Wildlife Service and the U.S. Army Corps of Engineers regarding their decision to allow phosphate mining on 50,000 acres of land in Manatee, DeSoto and Hardee counties (Aronson 2017; Newborn 2016). Their suit cited the Endangered Species Act claiming that mining threatened the indigo snake, wood storks, and crested caracara—all threatened and endangered species.

The Conspicuous Absence of Opposition and Partnerships

What is fascinating however about these organizations and their advocacy to stop phosphate mining in DeSoto County is that while each represents the environmental interests of DeSoto County, none of these organizations are headquartered in the county and none of the leaders of these organizations reside there either. While individual DeSoto citizens have expressed their concern over the opening of the DeSoto Mine (DeSoto County Commission 2010), there is no organized resistance to Mosaic originating in DeSoto County. The bulk of the organized opposition to the DeSoto Mine is being generated from surrounding counties, to include Charlotte County to the south.

Historically, the only discernable environmental advocacy group indigenous to DeSoto County was DeSoto Citizens Against Pollution (DCAP). DCAP was founded and led by one time Arcadia resident Alan Behrens in 1999. Behrens now resides in Hillsborough County. DCAP's mission involved protecting fish, wildlife and air and water resources, promoting environmental and public health and safety, alerting the public of environmental hazards, and discouraging / opposing activities deleterious to environmental and public health (FDEP 2006). In 2006 DCAP reported 52 members 27 of whom resided in Hardee County and 23 in DeSoto County. The bulk of the members either own property in or around Horse Creek or recreationally use the creek for fossil hunting, fishing and boating. The membership of DCAP was principally concerned that the clay settling areas that would be introduced into the area with mining would adversely impact water flow resulting in the degradation of the state of Horse Creek and its environs (FDEP 2006).

DCAP has been inactive since about 2009. It's leadership eventually migrated to the board of People for Protecting Peace River opposing phosphate mining in the county. DCAP appears to have operated in DeSoto county in the early nineties and advocated for the protection of Horse Creek in the face of Mosaic's predecessor IMC-Phosphate's decision to mine near the creek beginning in 2003. DCAP continued advocating for the protection of Horse Creek at least through 2009 in recognition that DeSoto County was situated in the terminus of the Bone Valley formation and would inevitably be mined for phosphate. As IMC asserted, mining in DeSoto and adjacent counties was necessary for the life-blood of the company, and that if the company "went away" some "40 percent of the Florida phosphate industry goes with us" (Pittman 1999).

During this period, DCAP allied itself with Manasota-88 in their desire to protect Horse Creek. However, then president of DCAP Alan Behrens made it clear that while he didn't personally like phosphate mining, opposition to phosphate mining in DeSoto County was not DCAP's principal goal—just the protection of Horse Creek (Pittman 1999). However, after FDEP signaled its intent to grant a mining permit to IMC in 2003, DCAP joined Charlotte County and Lee County and filed a petition for administrative proceedings to challenge permitting. These three petitions were eventually consolidated into a single petition for administrative hearings. In 2004, IMC revised its permit request to FDEP and reduced the proposed mine site to 4197 acres. Following revision FDEP approved the IMC permit. (Peace River/Manasota Water Authority v. Mosaic Fertilizer 2009).

In 2009, the Peace River/Manasota Water Authority and the Florida Sierra Club joined Charlotte, Lee and Sarasota counties in challenging the FDEP mining permit. In reviewing this appeal, it is interesting to note that not only did DCAP refrain from joining the appeal, they actually joined Mosaic Company and FDEP as appellees. While the reason for their change of heart remains a mystery, court records indicate that no representative of DCAP appeared for the final 2009 hearing before the Second District Court of Appeal (Florida). This appears to mark and end to DCAP activities in DeSoto County (Peace River/Manasota Water Authority v. Mosaic Fertilizer 2009).

Around 2009, DCAP transformed into Hardee Citizens Against Pollution (as Alan Behrens moved north) and eventually "morphed" again into People for Protecting Peace River. What is noteworthy, however, is as the organization changed and evolved over time, the organization and its leaders moved out of DeSoto County. This left DeSoto County without local environmental leadership and advocacy. While there is significant evidence of individual opposition to mining (DeSoto County Commission, 2010) all the organized opposition comes from beyond the county and is principally centered in Hardee, Manatee and Sarasota Counties.

In the face of no organized opposition in DeSoto County, Mosaic's job was rendered much easier regarding marketing the DeSoto Mine to the community. However, the absence of "loyal environmental opposition" also meant that Mosaic was not afforded the opportunity to enter productive corporate-community environmental partnerships. The virtual absence in this rural county of local environmental advocacy organizations is in part reflective of how such local nonprofits evolve and devolve. In the case of DCAP, the organizing impetus and life of the nonprofit largely centered around its founder Alan Behrens, and when Behrens ultimately left the county it appears that the organization died.

A similar pattern can be found in north Florida in the Suwannee River basin. In 1993 an organization called Save Our Suwannee emerged in response to a plan to build a giant landfill along the banks of the Suwannee River (Save Our Suwannee 2006). The organization persisted for 12 years before closing its doors in 2015. Per the last president of the organization, Merrillee Malwitz-Jipson, the organization basically folded its tent because it had successfully dealt with the immediate issues that brought it into existence and when those issues were resolved and leadership changed the organization lost its focus and reason for existing (Malwitz-Jipson 2017).

What Malwitz-Jipson relates regarding Save Our Suwannee (SOS) is in fact illustrative of much of what is well known about nonprofit organizations in general—of which local environmental organizations are a sub species. Small nonprofit organizations typically struggle to organize and sustain themselves and once organized they fight to maintain effective ongoing leadership (Landles-Cobb et al. 2015; Linshuang et al. 2011; Tierney 2006) and procure necessary funding and sponsorship (O'Connell 2010). Leadership is particularly a problem—especially leadership succession.

What too often happens in small local nonprofits is an indigenous leadership team emerges within a community to tackle a problem and that team organizes to create and run the nonprofit for a period of years. Inevitably, as the issue or issues that organized these nonprofits is resolved the organization's mission begins to drift until finally it closes its doors. Arguably this is in part what happened to SOS once they succeeded in halting the proposed landfill. With the objective of the organization realized, the leadership team may choose to declare victory and close shop. For other nonprofits organized around a larger set of issues or dealing with concerns that don't just go away, time spent battling the issues may divert attention away from the need to recruit and groom successive generations of leadership. When this necessary work is neglected then eventually the organization fails for lack of leadership (Landles-Cobb et al. 2015). This happened to DCAP and SOS.

There are, however, other forces that also contribute to the demise of local nonprofits to include remaining small (Bielefeld 2014) becoming isolated (Altman 2016; Andrews & Edwards 2005), and occupying too narrow a "niche" in the community to justify their ongoing existence (Hager & Searing 2015; Bielefeld 2014). Arguably DCAP exhibited each of these problems since it was isolated in rural DeSoto County, occupied a small "niche" of environmental advocacy inconsistent with the county's dominant ranching and agricultural ethos. Moreover, it does not appear that DCAP strongly affiliated itself with outside environmental organizations that might have served to bolster its resources and environmental mission. DCAP remained small and isolated in a community that might not have been forthcoming to a group who carried an "environmentalist" moniker and who opposed economic interests like phosphate mining that many saw as in the county's economic interest. DCAP also failed to groom organizational leadership and neglected recruiting and empowering a loyal and engaged volunteer membership.

DCAP's organizational model was more akin to a club of like-minded people with common interests who convened and adjourned their organization at their convenience and in response to their corporate and regulatory antagonists. They were probably never as much about functioning as an ongoing nonprofit organization as functioning as an issue-centered group with limited resources, leadership capacity, and financial wherewithal. Without the input of new leadership, capital and institutional relationships the resources of the core of the organization eventually dissipated and DCAP passed into history.

The loss of DCAP and the failure of similar organizations dedicated to the environment to emerge may have created a climate where corporate entities like Mosaic can operate without the need to defend themselves from local environmental opposition. Given the highly litigious nature of phosphate mining in Florida the relative absence of organized opposition to mining in DeSoto County is likely perceived by Mosaic's management as a fortuitous. The absence of local opposition makes it more likely the objectives of the company are maximized in the county. However, the absence of organized environmental advocacy in DeSoto County also means that there is a less likelihood that the environmental welfare of the area is protected. Granted, county commissioners and city officials are very much entrusted with looking out for the public welfare in the county—to include environmental welfare. However, these governmental functions would be even better served if local officials were bolstered in their efforts by involved, informed and active local citizens.

The absence of such local organized advocacy weakens government oversight and will. However, it also denies Mosaic the opportunity to engage in creative environmentally—oriented community partnerships that could do much to repair the company's image as an environmental tyrant. If Mosaic had been compelled to deal with locally organized environmental advocacy in DeSoto County they might have experienced the opportunity to forge a new cooperative community relationship that significantly redefined "reclamation" beyond its narrow meaning in state and federal regulation. Such reclamation would involve more than cosmetically restoring the surface layers of disturbed soil with mulch and native plant life. Ideally, such restoration could additionally entail restoring the various soil horizons to create a sustainable soil ecosystem—doing so as a part of an enterprise designed to realize sustainable economic as well as environmental outcomes. Such restoration could conceivably support a variety of economically viable land uses to include farming and ranching as well as land development for neighborhoods and businesses. Reclamation approached in this way—while undoubtedly more expensive to achieve—would assure generations of DeSoto County residents that natural environs and agriculturally viable land will be available indefinitely long after phosphate mining is over.

Ecopragmatic Principles Not Exemplified in DeSoto County

The virtual absence of grass-roots organizational opposition to Mosaic Fertilizer in DeSoto County created an environment where none of the principles of ecopragmatic dialogue and cooperation have emerged. Unfortunately, this void produced distant and distrustful relationships between advocacy groups like Florida Sierra, Manasota-88 and People for Protecting Peace River and Mosaic Fertilizer. Likewise, federal and state environmental agencies like FDEP, SWFWMD, and the U.S. Army Corps of Engineers have also found themselves at odds with regional environmental organizations who perceive the regulatory roles of these agencies as being influenced by their seemingly cozy relationships with "big phosphate." Without doubt, the presence of organized and involved local environmentalists "on the ground" in DeSoto County would have compelled Mosaic to engage in partnerships designed to fashion mutually useful economic and environmental goals.

What remains is a highly balkanized policy environment in which advocacy groups outside of the county regularly engage in pitched regulatory and legal battles over mine sites and reclamation practices with Mosaic and state and federal agencies. Based upon interviews with Mosaic staff; after reading the company's comments on their various websites and despite all their marketing communiques about being community partners in their company towns and cities in central Florida, Mosaic has adopted a "bunker mentality" where they are highly suspicious of all outsiders and ever vigilant about defending themselves in the courts and in the court of public opinion. The principal lesson to be learned from this final case study is that in the absence of local organized environmental involvement and advocacy there is simply no opportunity for environmental *discourse* among regulatory, governmental, business and environmental groups. In the absence of "discourse" confrontation, "distrust" and "discord" reigns.

While it is beyond question that there is an important place for advocacy, resistance and confrontation in the world of environmental policy, these options alone are not sufficient for realizing viable public policy. In each of the other case studies highlighted in this book one can find a healthy balance of cooperation and confrontation, discourse and disagreement; engagement and disengagement. In every case the essential ingredient for progress and compromise was the local presence of a group of organized environmental advocates. Granted that each of the cases discussed involved agencies and organizations that acted upon (not from within) local communities and these larger nonprofits and regulatory groups played critical roles in the collaboration of many "strange bedfellows" involving "regulatory/economic/ environmental partners."

As valuable as these larger organizational forces are, former House Speaker Tip O'Neill was prescient in observing that ultimately "all politics is local" (Gelman 2011). Without strong local advocacy groups acting on behalf of local environments and economics discourse and dialogue don't occur. These strong local advocates constitute the "network of responsibles" upon which successful partnerships depend. Such local people and institutions create the conditions around which teamwork and cooperation emerge and in their absence stakeholders become adversaries and cooperation devolves into confrontation. All that remains are "either—or" options that obfuscate "both-and" opportunities. In such scenarios, someone is wrong (and must be punished) and someone is right (and must be rewarded).

CONCLUSION

The DeSoto case, though not as rewarding and interesting as the other cases highlighted in this book, is of great importance principally because it speaks to the state-of-affairs in countless small counties nationwide where demographic and economic forces conspire to discourage the emergence of productive environmental and economic partnerships. In places like DeSoto County communities and the environment suffer with unresolved environmental issues embroiled in politics and litigation. Battle lines are drawn, policy opponents become irreconcilably Balkanized from one another and important environmental issues don't get solved (certainly not locally). If it were not for the resources of large powerful national NGO's like the Sierra Club and the Nature Conservancy then environmental resources in these remote areas would be completely at risk. Advocacy and opposition on the part of these groups keep federal and state agencies and corporate interests honest and engaged in environmental stewardship.

At the heart of ecopragmatics is the belief that environmental policy is best served when pursuing "cooperation" rather than "conflict" precipitated by locally organized and active environmental advocates and organizations. This ingredient, when coupled with outside economic and advocacy support, is what transforms stalemate into partnerships and progress. Thankfully, such local organizations emerge and dutifully serve their communities and their local environment. Their task, however, is tedious and difficult. They suffer with modest financial backing and have trouble attracting and sustaining membership and leadership. They need a great deal of care and feeding to remain in place—and its vitally important that they do so.

The need to support and sustain local environmental advocacy groups is so vital that organizations like the International Union for the Conservation of Nature (IUCN, 2015), Earth Policy Institute, Friends of the Earth, the Sierra Club, the Nature Conservancy and others have incorporated this task into the heart of their mission - partnering with local organizations and providing them with support and guidance (Stonebrook 2014; Witte, Brenner & Reinicke 2003; Streck 2002). Despite the emphasis upon environmental networking that has emerged internationally and across America, there is still an ongoing need for developing small isolated environmental organizations like the former DCAP so that—in conjunction with larger environmental organizations—they may play the role of local advocate - compelling even the largest and most powerful corporate adversary to engage them and their communities in mutually beneficial relationships that protect environments and economies. It is upon these foundations that future ecopragmatic relationships will be built and sustained.

REFERENCES

Altman, Ian. 2016. "Half of Nonprofits Are Set Up to Fail -- How About Your Favorite?" *Forbes.* (March 20), Accessed July 18, 2017 https://www.forbes.com/sites/ianaltman/2016/03/20/half-of-nonprofits-are-setup-to-fail-how-about-your-favorite/#634e8eaa4619

American Rivers. 2004. *America's Most Endangered Rivers of 2004.* Washington: American Rivers, Accessed July 10, 2017 https://s3.amazonaws.com/american-rivers-website/wp-content/uploads/2016/02/24220916/2004-mer-report.pdf.

Andrews, Kenneth T. and Bob Edwards. 2005 "The Organizational Structure of Local Environmentalism." *Mobilization: An International Journal.* 10(2): 213-234.

Aronson, Claire and Hannah Morse. 2017. "Mosaic Makes its Case for More Phosphate Mining," *Bradenton Herald.* (January 26), Accessed July 13, 2017 http://www.bradenton.com/news/business/article128875614.html

Bielefeld, Wolfgang. 2014. "The Challenges of New Nonprofits." *Nonprofit Quarterly.* (December 31), Accessed January 20, 2017 https://nonprofitquarterly.org/2014/12/31/the-challenges-of-new-nonprofits/

BEBR. 2016. "Florida Estimates of Population, 2016." Gainesville, FL: Bureau of Economic and Business Research, College of Arts and Sciences, University of Florida, Accessed July 4, 2017 https://www.bebr.ufl.edu/sites/default/files/Research%20Reports/estimates_2016.pdf.

Bartlett, Robert. 1987. *Booms & Busts on Bitter Creek: A History of Rock Springs, Wyoming.* Boulder: Pruett Publishing.

Barnett, Cynthia. 2008. "One Last Big Push for Phosphate Mining," *Florida Trend.* (May 1), Accessed July 4, 2017 http://www.floridatrend.com/article/7700/one-last-big-push-for-phosphate-mining.

Brown, Jr., Canter. 2005 *None Can Have Richer Memories, Polk County, 1940-2000.* Tampa: University of Tampa Press.

———. 2001. *In the Midst of All that Makes Life Worth Living, Polk County, Florida, to 1940, Polk County Historical Association.* Tallahassee: Sentry Press.

———. 1995. *Fort Meade: 1849-1900.* Tuscaloosa: University of Alabama Press.

Burnett, Gene. 1972. *Florida's Past: Volume 3.* Tallahassee: Pineapple Press.

Citrus County Historical Society. 2017. "The History of Floral City." Accessed July 7, 2017 https://www.cccourthouse.org/fchistory.php

Chow, Lorraine. 2016. "Florida Residents Sue Mosaic Over Massive Radioactive Sinkhole." *EcoWatch.* (September 24), Accessed July 13, 2017 https://www.ecowatch.com/mosaic-radioactive-sinkhole-2013749187.html

Cook, David. 2011. "Boom and Bust in Phosphate Mining." *Ocala Star-Tribune.* (January 22), Accessed July 4, 2017 http://www.ocala.com/news/20110122/boom-and-bust-in-phosphate-mining

———. 2010 "Ocala Begins Love Affair with Railroads." *Ocala Star-Banner.* (January 17), Accessed July 8, 2017 http://www.ocala.com/news/20100117/ocala-begins-love-affair-with-railroads

Demers, Nora. 2016. "Proposed Mining Limits," Mining Impacts: Compilation of Issues and Resources." Florida Gulf Coast University, Fort Myers, Florida, Accessed July 13, 2017 http://faculty.fgcu.edu/ndemers/Mining/phosphatenews.htm

Dewey, Scott. 2008. "The Fickle Finger of Phosphate: Central Florida Air Pollution and the Failure of Environmental Policy, 1957-1970." in *Other Souths: Diversity and Differences in the U.S. South Reconstruction to Present.* ed. by Pippa Holloway. Athens: University of Georgia Press.

DeSoto County Commission. 2010. "Public Meeting of the Board of County Commissioners." (May 25), Arcadia, FL, Accessed July 13, 2017 http://desotocountyfl.iqm2.com/Citizens/FileOpen.aspx?Type=15&ID=2654&Inline=Tru

DeSoto County Historical Society. 2017. "History of DeSoto County." Accessed July 8, 2017 http://www.historicdesoto.org/history.html

Ericson, W.A., L.P. Moore and L. D. Madrid. 1993. "Development of Florida's Phosphate Lands." *Third International Conference on Case Histories in Geotechnical Engineering*. Paper No. 8.13, St. Louis, MO, June 1-4, p. 1189-1196. Accessed September 20, 2017 http://scholarsmine.mst.edu/icchge/3icchge/3icchge-session08/2

Erwin, Kevin. 2008. "IMC's Strip Mining of the Peace River Basin: The Cost of Reclamation, the Price of Failure." Ecological Consultant Report on the IMC Ona Mine in Hardee County, Florida, Accessed June 23, 2017 http://www.ourphosphaterisk.com/downloads/Kevin%20Erwin%20Reclamation.pdf

———. 2006. "IMC's Strip Mining of the Peace River Basin," Report for Manasota-88. Accessed July 13, 2017 http://www.ourphosphaterisk.com/downloads/Kevin%20Erwin%20Reclamation.pdf

Floral City Heritage Council. 2017. "Introduction: The Discovery of Phosphate: Florida's Gold Rush." Accessed July 7, 2017 http://floralcityhc.org/images/Phosphate-Introduction.pdf

FloridaGenWeb.org. 2017. "John Logan—Sheriff of Polk County for 16 Years." Accessed July 17, 2017 http://fl-genweb.org/decole/Polk/PoUnifo/JohnLogan.html

Florida Department of Environmental Protection (FDEP). 2006. "Final Order: Peace River / Manasota Water Authority and Lee County versus IMC Phosphate and Department of Environmental Protection." State of Florida Department of Environmental Protection, DEP1088, Accessed July 18, 2017 http://www.dep.state.fl.us/legal/Final_Orders/2006/DEP06-1088.pdf

Florida Industrial and Phosphate Research Institute (FIPR). 2017. "Timeline of Phosphate Communities." Bartow, FL, Florida Polytechnic University, Accessed July 8, 2017 http://www.fipr.state.fl.us/about-us/phosphate-primer/timeline-of-phosphate-communities/

Gelman, Andrew. 2011 "All Politics is Local? Debate and the Graphs." *The New York Times*. (January 3), Accessed July 17, 2017 https://fivethirtyeight.blogs.nytimes.com/2011/01/03/all-politics-is-local-the-debate-and-the-graphs/

Graettinger v. IMC Phosphate. 2003. Motion to Relinquish Jurisdiction, State of Florida Division of Administrative Hearings, (November 14), Accessed July 10, 2017 https://www.doah.state.fl.us/DocDoc/2003/003692/03003692111403i01114258.pdf

Hager, Mark and Elizabeth Searing. 2015. "10 Ways to Kill Your Nonprofit." *Nonprofit Quarterly*. (January 6), Accessed July 20, 2017 https://nonprofitquarterly.org/2015/01/06/10-ways-to-kill-your-nonprofit/

Hirsch, Michael. 2016. "The Florida Sierra Club Objects to a New Phosphate Mine in DeSoto County." *WUSF-Tampa*. (September 30), Accessed July 4, 2017 http://wusfnews.wusf.usf.edu/post/florida-sierra-club-objects-new-phosphate-mine-desoto-county#stream/0

International Union for Conservation of Nature (IUCN). 2015. "Join the World's Largest Environmental Network: The Benefits of IUCN Membership." Gland, Switzerland, Accessed July 24, 2017 https://www.iucn.org/downloads/membership_brochure_en.pdf

Kinane, Sean. (2016) "Environmentalists Will Sue if Corps Permits Florida Phosphate Mining." *WMNF Listener Blog*. (December 21) Accessed Web July 13, 2017 http://www.wmnf.org/environmentalists-sue-corps-florida-phosphate-mining/

Landles-Cobb, Libbie, Kirk Kramer and Katie Smith Milway. 2015. "The Nonprofit Leadership Development Deficit." *Stanford Social Innovation Review*. (October 22), Accessed July 20, 2017 https://ssir.org/articles/entry/the_nonprofit_leadership_development_deficit

Levi, Steven C. 2007. *Boom and Bust in the Alaska Goldfields: A Multicultural Adventure*. Westport: Praeger.

Linshuang, Lao, Nancie Zane, Marian N. Ruderman, and Richard H. Price. 2011. *Emerging Leadership in Nonprofit Organization: Myths, Meaning, and Motivations.* Colorado Springs: Center for Creative Leadership. Accessed July 20, 2017 http://www.ccl.org/wp-content/uploads/2015/03/AMEXReportEmergingLeadership.pdf

Logan, Casey. 2016. "Arcadia to Build $7 Million Arena." *Fort Myers News Press.* (March 4), Acessed July 4, 2017 http://www.news-press.com/story/money/2016/03/04/arcadia-build-arena/81116082/

Mader v. IMC Phosphate. 2003. Petition for Formal Administrative Hearing, (October 10), Florida Department of Environmental Protection, Accessed July 10, 2017 https://www.doah.state.fl.us/DocDoc/2003/003790/03003790101003I02144933.pdf

Mahler, Carol. 2014. "History of DeSoto County." (June 25), DeSoto County Historical Society, Accessed July 4, 2017 http://www.historicDeSoto.org/history.html

Malwitz-Jipson, Merrilee. 2017. Private Conversation, June 18.

Manasota-88. 2008. "Ona Permit." Accessed July 10, 2017 http://www.ourphosphaterisk.com/permitting/ona-permit

Manfuso, Jamie. 2004. "Soil on Reclaimed Land at Center of Debate." *Herald-Tribune.* (May 9), Accessed July 13, 2017 http://www.heraldtribune.com/article/LK/20040509/News/605215780/SH/

Matson, George Charlton. 1915. *The Phosphate Deposits of Florida.* Bulletin 604. Washington, D.C.: United States Geological Survey.

Meyer, Susan. 2016. *Mining and Ranching in Early Colorado: Boom and Bust and Back Again.* Columbia: Tyrone Alderman.

Millar, C. C. Hoyer. 1892. Florida, South Carolina, and Canadian Phosphates. New York: The Scientific Publishing Company.

Mosaic in Desoto. 2017. "Permitting Process." Accessed July 11, 2017 http://mosaicindesoto.com/about/permitting-process/

———. 2016. "Just the Facts: The DeSoto Mine." Accessed July 4, 2017 http://mosaicindesoto.com/desoto-project/just-the-facts/

———. 2012. "Mosaic Mine Permitting Agencies." Accessed July 11, 2017 http://mosaicindesoto.com/files/2012/03/mosaic-mine-graphic.gif

Mosaic in Hardee. 2017. "Just the Facts: The Ona Mine." Accessed July 10, 2017 http://mosaicinhardee.com/just-the-facts/

Mosaic in Manatee. 2018. "Welcome to Mosaic in Manatee." Accessed September 17, 2017 http://mosaicinmanatee.com/

Mosaic International. 2017. "The Crop Nutrition Leader: Overview." Accessed July 4, 2017 http://www.mosaicco.com/Who_We_Are/overview.htm

Morse, Hannah. 2017. "Residents Send Hundreds of Comments Before Mosaic Hearing." *Bradenton Herald.* (January 24), Accessed July 13, 2017 http://www.bradenton.com/news/local/article128490099.html

Newborn, Steve. 2016. "Lawsuit Targets Phosphate Mining Expansion." *WUSF News.* (December 23), Accessed July 13, 2017 http://edwardwimberley.com/courses/10580/wusfnews.pdf

O'Connell, Jonathan. 2010. "Nonprofits Struggle to Survive and Maintain Services." *Washington Post.* (November 8), Accessed July 20, 2017 http://www.washingtonpost.com/wp-dyn/content/article/2010/11/05/AR2010110507410.html

Peace River / Manasota Water Authority v. Mosaic. 2009. Florida Second District Court of Appeal (February 10), Accessed July 17, 2017 http://www.2dca.org/opinions/Opinion_Pages/Opinion_Page_2009/February/February%2010,%202009/2D06-3891.pdf#search=casey

Pike, Jim. 2017. "Polk County Ghost Towns." *Flickr.* Accessed July 10, 2017 https://www.flickr.com/photos/mainmanwalkin/sets/72157604004388069/

Pittman, Craig. 2015. "Phosphate Giant Mosaic Agrees to Pay Nearly $2 Billion Over Mishandling of Hazardous Waste." *Tampa Bay Times.* (October, 1), Accessed July 13, 2017 http://www.

tampabay.com/news/environment/phosphate-giant-mosaic-agrees-to-pay-2-billion-over-mishandling-of/2247897

Pittman, Craig. 1999. "Campaign to Protect Creek Has Few Allies." *St. Petersburg Times.* (July 20), Accessed July 17, 2017 http://fluoridealert.org/news/campaign-to-protect-creek-has-few-allies/

Powers, Thomas Michael. 1996. *Lost Landscapes and Failed Economies: The Search for a Value of Place.* Washington: Island Press.

Quinones, Manuel. 2011. "Army Corps of Engineers Tries to Assess Impacts of Sprawling Phosphate Operations in FL." *New York Times.* (April 14), Accessed July 10, 2017 http://www.nytimes.com/gwire/2011/04/14/14greenwire-army-corps-tries-to-assess-impacts-of-sprawlin-83462.html?pagewanted=print

Raguse, Lou. 2016. "From Boom to Bust: Big Changes in ND Oil." *KARE Television*, Minneapolis, MN., Accessed July 4, http://www.kare11.com/news/from-boom-to-bust-big-changes-in-nd-oil/156422333

Ringholz, Raye C. 2003. *Uranium Frenzy: Saga of the Nuclear West.* Logan: Utah State University Press.

Ritchie, Tom, Frank Peters and Paulette Lash Ritchie. 2012. *Images of America: Floral City.* Charleston: Arcadia Publishing.

Save Our Suwannee. 2006. "About Us." Save Our Suwannee, Bell, FL, Accessed July 18, 2017 http://www.saveoursuwannee.org/about-us/

Stockfisch, Jerome R. 2015. "Digging In: Phosphate Producer Mosaic is in it for the Long Haul." *Tampa Bay Times.* (September 2), Accessed July 10, 2017 https://www.google.com/?gws_rd=ssl#q=mosaic+in+it+for+the+long+haul

Stonebrook, Shelley. 2014. "10 Environmental Organizations that are Changing the World." *Mother Earth News.* (June 25), July 24, 2017 https://www.cornucopia.org/2014/06/10-environmental-nonprofit-organizations-changing-world/

Streck, Charlotte. (2002) "Global Public Policy Networks as Coalitions for Change," in *Global Environmental Governance: Options and Opportunities.* ed. by Daniel Esty and Maria Ivanova. New Haven: Yale School of Forestry.

Thomas, Mabel W. and Laura Romain Thomas. 2017. *Gold Miner's Daughter: A Memoir of Boom, Bust and Bliss in the High Sierra.* Waukesha: Thomas Press.

USGS. 1985. "Fort Meade Mine—Cargill." United States Geological Society, (September), Accessed July 4, 2017 https://mrdata.usgs.gov/mrds/show-mrds.php?dep_id=10265790

Tierney, Thomas. 2006. "Nonprofit Sector's Leadership Deficit." *Bridgestar.* Accessed July 20, 2017 http://edwardwimberley.com/courses/10580/tierney.pdf

Ware, Lynne W. 1984. "The Peace River: A Forgotten Highway." *Tampa Bay History.* 6(2), (Fall/Winter): 19-30.

Weisskoff, Richard. 2016. "Long-term Adverse Economic Effects of Mining on Communities." A Report Prepared for Citizens Against Phosphate Mining in Union and Bradford Counties and Our Santa Fe River," (April 13), Accessed July 4, 2017 https://oursantaferiver.org/wp/wp-content/uploads/Weisskoff-Final-Report-on-Longterm-Adverse-Economic-Effects-of-Mining-in-Communities-041316.pdf

———. 2012. "Keep Farming, Not Mining." *Herald Tribune.* (February 29), Accessed July 13, 2017 http://www.heraldtribune.com/news/20120229/keep-farming-not-mining

White, Eugene N. 2009. "Lessons from the Great American Real Estate Bubble: Florida 1926." National Bureau of Economic Research (NBER) Summer Institute, NBER Working Paper No. 15573, Accessed July 7, 2017 http://econweb.rutgers.edu/ewhite/w15573.pdf

Witte, Jan Martin, Thorsten Brenner and Wolfgang H. Reinicke. 2003."Global Public Policy Networks: Lessons Learned and Challenges Ahead." *Brookings.* (March 1), Accessed July 24, 2017 https://www.brookings.edu/articles/global-public-policy-networks-lessons-learned-and-challenges-ahead/

Wynne, Nick. 2010. *Paradise for Sale: Florida's Booms and Busts.* Stroud: The History Press.

www.ingramcontent.com/pod-product-compliance
Lightning Source LLC
Chambersburg PA
CBHW052010030426

42334CB00029BA/3155